P9-DWY-730

GRACE AND GRIT

KEN WILBER

GRACE AND GRIT

Spirituality and Healing

in the Life and Death of

TREYA KILLAM WILBER

SHAMBHALA

Boston & London

1993

Shambhala Publications, Inc.
Horticultural Hall
300 Massachusetts Avenue
Boston, Massachusetts 02115

Shambhala Publications, Inc.
Random Century House
20 Vauxhall Bridge Road
London SW1V 2SA

© 1991 by Ken Wilber

All rights reserved. No part of this book may be reproduced in any form or by any means, electronic or mechanical, including photocopying, recording, or by any information storage and retrieval system, without permission in writing from the publisher.

9 8 7 6 5 4 3 2 1
First Paperback Edition

Printed in the United States of America on acid-free paper

Distributed in the United States by Random House, Inc., in Canada by Random House of Canada Ltd., and in the United Kingdom by Random House UK Ltd

The Library of Congress catalogues the hardcover edition of this work as follows:

Wilber, Ken.
Grace and Grit : spirituality and healing in the life and death of Treya
Killam Wilber / by Ken Wilber.—1st ed.
p.   cm.
ISBN 0-87773-635-9
ISBN 0-87773-698-7 (pbk.)
1. Wilber, Treya Killam—Health.   2. Wilber, Ken.   3. Cancer—
Patients—United States—Biography.   I. Title.
RC265.6.W55W55   1991
362.1'9699'40092—dc20   91-2176
[B]   CIP

To Sue and Radcliffe Killam,
   on the occasion of Rad's eightieth birthday;
To Vicky, Linda, Roger, Frances, Sam, Seymour, Warren, and Kati,
   for being there through thick and thin;
To David and Mary Lamar, for carrying on;
To Tracy and Michael, for putting up with me;
To Zahirudeen and Brad, for holding down the home fort;
To the women and men of the Cancer Support Community,
   Treya and Vicky's child;
To Ken and Lucy, for understanding our absence;
To Edith Zundel, our mother away from home;
And in memory of Rolf Zundel and Bob Doty,
   two of the most decent men we had ever known,
   casualties in this gruesome war

CONTENTS

Contents

GRACE AND GRIT

A NOTE TO THE READER

W H E N Treya and I first met, we had the strangest feeling that we had been looking for each other for lifetimes, but I don't know if that is literally true. But I do know that then commenced one of the most extraordinary stories I myself have ever heard. An unbelievable story, in many ways, and therefore I can assure you, a true story.

This book is two things: One, it is that story. But two, it is an introduction to the perennial philosophy, or the world's great wisdom traditions. Because, in the final analysis, the two are inseparable.

Treya had five main passions, I would say: nature and the environment (from conservation to recreation), crafts and arts, spirituality and meditation, psychology and psychotherapy, and service organizations. Nature, crafts, and service organizations are fairly self-explanatory. But what Treya meant by "spirituality" was contemplative or meditative spirituality, which is another way of saying the perennial philosophy. Treya didn't talk much about her mystical spirituality, which led many people, even some very close to her, to conclude it was peripheral to her concerns. Treya herself described it as the "guiding symbol of my life." It is, in other words, absolutely central to this story.

As it turned out, this interest in psychology and religion was also one I deeply shared, and, indeed, I had written several books on exactly that topic. And so woven into the following narrative are explanations of the great wisdom traditions (from Christianity to Hinduism to Buddhism), the nature of meditation, the relation of psychotherapy to spirituality, and the nature of health and healing. Indeed, the *main purpose* of this book is to provide an accessible introduction to just those topics.

Nonetheless, if you hit one of these explanatory sections—which occupy about one-third of the book, and which are very obvious—and all you are interested in at the moment is following Treya's story, feel free to fast-forward through these sections and pick up the story again. (Chapter 11 is particularly technical.) If you wish to come back later, you can peruse these sections at leisure.

I first met Treya in the summer of '83, at a friend's house, on a breezy night, on the edge of the San Francisco Bay. . . .

1

A FEW EMBRACES,
A FEW DREAMS

L O V E at first touch, she always called it.

It took me thirty-six years to connect with "the man of my dreams." Or as close as one gets these days to that ideal, which in my case is pretty damn close. Once I got used to his shaved head, that is. . . .

When I was growing up in south Texas, in the days when girls dreamt of such things, I never imagined I'd marry a six-foot-four philosopher-psychologist-transcendentalist who looks like he came from some faraway planet. Unique packaging and a unique combination of traits. What a sweetheart! And brilliant too. In all my past experience with men, the sweet ones weren't brilliant and the brilliant ones were definitely not sweet. I always wanted both.

Ken and I met on August 3, 1983. Within two weeks of that first meeting we had decided to get married. Yes, it was fast. But somehow we both seemed to know, almost right away. After all, I'd been dating for years and had a number of very satisfying relationships, but—I'm thirty-six years old, and I had *never* before met anyone I had even thought about marrying! I'd wondered if I was afraid, or too much a perfectionist, or too much an idealist, or simply hopelessly neurotic. After wondering (and worrying) about myself for awhile, I'd settle back comfortably into accepting my situation, until some event would bring on the self-questioning again, usually some event that made me doubt my "normality." Other people falling in love, getting married, being in relationships . . .

I suppose a part of each of us wants to be "normal" so we can be accepted. I know as a child I never wanted to attract attention for being different, and yet I wound up living a life that could scarcely be called normal. A normal education at one of the seven sisters colleges, a year of teaching, a normal M.A. in English literature, but then a sudden veering away from that path with a passion for environmental causes that led me to the mountains of Colorado. Environmental work, skiing, assorted odd jobs, teaching skiing. Then another unexpected, sudden change in direction. Born out of a deep longing for something I was at a loss to describe, a bicycle trip to Scotland took me through Findhorn, a spiritual community east of Inverness. There I found an answer, or part of an answer, to that longing, and there I lived for three years. I learned to recognize that longing as a spiritual longing, and there I learned various ways to begin to honor that need. That insistent call from within. I left only because friends called on me to help start another unconventional center [Windstar], in Colorado outside of Aspen, where I hoped my spiritual and environmental concerns could intertwine. From there on to graduate school, but again an unconventional one stressing interdisciplinary East/West and transcendental philosophy and psychology [the California Institute of Integral Studies].

It was there I first read the works of one Ken Wilber, considered by many, I heard, as the leading theorist in the new field of transpersonal psychology (a psychology that deals with all the things orthodox psychology deals with, but also studies the psychology of spiritual experience). He was already being called "the long-sought Einstein of consciousness research" and "a genius of our times." I loved his books—they illuminated many thorny issues I'd struggled with, illuminated them with a clarity I found refreshing and inspiring. I remember liking the picture on the back of one, A Sociable God. It showed an elegant-looking, shaved-headed man with glasses accenting an intense, concentrated look, the background a solid wall of books.

In the summer of '83 I went to the Annual Transpersonal Psychology Conference and heard that the famous Ken Wilber was there, but would not be speaking. I saw him from a distance a few times—hard to miss at six-foot-four and bald—surrounded by admirers and once sprawled by himself on a couch, looking lonely. I didn't think much of this until some weeks later when a friend, Frances Vaughan, who'd been with my travel group in India, called to invite me to dinner with Ken.

I couldn't believe that Frances and Roger had finally agreed on somebody. Terry Killam. Very beautiful, extremely intelligent, great sense of humor, gorgeous body, fellow meditator, enormously popular. This was all sounding a little too good to be true. If she's so great, why wasn't she with somebody? I was skeptical of the whole thing. That's all I needed, another blind date, I kept thinking as I phoned her. I loathed this whole dating routine; it was right up there with root canal. So what was so wrong with dying alone, miserable and wretched? Beats dating.

I had been staying with Frances Vaughan and Roger Walsh for the better part of a year, in Frances's lovely house in Tiburon, where a downstairs room was made available for me. Frances was an altogether remarkable woman—past president of the Association for Transpersonal Psychology, soon-to-be president of the Association for Humanistic Psychology, and author of several books, most notably *The Inward Arc*—not to mention the fact that she was quite beautiful and looked a decade younger than her mid-forty years. Roger was from Australia, but had been in the States for the past two decades. He was teaching at the University of California, Irvine, during the week and flying back on weekends to be with Frances. Roger, who in Australia had gotten the equivalent of an M.D. and a Ph.D., had also written several books, and he and Frances had coedited the most popular (and best) introduction to transpersonal psychology, *Beyond Ego*. Roger felt like a real brother to me—something that had never happened before—and we had all settled into Paradise Drive like a small and cozy family.

Except, of course, we were one person short—a partner for me—and so Frances and Roger dutifully looked around for any likely candidates. Frances would come up with a woman, and Roger would comment to me, "She's not terribly good-looking but then neither are you." Roger would come up with someone and Frances would tell me, "She's not very bright but then neither are you." What I remember, at any rate, about that year, was that in all the various dates I had, it seemed to me that Roger and Frances never really agreed on any of them.

After a year of this, Roger came in one day and said, "I can't believe it, I've got the perfect woman for you. I can't believe I didn't think of this before. Her name is Terry Killam." Sure, I thought, I've been here before. Think I'll take a skip on that.

Three days later, Frances came in and said, "I can't believe it. I've got the perfect woman for you. Can't believe I didn't think of this before. Her name is Terry Killam."

I was stunned. Frances and Roger agreeing? And not just agreeing but enthusiastic? This must be, I thought, a beautiful woman who is good for my soul. I looked at Frances, sort of kidding, and said "I'll marry her."

Our first meeting was unusual. Scheduling problems abounded, and we finally wound up getting together at the house of a mutual male friend who was dating a friend of mine from school (who was also a former girlfriend of Ken's). I came after 9:00 P.M. since I was seeing clients. Ken and I just barely had a chance to say "hello" when our two friends began to bring up some very deep problems in their relationship. Ken was asked to be facilitator, or "therapist for the evening," and the next three hours were spent dealing with their issues. You could tell this wasn't exactly how Ken had wanted to spend the evening, but he stayed right there, fully present, and was really wonderful, working with some extremely deep and difficult issues in their relationship.

Ken and I didn't say much to each other—we didn't have a chance! I spent most of the time trying to get used to his shaved head, which was disconcerting to me. I loved the way he looked from the front, but the side view . . . well, that would take some getting used to. But I was very impressed with the way he worked, with his gentleness and sensitivity and compassion, especially when it came to the woman and her agonizing issues about relationship, specifically about wanting a child.

At one point we all went into the kitchen for some tea. Ken put his arm around me. I felt a little uncomfortable since I hardly knew him, but slowly I put my arm around him. Then something moved me to put my other arm around him too and I closed my eyes. I felt something indescribable then. A warmth, a kind of merging, a sense of fitting together, of blending, of being completely one. I let myself float with it for a moment, then opened my eyes, surprised. My woman friend was looking straight at me. I wondered if she could see, if she could tell what had just happened.

What had just happened? Some kind of recognition, a recognition beyond this present world. It had nothing to do with how many words we'd shared. It was spooky, eerie, a once-in-a-lifetime feeling. When I finally left at 4:00 A.M. Ken held me before I got in my car. He said he

6

was surprised, he felt like he never wanted to let me go. That was just how I felt, like I belonged in some almost esoteric sense in his arms.

That night I dreamt about Ken. I dreamt I was driving over the [Golden Gate] bridge from the city, as I had the night before, but I was driving over a bridge that wasn't really there. Ken was following me in another car and we were to meet at a certain rendezvous. The bridge led to a magical town, a bit like a real town but with an ethereal quality that seemed suffused with meaning and import and, especially, beauty.

Love at first touch. We hadn't said five words to each other. And I could tell by the way she was looking at my shaved head that it definitely was not going to be love at first sight. I, like almost everybody, found Treya quite beautiful, but I really didn't even know her. But when I put my arm around her, I felt all separation and distance dissolve; there was some sort of merging, it seemed. It was as if Treya and I had been together for lifetimes. This seemed very real and very obvious, but I didn't know quite what to make of it. Treya and I still hadn't even talked to each other, so neither of us knew the same thing was happening to the other. I remember thinking, Oh great, it's four in the morning and I'm having some sort of weird mystical experience right in the kitchen of one of my best friends, merely by touching a woman I've never met before. This is not going to be easy to explain. . . .

I couldn't sleep that night; images of Treya poured over me. She was indeed beautiful. But what exactly was it? There was an energy that seemed literally to radiate from her in all directions; a very quiet and soothing energy, but enormously strong and powerful; an energy that was very intelligent and suffused with exceptional beauty, but mostly an energy that was *alive*. This woman said LIFE more than anybody I had ever known. The way she moved, the way she held her head, the ready smile that graced the most open and transparent face I had ever seen—God, she was alive!

Her eyes looked at, and through, everything. It wasn't that she had a penetrating glance—that's much too aggressive—it was simply that she seemed to see through things, and then perfectly accept what she saw, a kind of gentle and compassionate x-ray vision. Eyes committed to truth, I finally decided. When she looked directly at you, you could tell unmistakably that this was a person who would never lie to you. You trusted her immediately; an enormous integrity seemed to permeate even her smallest movements and mannerisms. She appeared the most self-confident person I had ever met, yet not proud or boastful in the least. I wondered if she ever got flustered; it was hard to imagine. Yet behind the almost intimidating solidness of her character, there were the dancing eyes, seeing everything, not ponderously, but wanting rather to play. I thought, this woman is game for anything; I don't think anything scares her. There was a lightness surrounding her, sincere but not serious; with her superabundance of life, she could afford to play, she could shed density and float all the way to the stars, if she wanted.

I finally drifted off, only to awaken with a start: I've found her. That's all I kept thinking: I've found her.

That same morning, Treya was writing a poem.

> A lovely evening last night, well-laced with brandy on all sides,
> The conversation punctuated by refilling glasses,
> making coffee,
> a kind of minuet of words and small actions
> interlacing with delicate probing and a deep caring,
> as he worked with their relationship.
> A gentleness, a softness, a willingness to support
>   through asking tough questions, probing deeper,
> panning for the gold of truth, coming up with bits of dust,
>   small pebbles, going slowly deeper to the mother load,
> and finding it.
> The whole process was lovely, how he continued on, probing,
>   caring,
> and then that lovely resolution, the softness in the air,
>   between us all.
> I feel my heart open at the memory of it,
> as it opened last night.
> To be touched like that,
> like he touched me,
> first through his words and what it showed of
>   him,
> the soft depths of his brown eyes,
> and then an easy melting body to body, something clearly
>   happened there,
> I closed my eyes to try to sense it, beyond words,
> but palpable, real, even if mostly
> inexpressible.
> I feel my heart open,
> I trust him more than
> I trust the universe.

A Few Embraces, A Few Dreams

As I lay in bed, I noticed a series of subtle energy currents running through my body, which felt very much like the so-called kundalini energy, which, in Eastern religions, is said to be the energy of spiritual awakening, an energy that lies dormant, asleep, until aroused by an appropriate person or event. I had felt these currents before—I'd been meditating for fifteen years, and these types of subtle energies are common in meditation—but never were they quite this clearly defined. Incredibly, the same thing was happening to Treya, and at exactly the same time.

Fascinating lying in bed this morning. Feeling little wavelets of vibration, very clear and distinct. Sensations in my arms and legs, but mostly localized in the lower half of my trunk. What is happening when this goes on? Are things loosening up, held tensions from the past dissolving?

I focused on my heart, felt an opening very, very clearly, from thinking of that sensation I had with Ken last night. An amazingly powerful surge from my heart, that then goes down into the center of my body, and then up toward the top of my head. So pleasurable and blissful it's almost painful, like an ache, a longing, a reaching out, a wanting, a desire, an openness, a vulnerability. Like how I would feel perhaps all the time if I weren't protected, if I dropped my defenses . . . and yet it feels wonderful, I love the feeling, it feels very alive and very real, full of energy and warmth. Jolts my inner core alive.

Just to make sure it's clear, Treya and I had not slept together. We had not even really talked. We had simply put our arms around each other, once in the kitchen, and once shortly thereafter, right before she left. We had had fifteen minutes of conversation. That was the sum total of our involvement at that point, and yet we were both startled by what was happening. It was all a bit much, and both of us tried to put a more sober and restrained face on the situation. With not much success.

I didn't see Ken for a week after that. He had told me he had to go to L.A. and would get in touch when he returned. I dreamt about him twice more while he was gone. I clearly knew on some deep level that this was a remarkable meeting of some import, but consciously I tried to play it down. I could be imagining things, I could be building castles in the air, after all there had been so many disappointments in the past. What did I have to go on, anyway? A few embraces, a few dreams.

9

When we finally did go out on our first real date a week later, Ken talked all through dinner about this girlfriend he'd gone to see in L.A. It embarrasses him to be reminded of this now, but I remember feeling comfortably amused. Turns out he was trying to hide his feelings by talking about somebody else. But we were together from then on. If we spent any time apart we knew what the other was doing. But we were mostly together, and we didn't like being separated. When we were together we liked being close together, touching. I felt somehow like I had long been thirsty for him, not just physically but emotionally and spiritually. The only way to begin to assuage this thirst was to be together as much as possible. I just drank him in on all levels.

One lovely early September evening, we sat on the deck of my house at Muir Beach, drinking wine, surrounded by the smells of the Pacific Ocean and the eucalyptus trees, softly serenaded by evening summer sounds, the breeze through the trees, a dog barking in the distance, waves breaking on the beach far below. We somehow managed to drink our wine while staying perfectly entwined in each other's arms, no mean feat! After some moments of silence Ken asked, "Has anything like this ever happened to you before?" It took not a moment's hesitation to answer, "No, never. Nothing like this. How about you?" "Never, not like this." We began laughing and in an exaggerated John Wayne voice he said, "It's bigger than the two of us, pilgrim."

I became obsessed with the thought of Ken. I loved the way he walked, talked, moved, dressed, everything. His face was with me every moment. This led to not a few mishaps during this period. Once I'd gone to a bookstore to buy copies of some of his books. Thinking intently of him, as usual, I pulled out of my parallel parking place directly into the path of an oncoming van. In all my years of driving I have never had an accident. Another evening I was going to meet Ken, again obsessed with thoughts of him and oblivious of all else. I ran out of gas near the entrance to the Golden Gate Bridge. That brought me back to earth in a hurry, though I arrived hours late.

It seemed, to both of us, like we were already married, and all that was required was to let people know about it. Treya and I never once talked about marriage; I don't think it seemed necessary to either of us. It was simply going to be.

What amazed me was that we had both given up finding the mythical "right person." Treya hadn't accepted a date in over two years; she had resigned herself to going it alone. I felt the same; and yet here we were, both so sure we would be married that we hadn't even felt it necessary to discuss it once.

But before the formalities—before I actually asked her to marry me—I wanted her to meet a dear friend, Sam Bercholz. Sam was living in Boulder with his wife Hazel and their kids Sara and Ivan (the terrible).

Sam was founder and president of Shambhala Publications, generally regarded as the finest publishing house in the world for East/West studies, Buddhism, and esoteric philosophy and psychology. Sam and I went back a long way. In addition to the publishing company, which was then located in Boulder, Colorado, Sam had started Shambhala Booksellers, an altogether extraordinary and now rather famous bookstore in Berkeley. When Sam first began the bookstore—at age twenty—he used to fill mail orders himself, working in the basement late into the night packing and shipping books to various customers. And once a month, like clockwork, he would receive a huge order from some kid in Lincoln, Nebraska. Sam kept thinking, "If this guy is actually reading all these books, we're going to hear from him."

I actually *was* reading all those books. I was twenty-two and right in the middle of completing my graduate studies in biochemistry. Originally I had wanted to be a doctor, and had entered the premed program at Duke University in Durham, North Carolina, which I pursued for two years, until I decided the practice of medicine wasn't creative enough for my intellectual tastes. One simply memorized facts and information, and then rather mechanically applied them to nice unsuspecting people. It struck me as a glorified plumbing job. It also struck me as a not-nice way to treat a human being. So I left Duke and returned home (my dad was in the Air Force; he and Mom were stationed at Offut Air Force Base, right outside Omaha, Nebraska). I took a double major (one in chemistry, one in biology) and then went to graduate school in biochemistry at the University of Nebraska at Lincoln. At least biochemistry was creative; at least I could do research; at least I could discover something, or bring forth new information, new ideas, new theories, and not merely apply that which had been taught me.

Nonetheless, although I graduated with honors, my heart wasn't in it. Biochemistry, medicine, and science in general simply were not addressing the questions that were becoming of fundamental importance to me—silly questions like, "Who am I?" "What's the meaning of life?" "Why am I here?"

Like Treya, I was looking for something, something that science simply could not provide. I began an obsessive study of the world's great religions, philosophies, and psychologies, both East and West. I read two and three books a day, cutting biochemistry classes and shortchanging my laboratory work (which consisted of the positively revolting task of cutting up hundreds of cow eyes a week so as to perform research on the retinas). My wandering interests greatly worried my professors, who suspected I was up to something no good—that is, something not scientific. Once, when I was scheduled to give a biochemistry lecture to faculty and students on something fascinating like "The photoisomerization of rhodopsin isolated from bovine rod outer segments," I instead gave a two-hour lecture brashly entitled "What Is Reality and How Do We Know It?," a scathing attack on the inadequacy of empirical scientific methodology. The assembled faculty listened very intently, asked numerous intelligent and thoughtful questions, and followed the arguments perfectly. Then, right as I had finished the presentation, came a whispered but clearly audible comment from the back of the room, a comment that summarized virtually everybody's feelings: "Whew! Now back to reality."

That was genuinely funny, and we all laughed. But the sad thing was that what "reality" meant, of course, was empiric-scientific reality, which basically meant only that which could be perceived by the human senses or their instrumental extensions (microscopes, telescopes, photographic plates, and so on). *Anything* outside of that narrow world—anything that might have something to do with the human soul or Spirit or God or eternity—was deemed unscientific and thus "unreal." I had spent my entire life studying science, only to be met with the wretched realization that science was, not wrong, but brutally limited and narrow in scope. If human beings are composed of matter, body, mind, soul, and spirit, then science deals handsomely with matter and body, but poorly with mind and not at all with soul and spirit.

I did not want to know more about matter and bodies; I was choking on truths about matter and bodies. I wanted to know about mind, and especially about soul and spirit. I wanted some meaning in the mess of facts I was ingesting.

And so there I was, going through the mail-order catalogue of Shambhala Booksellers. I had left graduate school, cutting short my doctorate and taking a master's instead; the last clear memory I have of the place being the look of horror in my professors' faces as I told them of my plans to write a book on "consciousness and philosophy and the soul and stuff."

I took a job as a dishwasher in order to pay rent. I was making $350 a month and sending $100 of that to Shambhala for mail-order books.

I did write that book. I was twenty-three years old; the book was called *The Spectrum of Consciousness*. Fortunately, the reviews were enthusiastic. It was largely the positive feedback I got on *Spectrum* that kept me going. For the next five years, I washed dishes, bused tables, worked at a grocery store, and wrote five more books.* By that time I had been practicing Zen meditation for almost ten years; the books were a great success; I was quite content. I was happily married for nine years, then happily divorced (we're friends to this day).

In 1981 I moved to Cambridge, Massachusetts, in order to try to salvage *ReVISION Journal*, a journal that Jack Crittenden and I had cofounded three years earlier. *ReVISION* was in many ways a remarkable journal, largely due to Jack's guiding energy and insight. At a time when cross-cultural philosophy and interdisciplinary studies were largely ignored, *ReVISION* was something of a beacon to many scholars and intellectuals interested in East/West studies and the interface between science and religion. We were, for example, the first to publish extensive papers on the holographic paradigm, with contributions by Karl Pribram, David Bohm, Fritjof Capra, and others. I later drew these papers together into a book entitled *The Holographic Paradigm: Exploring the Leading Edge of Science*.

Incredibly, *ReVISION* was a two-man show. I did the general editing from Lincoln, and Jack, in Cambridge, did absolutely everything else, from line editing to pasteup to assembly to printing to mailing. He finally hired an extremely intelligent (and very beautiful) woman to be the subscription department, and then promptly married the subscription department, who promptly got pregnant. Jack had to leave *ReVISION* in order to get a real job, and so I soon found myself on the way to Cambridge to see if I could rescue *ReVISION*.

It was in Cambridge that I finally met Sam in the flesh. We hit it off immediately. A hefty man with a beard, a genius for business, a globally inclined mind, and an extraordinarily warm heart, Sam reminded me of nothing so much as a great big teddy bear. He was in town to check out the possibility of moving Shambhala Publications to Boston, which he eventually did.

---

* No Boundary: Eastern and Western Approaches to Personal Growth; The Atman Project: A Transpersonal View of Human Development; A Sociable God: A Brief Introduction to a Transcendental Sociology; Up from Eden: A Transpersonal View of Human Evolution; Eye to Eye: The Quest for the New Paradigm.

But by the end of a year in Cambridge, I had had it. My friends all thought I would love Cambridge because of the intellectual stimulation, but I found it not so much stimulating as irritating. People seemed to confuse the sound of grinding teeth with thinking. *ReVISION* was eventually salvaged by moving it to Heldreff Publications, and I fled Cambridge for San Francisco—Tiburon, more precisely, where I lived with Frances and Roger, who, a year later, introduced me to Treya.

Sam was back in Boulder with his family, and—before I proposed to Treya—I wanted Sam and Treya to check each other out. And so on our way to Aspen to meet Treya's family, we stopped in Boulder. After talking with Treya for about five minutes, Sam pulled me aside and said, "Not only do I approve, I'm worried about her getting shortchanged."

I proposed to Treya that night, on a sidewalk in Boulder, outside of Rudi's restaurant on Pearl Street. All she said was, "If you didn't ask me, I was going to ask you."

I had previously planned a visit to Colorado with my parents. Although Ken and I had known each other less than two weeks, I desperately wanted him to meet them. We arranged for him to combine a business trip to Shambhala Publications in Boulder with a visit to Aspen. I flew out first and, throwing all caution to the winds, spent three days raving to my parents and old friends about this wonderful, unique, totally lovable man. I didn't care what they thought, even though I had never raved about a man in my entire life, and even though I hadn't even dated a man in over two years! I was for some reason unafraid of making a fool of myself; I felt certain of how I felt. Many of these friends had known me for well over ten years and were mostly convinced I would probably never get married. My mother couldn't control herself, she simply had to ask if I thought we'd get married, even though I hadn't mentioned that possibility and Ken and I had never discussed it. What could I say? I had to tell the truth. Yes, we would get married.

When I flew to Denver to meet Ken at the airport I was suddenly terribly nervous. I had a drink, very unusual for me, while waiting for him. I nervously watched everyone get off the plane, somehow secretly hoping he wouldn't be there. Who was this tall, bald, completely unusual man I was expecting anyway? Was I ready for this? No, at that moment, I was not ready.

And he was not on the plane. That gave me time to reconsider. From the fear of his arrival to the relief at not seeing him to disappointment to near panic that he would not show up. What if he turned out to be some figment of my dreams? What if he was real but had stayed on in L.A. with his old girlfriend? What if . . . I suddenly wanted wholeheartedly to see him again.

And yes, there he was, on the next plane. Unmistakable, impossible to miss. With a mixture of nervousness, embarrassment, and pure delight I greeted him, still unaccustomed to the attention his striking looks always attracted.

We spent the next few days in Boulder with his friends. Since Ken and I were always somehow physically attached to each other, in public or in private, I began to wonder what his friends thought of me. One evening after dinner, standing outside the restaurant where we had just eaten with Sam and Hazel, I asked him what he had told Sam about me. He held my hands and looked at me with those huge brown eyes and said, "I told Sam that if she'll have me, this is the woman I want to marry." Without a moment's reflection or hesitation I said "Of course." (I was thinking—or maybe I said—"I was going to ask you.") We all went out to celebrate with champagne, a mere ten days after our first date. It was a lovely, windy late-summer evening, fresh, clear, charged with energy. I felt the presence of the Colorado Rockies looming behind us, witnessing this promise, conferring their blessing. My favorite mountains. The man of my dreams. I felt delirious and dizzy with happiness.

In a few days we went to Aspen, where I had lived for almost ten years. My parents loved him. My brother and sister-in-law loved him. All my friends loved him. One sister called to congratulate me. The other called, concerned, to ask me questions she felt would reveal if this were genuine or not; I passed. Ken and I walked along my favorite path, up Conundrum Creek, flanked on either side by beautifully sculpted mountainsides. A perfect glacial valley filled with graceful aspen trees and strong evergreens, with rock outcroppings leading to complex ridgelines etched against the crystalline deep-blue sky. This was a path I had walked and run many, many times in the past. This was the valley I always visualized when I needed to feel at peace. And here we were, the peaceful murmur of the stream accompanying us, an occasional hummingbird darting by, the gentle rustling sound of the aspen leaves filling the air around us, Indian paintbrush and gentians and asters and cow parsnip and columbine, always the lovely columbine, scattered all about us.

That evening we went for some quiet time alone to a little cabin in the aspen forest. You might think gnomes or elves had built it. A large, reddish, lichen-covered rock formed one wall; its corners were living aspen trees and its other walls made of hand-hewn aspens. A person could walk by this cabin without noticing it, it blends so naturally into its surroundings. The chipmunks are as much at home inside as outside. There Ken and I talked of the future and fell happily asleep in each other's arms.

We are alone, sitting in front of the fireplace, fire blazing against the cool night, the electricity in the house, once again, not working. "Right there, on your left shoulder," Treya says. "Can't you see it?"

"See it, no I can't see it. See what?"

"Death. It's right there, on your left shoulder."

"Are you serious? You're kidding, right? I don't understand."

"We were talking about how death is a great teacher, and suddenly, on your left shoulder, I saw this dark but powerful figure. It's death, I'm sure."

"Do you hallucinate often?"

"No, never. It's just that I saw death on your left shoulder. I don't know what it means."

I can't help it. I look at my left shoulder. I don't see anything.

2

BEYOND PHYSICS

T H E wedding was set for November 26, a few months away. In the meantime we busied ourselves with all the necessary preparations. That is to say,
Treya busied herself with all the necessary preparations. I wrote a book.

This particular book, *Quantum Questions*, centered on the remarkable
fact that virtually every one of the great pioneers of modern physics—men
like Einstein and Schrödinger and Heisenberg—were spiritual *mystics* of
one sort or another, an altogether extraordinary situation. The hardest of
the sciences, physics, had run smack into the tenderest of religions,
mysticism. Why? And what exactly *was* mysticism, anyway?

So I collected the writings of Einstein, Heisenberg, Schrödinger, Louis
de Broglie, Max Planck, Niels Bohr, Wolfgang Pauli, Sir Arthur Eddington, and Sir James Jeans. The scientific genius of these men is beyond
dispute (all but two were Nobel laureates); what is so amazing, as I said, is
that they all shared a profoundly spiritual or mystical worldview, which is
perhaps the last thing one would expect from pioneering scientists.

The essence of mysticism is that in the deepest part of your own being,
in the very center of your own pure awareness, you are fundamentally one
with Spirit, one with Godhead, one with the All, in a timeless and eternal
and unchanging fashion. Sound far out? Listen to Erwin Schrödinger,
Nobel-prizewinning cofounder of modern quantum mechanics:

"It is not possible that this unity of knowledge, feeling, and choice that
you call *your own* should have sprung into being from nothingness at a
given moment not so long ago; rather, this knowledge, feeling and choice

are essentially eternal and unchangeable and numerically *one* in all men, nay, in all sensitive beings. Inconceivable as it seems to ordinary reason, you—and all other conscious beings as such—are all in all. Hence this life of yours which you are living is not merely a piece of the entire existence, but is, in a certain sense, the *whole*. . . . This is that sacred, mystic formula which is so simple and so clear: 'I am in the east and in the west, I am above and below, *I am this whole world.*'

"Thus you can throw yourself flat on the ground, stretched out upon Mother Earth, with the certain conviction that you are one with her and she with you. You are as firmly established, as invulnerable, as she—indeed, a thousand times firmer and more invulnerable. As surely as she will engulf you tomorrow, so surely will she bring you forth anew. And not merely 'someday': now, today, every day she is bringing you forth, not *once*, but thousands upon thousands of times, just as every day she engulfs you a thousand times over. For eternally and always there is only *now*, one and the same now; the present is the only thing that has no end."*

According to the mystics, when we go beyond or transcend our separate-self sense, our limited ego, we discover instead a Supreme Identity, an identity with the All, with universal Spirit, infinite and all-pervading, eternal and unchanging. As Einstein explains: "A human being is part of the whole, called by us 'Universe'; a part limited in time and space. He experiences himself, his thoughts and feelings as something separated from the rest—a kind of optical delusion of his consciousness. This delusion is a kind of prison for us, restricting us to our personal desires and to affection for a few persons nearest us. Our task must be to free ourselves from this prison."

Indeed, the whole point of meditation or contemplation—whether it appears in the East or in the West, whether Christian, Muslim, Buddhist, or Hindu—is to free ourselves from the "optical delusion" that we are merely separate egos set apart from each other and from eternal Spirit, and to discover instead that, once released from the prison of individuality, we are one with Godhead and thus one with all manifestation, in a perfectly timeless and eternal fashion.

And this is not a mere theoretical *idea*; it is a direct and immediate *experience*, which has been reported the world over from time immemorial, and which is essentially identical wherever it appears. As Schrödinger put it, "Within a cultural milieu where certain conceptions have

---

* All quotes in this section are from *Quantum Questions*.

been limited and specialized, it is daring to give this conclusion the simple wording that it requires. In Christian terminology to say: 'Hence I am God Almighty' sounds both blasphemous and lunatic. But please disregard these connotations for a moment, and consider that in itself, the insight is not new. In Indian thought it is considered, far from being blasphemous, to represent the quintessence of deepest insight into the happenings of the world. Again, the mystics of many centuries, independently, yet in perfect harmony with each other (somewhat like the particles in an ideal gas) have described, each of them, the unique experience of his or her life in terms that can be condensed in the phrase *Deus factus sum*—I have become God."

Not in the sense that my particular ego is God—far from it—but rather that, in the deepest part of my own awareness, I directly intersect eternity. And it was this direct intersection, this mystical awareness, that so interested these pioneering physicists.

In *Quantum Questions*, I wanted to show how and why these great physicists were all mystics, and I wanted them to be able to speak eloquently for themselves about why "the most beautiful emotion we can experience is the mystical" (Einstein), about how "the mechanism demands a mysticism" (de Broglie), about existing "in the mind of some eternal Spirit" (Jeans), about why "a synthesis embracing both rational understanding and the mystical experience of unity is the mythos, spoken or unspoken, of our present day and age" (Wolfgang Pauli), and about the most important relationship of all: "that of a human soul to a divine spirit" (Eddington).

Notice I was *not* saying that modern physics itself supports or proves a mystical worldview. I was saying the physicists themselves were mystics, and not that their discipline was a mystical or somehow spiritual endeavor resulting in a religious worldview. In other words, I disagreed entirely with books such as *The Tao of Physics* and *The Dancing Wu Li Masters*, which had claimed that modern physics supported or even proved Eastern mysticism.* This is a colossal error. Physics is a limited, finite, relative, and partial endeavor, dealing with a very limited aspect of reality. It does *not*, for example, deal with biological, psychological, economic, literary, or historical truths; whereas mysticism deals with all of that, with the Whole. To say physics proves mysticism is like saying the tail proves the dog.

---

* Fritjof Capra, the author of *The Tao of Physics* (now in a third, updated edition published by Shambhala) has since refined his views considerably; it is not so much Capra but his pale imitators, such as Gary Zukov and Fred Alan Wolf, that I have in mind.

To use Plato's analogy of the Cave: physics gives us a detailed picture of the shadows in the Cave (relative truth), whereas mysticism gives us a direct introduction to the Light beyond the Cave (absolute truth). Study the shadows all you want, you still won't have Light.

Moreover, *none* of these founding physicists believed that modern physics supports a mystical or religious worldview. They believed, rather, that modern science could no longer *object* to a religious worldview, simply because modern physics, unlike classical physics, had become acutely conscious of its extremely limited and partial role, of its total inadequacy in dealing with ultimate realities. As Eddington put it, also using Plato's analogy: "The frank realization that physical science is dealing with a world of shadows is one of the most significant of recent advances."

All of these pioneering physicists were mystics precisely because they wanted to go beyond the intrinsic limitations of physics itself to an interior and mystical awareness that, in transcending the world of shadow forms, revealed higher and more enduring realities. They were mystics, not because of physics, but in spite of physics. In other words, they wanted mysticism as meta-physics, which means "beyond physics."

And as for the attempt to support a particular religious worldview by interpretations from modern physics? Einstein, representing the majority of these physicists, called the whole attempt "reprehensible." Schrödinger actually called it "sinister," and explained: "Physics has nothing to do with it. Physics takes its start from everyday experience, which it continues by more subtle means. It remains akin to it, does not transcend it generically, it cannot enter into another realm . . . because [religion's] true domain is far beyond anything in reach of scientific explanation." And Eddington was decisive: "I do not suggest that the new physics 'proves religion' or indeed gives any positive grounds for religious faith. *For my own part I am wholly opposed to any such attempt*" (italics his).

Why? Simply imagine what would happen if we indeed said that modern physics supports mysticism. What happens, for example, if we say that today's physics is in perfect agreement with Buddha's enlightenment? What happens when tomorrow's physics supplants or replaces today's physics (which it most definitely will)? Does poor Buddha then lose his enlightenment? You see the problem. If you hook your God to today's physics, then when that physics slips, that God slips with it. And *that* is what concerned these mystical physicists. They wanted neither physics distorted nor mysticism cheapened by a shotgun wedding.

Treya watched all this with great interest—she soon became my best editor and most trusted critic. This was a particularly satisfying book. Treya and I were both meditators; that is, we both shared a contemplative or mystical worldview, and our meditation practice was a direct way to practice going beyond individuality, going beyond ego, and discovering a Self and Source beyond the mundane. That so many of the world's great physicists were also outspoken mystics was a great support. I had long ago decided that there were two types of people who believed in universal Spirit—those who were not too bright (e.g., Oral Roberts), and those who were extremely bright (e.g., Einstein). Those in between made it a point of "intellectual" merit not to believe in God, or anything transrational for that matter. Anyway, Treya and I believed in God, as one's own deepest Ground and Goal, which meant we were either very bright or slightly dumb. And by "God" I do not mean an anthropomorphic father figure (or mother figure), but rather a pure awareness, or consciousness as such, that is *what* there is and *all* there is, a consciousness that one cultivates in meditation and actualizes in daily life. This mystical understanding was absolutely central to Treya, and to me, and to our life together.

Treya watched the assembly of this book with much amusement, too. She decided that, whatever else I was doing, I was also trying to duck my responsibilities for the upcoming wedding. Probably true.

My connection with Treya continued to deepen, if that were possible. We were way, way, way "beyond physics"! Love is a time-honored way to transcend the separate-self sense and leap into the sublime; Treya and I held hands, closed our eyes, and jumped.

Looking back on it, we had these four pitifully short months to cement our relationship before cruel disaster would strike. The bond we formed in those few ecstatic months would have to last us through the ensuing five years of a nightmarish tour through medical hell. The ordeal was so grueling that eventually Treya and I both broke. Our love almost shattered, only to resurface and literally put us both back together.

In the meantime we were calling and writing our friends, who were kind and patient with two people who had obviously gone stark raving berserk. My friends took one look at Treya and had no trouble understanding why I was babbling and spitting up on myself. Treya's friends, who had never seen her babble over anything, found the whole situation immensely

enjoyable. I was uncharacteristically short-spoken; Treya uncharacteristically long-winded.

Muir Beach
September 2, 1983

Dear Bob,

I'll make this short. I've found her. I'm not sure exactly what that
means, but I've found her. Her name is Terry Killam, and she's, well . . .
She's gorgeous, intelligent, even brilliant, caring, loving, warm, compassionate, . . . did I say gorgeous? did I say brilliant? . . . and something
else: she has more courage and integrity than any person (male or female)
I've ever known. I don't know, Bob, I'd follow this woman anywhere. She's
not that bright, actually, because she feels the same way about me. Ten
days after we met I asked her to marry me. You believe that? She said
yes, you believe *that*? Wedding invite to follow. Bring a friend, if you can
find one.

Later,
Ken

P.S. I know, you'll be there on the second day, if there is one.

Muir Beach
September 24, 1983

Dear Alyson,

Well, love, I've finally found him. Remember those lists we made,
well-lubricated with sherry, our "wish-list" for the perfect man? How
many years ago was that and what deadline did I choose? Who knows . . .
and I had long ago given up. I never, ever thought anything like this would
happen to me.

His name is Ken Wilber—you've probably heard of his writings and
may have read some of his books. He writes about consciousness and
transpersonal psychology and his books are used a great deal at various
universities (including mine, the California Institute of Integral Studies).
If you haven't read his stuff I think you'd be interested, and I'll send you
some of his books. He's considered by many to be the leading theorist in
transpersonal studies. Ken jokes that "being called the foremost theorist in
transpersonal psychology is like being called the tallest building in Kansas
City."

22

Meeting him made me realize that inside I had pretty much decided I would never find anyone I wanted to marry and would carry on through life in my old, comfortable, independent style. I've never even considered marrying someone before, even though I am thirty-six, and then along comes Mr. Ken Wilber!

We feel like we've been together forever. I have never felt such a connection with any man before in my life; it's as if the very cells of my being are connected to him, and as if that kind of connection is simply the most concrete and immediate expression of a connection between us that exists on all levels, even the most subtle. I have never felt so loved and accepted, or so loving and accepting of another person, in my life. He is definitely the man for me! Actually, the hardest thing for me was getting used to the fact that he shaves his head (he's a Zen Buddhist and has been practicing meditation for twelve or thirteen years, and he got in the habit of shaving his head). He's thirty-four years old, six-foot-four, thin, with a beautiful and very clear face and a wonderful body. I'll try to enclose a picture, and I'll also send you some of his books.

Finding him also made me feel somewhat vindicated . . . that sounds like a strong way to describe it, but it's the sense I had. That following my own inner sense of direction, as confused as it may have looked on the surface, really was leading me somewhere. The sense we have is that we've known each other before and have been looking for each other again in this lifetime. . . . I don't know if I believe that way of describing things actually, but it's an accurate metaphor for how we feel. He does feel like my soulmate, corny as that word sounds. Being with Ken is filling up some of those inner places of self-doubt and doubt of the universe. I have great respect for his work and his intelligence, and I love the way his intelligence shows through in all aspects of his life. He's also got an incredible sense of humor—he keeps me laughing all the time!— and a lightness about how he lives his life, which is good for me. I feel very loved and recognized by him, in a way I've never experienced before. He is the most loving, kind, supportive man I've ever known. The relationship feels very natural, very easy, not a lot of issues to work through. More like, oh, there you are, I've been looking for you. We make a great team and I'm really excited to see how our lives together shape up in the future. An amazing thought to look ahead twenty years and know we'll still be together . . . quite an adventure! I'm really looking forward to a long life with him.

I can't quite believe it sometimes, I don't really trust the universe to let it happen, like something might change, etc. But we feel very committed to each other and I think it will be fascinating to watch the relationship and our work take shape over the years. He's pretty much moved in already and plans are moving for the wedding, which seems odd, too, to be planning a wedding. We feel already married, really, and the ceremony feels like it's mostly for the family.

Well, love, that's my big news. All I've been doing lately is hanging out with Ken and keeping up with my counseling clients. It's late now and I'm tired. I'll tell you more when I see you . . . at my wedding!

Love,
Terry

I keep looking at my left shoulder, staring actually, because I can't see anything. I think Treya is probably kidding; I don't know her that well. "You mean, you figuratively see it."

"I don't know what it means, but I definitely saw a figure of death sitting on your left shoulder, just as plainly as I'm now looking at your face. It looked like, I don't know, like a black gremlin, just sitting there, smiling."

"You're sure this doesn't happen to you often?"

"Never. I'm sure."

"Why my left shoulder? Why me?" This is starting to get a little bizarre. With no light in the room except that cast by the dwindling fire, it's also slightly eerie.

"I don't know. But it seems very important. I'm serious."

She is so earnest I cannot help it: once again I actually look at my left shoulder. Once again I see nothing.

A month before the ceremony, Treya went in for a physical.

So here I lie on my doctor's examination table, legs spread wide, a white sheet draped over my knees, exposed to the cool air and the doctor's probing hands—the classic position for a gynecological exam. Having a general physical seems like a good idea at this time, since I'm just about to be married. My parents have these checkups regularly, I have them irregularly. Of course, I feel fine. I've always been healthy as a, pardon the expression, horse. I assume Ken is getting a healthy wife.

I visualize an African chieftain examining a girl's teeth and shins before approving the marriage with his son.

My head is full of plans and questions: where to hold the wedding, how many to invite, what crystal and china patterns to select, all the earthshaking issues that must be decided before this union can be sanctified. There's not much time for all these preparations. We decided to get married about a week after we first met and set the date for three months after that.

The doctor's examination continues. He is now poking and pushing my abdomen and my stomach. He's a nice man, a nice doctor. I like him a lot. He's a general practitioner and interested in health on all levels, so he not only practices as an M.D. but as a therapist. This shows in the way he works with his patients, in the atmosphere in his office. A nice man.

Now he's examining my breasts. First the left one. They're big breasts, have been ever since I was about twelve. I remember being afraid they wouldn't grow, times I sat in a bathtub with a girl friend, both of us massaging and pulling on our nipples to hasten our progress into womanhood. They did grow, suddenly and too much, a situation that became obvious at a summer camp when I had to borrow a well-used bra. My breasts—such an embarrassment so many times. When I was young boys accidentally brushed up against me on uncrowded town streets. When I was older, men's eyes seemed unable to focus on my face. Blouses pull between the buttons in front, clothes that looked good on others don't on me, overblouses make me look fat or pregnant, tucking blouses in makes me look fat and busty. All my life I've been what I learned men refer to as a four-hook woman. Bra straps cut into my shoulders. They don't make pretty, lacy, sexy bras in my size. I always have to wear a bra, and I need an especially strong one to go riding or jogging. Bikinis and even two piece suits, when I can find them in my size, look, in my eyes, obscene. One piece suits never give me enough support.

But I got used to the adjustments this peculiarity requires and grew to like my breasts. They are soft and firm and rather pretty, in a *Playboy* magazine kind of way. Apparently I inherited this trait from my father's mother. I'm the only one of the four women in my family with this problem. Mother once suggested I have my breasts reduced. I think she was concerned about my problems in finding clothes. I thought this was unnecessary, but I went to see a plastic surgeon many years ago. The doctor explained the surgical procedure but agreed with me. My breasts were big, but not big enough to warrant such drastic measures.

Now the doctor begins examining my right breast. A careful examination, the kind I should give myself each month. I vaguely remember being told to do breast self-examinations, but I'm quite certain that I was never taught how to do it. My doctor continued his examination.

"Do you know you have a lump in your right breast?"

What? A lump? "Why no, I didn't know."

"It's right here, in the lower outer quadrant of your right breast. You should be able to feel it easily."

He guides my hand to the area. Yes, I can feel it easily. Too easily. It would have been a cinch to find something this size if I'd only been looking. "What do you think it is, doctor?"

"Well, it's fairly large and quite hard. But it's not attached to the muscle underneath and it moves easily. My guess is with those characteristics and in a woman your age it's nothing to worry about. It may be just a cyst."

"What do you think we should do?" No mention yet of the word *cancer.*

"Considering your age, which makes it unlikely that this is cancer, why don't we wait a month and see if the lump changes size? It could change with your menstrual cycle. Come back and see me in a month."

I am relieved. I get dressed, say goodbye, and leave. My head is full of wedding plans, people to call, decisions to make. I'm also working on a master's degree in psychology and counseling, so there's reading and studying and work at the counseling center to do. Yet underneath it all now lies this cold current of fear. Could this be breast cancer? I knew I was afraid. It was not anything I could put into words, just a feeling of dread, of somehow knowing. Was this a premonition? Or was it simply the fear any woman would feel at such a time? I busy myself with all there is to do at this exciting time. Still, still, I find my fingers furtively reaching for that hard, definite, unchanging lump. Alas, it's always there. Walking briskly through downtown San Francisco while shopping for wedding shoes—it's still there. Sitting in a psychology class at graduate school—still there. Sitting at my desk making phone calls to arrange things for the wedding—still there. Right where my breast touches the futon as I lie each night next to my husband-to-be, snuggling into my favorite place with his long arms wrapped around me—still there.

I thought the lump was nothing. It was extremely hard, like a rock, which was bad; but it was symmetrical and detached, which was good. And anyway, there was only a one in ten chance it was cancer. All of our friends thought it was nothing. Besides, we were in love. What could possibly go wrong? The only thing on our horizon was a wedding, followed by "lived happily ever after."

I rushed around, getting things ready for the wedding three weeks away. It was incredibly exciting, I was so sure, though still nervous. Here I was, preparing for an event I had no idea would be so complicated. And occasionally I'd feel shooting pains in my right breast and worry; feel again for that hard, smooth lump and wonder.

There was a lot to do. We'd recently returned from a quick trip to the East coast to meet Ken's parents. My parents came up for a weekend of preparations, helping us scout possible locations for the ceremony, helping me choose the engraving for the invitations.

We could have waited, of course. I'd always wanted to be married in a green mountain meadow in the Colorado Rockies, if that unexpected event ever took place. But I didn't want to wait until next summer, even if it meant being married in the same month as my birthday, and tucked in between Thanksgiving and Christmas. It would be nice to celebrate our anniversary in a less crowded month, to be sure. But I was in a hurry. I remember saying, "For some reason, I seem to be in a real hurry to get married." I remember that distinctly, even before the lump was discovered.

So, after all those years of fears that I was searching for impossible perfection or was secretly afraid to make a commitment, we were married. I'd known Ken less than four months, but I was sure. He whispered wonderful things to me in the limousine on our way to the ceremony, about searching for me for lifetimes, slaying dragons to find me, romantic, poetic, lovely things that felt deeply true. I was even a little embarrassed because I wondered if my mother and father could hear too.

Our wedding day was a beautifully clear, brilliantly sunny day, the first nice day after a week of wild, blustery storms. Everything glistened in the sunshine; the air itself seemed full of light. A magical day. We were married by two dear friends, David Wilkinson, a Methodist minister I'd known during my years at Findhorn, and Father Michael Abdo, the abbot of a Catholic monastery near my previous home in

Colorado. (When Ken and I were engaged, I sent Father Michael a box of Ken's books, along with a letter saying we were getting married. Father Michael opened the box and said, "Oh, I see Terry has discovered my favorite writer." Then he opened the letter and said, "Oh, I see Terry is *marrying* my favorite writer.") My Methodist friend reminded us that marriage could be a prison—behind us Alcatraz rose out of the glistening San Francisco Bay—or bring beauty and freedom, and he gestured toward the sweeping arch of the Golden Gate Bridge joining two pieces of land, as we were that day joined.

The reception was great fun, mingling families and friends with the requisite copious amounts of champagne and assorted goodies. I liked what Judith Skutch, publisher of A *Course in Miracles*, said: "This is a marriage made by royalty!" I was delirious! I wished afterward that I had stopped for a few moments during the whirl of things to let it all sink in. And that night I slept curled in my husband's arms, elated and exhausted.

That day and the next there wasn't time for fear, nor time to check for the lump. By now my initial sense that there might indeed be something wrong had faded as others reassured me and wedding plans engulfed me. I felt quite carefree as I returned to the doctor's for another check.

Our Hawaiian honeymoon was planned for two weeks later, since Treya had to finish classes and take final exams. Almost everybody had quit worrying by then.

"Well, it's still there. Doesn't look like it's changed at all," my doctor says. "Have you noticed any changes?"

"Not in its size or the way it feels, no. I have noticed some shooting pains in my breast that I don't remember before, but they're in other parts of the breast. I still don't feel anything around the lump," I answer. There's silence for a time. I can feel the wheels turning as my doctor ponders what to do.

"Well," he finally says. "This is a difficult case to call. I don't think the lump is anything, probably just a cyst. The way it feels, your age, your health, everything leads me to think it's nothing. But, again because of your age, I think, just to be sure, you should have it taken out. It's the safest course."

"OK, if you say so. I've got plenty of spare breast tissue! When do you think I should have it done? Ken and I leave for our honeymoon in a week and we'll be gone two weeks over Christmas. Can it wait three weeks?" I am mostly concerned with travel plans.

"Yes, I think so. No danger in waiting three weeks. It'll be nicer not to have an incision with stitches to worry about on your honeymoon anyway," he says. "I'd also like you to see another doctor, a surgeon, for a second opinion. Here's his name. His office is close to Marin General."

Thinking very little of all this—after all, I'm only taking the necessary precautions—I find myself the next day in this surgeon's office. He examines the lump and my breast carefully. He has me raise my hand above my head, tense my muscles, then put my hands on my knees with my elbows out and tense the muscles. He looks carefully at the skin over the lump. I don't know it at the time, but there are ways to guess from this kind of external examination if a lump might be malignant or not. If malignant there is often a slight puckering of the skin over the lump. Since my skin does not do that and the lump is unattached to anything, this doctor also feels that it is probably just a cyst. He proceeds to try to aspirate the lump, sounding quite confident. For this procedure a wide needle is used; if the lump is a fluid-filled cyst, the fluid is drained out through the needle and voilà, only seconds later no lump. But when he tries this with my lump, the needle jams up against something hard. The doctor seems surprised and slightly startled. Oh, he says, it must after all be a fibroadenoma, a benign growth. He recommends having it removed, and he also thinks it would be fine to wait until after our three week honeymoon/Christmas trip to have the procedure done. So I walk out of that office with a bruise on my breast and the lump still inside. . . .

So that decided it. The doctors were convinced the lump was nothing to worry about, even though it should be removed, and so everybody pretty much stopped worrying. Except Sue, Treya's mother.

Mother is quite insistent. She wants me to see an oncological surgeon, someone who specializes in cancer, for yet a third opinion. This is in spite of the fact that we leave on our honeymoon in four days and I have two final exams before then. I resist, then reluctantly agree. After all, she knows whereof she speaks. This is the same mother who fifteen years before shocked and frightened the whole family when it was discovered she had colon cancer.

I remember well the absolute terror and confusion of the days surrounding the discovery and her operation, which happened the summer after I graduated from college. I remember well how shocked and dazed and somehow uncomprehending we all were, wandering glassy-eyed around the huge complex of M. D. Anderson Cancer Center in Houston. I remember well Mother in her hospital bed, tubes seemingly coming to and from everywhere. It all seems like a blur to me now, the rush home, the feeling of not knowing, the flight to Houston and M. D. Anderson Hospital, the hotel room, my dear father pacing up and down in the room, in the parking lot, in the hospital, trying to take care of Mom, trying to explain to us, living with his own fear, making all the arrangements and decisions. Somehow I don't think it ever really hit me, the seriousness of it all. I went through the whole thing in a daze. I didn't really understand what cancer was. Not then, not even when we visited Mom after the operation, still groggy from the sedative, not even when I felt the tension and fear in the house go up each time she returned to M. D. Anderson for a checkup over the following years.

Now it's fifteen years later. She's passed each checkup. And each time our family would breathe a collective sigh of relief. Each time the level of fear would drop just a bit. The world seemed a little more stable, a little more trustworthy. I worried less about what Daddy would do without Mother; they were so close I simply couldn't imagine either of them living without the other. I never once thought to worry about what it might be like for Mother to die from cancer. I knew too little then to worry about such things. At least my ignorance saved me unnecessary worry, for here she was fifteen years later, feeling fine and sounding quite adamant about my getting yet a third opinion.

This time from an oncologist, a cancer specialist. Perhaps I should come to M. D. Anderson? she suggests. Over the years my parents had become more involved in Anderson out of gratitude for the excellent care my mother had received and out of interest in supporting cancer research. They had recently endowed a chair for research into genetics and cancer.

But I want to go to Hawaii, not Houston. I call a cousin who is a gynecologist in the city to see if he can recommend an oncologist. He does, and I make an appointment. Mother wants to know more about this Doctor Peter Richards before turning me over to him. It turns out that Dr. Richards trained at M. D. Anderson with the surgeon who performed my mother's operation fifteen years earlier! What luck . . . and he comes highly recommended by M. D. Anderson. He was one of the best to come along in years, they say, and they had wanted him to stay. But he had chosen to return to Children's Hospital in San Francisco, where his father was Chief of Surgery. That's nice, I keep thinking. I like that touch, and mother is satisfied.

The next day I find myself in the office of Peter Richards. I like him immediately. He's young, personable, and obviously very capable. I feel comfortable in his office; by contrast the last office I was in seems seedy, out of date. After his examination of the lump and of both breasts, he too suggests removal of the lump. However, he does not want to wait for three weeks. He feels the lump should come out right away. It's probably nothing, he reassures me, but he'll feel more comfortable taking it out now.

Perhaps I'm still high on the wedding, high on being in love, high on the thought of Hawaii. None of this bothers me. We schedule a lumpectomy for the next day, Thursday, at 4:00 P.M., which would leave just enough time for the lab to examine a frozen section and give us a report. Since this is same-day surgery with only a local anaesthetic, I assume I'll feel just fine for my final exam the following morning. We plan on leaving for Hawaii right after the exam.

"What if there's a problem?" Dr. Richards asks delicately. "Then we won't go," I answer, happy in my ignorance. After a few weeks of the creeping, shadowy fear that followed the discovery of the lump, I have now adopted the cheery attitude of I'll deal with it when/if it happens.

I spend the evening and most of the next day preparing for my exam. Ken is working hard to finish *Quantum Questions*. I am so confident I tell Ken he doesn't have to come to the hospital with me, since I don't want to interrupt his work. I'm used to doing things on my own, after so many years; what I'm not used to is asking people for help. Ken is shocked by my suggestion that I go alone. I'm secretly relieved that he's coming with me.

Treya and I talked of Hawaii on our way to Children's Hospital. We found the same-day-surgery section, and began the formalities. All of a sudden I became quite apprehensive and nervous. The procedure hadn't even begun, and yet I felt something was terribly wrong.

Ken is more nervous than I am. I undress, put on the gown, lock my clothes away, am given my hospital ID bracelet. More waiting time. A young Scandinavian doctor comes by to ask some questions. He will be assisting Dr. Richards, he says. His questions seem innocuous enough; only later do I understand their import.

"How old were you when you started menstruating?"

"I think fourteen. A bit later than most." (Women who begin menstruating early are at higher risk for breast cancer.)

"Have you ever had a child?"

"No, I've never even been pregnant." (Women who have not had a child by the age of thirty are at higher risk for breast cancer.)

"Has anyone in your family had breast cancer?"

"Not that I know of." (Somehow I had completely forgotten—blocked?—that my mother's sister had breast cancer five years earlier. She has been fine since. Women with breast cancer in their family are at higher risk.)

"Does the lump hurt? Has it ever hurt?"

"No, never." (Cancerous lumps almost never hurt.)

"How do you feel about the operation? If you are nervous or afraid we can give you something."

"That won't be necessary. I feel fine." (Studies have shown that women who are most afraid before having a lumpectomy for suspected malignancy are less likely to have cancer; those who are calm are more likely to have cancer.)

"Are you both vegetarians? I have a theory that I can tell by the color of people's skins."

"Yes, we both are. I've been a vegetarian since 1972, over ten years." (A diet high in animal fat—the type of diet I was raised on—has been implicated in breast cancer.)

I soon find myself flat on my back on a stretcher being wheeled through hallways known to me only by their ceilings. What's the opposite of a bird's eye view? because that's what I have for the next hour or so. The operating room turns out to be surprisingly cold—this makes it less hospitable to bacteria. A nurse brings me another sheet, this one deliciously warm, as if fresh out of the oven. I chat with the nurse as she makes preparations, interested in all the proceedings and wanting an explanation of everything. She hooks me up to the heart monitor, explaining that it will sound an alarm if my heartbeat falls below sixty. I tell her my heartbeat is fairly slow anyway and she lowers the level to fifty-six.

There we are, the friendly nurse, the nice Scandinavian doctor, and my pal Dr. Richards, talking about all sorts of things—vacations, skiing, hiking (we all love the outdoors), families, philosophies. A thin barrier has been erected between my searching eyes and the arena of action, my right breast. I wish I could see what's going on in a mirror somehow, then decide that it's probably too bloody to see much anyway. The local anaesthetic given earlier to my outer, lower right breast has taken effect, though as Dr. Richards cuts deeper a few more shots are needed. My imagination paints a vivid but probably inaccurate picture of the proceedings. A few times the heart monitor beeps to say my pulse is below fifty-six, so calm am I. Dr. Richards makes a few comments to the second doctor about subcutaneous stitching technique, and then it is all over.

But when I hear Dr. Richards say "Call Dr. X" my heart suddenly jumps. "Is there anything wrong?" I ask, panic in my voice and my heart suddenly pounding way past fifty-six. "Oh no," Dr. Richards says. "We're just calling for the pathologist who's waiting to look at the tumor."

I relax. All has gone normally. I can't understand why I suddenly panicked at that moment. I am unwrapped, cleaned up, and moved to a wheelchair for my return journey, feeling much less helpless than when flat on my back but still lost in anonymous hallways. I am wheeled out to the nurse's desk then given yet more papers to fill out. I am thinking of my test the next day when Dr. Richards shows up to ask where Ken is. Unconcerned, I say he's in the waiting room.

I knew Treya had cancer when I saw Peter come down and ask the duty nurse for a private conference room.

A few minutes later the three of us are in a private room. Dr. Richards mumbles something like I'm sorry but the tumor is malignant. I am shocked, almost frozen. I don't cry. In a dazed kind of calm I ask several intelligent questions, trying to hold on, not daring yet to look at Ken. But when Dr. Richards leaves to call a nurse, then, and only then, I turn to look at Ken, stricken. I burst into tears, everything dissolves around me. Somehow I am out of my wheelchair and into his arms, sobbing, sobbing.

Strange things happen to the mind when catastrophe strikes. It felt like the universe turned into a thin paper tissue, and then someone simply tore the tissue in half right in front of my eyes. I was so stunned that it was as if absolutely nothing had happened. A tremendous strength descended on me, the strength of being both totally jolted and totally stupefied. I was clear, present, and very determined. As Samuel Johnson drily commented, the prospect of death marvelously concentrates the mind. I felt marvelously concentrated, all right; it was only that our universe had just been torn right down the middle. The rest of the afternoon and all of that evening unfolded in slow-motion freeze-frames, one clear and exquisitely painful frame after the next, no filters, no protection.

I only remember pieces of the rest. Ken held me while I cried. How foolish I'd been to even think of coming alone! It felt like I cried constantly for the next three days, not really understanding anything. Dr. Richards returned to explain our alternatives, something about mastectomy, radiation, implantation, lymph nodes. He assured us he didn't expect us to remember much of this and he'd be glad to go over it again anytime. We had a week to ten days to think about it and make up our minds. A nurse from the breast health information center arrived with a packet of information and an explanation that was too elementary to be very interesting; besides, we were too devastated to listen.

I suddenly wanted out, out of that hospital, out into the air, out where things smelled normal again and no one wore white robes. Somehow I felt terribly like damaged goods, like I wanted to apologize to Ken. Here was this wonderful man, my husband of a mere ten days, and his new wife turns out to have CANCER. Like opening a long-awaited present only to find the lovely crystal inside smashed. It seemed unfair to burden him with something this major so soon in our married life. It just seemed too much to ask him to have to deal with this.

Ken stopped that kind of thinking right away. He didn't make me feel silly for thinking like that. He understood how I might feel that way but said my having cancer made no difference. "I've been looking for you for ages, and I'm just glad to have you. None of this matters. I'll never let you go, I'll always be here with you. You're not damaged goods, you're my wife, my soulmate, the light of my life." He wasn't going to let me go it alone, no sense my even trying. So there. No doubt at all that he would be there for me in every way possible, as I found out in the long months ahead. What if he'd let me talk him out of going to the hospital with me?

I remember driving home. I remember Ken asking me if I felt embarrassed at having cancer. I said no, that emotion hadn't occurred to me. I didn't feel it was my fault in any direct way, more the luck of the draw and life in these modern times. One out of four Americans gets cancer; one out of ten women gets breast cancer. But most get it when they're older. They usually don't even begin looking for breast cancer in women until they're thirty-five. I was thirty-six, just over the line. Never really heard that big, lumpy breasts put you at more risk. But having a child before you're thirty seems to confer some kind of protection . . . not that I could have done much about that, my life developing as it did. Can just imagine the operating manual for girl babies destined to grow big breasts. Check "Breasts, precautions" in the index and find, along with warnings about sunburn and clandestine breast squeezers who operate in crowds, there'd be this recommendation: "advisable to use for original design purposes before the age of thirty."

We returned to our Muir Beach home, only to be faced with the difficult task of all-night phone calls.

At home I sat huddled on the couch, crying. Tears felt like an automatic, knee-jerk, reflexive response to the word CANCER, like the only sane and appropriate response. I simply sat there and cried as Ken called family and friends with the bad news. Sometimes I sobbed, sometimes the tears trickled steadily; I was in no shape to talk to anyone. Ken back and forth, hugging me, talking on the phone, hugging me, talking on the phone. . . .

After a while something shifted. Self-pity lost its savor. The drumbeat of CANCER-CANCER-CANCER pounding in the back of my head became less insistent. Tears no longer satisfied, like when you've eaten too many cookies and the taste is lost. By the time Ken reached the last few people to call I was calm enough to talk a bit on the phone. That felt better than sitting like a sodden, leaking lump on the couch. "Why me?" was a question that soon lost its punch. "What now?" replaced it.

The freeze-frames clicked by, slowly, painfully, vividly. A few phone calls came in from the hospital, all bearing bad news. The lump had been 2.5 centimeters, fairly large. That technically put Treya in the stage two category, which meant a higher chance for lymph node involvement. Worse, the pathology report revealed that the cells in the tumor were extremely poorly differentiated (which meant, basically, very cancerous). On a scale from one to four, four being the worst, Treya had a particularly bad grade four tumor—vicious, hard to kill, and very fast-growing, though at the time we understood virtually none of this.

Although everything was happening in painfully slow motion, each frame contained too much experience and too much information, which produced the bizarre sensation that things were happening both very rapidly and very slowly, somehow at the same time. I kept having the image of myself playing baseball: I am standing there with my glove on, with several people throwing baseballs at me, which I am supposed to catch. But so many balls are being thrown at me that they bounce off my face and body and land on the ground, while I stand there with a stupid-looking expression. "Gee, guys, want to slow down and give me a chance? No? . . ." The bad-news phone calls continued.

Why couldn't someone call with good news, I thought? Isn't this enough for now? How about a ray of hope somewhere? With each call I went through a period of renewed self-pity, why me? I let myself react, and then after some time passed I could accept the news calmly as simple factual information. This is the way it is. I had a 2.5 centimeter lump removed. It was invasive carcinoma. The cells were poorly differentiated.

That's all we knew for now.

It was late. Ken went in the kitchen to get us some tea. The world lay quiet, resting, and my tears began again. Quiet tears, despairing tears. This was true, this was real, this was happening to me. Ken came back in, looked at me; didn't say a thing; sat down, put his arms around me; held me very tight; we stared into the darkness, not saying a word.

3

CONDEMNED TO MEANING

❦

S U D D E N L Y, I am awake. Uneasy, disoriented. It must be three or four in the morning. Something is terribly, terribly wrong. Ken breathes deeply beside me. The night is dark and still; I can see the stars through the skylight. A terrible ache rushes into my heart, tightens my throat. Fear. Of what? I notice my hand, resting on my right breast, stroking the bandages, sensing the stitches beneath. I remember. Oh no, no. My eyes squeeze shut, my face contorts, my throat closes in fear. Yes, I remember. I don't want to remember; I don't want to know. But here it is. Cancer. Cancer awakens me in the stillness of this dark night, this fifth night past my wedding night. I have cancer. I have breast cancer. A hard lump was removed from my right breast only hours ago. It was not benign. I have cancer.

This is real. This is happening to me. I lie in bed rigid with shock and disbelief as the world lies quiet around me. Ken lies next to me; I can feel his comforting presence, warm and strong. But suddenly I feel terribly alone. I have cancer. I have breast cancer. I believe this is true and, at the same time, I do not believe it; I cannot let it in. And yet this knowledge awakens me in the night, it catches in my throat and leaks out of my eyes and sets my heart pounding. So loud in this still, soft night with Ken breathing deeply beside me.

Yes, there it is, the fresh incision in my breast. Unmistakable, undeniable. No, I cannot sleep. Not with this ache in my throat and in my chest, not with my eyes squeezed tight against what I know to be true but cannot accept, not with this terrible fear of the unknown massed densely all about me. What to do? I get up, crawling carefully over Ken. He stirs, settles again to a restless sleep. I can see dim, familiar shapes about me. The house is cold. I find my pink terrycloth robe, wrap myself in its comforting familiarity. It is December and we have no central heating in this house here on the edge of the Pacific. I hear the waves of Muir Beach breaking far below, ghostly in the night. I do not build a fire but wrap myself in a blanket against the cold.

Now I am awake, terribly awake. Alone with my shock and my fear. What to do? I'm not hungry, I can't meditate, reading seems irrelevant. Suddenly I remember the package of information the nurse gave me, the nurse from the Breast Health Education Center. Of course, of course. I'll read that. It seems a lifesaver to me, something relevant to read, something to calm my fear, something to reduce the ignorance that feeds the fear.

I curl up on the couch, pulling my blanket tighter around me. All is quiet, very still. How many other women, I wonder, have also awakened in the middle of this same night with the same stark knowledge? How many awakened last night, how many will awaken nights to come? How many women have heard this word CANCER pounding like an endless drumbeat inside their heads, relentless, unforgiving. CANCER. CANCER. CANCER. This cannot be undone, this cannot be erased. CANCER. A cloud of voices, images, ideas, fears, stories, photographs, advertisements, articles, movies, television shows arises around me, vague, shapeless, but dense, ominous. These are the stories my culture has collected around this thing, "the big C." These voices and stories and images around me are full of fear and pain and helplessness. This big C is not a good thing. Most die from it, the stories tell me, their deaths often protracted and painful, terrible indeed. I don't know the details. I know very little about cancer, really, but these stories tell me it is terrible and painful and uncontrollable and mysterious and powerful, especially in its mystery. No one understands it, this growth gone out of control. No way to stop it or direct it or ultimately to contain it. A wild, blind growth that ultimately destroys itself and its host with its voraciousness. Blind, self-destructive, malevolent. No one understands it, not how it begins or how to stop it.

And this is what has been growing inside me. I shiver slightly, pulling my blanket tighter, wrapping myself in a cocoon against this terrible thing. But it is here inside me, it has been here all the time I felt so well, all the time I ran twelve miles a week, all the time I ate good food, raw salads and steamed vegetables, all the time I meditated regularly, studied, led a quiet life. Who can understand this? Why now, why me, why anyone?

I sit here, on this couch, wrapped in my blanket, these papers and pamphlets piled in my lap. I turn to them, obsessed with wanting to know more. Is there more than these stories my culture has told me? Perhaps there is. I know that not-knowing feeds my fear, the cloud around me billows larger. So I read. About the woman who found her lump when it was the size of an apple seed. Mine was 2.5 centimeters, just under an inch. About children with leukemia, how can such a thing happen, for children to suffer so. About types of cancer I knew nothing about; they never before existed in my world. About surgery and chemotherapy and radiation. About survival rates, those crucial numbers for cancer patients. These numbers mean people, people like me. After five years such-and-such percent survive, such-and-such percent die. Where will I be? In which percent? I want to know now. I cannot bear this not-knowing, this groping in the dark, this trembling in the night. I want to know now. Should I prepare to live? Or should I prepare to die? I do not know. No one can tell me. They can give me figures, but no one can tell me.

I dive further into these words, these pictures, these figures. They keep me occupied, keep my mind from spinning its own fearful tales. I eye the full color pictures of patients under huge machines, lying on operating tables, conferring with concerned doctors, posing with their families all smiling at the camera. Soon this will be me. I am about to become a patient, and eventually a cancer statistic. These things will be done to me, as they have been done to so many others. I am not alone in this, the pictures make that clear. So many people involved in this "war against cancer," a war now to be fought in my own body.

The reading soothes me. This night information is my lifeline out of useless fear and worry. This night information was the best kind of therapy. I was to find this was always true for me in the future. The more I knew, the more secure I felt, even if the news was bad. Ignorance frightens me; knowledge soothes me. The worst part is not knowing . . . definitely the worst part is not knowing.

I crawl back into bed, push against Ken's warm body. He is awake, silently looking at the skylight. "I'm not going to leave you, you know." "I know." "I really think we can beat this, kid. We just have to figure out what the hell we're going to do. . . ."

As Treya realized, our immediate problem was not cancer; our immediate problem was information. And the first thing you learn about cancer information is: basically, none of it is true.

Let me explain. In any disease, a person is confronted with two very different entities. One, the person is faced with the actual disease process itself—a broken bone, a case of influenza, a heart attack, a malignant tumor. Call this aspect of disease "illness." Cancer, for example, is an illness, a specific disease with medical and scientific dimensions. Illness is more or less value-free; it's not true or false, good or bad, it just is—just like a mountain isn't good or bad, it just is.

But two, the person is also faced with how his or her society or culture deals with that illness—with all the judgments, fears, hopes, myths, stories, values, and meanings that a particular society hangs on each illness. Call this aspect of disease "sickness." Cancer is not only an illness, a scientific and medical phenomenon; it is also a sickness, a phenomenon loaded with cultural and social meanings. Science tells you when and how you are ill; your particular culture or subculture tells you when and how you are sick.

This is not necessarily or even especially a bad thing. If a culture treats a particular illness with compassion and enlightened understanding, then sickness can be seen as a challenge, as a healing crisis and opportunity. Being "sick" is then not a condemnation or a moral judgment, but a movement in a larger process of healing and restoration. When sickness is viewed positively and in supportive terms, then illness has a much better chance to heal, with the concomitant result that the entire person may grow and be enriched in the process.

Men and women are condemned to meaning, condemned to creating values and judgments. It is not enough to know *that* I have a disease; *that* I have a disease is my illness. But I also need to know *why* I have that disease. Why me? What does it mean? What did I do wrong? How did this happen? I need, in other words, to attach some sort of *meaning* to this illness. And for this meaning I am dependent first and foremost on my society, on all the stories and values and meanings in which my culture dresses a particular disease. My sickness, as opposed to my illness, is defined largely by the society—the culture or subculture—in which I find myself.

Consider, for example, gonorrhea. As an illness it is fairly straightforward: an infection chiefly of the mucosal lining of the genitourinary tract, spread by sexual contact among infected partners, and highly sensitive to treatment by antibiotics, especially penicillin.

That's gonorrhea as an illness, as a medical entity. But our society attaches a great number of meanings and judgments to gonorrhea as a sickness—society has much to say about the disease and those who contract it, some of which is true, much of which is false and cruel. Those who contract gonorrhea are unclean, or perverts, or morally degenerate; gonorrhea is a moral disease, which is its own painful punishment; those who get gonorrhea deserve it, since they are morally unfit—and so on.

Long after penicillin has destroyed the illness, the sickness may still remain, its judgments and condemnations eating away at the person's soul the way the simpler bacteria once ate at the body. "I'm a rotten person, I'm no good, how horrible of me. . . ."

Thus, it is through science that I seek to *explain* my illness (in this case, a genitourinary infection caused by *Neisseria gonorrheae*), but it is through my society that I seek to *understand* my sickness—what does it *mean*? (In this case, it means you are morally defective.) Whatever culture or subcultures I belong to will offer up an entire battery of meanings and judgments for my sickness, and to the extent that I am *in* a particular culture, then that culture's meanings and judgments are *in* me, internalized as part of the very fabric of how I will understand myself and my sickness. And the point is that the meaning of that sickness—negative or positive, redemptive or punitive, supportive or condemnatory—can have an enormous impact on me and on the course of my disease: the sickness is often more destructive than the illness.

Most disturbing is the fact that when society judges a sickness to be "bad," when it judges a sickness negatively, it almost always does so exclusively out of fear and ignorance. Before it was understood that gout is a hereditary disease, it was ascribed to moral weakness. A blameless illness became a guilt-ridden sickness, simply through lack of accurate scientific information. Likewise, before it was understood that tuberculosis is caused by the tubercle bacillus, it was thought to be a process of "consumption," whereby a person with weak character was slowly "consumed." A bacterial illness became a sickness indicative of a weak character. And even earlier, plagues and famines were thought to be a direct intervention of a vengeful God, punitive retribution for the collective sins of a particular people.

Condemned to meaning: we would much prefer to be saddled with a harmful and negative meaning than to have no meaning at all. And so whenever illness strikes, society is on hand with a huge supply of ready-made meanings and judgments through which the individual seeks to understand his or her sickness. And when that society is in fact ignorant of the true cause of an illness, this ignorance usually breeds fear, which in turn breeds negative judgments about the character of the person unlucky enough to come down with the illness. The person is not only ill but sick, and this sickness, defined by society's judgments, all too often becomes a self-fulfilling and self-reinforcing prophecy: Why me? Why am I sick? Because you've been bad. But how do you know I've been bad? Because you're sick.

In short, the less the actual medical causes of an illness are understood, then the more it tends to become a sickness surrounded by desultory myths and metaphors; the more it tends to be treated as a sickness due to character weakness or moral flaws of the afflicted individual; the more it is misunderstood as a sickness of the soul, a personality defect, a moral infirmity.

Now of course there are cases when moral weakness or weakness of will (say, a refusal to stop smoking) or personality factors (say, depression) can contribute directly to illness. Mental and emotional factors can most definitely play a significant role in some illnesses (as we will see). But this is entirely different from an illness with major medical causes being wholly misinterpreted, through ignorance and lack of information, as caused by moral defect or weakness. This is a simple case of society's trying to understand a disease by condemning a soul.

Now cancer is a disease, an illness, about which very little is actually known (and there is virtually nothing known about how to cure it). And therefore, cancer is a disease around which an enormous number of myths and stories have grown up. As an illness, cancer is poorly understood. As a sickness, it has assumed awesome proportions. And as difficult as the illness of cancer is, the sickness of cancer is absolutely overwhelming.

So the first thing you have to understand when you get cancer is that almost all the information you will receive is shot through with myths.

And because medical science has so far largely failed to explain the cause and cure of cancer, it—the medical establishment—is itself infected with an enormous number of myths and falsehoods.

To give only one example: The National Cancer Association claims in its national advertising that "half of all cancers are now curable." Fact: In the last forty years there has been no significant increase whatsoever in the average survival rates of cancer patients—despite the much vaunted "war on cancer" and the introduction of more sophisticated radiation techniques, chemotherapies, and surgeries. All of that has had no significant impact on cancer survival rates at all. (The one happy exception is the blood cancers—Hodgkin's and leukemia—which respond well to chemotherapy. The pathetic 2% or so increase in survival rates for the remaining cancers are due almost entirely to early detection; the rest of the cancer rates have not budged an inch, literally.) And as for breast cancer, the survival rates have actually gone down!*

Now, doctors know this. They know the statistics. And on rare occasions you can get a doctor to admit it. Peter Richards, to his credit, did exactly that with Treya and I: "If you look at the cancer statistics over the last four decades, you'll see that none of our treatments has extended the patients' survival rates. It's as if, when a cancer cell enters your body, it has a date written on it [that is, the date you will die]. We can sometimes extend the disease-free interval, but we can't change that date. If that cancer cell has five years written on it, then we can keep you fairly disease-free and functioning right up to five years, but none of our treatments seem to extend that five years. That's why cancer survival rates haven't improved in almost forty years. It's going to take some major breakthroughs on a biochemical-genetic level before any real advances are made in cancer treatment."

So what's a typical doctor to do? He knows that his medical interventions—surgery, chemotherapy, radiation—are ultimately not very effective, and yet he has got to do something. And so this is what he does: Since he can't really control the illness, he attempts to control the sickness. That is, the attempts to define the *meaning* of the disease by prescribing a certain way that the patient should think about the cancer—

New York Times, April 24, 1988: "Statistics released recently suggest that, far from winning the war on breast cancer, we may actually be losing ground. . . . Women over 50 survive the disease no longer today than they did a decade ago, and women under 50 had a 5 percent greater mortality rate in 1985 than in 1975."

namely, that the disease is an entity that the doctor understands and that the doctor can medically treat, and that other approaches are useless or even harmful.

In practice, this means that the doctor will, for example, sometimes prescribe chemotherapy *even when he knows it won't work*. This came as a complete shock to Treya and me, but the practice is quite common. In a highly respected and authoritative text on cancer—*The Wayward Cell* by Dr. Victor Richards (who is, incidentally, Peter Richards's father)—the author presents a long discussion of why, under many circumstances, chemotherapy doesn't work, and then he goes on to state that nonetheless under the same circumstances chemotherapy should still be prescribed. Why? Because, he says, it "keeps the patient oriented toward the proper medical authorities." Put bluntly, it stops the patient from looking elsewhere for treatment—it keeps the patient oriented toward *orthodox* medicine, whether or not that medicine actually works in this case.

Now that is *not* treating the illness; that is treating the sickness—it is attempting to control how the patient understands the disease and therefore the types of treatment the patient will seek. The point is that the treatments might not significantly affect the illness, but they do affect the sickness, or how one *orients oneself* toward the illness: the types of authorities one will listen to and the types of medicines one will accept.

A good friend of ours who had advanced cancer was given the very strong recommendation, by her doctors, that she undertake yet another course of very intensive chemotherapy. If she did so, the doctors told her, she could expect to live an average of twelve months. It finally dawned on her to ask: How long can I be expected to live without the chemotherapy? The answer came back: Fourteen months. The doctors' recommendation: Do the chemotherapy. (People who haven't actually gone through something like this have a very hard time understanding that these kinds of things happen all the time—which is testament to just how thoroughly we have accepted the orthodox medical interpretation and "treatment" of the sickness.)

I really don't blame doctors for this; they are largely helpless in the face of desperate patient expectations. Nor have I ever met a single doctor that I thought was maliciously trying to manipulate patients. By and large these physicians are incredibly decent men and women doing the very best they can in impossible circumstances. They're as helpless as we are. It's simply that, whereas illness is a fairly clearcut scientific entity, sickness is a religion. Since cancer the illness is largely unresponsive, doctors are forced to try to treat cancer the sickness, at which point they must act more like priests than like scientists, a role they are ill-equipped and ill-trained to play. But in a democracy of the sick, the high priest is the doctor, by popular demand.

And so this is the point that I began with: a lot of the information that decent doctors will give you about cancer is shot through with myths, simply because they are forced to act not just as doctors but also as priests, as manipulators of the *meaning* that your illness has. They are dispensing not just science but religion. Follow their treatments and you will be saved; go elsewhere for treatment and you will be damned.

And so, starting in that horrible first week, the week after the original diagnosis and before Treya began treatment—and stretching out unrelentingly over the next five years—this is what we were *always* faced with: separating the illness of cancer from the sickness of cancer. And trying to learn the best way to *treat* the illness, and the sanest way to *understand* the sickness.

As for the illness, Treya and I began a panic-driven crash course in oncology. Starting the very night of the diagnosis, both Treya and I read everything we could get our hands on. By the end of the week we had gone through over three dozen books (most medical texts, some popular accounts) and as many journal articles. We wanted as much pure information as we could get. Unfortunately, much of the scientific information on cancer research is either inconclusive or disheartening, and what information there is changes at a horrifyingly fast rate.

We also began an intensive investigation of virtually every type of alternative treatment available: macrobiotics, Gerson diet, Kelley enzymes, Burton, Burzynski, psychic surgery, faith healing, Livingston-Wheeler, Hoxsey, laetrile, megavitamins, immunotherapy, visualization, acupuncture, affirmations, and so on (many of which I will describe later). And where most medical-scientific information is either inconclusive or honestly negative, most alternative "information" is anecdotal and unrelentingly positive. Reading alternative literature, you begin to get the giddy feeling that *everybody* treated by orthodox medicine dies, and *everybody* treated by alternative medicine lives (except those who were *first* treated by orthodox methods; they all die). You soon realize that whatever genuine benefits alternative medicine might have against the *illness* of cancer (and there are many, as we will see), the alternatives are mostly in the business of treating the *sickness* of cancer, of providing positive meaning, moral support, and above all hope to those stricken with the illness.

That is, they are acting largely in a religious and not medical capacity, which is why virtually all of their literature contains no scientific studies at all, but hundreds of *testimonials.*

So our first task was to dig through all of this literature, both orthodox and alternative, and try to collect at least a handful of facts (as opposed to propaganda) on which we could depend.

The second task we had to face was dealing with the sickness of cancer, dealing with all the various meanings and judgments that our different cultures and subcultures attached to this illness, that "cloud of voices, images, ideas, fears, stories, photographs, advertisements, articles, movies, television shows . . . vague, shapeless, but dense, ominous . . . full of fear and pain and helplessness," as Treya said.

And it wasn't just the general society at large that supplied various stories. Treya and I were exposed to several different cultures and subcultures, each of which had something very definite to say. Here are just a few:

1. Christian—The fundamentalist message: Illness is basically a punishment from God for some sort of sin. The worse the illness, the more unspeakable the sin.
2. New Age—Illness is a lesson. You are giving yourself this disease because there is something important you have to learn from it in order to continue your spiritual growth and evolution. Mind alone causes illness and mind alone can cure it. A yuppified postmodern version of Christian Science.
3. Medical—Illness is fundamentally a biophysical disorder, caused by biophysical factors (from viruses to trauma to genetic predisposition to environmental triggering agents). You needn't worry about psychological or spiritual treatments for most illnesses, because such alternative treatments are usually ineffectual and may actually prevent you from getting the proper medical attention.
4. Karma—Illness is the result of negative karma; that is, some nonvirtuous past actions are now coming to fruition in the form of a disease. The disease is "bad" in the sense that it represents past nonvirtue; but it is "good" in the sense that the disease process itself represents the burning up and the purifying of the past misdeed; it's a purgation, a cleansing.
5. Psychological—As Woody Allen put it, "I don't get angry; I

grow tumors instead." The idea is that, at least in pop psychology, repressed emotions cause illness. The extreme form: Illness as death wish.

6. Gnostic—Illness is an illusion. The entire manifest universe is a dream, a shadow, and one is free of illness only when one is free from illusory manifestation altogether, only when one awakens from the dream and discovers instead the One reality beyond the manifest universe. Spirit is the only reality, and in Spirit there is no illness. An extreme and somewhat off-centered version of mysticism.

7. Existential—Illness itself is without meaning. Accordingly it can take any meaning I *choose* to give it, and I am solely responsible for these choices. Men and women are finite and mortal, and the authentic response is to accept illness as part of one's finitude even while imbuing it with personal meaning.

8. Holistic—Illness is a product of physical, emotional, mental, and spiritual factors, none of which can be isolated from the others, none of which can be ignored. Treatment must involve all of these dimensions (although in practice this often translates into an eschewal of orthodox treatments, even when they might help).

9. Magical—Illness is retribution. "I deserve this because I wished So-and-so would die." Or, "I better not excel too much, something bad will happen to me." Or, "If too many good things happen to me, something bad has to happen." And so on.

10. Buddhist—Illness is an inescapable part of the manifest world; asking why there is illness is like asking why there is air. Birth, old age, sickness, and death—these are the marks of this world, all of whose phenomena are characterized by impermanence, suffering, and selflessness. Only in enlightenment, in the pure awareness of nirvana, is illness finally transcended, because then the entire phenomenal world is transcended as well.

11. Scientific—Whatever the illness is, it has a specific cause or cluster of causes. Some of these causes are determined, others are simply random or due to pure chance. Either way, there is no "meaning" to illness, there is only chance or necessity.

Men and women necessarily and intrinsically swim in the ocean of meaning; Treya and I were about to drown in it. On the way home in the car, on that first day, the various meanings were already flooding through us, and nearly choking Treya.

And what was the symbolical meaning to me, personally, of having such a cell and now a large collection of such cells in my right breast? That's all I could think about as Ken resolutely drove. A rapid growth inside myself that doesn't know when or how to stop. A growth that takes nutrients from neighboring tissues. A growth that might shed cells to travel through my lymph or blood system, cells that might seed other such growths if my immune system somehow missed deactivating them. Left unchecked, it would certainly kill me. Was there some secret death wish here? Had I been too hard on myself, too judgmental and self-critical, such that secret self-hatred caused this? Or had I been too nice, repressing my anger and my judgments, so they eventually manifested as this physical symptom? Was I being punished somehow for having been given so much in this life, a family I really enjoyed, intelligence and a good education, attractive looks, and now this fantastically-beyond-belief husband? Was one only allowed so much, so that going beyond triggered adversity of some kind? Had I somehow earned this through the karma of some previous lifetime? Did this experience contain in it a lesson I needed to learn or the necessary push to move on in my spiritual evolution? Perhaps, after all these years of rather anxiously looking for my life's work, coming down with cancer contained the seeds of this work, if only I could recognize it?

We would come back to this issue again and again and again, back to the meaning of getting cancer. The issue popped up everywhere; everybody had some theory about it; it hung in the air always; it became an unwanted but inescapably dominant theme of our lives, against which so much else paled in significance. Treating cancer the illness took an average of a few days each month; treating cancer the sickness was a full-time job—it permeated every aspect of our lives, our work, our play; it invaded our dreams and refused to let us forget; it was there in the morning, smiling, the skull that would grin in at the banquet, the constant reminder, the wayward cell that had entered her body, the cell that had a date on it.

"So what do you think?" I finally asked Ken. I had been diagnosed just two days earlier, and we were having lunch in between doctors' appointments. "Why do you think I got cancer? I know all this is a simplistic application of the idea that the mind affects the body, but the fear that goes with cancer makes it hard to make fine distinctions! Whenever I come up with a theory about the emotional cause of my cancer, as opposed to the environmental and genetic causes, it's hard not to blame myself. I feel I might have done something wrong, somehow, thought wrongly or felt wrongly. At times I wonder if others will make up theories about me when they find out I have cancer. Perhaps they'll think I repressed my emotions too much or was too aloof, too cool. Maybe they'll think I am too compliant, too nice, too good to be true. Maybe that I was too confident, too smug, I deserved some hard times in my life. I'm not as bad as the woman I heard of who felt like a failure in life for having gotten cancer, but when I'm in that kind of mood I understand what she means. What do you think?"

"Hell, kid, I don't know what I think. Why don't you make a list? Try it now. Write down all the things that you think contributed to your getting cancer."

Here is what I wrote, waiting for my vegetable soup to arrive:

- repressing my emotions, especially anger and sadness
- a period of major life change and stress and depression I went through a few years ago, during which I cried almost every day for two months
- being much too self-critical
- too much animal fat in my diet when younger and too much coffee
- worrying about my real purpose in life; internal pressure to find my calling, my work
- feeling very lonely and hopeless as a child, isolated and alone and unable to express my feelings
- a long-standing tendency to be self-contained, independent, and in control
- failure to more vigorously pursue a spiritual path, like meditation, since this has always been my fundamental goal
- not meeting Ken sooner

"So what do you think. You still haven't said."

Ken looked at the list. "Ah, sweetie, I like the last one. Okay, what do I think. I think cancer is caused by dozens of different things. As Frances [Vaughan] would say, human beings have physical, emotional, mental, existential, and spiritual dimensions, and I would guess that problems on any and all of those levels can contribute to illness. Physical causes: diet, environmental toxins, radiation, smoking, genetic predisposition, and so on. Emotional causes: depression; rigid self-control and hyperindependence. Mental: constant self-criticism, constant pessimistic outlook, especially depression, which seems to affect the immune system. Existential: exaggerated fear of death causing exaggerated fear of life. Spiritual: failure to listen to one's inner voice.

"Maybe all of those contribute to a physical illness. My problem is, I don't know how much weight to give each level. Is the mental or psychological cause of cancer worth 60% or 2%? But that's the whole point, you see? That's the whole issue. Right now, from all the evidence I've seen, I'd say that with cancer it's about 30% genetic, 55% environmental [drinking, smoking, dietary fat, fiber, toxins, sunlight, electromagnetic radiation, etc.], and 15% everything else—emotional, mental, existential, spiritual. But that means that at least 85% of the causes are physical, seems to me."

My soup arrived. "Basically none of this would matter much except for my fear that, somehow, if I was responsible for cancer this time around I might do this to myself again. Why even get treatment if I just repeat it? I almost wish I could see the whole thing as something that accidentally happened to me, perhaps because of a genetic predisposition or X-ray treatments when I was young or living next to a toxic waste dump or whatever. Now I'm afraid if I get depressed my will to live and my white cell count may go down. If I get flashes of hospital deathbed scenes, I fear I may be giving energy to such an outcome, almost 'creating' it. I just can't get it out of my head—what did I do to cause this? What did I do wrong? What am I saying to myself by getting cancer? Do I somehow not want to live? Is my will strong enough now? Am I punishing myself somehow?" I began sobbing again, this time into my vegetable soup. Ken pulled his chair around and held me. "That's good soup, you know."

"I don't want you to have to worry about me," I finally said.

"Sweetie, as long as you're breathing and crying, I won't worry about you. If you stop either one, then I'll worry."

"I'm frightened. How do I need to change? Do I need to change? I want you to tell me what you honestly think."

"I don't know what caused the cancer, and I don't think anybody does. The people that go around saying that cancer is caused primarily by repressed emotions or low self-esteem or spiritual anemia—they don't know what they're talking about. There is no credible evidence whatsoever for those notions; they're basically put forward by people who are trying to sell you something anyway.

"Since nobody knows what caused your cancer, I don't know what you should change in order to help cure it. So why don't you try this. Why don't you use cancer as a metaphor and a spur to change all those things in your life that you wanted to change anyway. In other words, repressing certain emotions may or may not have helped cause the cancer, but since you want to stop repressing those emotions anyway, then use the cancer as a reason, as an excuse, to do so. I know advice is cheap here, but why not take the cancer as an opportunity to change all those things on your list that can be changed?"

The whole idea was a great relief, and I started smiling. Ken added, "And don't change them because you think they caused cancer—that will just make you feel guilty—change them simply because they should be changed in any event. You don't need cancer to tell you what you need to work on. You already know. So let's start. Let's make it a new beginning. I'll help. It'll be fun. Really. Am I getting goofy or what? We could call it Fun with Cancer." We both started laughing out loud.

But that made perfect sense, and I felt a kind of clarity and determination. Ultimately, of course, there was probably no "preordained" meaning to my getting cancer, though people of earlier times might indeed have been drawn to such interpretations. I was also not especially satisfied by the general medical approach, which I felt would reduce it to a chance combination of various material circumstances (diet, genetics, environmental pollutants). That's an adequate explanation on one level, and true on that level, but it didn't go far enough for me. I wanted—and needed—for this experience to have some meaning and purpose. The only way that could happen with any certainty was for me to act "as if" it did, to imbue it with meaning through my thoughts and actions.

I hadn't even decided on a course of treatment yet, and this is what I was thinking about. I didn't want to simply treat the disease and then relegate it to some dark closet in my life I hoped I'd never have to open or do anything about. Cancer would certainly be a part of my life from now on, but not simply in terms of constant checkups or constant awareness of the possibility of a recurrence. I was going to use it in as many ways as possible. Philosophically, to get me to look at death more closely, to help me prepare to die when the time came, to look at the meaning and purpose of my life. Spiritually, to rekindle my interest in finding and following a contemplative path, one that is at least generally suitable to me and stop delaying by looking for the perfect one. Psychologically, to be kinder and more loving to myself and others, to express my anger more easily, to lower my defenses against intimacy and my tendency to retreat into myself. Materially, to eat mainly fresh, well-washed, and whole foods and to start exercising again. And most of all, to be gentle with myself about meeting or not meeting those goals.

We finished our lunch, what we would later jokingly call The Great Vegetable Soup Incident, or Fun with Cancer. It marked a major turning point in how we would both deal with the "meaning" of Treya's cancer, and especially how we would view all the changes in her life-style that she would subsequently make—change them, not because of cancer, but because they needed to be changed, period.

"Well, I don't think you can see it, or could see it. It's just something I saw."
"Is it still there?" The thought is disturbing.
"I don't see anything, but it feels like it's still there." Treya is discussing this as if it were the most natural thing in the world, to have death sitting on your honey's shoulder.
"I don't suppose you could just brush it off or something?"
"Don't be silly," is all she says.

Treya and I finally worked out our own meaning for this sickness, and evolved our own theories of health and healing (as we'll see). But in the meantime, we had to treat the illness, and we had to treat it very quickly.
We were late for our appointment with Peter Richards.

4

A QUESTION
OF BALANCE

❧

"IT'S a new procedure pioneered in Europe. I think you're a good candidate for it."

Peter Richards looked pained. He obviously had a great deal of affection for Treya; how hard, I thought, to treat cancer patients. Peter outlined the options: mastectomy with removal of all the lymph nodes; leaving the breast but removing the lymph nodes, then treating the breast with radiation implants; segmental or partial mastectomy (removing about one-quarter of the breast tissue), removal of about half the lymph nodes, then five or six weeks of radiation to the breast area; segmental mastectomy with removal of all lymph nodes. It was hard to escape the impression that we were all calmly discussing medieval torture techniques. "Oh, yes ma'am, we have something lovely in a size eight Iron Maiden."

Treya had already hit upon a general plan of action. Although we were both great fans of alternative and holistic medicine, a careful scrutiny showed that none of the alternatives—including Simonton visualization, Gerson diet, and Burton in the Bahamas—had any substantial success against grade four tumors. These tumors are the Nazis of the cancer crowd, and they are not terribly impressed with wheat grass juice and sweet thoughts. You have to nuke these bastards if you're going to have any chance at all—and that's where white man's medicine comes in.

53

Treya decided, after carefully looking at all the options, that the most sensible course of action was to use orthodox treatments for the first step, and then combine them with a full spectrum of holistic auxiliary treatments. Holistic practitioners, of course, usually discourage the use of any orthodox treatments, like radiation or chemotherapy, because, it is said, they permanently compromise the immune system, thus making the holistic treatments less likely to succeed.

There is some truth to that, but the situation is much more subtle and complex than most holistic practitioners seem to realize. First of all, it is true that radiation, for example, will lower the number of white blood cells, one of the body's front lines of immunity. Most of this is temporary, however, and the slight long-term reduction has not been correlated with immune deficiency, simply because there is no direct link between the *quantity* of white blood cells and the *quality* of immune protection. For example, people who receive chemotherapy have on average no long-term higher incidence of colds, flu, general infections, or secondary cancers, even though portions of their white blood count might be lower. It is not obvious at all that these people have an "impaired" immune system. The hard fact is, many people who use holistic treatments die, and the most convenient excuse is, "You should have come to us first."

Treya decided that, given the present state of medical knowledge, the only prudent course was to aggressively combine orthodox and alternative methods. As for the orthodox, studies in Europe had demonstrated that the segmental mastectomy followed by radiation was as effective as the gruesome modified radical mastectomy. All three of us—Peter, Treya, and myself—felt that the segmental mastectomy was the reasonable course. (Treya had little vanity; she chose the procedure not because it saved most of the breast but because it saved a lot of the lymph nodes.)

And so, on December 15, 1983, Treya and I spent our honeymoon in room 203, second floor, Children's Hospital, San Francisco.

"What are you doing?"

"I'm having them send up a cot. I'm sleeping in the room."

"They won't let you."

Ken made his eyes-rolled-up-you've-got-to-be-kidding look. "Kid, a hospital is a terrible place to be if you're a sick person. There are germs in a hospital that you can get nowhere else in the world. If the germs don't get you, the food will. I'm staying. Besides, this is our honeymoon; I'm not going to leave you." He got a cot and spent the entire time with me in my room, a large part of his six-foot-four frame dangling off the very small cot they put in. Right before surgery he brought in beautiful flowers. The note said, "For the other half of my soul."

Treya seemed to have rapidly regained her footing. Her natural and enormous courage resurfaced, and she literally breezed through the whole ordeal.

12/11—All three of us [Peter Richards, Treya, and Ken] came to the same decision—segmental, partial axillary [removal of about half the lymph nodes], radiation. That felt good. Feeling fine, joking about it, doing great. Lunch at Max's, Xmas shopping with Ken. Home late and exhausted, but with more of those *endless* errands done. Outpouring of my love for Ken, then wanting to forgive and send my love to everybody in my life, especially my family.

12/14—First acupuncture treatment. Nap, packed. To hotel, dinner Mom and Dad, more wedding presents. Called Kati [a sister] to come. Snuggle with Ken.

12/15—Nine o'clock to hospital—prepped—waiting room—to my room—two hr. delay. Felt fine going into surgery—fine coming out, not too dopey. Woke at five—Ken, Dad, Mom, Kati there. Ken got a cot—"other half of my soul." Morphine that night. Interesting sensations—drifty, dreamy, similar to meditation sometimes. Woke me practically every hour for temp. and blood pressure. My b.p. is naturally so low, Ken had to wake up each hour and assure the nurse, who couldn't even find a pulse, that I was alive.

12/16—Slept all day—walked down hall with Ken slowly. Mom, Dad, Kati, Joan [a friend]. Dr. R. in, twenty nodes out, all negative [no cancer in her lymph nodes, extremely good news]. Walked with Suzannah. Couldn't sleep that night, called for med. at four, morphine and Tylenol. Great to have Ken there all the time; glad he insisted.

12/17—Called various people—read a lot—Dr. R. by—family left—Ken Xmas shopping—feeling very good.

12/18—Lots of visitors—Ken on errands—walked a lot—reading *The Color Purple*. Am still sore, fluid still draining.

12/19—Checked out—lunch at Max's—Xmas shopping with

Ken—home. Sort of wish I'd written more about all this—am feeling fine, confident—some pain the first day, esp. where the [drainage] tubes were—feeling so good I sometimes worry I'm overconfident!

The immediate impact of the surgery was psychological: Treya took the time to begin an almost complete reassessment of what she always called her "life's work"—namely, what *was* her life's work supposed to be? As she explained it to me, this question centered around issues of being versus doing, which in this culture also means issues of masculine versus feminine roles. Treya, by her account, had always valued *doing*, which is often (but not necessarily) associated with the masculine, and she devalued *being*, which is often (but not necessarily) associated with the feminine. * Doing values are values of producing something, making something, achieving something; they are often aggressive, competitive, and hierarchical; they are oriented toward the future; and they depend upon rules and judgment. Basically, doing values attempt to *change* the present into something "better."

Being values, on the other hand, are values of *embracing* the present; values of accepting a person for what they *are*, not for what they can *do*; values of relationship, inclusion, acceptance, compassion, and care.

Both of these values—doing and being—are equally important, I think. But the point is that, since being values are often associated with the feminine, Treya felt that in overvaluing the doing/masculine, she had actually repressed in herself a whole range of being/feminine.

This was not just a passing curiosity for Treya. Rather, I would say that, in its various forms, it was *the* major psychological issue in Treya's life. Among many other things, it was directly responsible for her eventually changing her name from "Terry" to "Treya"—Terry, she felt, was a man's name.

A lot of issues are becoming clearer to me. For as long as I can remember I have beat myself up with the question "What is my life's

---

*Throughout this account Treya speaks of the traditional association of masculine with doing, with the mind, with Heaven (logic), and the feminine with being, with the body, with the Earth. Needless to say, these are not hard and fast divisions but personal preferences, nor does it imply that men can't be or women can't do. It is simply the way Treya herself came to think of these distinctions as they appeared in herself and in me. Treya felt that the first wave of feminism was proving that women could do just as well as men, but the second wave would be returning to the ways of being that women seem natively to better understand. I am going to follow Treya in this terminology when it comes to this area, since she has been my main teacher here.

work?" I think that perhaps I put too much emphasis on doing, not enough on being. I was the oldest of four children, and as I grew up I wanted to be my father's eldest *son*. After all, in Texas at that time the really important "jobs" were men's jobs—men did all the really *productive* work. I valued men's values, and I did not want to be a Texas wife—so I threw over many feminine values, and fought them in myself, fought them any time they came up in me. A denial, I believe, of my feminine side, my body, my nurturing, my sexuality, while I aligned myself with my head, my father, my logic, my society's values.

In facing this cancer, I now think the answer to that burning question—what is my work?—comes in two parts.

1. Ironically—in light of my constant resistance to finding myself through a man—part of my work is definitely taking care of Ken, supporting his work in whatever way I can, learning how to do that without losing my autonomy, how to let that old fear die away slowly as I grow into this work—which begins first by simply being his wife and support and keeping a nice house, a nice place for him to work (hire a maid!) and seeing what else that might grow into. But it begins by supporting him and his work in all those invisible ways a wife does that my ego always revolted against. But now it's no longer an idea, the situation is nothing like the Texas model my ego rebelled against; my ego's not in the same state it was then. His work is, I believe, incredibly important and on a level of contribution to the whole way beyond what I could get up to (not meant to be self-denigrating, just honest), and besides, it's *Ken* I'm talking about, and I absolutely love him. He is clearly, absolutely, at the center of my work. I don't think I could come to this place at all if Ken actually wanted me to do this, if he wanted me to be the good "wife." He puts no demands on me at all. If anything, he's been the wife, taking care of me!

2. The second element that seems to be coming up, and connected with the counseling and group work I've done, is cancer work. That feels more and more what I might do. Start by doing a book on my experience with cancer; various theories of healing; interview therapists on body-mind connection; interview other cancer patients. Then maybe a video—we'll see. But definitely this feels like something central to my work.

I see that both of these are forms of "selfless service," ways to get my ego out of the way and serve others. So both of them directly tie into my lifelong desire to pursue a spiritual discipline. Everything is starting to come together!

I am feeling an opening in my being
Feeling an opening between my head and my heart,
    my father and mother, my mind and my body,
My male and female, my scientist and my artist.
One the feature writer, the other the poet.
One the responsible eldest child, taking after her father
Who kept his family together;
The other the playful, explorer, adventurer, mystic

This was by no means the solution or the final version of Treya's search for her vocation, for her "true work," but it was a start. I could sense a shift in her, an inner healing of sorts, an integrating, a balancing.

We came to refer to her search for her "work" as a search for her "daemon"—the Greek word that in classical mythology refers to "a god within," one's inner deity or guiding spirit, also known as a genii or jinn, the tutelary deity or genius of a person; one's daemon or genii is also said to be synonymous with one's fate or fortune. Treya had not yet found her fate, her genius, her destiny, her daemon, not in its final form, anyway. I was to be a part of that fate, but not quite the main focus that Treya thought; I was more of a catalyst. Her daemon, really, was her own higher Self, and it would soon be expressed, not in work, but in art.

I, on the other hand, had found my fate, my daemon, and it was my writing. I knew exactly what I wanted to do, why I wanted to do it; I knew why I was put here, and what I was supposed to accomplish. When I was writing I was expressing my own higher Self; I had no doubt or hesitation about that at all. Two paragraphs into the writing of my first book, when I was twenty-three years old, I knew I had come home, found myself, found my purpose, found my god. I have since never doubted it once.

But there is a strange and horrible thing about one's daemon: When honored and acted upon, it is indeed one's guiding spirit; those who bear a god within bring genius to their work. When, however, one's daemon is heard but unheeded, it is said that the daemon becomes a demon, or evil spirit—divine energy and talent degenerates into self-destructive activity. The Christian mystics, for example, say that the flames of Hell are but God's love denied, angels reduced to demons.

Got a little edgy when Ken and Janice [a friend] were talking about how much alike they are because if they don't work they get weird. Ken handles his not working with drink and other relaxations; Janice says she works to keep from being suicidal. Seems to me they are different motivations—Ken has a daemon that makes him work to fulfill it; Janice has a demon that she works to avoid. But the point is Ken was trying to make a connection, understandable, and I got a bit weird about it because of my insecurity about what I'm doing now. Same old story—don't have to work because of some inner demon (Janice), and I haven't found my daemon (Ken), the work I deeply want to do. Sometimes I think my real problem is that I just don't believe I could ever get really good at something, that I have an inflated idea of how good others are, and that maybe by the time I'm fifty that will have been cut down by experience to match reality and I'll then know I could be good enough. And sometimes I think I just have to stop chasing my daemon long enough to let some space in my life for it to begin to show itself and grow. I want a full-blown plant right away and have been too impatient to nourish the small shoots enough to see which one I choose or chooses me.

I need to learn how to read the depths of my being, find my own "guidance" and daemon. I don't want to live without some kind of faith in a greater purpose, even if it is only evolution! So I don't want to let any anger on my part [about getting cancer] diminish mystical experiences and their power to change people in any way. I don't want to let any bitterness erode my sense of the sacred and the meaningful in life, but use it instead to deepen the need for those explorations and understandings. Even anger can be the "stuff" through which God or this evolutionary force manifests and works. I'm still interested in how people change, how they find meaning and purpose in their lives. I definitely recognize in myself a need for a work, a kind of foundation for the more amorphous work of the Findhorns and Windstars. I feel Ken and cancer work are a big part of that foundation. But I need in myself the counterpart of Ken's writing, Steven's architecture, Cathy's dance. I recognize in me [what Haridas Chaudhuri calls] "the need for self-creation and creative accomplishment," my "will to self-unfoldment."

To continue on that path I need to find ways to get in better touch with my deep psyche, the inner principle of ongoing personal growth. That is as close as I can get to God within me; learning to understand

and follow that is the same as hearing and obeying God's will. Going within and getting in touch with the deepest, most true part of oneself . . . getting to know it, nourish it, let it grow more mature . . . invest it with power (recognizing it as the inner God) . . . and develop the will to follow that inner direction . . . the ability to test its truth and the faith and courage to follow it even when it contradicts the rational mind of our consensus reality.

So that's my task now. . . .

In the coming nightmare that Treya and I endured, part of her torment was that she had not yet found her daemon; my torment was that, once having had mine, I watched it slip away. My angels starved into demons, and I was very nearly destroyed by that particular variety of hell.

We spent Christmas in Laredo with the family (after a brief stop in Houston at M. D. Anderson Hospital), and then returned to Muir Beach for Treya to begin her radiation treatments with Dr. Simeon Cantril, "Sim" to his friends. Sim was a brilliant, very likable man, who had lost a wife to cancer; but his intellectual intensity sometimes came across as a personal brusqueness, or even coldness, which, although a false impression, was nonetheless intimidating. Thus, in addition to giving Treya top-notch radiotherapy, he gave her the chance to polish her assertiveness training with doctors, a training she brought to the brink of perfection.

They don't give you the whip. You have to push, and ask, and push, and above all, don't feel foolish. And especially don't be put off by their air of busyness, the feeling that their time is so valuable they can hardly answer questions. It's your life that's at stake. Ask your questions.

This assertiveness was simply part of a "take-charge" attitude that Treya increasingly brought to her illness. During the five and one-half weeks of daily radiation treatment—itself a painless procedure whose only major side effect was a mild but growing fatigue, with occasional flulike symptoms—during this period, Treya began to implement her main agenda: change those things in your life that need changing anyway.

Started radiation treatment today. I'm feeling very excited over the discipline/regularity of the process, doing it on a daily basis, helping with my discipline in other areas. I've started taking long daily walks. I

60

feel I need a project, some work focus to see me through this time—I need to express my energy outward rather than turning it in on myself, so I'm working on my book on cancer. Ken is doing the megavitamin therapy for me—he's a trained biochemist, after all! He buys huge batches of over fifty nutrients and mixes them up in the kitchen sink, while he makes funny mad scientist sounds. He's also taken over most of the cooking, becoming my dietician as well. He is a fabulous cook! And his unofficial job is to keep me laughing. I came home yesterday, and asked him how he was doing. He said, "Oh Christ, horrible day. Smashed the car, burnt the dinner, beat my wife. Oh, hell, forgot to beat my wife . . ." and started chasing me around the kitchen table.

In addition to meditation, exercise, acupuncture, vitamins, diet, and my book, I've started visualization, I'm seeing two holistic doctors, and I'm putting more energy into this journal! Keeping this journal is part of the cure. Only regret over Xmas is that I was lazy about all this, ate what was there, didn't meditate or exercise, let it all get pretty murky, slip away from me.

Now feel I'm taking charge, asking questions, taking responsibility. In only two days the pain [from surgery] went away, is there a causal connection? It's important to feel I can do something to help, to get better, not just throw myself over to the doctors.

Reading [Norman] Cousins's *The Healing Heart*—says he never got depressed, always focused on what he could do to recover. That's great, but I get depressed—feel part of it is the uncertainty around what caused the cancer, why I got it. It's much clearer with heart disease—stress and diet. But I do know what I need to change, so I'm focusing on that! I know that as long as I'm reading and thinking and working at it, my spirits stay high. When I feel like a victim or leave it up to the doctor or want Ken to do it, I get depressed. Lesson in will to live.

As important as this "take-charge" attitude was, it was still only half the equation. In addition to learning how to take control and assume responsibility, a person also needs to learn when and how to let go, to surrender, to go with the flow and not resist or fight it. Letting go versus taking control—this is, of course, just another version of being versus doing, that primordial polarity of yin and yang that assumes a thousand different forms and is never exhausted. It is not that yin or yang is right, that being is better than doing—it's a question of finding the right balance, finding the natural harmony between yin and yang that the ancient Chinese called the Tao. Finding that balance—between doing and being, controlling and allowing, resisting and opening, fighting and surrendering, willing and accepting—finding that balance became *the* central issue in Treya's confrontation with cancer (just as it was her main psychological issue as well). We would both come back to this question of balance again and again and again, each time with a slightly different perspective.

Balance the will to live with the acceptance of death. Both needed. I need to learn that balance. I feel that I already accept death; I'm worried that I am not afraid to die, worried that means I might want to die. But I don't want to die; I'm just not afraid of it. I don't want to leave Ken! So I'm going to fight!

But I also know, from recently spending time with Jerry Jampolsky [who wrote several books based on A *Course in Miracles*, most notably *Love is Letting Go of Fear*] that I need to learn to *let go*—as Jerry says, "Let go and let God." He really shook me out of my stuff. Instead of trying to change myself or others, try forgiveness, forgiving myself and forgiving others. And if I can't forgive somebody (if my ego won't let me forgive somebody), then ask the Holy Spirit in me to forgive. It's like asking my higher Self to forgive others, and forgive me. "God is the love in which I forgive," as the *Course* says.

Forgiving myself means accepting myself. Gulp! This means giving up an old friend of mine—self-criticism. My scorpion companion. When I visualize all the things that keep me from feeling right about myself, then, up higher than the rest, as a kind of backdrop to all my other "problems," is a figure of a scorpion with its tail arched over its back. On the verge of stinging itself. This is my self-criticism, cutting myself down relentlessly, feeling unlovable, the background feeling behind all the other problems, the grievances against myself that keep me from seeing the light and the miracles that can only be seen in that light. Hmmm. The big one. Getting better, but still the big one. A touch of an acid feeling in my stomach when I think of it. What the poison I give myself feels like when I swallow it.

I used to write down nice things people would say about me because I couldn't quite believe someone felt that way about me. I sometimes seem to have trouble believing that someone could really love me—like there's a gap between my knowing I'm a good person, people really like being around me, I'm intelligent, pretty, etc.—and yet sometimes I don't see why anyone (a man, especially) could/would really love me.

It wasn't that Treya hadn't "accomplished" a lot, "done" a lot, for she had. She had graduated with distinction from Mount Holyoke, and taught English literature before returning to Boston University for a master's degree; had helped found Windstar and served as its director of education for three years; had received a master's in psychological counseling from the California Institute of Integral Studies; had worked at Findhorn for three years; was on the board of the Rocky Mountain Institute; a member of the Threshold Foundation; facilitator in the U.S.-U.S.S.R. Youth Exchange Program. And her "list of doing," as she called it, would continue to grow to incredibly impressive dimensions—among other things, her writings on cancer and illness alone would reach an estimated *one million* people around the world.

And yet, particularly at this point in time, because Treya didn't very much acknowledge or value the being aspects of herself, she honestly could not figure out why people liked her so much, loved her so much, wanted to be around her so much. It was her extraordinary being they were attracted to, not some list of doing, as important as all that is, and Treya seemed to be overlooking this, devaluing this, entirely.

There were times that she was totally flabbergasted that I loved her, which *totally* flabbergasted me. During that first year, we had this conversation a dozen times: "You don't see why I love you? Are you kidding me? You're serious, aren't you? I love you totally, sweetie, and you know it. I'm here for you twenty-four hours a day because I'm crazy about you! You think that because you haven't found your ultimate vocation—you think you are worthless. You'll find it, I'm sure, but in the meantime you completely overlook your being, your presence, your energy, your integrity. Are you kidding? People are absolutely nuts about you, you know that. I have *never* seen anybody with the number of amazing and totally dedicated friends that you have. We all love you for what you are, not what you do."

That message is slowly but definitely sinking in. Jerry went over the same point. "You are lovable as you are, right now, and you don't need anything else added. If you can't think of any reason that you're lovable, then think this: you are God's creation, you are as God created you." I can feel that in the present moment—right now I feel lovable—but when I add past and future I still feel I need to do something.

With Ken it's still so new. I trust him completely, but there's still that little girl who's afraid someday he won't be there. And I don't know how to satisfy that little girl, that hole at the center. Will only time prove her otherwise, Ken being there year after year, or will that hole never be filled? He's been so fantastic I have to let that in! When I ask him if he's going to be around, he always says, "Hell, kid, I don't know; ask me in twenty years." What clearer proof do I need that God loves me than to have Ken by my side?

My fear of dependence, depending on somebody, a determination to do it all myself—part of not wanting others to do anything for me is a fear of depending on them and then being let down. Last night I dreamt that an earthquake was coming—I and others were preparing for it. At the last minute I doubted that my preparations were enough (enough food, etc.) and asked another woman if I could go with her to her shelter. A sense of trying to do it on my own first and then asking for help?

I felt I turned a corner with Jerry—a sense of how I don't need to be in charge of everything! I can just be, not have to do all the time. And so I have let go into the radiation, am no longer resisting it. I visualize healthy tissue growing back in. My initial resistance to radiation is similar to other resistances to letting go. So just: Let go and let God.

On the whole this experience [of cancer and the radiation treatment] has felt like an invitation to live more fully, less tentatively. I figure it's also an invitation to be kinder to myself—to let up on myself, to just drop the constant scorpion of self-criticism and "unlovability." I can put it very simply: I live life easier these days.

And so the lesson for both of us was very clear, if tricky to implement: balance being and doing, balance an acceptance of yourself, just as you, with a determination to change those things about yourself that need to be changed. Being meant: letting go and letting God, accepting, trusting, faith, forgiving. Doing meant: assuming responsibility for those things, and only those things, that can be changed, and then working as hard as you can toward changing them. This is the time-honored wisdom in the simple and profound prayer:

> God grant me the serenity to accept
> the things I cannot change,
> The courage to change the things I can,
> And the wisdom to know the difference.

Treya and I spent the summer in Aspen. Treya had lived there on and off for ten years; she considered it in many ways her home. After leaving

Findhorn, Treya had returned to Aspen, where she helped found Windstar with John Denver, Thomas Crum, Steven Conger, and several others (it became the favorite haunt of Bucky Fuller). She also joined the board of the Rocky Mountain Institute, which is run by her friends Amory and Hunter Lovins and is generally regarded as the finest alternative energy think tank in the world. So many good friends—Stuart Mace, the original pioneer (technical consultant on "Sergeant Yukon of the Royal Mounties"), best friend Linda Conger, Kathy Crum, Annie Denver, Bruce Gordon; Father Michael Abdo (who presided at our wedding) and Father Thomas Keating, who run the Cistercian monastery at Old Snowmass. It was these friends and centers, along with the stunning natural beauty of the trails and mountains—and not the rather disquieting glitterati that even then was beginning to ooze over Aspen—that made Treya consider it home.

What a summer it was. Treya had so many wonderful friends, all of whom I liked immediately. I myself honestly had never known anybody who generated such open love and devotion in people; the energy and integrity that seemed to radiate from Treya attracted both men and women like a benevolent Siren. People just wanted to be around her, be in her presence, and she always responded, never turned away.

I, of course, was writing a book, *Transformations of Consciousness: Contemplative and Conventional Perspectives on Development*, which I coauthored with Jack Engler and Daniel P. Brown, two Harvard professors who specialized in East/West psychology. The essence of this book was that if we take the various *psychological* models offered by the West (Freudian, cognitive, linguistic, object relational, etc.) and combine them with the *spiritual* models of the East (and Western mystics), then we arrive at a full-spectrum model of human growth and development, a model that traces human growth from body to mind to soul to spirit. What's more, using this overall map of human development, we can rather easily pinpoint the various types of "neuroses" that men and women may develop, and consequently choose more accurately the type of treatment or therapy that would be most appropriate and effective for each problem. The *New York Times* called it "the most important and sophisticated synthesis of psychologies East and West to emerge yet."

As for Treya and me, our favorite activity was still very simple: sitting on the sofa, our arms around each other, feeling the dancing energies in our body. So often we were taken beyond ourselves to that place where death is a stranger and love alone shines, where souls unite for all eternity and a single embrace lights up the spheres—the simplest way to discover that God most definitely is embodied, love of the two-armed form.

And yet this brought its own dilemma for me: the more I loved Treya, the more I feared and was obsessed with her death. This was a constant reminder of one of the central tenets of Buddhism (and mysticism in general): everything is impermanent, everything passes, nothing remains, nothing lasts. Only the whole endures eternally; all parts are doomed to death and decay. In meditative or mystical awareness, beyond the prison of individuality, one can taste the whole and escape the fate of a part; one is released from suffering and from the terror of mortality. But in my meditation I could not sustain that awareness for very long; I was still a novice in mystical practice. And although Treya and I could often enter the whole by a simple embrace, that too would soon fade, as if both of our souls had not yet grown enough to contain the largess offered.

And so I would return to the ordinary world of manyness, not where Ken and Treya were one beyond time, but where this part Ken loved that part Treya, and that part Treya might die. The thought of losing her was unbearable. The only recourse I had was to try to stay in the awareness of impermanence, where you love things precisely *because* they are fleeting. I was slowly learning that love did *not* mean holding on, which I had always thought, but rather letting go.

It was during this otherwise beautiful summer that Treya and I realized one of the real nightmares of being a cancer patient. If I wake up in the morning and I have a headache, or my joints hurt, or I have a sore throat, I will probably just shrug it off and go about my day. If a cancer patient wakes up with any of those symptoms, however, they mean: possible brain tumor, possible bone metastases, possible throat cancer. Every little twitch and twinge assumes ominous and threatening proportions. In the weeks, months, even years after a brush with cancer, your body's sensations conspire to inflict a kind of emotional Chinese water torture on you.

Toward the end of the summer in Aspen, this subtle torture was having its cumulative effect on both of us, and especially, of course, on Treya.

I had been feeling badly for some time, sleeping late, sometimes till noon, always till nine, and worrying. What does this mean? Could it be a return of cancer? Then the voice of reason on the other side. Don't be foolish, you're overreacting. You're turning into a hypochondriac. Just wait till you get back to California for your blood test. Maybe you're just depressed with nothing challenging to do right now.

But I'd long ago promised myself to follow up on these feelings. Even if most of the time I'm scaring myself with false cries of "the wolf is coming," I want to be sure not to miss a real wolf, a real symptom, by calling myself a hypochondriac. Maybe I am, but there is nothing better than early detection if something is really happening. So I called my old doctor in Aspen.

As I walked into the building, the tears began to well up inside. A strange mixture of fear, feeling sorry for myself, and simply needing to cry about the whole thing. The worry about possible recurrence, the fear I might not have that much longer with Ken, the wrenching inner adjustments of facing life and death in a new way . . . all that builds up and every so often tears are the best way to release the tension. Almost like lancing a wound so it can heal more quickly.

Once in the doctor's office I told the nurse what I'd come for. And all the while the tears were so, so close to the surface. I used to have such good control, I remember thinking. That's been swept away by all this. I never thought I'd be unable to call on that control when I really needed it. When the nurse left, I grabbed a kleenex and stared at a *People* magazine and struggled with my thoughts while the tears leaked slowly out of my eyes. So what, if I cry, I cry, I decided. And it'll probably feel good, too. Wonder why I'm still embarrassed by crying.

My doctor came in. Dr. Whitcomb. He's a sweetheart of a man; I've always really trusted him, both as a person and as a doctor. He was wonderful. He assured me that the trauma my immune system had suffered under general anaesthetic and radiation, combined with the hay fever and allergies I always suffer from during my beloved Colorado summers, was enough to account for my tiredness. He also lectured me—I need to hear this lecture every year or so—about my diet. Eat only vegetables, fruit, and whole grains; be sure to wash everything well to get the pesticides off; don't drink chlorinated water; don't eat meat because of the hormones and antibiotics animals are fed, though white fish every so often is fine; and start exercising again. Take as much buffered vitamin C as your body can handle to help your allergies. Don't take antihistamines unless you really need to; they only mask your symptoms. Be careful of yeast-based vitamins, especially the B vitamins, since people with allergies usually react to yeast. Use hypoallergenic vitamins. Take acidophilus.

There was more. I cried. I felt it was OK, he empathized with what I'd been through and what might lie ahead. I felt understood. And I felt much better when I walked out of there, armed with my hypoallergenic vitamins. Certainly a high percentage of a doctor's work involves emotional and psychological healing.

One of Ken's books turned out to be surprisingly healing too. Reading *Up from Eden* gave me a deeper understanding of how and why people repress death, or deny and hide from their own mortality. Ken traced four major historical epochs—archaic, magic, mythic, and mental—and showed how human beings at each stage tried to avoid death by constructing "immortality symbols." The great repression is of death, not sex. Death is the last and great taboo. Seeing the almost infinite number of ways that mankind has tried to deny death, repress it, avoid it, helped me look at death more openly and not try to deny it or push it away. And besides, Ken's whole point was that coming to terms with death, accepting death, was necessary in order for spiritual growth to occur at all. You have to die to the ego in order to awaken as Spirit. The message of the book was that the denial of death is the denial of God.

I remember very well my attitude when I first discovered I had breast cancer. It went something like well, if I'm going to die, I'm going to die. It's bound to happen sometime. I didn't feel terribly afraid of death itself, though the prospect of a long and painful process of dying was frightening. I felt quite accepting, even resigned, all intermixed with the fear of not knowing and grief at the shock of this discovery. But the main feeling was, if this is the way it was going to be, so be it.

But then that feeling began to change. As I read more and talked to more people I decided this accepting posture might be dangerous. I became afraid that if I didn't will to live more strongly I might bring upon myself an earlier death. I decided that I have to choose, very specifically and definitely, to live, that I had to force myself to choose to live.

Well, that was all fine. It led to some quick decisions about making changes. But I also began to worry more. The easiest way to recognize that worry was my reaction to the odd aches and pains we all have. It might be a recurrence, I would think. Oh no, better call the doctor. Etc., etc. Not a fun way to live each day, to be sure. But it crept up on me so gradually over the months I both did and didn't see it.

Reading *Up from Eden* tore away the last veil of self-deception about what I was doing to myself, because it helped me see how and why I was doing it. Our culture had evolved to the point where death is perceived more keenly than before. So we develop ever stronger and more subtle ways to deny death, to avoid both its imminence and its necessity. Existential philosophers have pointed out, in numerous ways, how this denial of death results in a less active life. Indeed, it's a kind of denial of life since life and death go hand in hand. If I'm afraid of death, then I will become extremely cautious and worried in life, since something might happen to me. So the more I fear death the more I fear life, and the less I live.

I realized that I had become gradually more and more indoctrinated with a fear of death. That's why I'd begun to worry about my symptoms. I hadn't seen that the other side of willing to live, the inevitable shadow side, is fear of not living, fear of dying. Holding on to life comes to mean fear of letting go.

So now I try to hold everything a bit more lightly, not so tightly. It's the tight grasp that leads me into thinking in an either/or kind of way; either I want to live or I will die. A light touch, it seems to me, lets me think in a both/and kind of way: I can both desire to live and be willing to let go when the time comes.

It's a new feeling and I haven't quite got the hang of it yet. I still worry some when I feel tired or my eyes hurt. But I feel more accepting, more willing to go through with whatever happens. It's easier now to just note the symptom and resolve to see the doctor when I can, whereas before I kind of hung on to the symptom and worried at it in the days before I could get to the doctor.

Like balancing on the edge of a razor, trying/efforting/concentrating/disciplining while at the same time remaining open/allowing/relaxing/just being. Back and forth, back and forth. I know I'm out of balance—which is most of the time—when I become aware of the effort or when I slide into laziness. And I use my worry as a clue that I'm out of balance, that I'm hanging on to life too tightly. The balance between will to live and acceptance of what is. Tricky. But it all feels much better this way. Worry is a bummer, plain and simple.

This also meant that Treya relaxed a bit about the strictness of her "healing agenda": She would still work on herself (and with a discipline that most people found astonishing), and yet, in her own awareness, she was holding it all much more lightly, much less obsessively.

Dinner with Nathaniel Branden and his wife, Devers. Nathaniel's an old friend of Ken's; I really like them both. He asked if I'd been doing much visualization and I told him I had during the radiation treatment. I said I found it helpful then, visualizing the radiation killing bad cells and the good cells repairing themselves quickly; it gave me some feeling of participation in the process, some sense of partial control or containment. But afterwards I kept it up for a while then stopped, because it seemed I had to postulate an enemy to continue—you are supposed to visualize the cancer cells being attacked, and I saw no reason to visualize cancer cells at all. The only "healthy" thing I could have continued with was imaging the breast cells continuing to repair themselves. Every now and then I imagine the immune system active and on guard. But if I obsessively do that, in a type of panic, I'm just buying into fear of death.

Nathaniel had picked up too on the possibility of blaming oneself as a negative side result of Simonton's approach. If I can make myself well, then I must have made myself sick. Ken's approach seems best there . . . perhaps 10% to 20% of getting sick is due to psychological factors (varies with the disease), but a higher percentage, say 40%, of getting well can be attributed in part to psychological factors.

Nathaniel and Ken had the same friendly argument they always have. I don't think either of them will ever give up! Nathaniel: "I think you are the clearest writer on mysticism around, and yet your whole position is self-contradictory. You say that mysticism is becoming one with the whole. But if I become one with the whole, there would be no motivation left to me as an individual. I might as well just roll over and die. Human beings are individuals, not amorphous wholes, so if I succeed in becoming one with all, there wouldn't even be any reason left for me to eat, let alone do anything else."

Ken: "Whole and part are not mutually exclusive. Mystics still feel pain, and hunger, and laughter, and joy. To be part of a larger whole doesn't mean that the part evaporates, just that the part finds its ground or its meaning. You are an individual, yet you also feel that you are a part of the larger unit of a family, which is part of the larger unit of a society. You already feel that, you already feel that you are a part of several larger wholes, and those wholes—like your life with Devers—give your life much value and meaning. Mysticism is just the even larger identity of also feeling part of the cosmos at large, and thus finding even greater meaning and value. Nothing contradictory about that. It's a direct experience of a larger identity, it doesn't mean your arms fall off."

And so it went!

Driving home I kept telling Ken little things he does that I love. He said he has dozens of things that are proof of how much he loves me but he's only going to tell me them one at a time, one a year. I badgered him to at least tell me one every six months, come on honey. Turns out this is one of his ways to keep me around . . . he figures I'll want to hear these things enough for it to be an extra little incentive for me to live longer and not leave him. He says he doesn't know what he'll do if I leave him. Reminded me of his earlier little allegory about if I die he'll come get me in the bardo. He's always promised to find me again, whatever happens.

That summer an event occurred that had an enormous impact on our lives and on our future plans. Treya got pregnant. This came as a shock to her, because she had never gotten pregnant before and had assumed that she probably couldn't. Treya was elated, I was stunned—and then the cruel reality of the situation settled in on us. Treya's doctors were unanimous: abort the pregnancy. The hormonal shifts concomitant with being pregnant would act like fertilizer for any remaining cancer cells in Treya's body (her tumor was estrogen positive).

I was ambivalent about fathering a child (a situation that eventually changed), and my lukewarm response to Treya's pregnancy—before we knew it had to be aborted—was a big disappointment to her. In my defense I rather lamely tried to point out that most of my friends who were fathers didn't get really excited about the child until it was born and actually placed in their arms; prior to that point, most guys are just various degrees of panic-stricken. But place the babe in their arms and they become slobbering drooling fathering fools, whereas mothers seem to beam from the minute of conception. Treya found none of it convincing; she experienced my lack of enthusiasm as an abandonment. It was the first time I had deeply disappointed her in the year we had been together; it hung over us like an ominous portent. And it was the nature of the thing itself that made it so difficult: pregnancy and abortion, life and death . . . as if we needed more of that.

I finally came to the point that, although I was still somewhat ambivalent, I was at least game: Let's go for it; let's get Treya better and then start a family. Definitely.

This unleashed the nesting instincts in both of us, and we began to make rather radical life changes. Up to that point both Treya and I had lived fairly monkish lives. Treya was practicing voluntary simplicity, and I was in effect a Zen monk. When I met Treya I owned one desk chair, a typewriter, and four thousand books; Treya had not much more.

All of this would change, and change dramatically, once we decided that we were going to raise a family. First, we needed a house . . . a big, big house, ready to hold a family. . . .

September 16, 1984
Muir Beach

Dear Martha,

Can't thank you enough for the atlas—an original and really great wedding present. As you know, I once studied geography, was in fact two courses shy of an M.A. in the field, so I love maps. One of my favorite courses in grad school was cartography! Many thanks from us both.

The big news in our lives is that we're moving to Lake Tahoe (Incline Village, northeast shore, to be exact). All came about because I accidentally got pregnant—first time in my life. Ironically I discovered this one week after I'd gone to a doctor to see whether or not we could eventually have a child, my having had cancer and all. The gynecologist said I should *never* get pregnant, because of the kind of tumor I'd had. I was devastated. Ken is wonderful, but I don't think he really understood what it meant to me. He was ambivalent and sometimes distant. He later apologized. But I cried for a week over this, his response was very upsetting—it made me realize how much I really wanted his child.

Then the discovery that I actually was pregnant! First time in my life. (Guess my body knows who the father's meant to be!) Absolute devastation. So we had to have it aborted. A very traumatic experience, but it was the right decision. I'm enough of a hypochondriac as it is now, checking out every pain or symptom with the doctor. I can't imagine how unnerving it would be to be pregnant now, not knowing how it was affecting any possible remnant of cancer or precancerous area, dealing with all the odd symptoms of pregnancy itself. So it feels right, though a lot of tears were shed over it and still are at times. So much for my righteous sense I'd get though this lifetime without having had an abortion!

The doctors did agree, however, that if I'm free of cancer in two years, then I can get pregnant again. Even though Ken is still a little ambivalent, he'll make a great father. Kids love him. He quips that's because he's the same emotional age as they are. Anyway, this stirred up our nesting instinct, which eventually led to our buying a beautiful house in Lake Tahoe!

We'd thought about Lake Tahoe before—in the mountains, which I love, and close to San Francisco (only four hours away). Our first trip up there we drove in through South Lake Tahoe, which was awful. But the north shore was really nice, especially Incline Village. It's a fairly recent planned town, maybe fifteen years old, with a small ski area, two golf courses, and two private beaches for people in the town. Ken thinks that's all a "bit much," as he says. "My God, we're moving into a country club. I need this like I need another satori." But he loves the lake, especially the kind of aqua color around the edges where there are white sandy beaches, and he's as anxious to get out of San Francisco as I am (he wants some quiet time to write). We looked at a bunch of houses on a few different trips and again on our way to Aspen for the summer, and finally found the right one.

We're extremely excited about it. . . . Easy access, a fantastic view, best of any we saw, and a layout that works really well for Ken's office. The house is still under construction, so we can specify all the interior details—carpets, wallpaper, paint colors, etc. I know you'll be out of the country for two more years, but then you must come and see us. Maybe we'll have a kid by then!

Thanks again so much for the atlas.

Love,
Terry

"Where are you going?" I ask her.

"I'll be right back. I'm just going to make a cup of tea. You're not afraid, are you?"

"Me? Oh, no. Fine, just fine." The fire has died down to a few glowing coals. Treya seems to be gone for minutes, but then the minutes seem to run into hours. It is very cold.

"Treya? Honey? Treya?"

Treya and I eagerly, almost desperately, looked forward to settling down in Tahoe. It took on the aura of refuge, of safety, of time out from turmoil. We were ready to raise a family; I was ready to get back to writing; life was starting to look very good.

For the first time in a year, Treya and I relaxed.

5

A UNIVERSE
WITHIN

Why in the past have I wanted to travel so much?
Why do I feel so constrained when I can't just pick up and go?
I twist in this new form, resist, feel confined.
I squirm, wonder if this is after all, really just another search for inner God
    displaced and sought "out there"?
If I let myself live more freely within myself, a whole being,
On my side, in support of myself completely,
Perhaps the foreign land will emerge within myself,
Strange sights and smells and thoughts swirling inside,
Pulling me into another land that begs to be experienced and felt
And shared with others and shaped and molded
In some way that satisfies that deep need.
An African bazaar within my belly,
Incense-soaked Indian temple festooned with monkeys in my chest,
High white Himalayan expanses with endless sky
In my head, limbos dancing to balmy Jamaican breezes,
The Louvre, the Sorbonne, washed down with a café au lait.
This planet, our home, a tiny land in my heart.

(Treya, 1975)

T R E Y A and I had both been meditating for many years, but, with the twist of the previous year's events, meditation began to take on a certain urgency. And so, just as we were getting ready for our move to Tahoe, Treya went on a ten-day meditation retreat with one of her favorite teachers, Goenka, who teaches a form of Buddhist meditation known as *vipassana* or insight meditation.

There are many ways to explain meditation, what it is, what it does, how it works. Meditation, it is said, is a way to evoke the relaxation response. Meditation, others say, is a way to train and strengthen awareness; a method for centering and focusing the self; a way to halt constant verbal thinking and relax the bodymind; a technique for calming the central nervous system; a way to relieve stress, bolster self-esteem, reduce anxiety, and alleviate depression.

All of those are true enough; meditation has been clinically demonstrated to do all of those things. But I would like to emphasize that meditation itself is, and always has been, a *spiritual* practice. Meditation, whether Christian, Buddhist, Hindu, Taoist, or Muslim, was invented as a way for the soul to venture inward, there ultimately to find a supreme identity with Godhead. "The Kingdom of Heaven is within"—and meditation, from the very beginning, has been the royal road to that Kingdom. Whatever else it does, and it does many beneficial things, meditation is first and foremost a search for the God within.

I would say meditation is spiritual, but not religious. Spiritual has to do with actual experience, not mere beliefs; with God as the Ground of Being, not a cosmic Daddy figure; with awakening to one's true Self, not praying for one's little self; with the disciplining of awareness, not preachy and churchy moralisms about drinking and smoking and sexing; with Spirit found in everyone's Heart, not anything done in this or that church. Mahatma Gandhi is spiritual; Oral Roberts is religious. Albert Einstein, Martin Luther King, Albert Schweitzer, Emerson and Thoreau, Saint Teresa of Ávila, Dame Julian of Norwich, William James—spiritual. Billy Graham, Archbishop Sheen, Robert Schuller, Pat Robertson, Cardinal O'Connor—religious.

Meditation is spiritual; prayer is religious. That is, petitionary prayer, in which I ask God to give me a new car, help with my promotion, etc., is religious; it simply wishes to bolster the little ego in its wants and desires. Meditation, on the other hand, seeks to go beyond the ego altogether; it asks nothing from God, real or imagined, but rather offers itself up as a sacrifice toward a greater awareness.

Meditation, then, is not so much a part of this or that particular religion, but rather part of the universal spiritual culture of all humankind—an effort to bring awareness to bear on all aspects of life. It is, in other words, part of what has been called the perennial philosophy.

Right before Treya and I moved to Tahoe, I was scheduled to give an interview on exactly this topic. We were in the process of moving and I could not meet with the original interviewers, so I asked them to send a list of questions instead. Treya, who understood this topic as well as I, then read the questions, added her own, and played the naive interviewer. She also played an aggressive devil's advocate.

One of the main topics discussed in this interview was the fundamental mystical doctrine that one has to die to the separate self in order to find the universal Self or God. The always-lurking possibility of Treya's physical death added a certain poignancy to the interview, and at one point I found it hard to continue. The transcripts simply say "Long pause," as if I were thinking about some difficult answer.

But that was the whole point: Treya's possible death became a profound spiritual teacher for both of us. Physical death made psychological death all the more cogent. As the mystics everywhere have repeatedly told us, it is only in accepting death that real life is found.

TREYA KILLAM WILBER: Why don't you start by explaining what you mean by the "perennial philosophy"?

KEN WILBER: The perennial philosophy is the worldview that has been embraced by the vast majority of the world's greatest spiritual teachers, philosophers, thinkers, and even scientists. It's called "perennial" or "universal" because it shows up in virtually all cultures across the globe and across the ages. We find it in India, Mexico, China, Japan, Mesopotamia, Egypt, Tibet, Germany, Greece. . . .

And wherever we find it, it has essentially similar features, it is in essential agreement the world over. We moderns, who can hardly agree on anything, find this rather hard to believe. But as Alan Watts summarized the available evidence—I'll have to read this—"Thus we are hardly aware of the extreme peculiarity of our own position, and find it difficult to recognize the plain fact that there has otherwise been a single philosophical consensus of universal extent. It has been held by [men and women] who report the same insights and teach the same essential doctrine whether living today or six thousand years ago, whether from New Mexico in the Far West or from Japan in the Far East."

This is really quite remarkable. I think, fundamentally, it's a testament to the universal nature of these truths, to the universal experience of a collective humanity that has everywhere agreed to certain profound truths about the human condition and about its access to the Divine. That's one way to describe the *philosophia perennis*.

TKW: Now you say that the perennial philosophy is essentially the same in various cultures. But what about the modern argument that all knowledge is molded by language and culture, and since cultures and languages differ dramatically from one another, there is simply no way that any sort of universal or collective truths about the human condition could be found? There is no human condition, there is only human history, and these histories are everywhere quite different. What about this whole notion of cultural relativity?

KW: There is much truth to that—there are indeed quite different cultures of "local knowledge," and exploring those differences is a very important endeavor. But cultural relativity is not the whole truth. In addition to obvious cultural differences, such as food styles or linguistic structures or mating customs, there are many phenomena of human existence that are largely universal or collective. The human body, for example, has two hundred and eight bones, one heart, two kidneys, and so on, whether it appears in Manhattan or Mozambique, whether it appears today or a thousand years ago. These universal features we call "deep structures," because they are everywhere essentially the same. On the other hand, this doesn't stop various cultures from using these deep structures in quite different ways, from Chinese footbinding to Ubangi lip-stretching to body painting to clothing styles to modes of bodily play, sex, and labor, all of which vary considerably from culture to culture. These variables we call "surface structures," since they are local and not universal.

We see the same thing in the area of the human mind. In addition to surface structures that vary from culture to culture, the human mind, like the body, has deep structures that are essentially similar across cultures. That is, wherever human minds emerge, they all have the capacity to form images, symbols, concepts, and rules. The *particular* images and symbols vary from culture to culture, it is true, but the very capacity to form these mental and linguistic structures, and the very structures themselves, are essentially similar wherever they appear. Just as the human body grows hair, the human

78

mind grows symbols. The mental surface structures vary considerably, but the mental deep structures are quite similar.

Now, just as the human body universally grows hair and the human mind universally grows ideas, so the human spirit universally grows intuitions of the Divine. And those intuitions and insights form the core of the world's great spiritual or wisdom traditions. And again, although the surface structures of the great traditions are most certainly quite different, their deep structures are quite similar, often identical. Thus, it's mostly the deep structures of the human encounter with the Divine that the perennial philosophy is interested in. Because when you can find a truth that the Hindus and Christians and Buddhists and Taoists and Sufis *all agree on*, then you have probably found something that is profoundly important, something that tells you about universal truths and ultimate meanings, something that touches the very core of the human condition.

TKW: At first glance, it's hard to see what Buddhism and Christianity would agree on. So what exactly are some of the essentials of the perennial philosophy? Could you go over its major points? How many profound truths or points of agreement are there?

KW: Dozens. I'll give you seven of what I think are the most important. One, Spirit exists, and Two, Spirit is found within. Three, most of us don't realize this Spirit within, however, because we are living in a world of sin, separation, and duality—that is, we are living in a fallen or illusory state. Four, there is a way out of this fallen state of sin and illusion, there is a Path to our liberation. Five, if we follow this Path to its conclusion, the result is a Rebirth or Enlightenment, a *direct experience* of Spirit within, a Supreme Liberation, which—Six—marks the end of sin and suffering, and which—Seven—issues in social action of mercy and compassion on behalf of all sentient beings.

TKW: That's a lot of information! Let's go over them one at a time. Spirit exists.

KW: Spirit exists, God exists, a Supreme Reality exists. Brahman, Dharmakaya, Kether, Tao, Allah, Shiva, Yahweh, Aton—"They call Him many who is really One."

TKW: But how do you know Spirit exists? The mystics say it does, but on what do they base their claims?

KW: On direct experience. Their claims are based, not on mere beliefs or ideas, theories or dogmas, but rather on direct experience, actual spiritual experience. This is what sets the mystics apart from merely dogmatic religious beliefs.

TKW: But what about the argument that the mystical experience is not valid knowledge because it is ineffable and therefore incommunicable?

KW: The mystical experience is indeed ineffable, or not capable of being entirely put into words. Like any experience—a sunset, eating a piece of cake, listening to Bach—one has to have the actual experience to see what it's like. But we don't therefore conclude that sunset, cake, and music don't exist or aren't valid. Further, even though the mystical experience is largely ineffable, it *can* be communicated or transmitted. Namely, by taking up spiritual practice under the guidance of a spiritual master or teacher, just like, for example, judo can be taught but not spoken.

TKW: But the mystical experience, which seems so certain to the mystic, could in fact simply be mistaken. The mystics might think they are becoming one with God, but that doesn't necessarily mean that's what's actually happening. No knowledge can be absolutely certain.

KW: I agree that mystical experiences are in principle no more certain than any other direct experiences. But far from pulling down the mystics' claims, that argument actually elevates their claims to a status equal to all other experiential knowledge, a status I would definitely accept. In other words, this argument against mystical knowledge actually applies to all forms of knowledge based on experiential evidence, including empirical sciences. I think I'm looking at the moon, but I could be mistaken; physicists think electrons exist, but they could be mistaken; critics think *Hamlet* was written by a historical person called Shakespeare, but they could be mistaken; and so on. How do we find out? We check it against more experience—which is also exactly what the mystics have historically done, checking and refining their experiences over the decades, centuries, and even millennia, a track record that makes modern science look like a johnny-come-lately. The point is that, far from tossing out the mystics' claims, this argument actually and correctly gives their claims exactly the same status as informed experts in any other field that relies on evidence to decide issues.

TKW: Fair enough. But I've often heard it said that the mystical vision could in fact be schizophrenic. How do you respond to that common charge?

KW: I don't think anybody doubts that a few mystics might also manifest some schizophrenic elements, and that some schizophrenics might also evidence mystical insights. But I don't know any authority in the field who believes mystical experiences are basically and primarily schizophrenic hallucinations. I know a fair number of nonauthorities who think so, and it's hard to convince them otherwise in a short space. So let me just say that the spiritual and contemplative practices used by mystics—such as contemplative prayer or meditation—can be fairly strong, but they simply are not strong enough to take wholesale numbers of normal, healthy, adult men and women and turn them, in the space of a few years, into floridly hallucinating schizophrenics. Zen Master Hakuin left behind him eighty-three fully transmitted students, who together revitalized and organized Japanese Zen. Eighty-three hallucinating schizophrenics couldn't organize a trip to the toilet, let alone Japanese Zen.

TKW: [Laughing] One last objection: The notion of being "one with Spirit" is just a regressive defense mechanism designed to shield a person from the horrors of mortality and finititude.

KW: If "oneness with Spirit" is merely believed in, as an idea or a hope, then it is frequently part of a person's "immortality project," a system of defenses designed to magically or regressively ward off death and promise an expansion or continuation of life, as I tried to explain in *Up from Eden* and *A Sociable God*. But the *experience* of timeless unity with Spirit is not an idea or a wish; it is a direct apprehension, and we can treat that *direct experience* in one of three ways: claim it is hallucinatory, which I just answered; claim it is mistaken, which I also just answered; or accept it as it announces itself to be, a direct experience of Spirit.

TKW: So you're saying, in effect, that genuine mysticism, as opposed to dogmatic religion, is very scientific, because it relies on direct experiential evidence and testing.

KW: Yes, that's right. The mystics ask you to take nothing on mere belief. Rather, they give you a set of experiments to test in your own awareness and experience. The laboratory is your own mind, the experiment is meditation. You yourself try it, and compare your test results with others who have also performed the experiment. Out of this consensually validated pool of experiential knowledge, you arrive at certain laws of the spirit—at certain "profound truths," if you will. And the first is: God is.

TKW: So that brings us back to the perennial philosophy, or mystical philosophy, and seven of its major points. The second was, Spirit within.

KW: Spirit within, there is a universe within. The stunning message of the mystics is that in the very core of your being, you are God. Strictly speaking, God is neither within nor without—Spirit transcends all duality. But one discovers this by consistently looking *within*, until "within" becomes "beyond." The most famous version of this perennial truth occurs in the *Chandogya Upanishad*, where it says, "In this very being of yours, you do not perceive the True; but there in fact it is. In that which is the subtle essence of your own being, all that exists has its Self. An invisible and subtle essence is the Spirit of the whole universe. That is the True, that is the Self, and thou, thou art That."

Thou are That—*tat tvam asi*. Needless to say, the "thou" that is "That," the you that is God, is not your individual and isolated self or ego, this or that self, Mr. or Ms. So-and-so. In fact, the individual self or ego is precisely what blocks the realization of the Supreme Identity in the first place. Rather, the "you" in question is the deepest part of you—or, if you wish, the highest part of you—the subtle essence, as the Upanishad put it, that transcends your mortal ego and directly partakes of the Divine. In Judaism it is called the *ruach*, the divine and supraindividual spirit in each and every person, and not the *nefesh*, or the individual ego. In Christianity, it is the indwelling *pneuma* or spirit that is of one essence with God, and not the individual *psyche* or soul, which at best can worship God. As Coomaraswamy said, the distinction between a person's immortal-eternal spirit and a person's individual-mortal soul (meaning ego) is a fundamental tenet of the perennial philosophy. I think this is the only way to understand, for example, Christ's otherwise strange remarks that a person could not be a true Christian "unless he hateth his own soul." It is only by "hating" or "throwing out" or "transcending" your mortal soul that you discover your immortal spirit, one with All.

TKW: St. Paul said, "I live, yet not I, but Christ in me." You're saying that St. Paul discovered his true Self, which is one with Christ, and this replaced his old or lower self, his individual soul or psyche.

KW: Yes. Your ruach, or ground, is the Supreme Reality, not your nefesh, or ego. Obviously, if you think that your individual ego is God, you're in big trouble. You would, in fact, be suffering from psychoses, from paranoid schizophrenia. That's obviously not what the world's greatest philosophers and sages have in mind.

TKW: But why, then, aren't more people aware of that? If Spirit is in fact within, why isn't it obvious to everybody?

KW: Well, that's the third point. If I am really one with God, why don't I realize that? Something must separate me from Spirit. Why this Fall? What's the sin?

TKW: It's not eating an apple.

KW: [Laughing] It's not eating an apple.

The various traditions give many answers to this question, but they all essentially come down to this: I cannot perceive my own true identity, or my union with Spirit, because my awareness is clouded and obstructed by a certain activity that I am now engaged in. And that activity, although known by many different names, is simply the activity of contracting and focusing awareness on my individual self or personal ego. My awareness is not open, relaxed, and God-centered, it is closed, contracted, and self-centered. And precisely because I am identified with the self-contraction to the exclusion of everything else, I can't find or discover my prior identity, my true identity, with the All. My individual nature, "the natural man," is thus fallen, or lives in sin and separation and alienation from Spirit and from the rest of the world. I am set apart and isolated from the world "out there," which I perceive as if it were entirely external and alien and hostile to my own being. And as for my own being itself, it certainly does not seem to be one with the All, one with everything that exists, one with infinite Spirit; rather, it seems completely boxed up and imprisoned in this isolated wall of mortal flesh.

TKW: This situation is often called "dualism," isn't it?

KW: Yes, that's right. I split myself as "subject" apart from the world of "objects" out there, and then based upon this original dualism, I continue to split the world into all sorts of conflicting opposites: pleasure versus pain, good versus evil, true versus false, and so on. And according to the perennial philosophy, awareness dominated by the self-contraction, by the subject/object dualism, cannot perceive reality as it is, reality in its wholeness, reality as the Supreme Identity. Sin, in other words, *is* the self-contraction, the separate-self sense, the ego. Sin is not something the self *does*, it is something the self *is*.

Furthermore, the self-contraction, the isolated subject "in here," precisely because it does not recognize its true identity with the All, feels an acute sense of lack, of deprivation, of fragmentation. The separate-self sense, in other words, is born in suffering—it is born "fallen." Suffering is not something that *happens* to the separate self, it is something that is *inherent* in the separate self. "Sin," "suffering," and "self" are so many names for the same process, the same contraction or fragmentation of awareness. You cannot rescue the self from suffering. As Gautama Buddha put it, to end suffering you must end the self—they rise and fall together.

TKW: So this dualistic world is a fallen world, and the original sin is the self-contraction, in each of us. And you're saying that not just the Eastern mystics but also the Western mystics actually define sin and Hell as being due to the separate self?

KW: The separate self and its loveless grasping, desiring, avoiding— yes, definitely. It's true that the equation of Hell or *samsara* with the separate self is strongly emphasized in the East, particularly in Hinduism and Buddhism. But you find an essentially similar theme in the writings of the Catholic, Gnostic, Quaker, Kabbalistic and Islamic mystics. My favorite is from the remarkable William Law, an eighteenth-century Christian mystic from England; I'll read it to you: "See here the whole truth in short. All sin, death, damnation, and hell is nothing else but this kingdom of self, or the various operations of self-love, self-esteem, and self-seeking which separate the soul from God and end in eternal death and hell." Or remember the great Islamic mystic Jalaluddin Rumi's famous saying, "If you have not seen the devil, look at your own self." Or the Sufi Abi 'l-Khayr: "There is no Hell but selfhood, no Paradise but selflessness." This is also behind the Christian mystics' assertion that, as the *Theologia Germanica* put it, nothing burns in Hell but self-will.

TKW: Yes, I see. So the transcendence of the "small self" is the discovery of the "big Self."

KW: Yes. This "small self" or individual soul is known in Sanskrit as the *ahamkara*, which means "knot" or "contraction," and it is this ahamkara, this dualistic or egocentric contraction in awareness, that is at the root of our fallen state.

But that brings us to the fourth major point of the perennial philosophy: There is a way to reverse the Fall, a way to reverse this brutal state of affairs, a way to untie the knot of illusion.

TKW: Ditch the small self.

KW: [Laughing] Ditch the small self, yes. Surrender or die to the separate-self sense, the small self, the self-contraction. If we want to discover our identity with the All, then our case of mistaken identity with the isolated ego must be let go. Now this Fall can be reversed instantly by understanding that in reality it never actually happened—there is only God, the separate self is an illusion. But for most of us, the Fall has to be reversed gradually, step by step.

In other words, the fourth point of the perennial philosophy is that a Path exists—a Path that, if followed properly, will lead us from our fallen state to our enlightened state, from samsara to nirvana, from Hell to Heaven. As Plotinus put it, a flight of the alone to the Alone—that is, from the self to the Self.

TKW: This Path is meditation?

KW: Well, we might say that there are several "paths" that constitute what I am generically calling "the Path"—again, various surface structures sharing the same deep structures. For example, in Hinduism it is said that there are five major paths or yogas. "Yoga" simply means "union," a way to unite the soul with Godhead. In English the word is "yoke." When Christ says, "My yoke is easy," he means "My yoga is easy." We see the same root in the Hittite *yugan*, the Latin *jugum*, the Greek *zugon*, and so on.

But maybe I could simplify the whole thing by saying that all these paths, whether found in Hinduism or in any of the other wisdom traditions, break down into just two major paths. I have another quote here for you, if I can find it—this is from Swami Ramdas:

"There are two ways: one is to expand your ego to infinity, and the other is to reduce it to nothing, the former by knowledge, and the latter by devotion. The Jnani [knowledge holder] says: 'I am God—the Universal Truth.' The devotee says: 'I am nothing, O God, You are everything.' In both cases, the ego-sense disappears."

The point is that, in either case, an individual on the Path transcends the small self, or dies to the small self, and thus rediscovers or resurrects his or her Supreme Identity with universal Spirit. And that brings us to the fifth major point of the perennial philosophy, namely, that of a Rebirth, Resurrection, or Enlightenment. In your own being, the small self must die so that the big Self may resurrect.

This death and new birth is described in several different terms by the traditions. In Christianity, of course, it finds its prototype in the figures of Adam and Jesus—Adam, whom the mystics call the "Old Man" or "Outer Man," is said to have opened the gates of Hell, while Jesus Christ, the "New Man" or "Inner Man," opens the gates of Paradise. Specifically, Jesus' own death and resurrection, according to the mystics, is the archetype of the death of the separate self and the resurrection of a new and eternal destiny from the stream of consciousness, namely, the divine or Christic Self and its Ascension. As St. Augustine said, "God became man so that man may become God." This process of turning from "manhood" to "Godhood," or from the outer person to the inner person, or from the self to the Self, is known in Christianity as *metanoia*, which means both "repentance" and "transformation"—we repent of the self (or sin) and transform as the Self (or Christ), so that, as you said, "not I but Christ liveth in me." Similarly, Islam views this death-and-resurrection as both *tawbah*, which means "repentance," and *galb*, which means "transformation," both of which are summarized in al-Bistami's succinct phrase, "Forgetfulness of self is remembrance of God."

In both Hinduism and Buddhism, this death-and-resurrection is always described as the death of the individual soul (*jivatman*) and the reawakening of one's true nature, which metaphorically the Hindus describe as All Being (*Brahman*) and the Buddhists as Pure Openness (*shunyata*). The actual moment of rebirth or breakthrough is known as enlightenment or liberation (*moksha* or *bodhi*). The *Lankavatara Sutra* describes this enlightenment experience as a "complete turning about in the deepest seat of consciousness." This "turning about" is simply the undoing of the habitual tendency to create a separate and substantial self where there is in fact only vast, open, clear awareness. This turning about or metanoia, Zen calls *satori* or *kensho*. "Ken" means true nature and "sho" means "directly seeing." Directly seeing one's true nature is becoming Buddha. As Meister Eckhart put it, "In this breaking through I find that God and I are both the same."

TKW: Is enlightenment actually experienced as a real death, or is that just a common metaphor?

KW: Actual ego-death, yes. It's no metaphor. The accounts of this experience, which may be very dramatic but can also be fairly simple and nondramatic, make it clear that all of a sudden you simply wake up and discover that, among other things, your real being is *everything* you are now looking at, that you are literally one with all manifestation, one with the universe, however corny that might sound, and that you did not actually *become* one with God and All, you have eternally been that oneness but didn't realize it.

Along with that feeling, or the discovery of the all-pervading Self, goes the very concrete feeling that your small self simply died, actually died. Zen calls satori "the Great Death." Eckhart was just as blunt: "The soul," he said, "must put itself to death." Coomaraswamy explains: "It is only by making stepping stones of our dead selves, until we realize at last that there is literally nothing with which we can identify our Self, that we can become what we are." Or Eckhart again, "The kingdom of God is for none but the thoroughly dead."

TKW: Dying to the small self is the discovery of eternity.

KW: [Long pause] Yes, provided we don't think of eternity as being everlasting time but a point without time, the so-called eternal present or timeless now. The Self doesn't live forever in time, it lives in the timeless present prior to time, prior to history, change, succession. The Self is present as Pure Presence, not as everlasting duration, a rather horrible notion.

Anyway, that brings us to the sixth major point of the perennial philosophy, namely, that enlightenment or liberation brings an end to suffering. Gautama Buddha, for example, said that he only taught two things, what causes suffering and how to end it. What causes suffering is the grasping and desiring of the separate self, and what ends it is the meditative path that transcends self and desire. The point is that suffering is inherent in the knot or contraction known as self, and the only way to end suffering is to end the self. It's not that after enlightenment, or after spiritual practice in general, you no longer feel pain or anguish or fear or hurt. You do. It's simply that they no longer threaten your existence, and so they cease to be problematic. You are no longer identified with them, dramatizing them, energizing them, threatened by them. On the one hand, there is no longer any fragmented self to threaten, and on the other, the big Self can't be threatened since, being the All, there is nothing outside of it that could harm it. A profound relaxing and uncoiling occurs in the heart. The individual realizes that, no matter how much suffering might occur, it doesn't fundamentally affect his or her real Being. Suffering comes and goes, but the person now possesses the "peace that surpasseth understanding." The sage feels suffering, but it doesn't "hurt." Because the sage is aware of suffering, he or she is motivated by compassion, by a desire to help all those who suffer and think it's real.

TKW: Which brings us to the seventh point, about enlightened motivation.

KW: Yes. True enlightenment is said to issue in social action driven by mercy, compassion, and skillful means, in an attempt to help all beings attain the supreme liberation. Enlightened activity is simply selfless service. Since we are all one in the same Self, or the same mystical body of Christ, or the same Dharmakaya, then in serving others I am serving my own Self. I think when Christ said, "Love your neighbor as yourself," he must have meant "Love your neighbor as your Self."

TKW: Thank you.*

---

* In these days of "politically correct" (PC) thinking, the one thing that is consistently overlooked, of course, is the perennial philosophy. The PC claim is that all of modern civilization is now dominated by thinking that is Eurocentric, logocentric, and sexist, and that the only politically adequate or correct view is therefore one that is, by contrast, radically egalitarian and pluralistic, and denies that any worldview can be "better" than another. The problem with this view is that, while it claims to be admirably liberal—in that nothing can be said to be "better" or "higher"—it ends up absolutely reactionary: if nothing is better, then there is and can be no liberal agenda, there can be no impetus to improve a present state of affairs according to a blueprint of a "better" state of affairs. It utterly lacks a coherent and integrative vision of human possibilities. Moreover, radical pluralism is itself a Eurocentric, logocentric notion.

The perennial philosophy, on the other hand, first arose in the matriarchy, and thus cannot be

What I kept thinking after that interview was, *that's* the person I love more than my self, big *s* or small *s*.

"I am come as Time, the waster of peoples, ready for the hour that ripens to their ruin."
"What, I couldn't hear that. What did you say?"
"Ready for the hour that ripens to their ruin . . ."
"Who's there? Treya, that you? Sweetie?"

When Treya first hit adolescence, she had a powerful and quite profound mystical experience, an experience that was probably the single most influential event in her life.

"When did this happen?" I asked her one evening shortly after we had met.

"I was thirteen. I was sitting in front of a fireplace, by myself, watching the fire, and all of a sudden I became the smoke from the fire and I began to rise up into the sky, higher and higher, until I became one with all space."

"You were no longer identified with your individual self and body?"

"I completely dissolved, I became one with everything. There was no individual self at all."

"You were still conscious?"

"Wide awake."

"But that was very real, right?"

"Completely real. It felt like I was coming home, like I was finally where I belonged. I know all the names for this—I had found my real Self, or God, or Tao, and so on—but I didn't know those terms then. I only knew I was home, I was perfectly safe, or saved I guess. This wasn't a dream; everything else seemed like a dream, the ordinary world seemed like a dream; this was real."

That mystical experience became the central guiding principle in Treya's life, even though she didn't talk about it much ("those who know don't speak . . ."). It was part of her lifelong interest in spirituality and meditation; it was behind her changing her name to Treya; it was part of the strength and courage with which she would face cancer.

---

charged with inherent sexism; it arose in illiterate peoples, and thus is not logocentric; and it first flourished in what are now Second and Third World countries—it is hardly Eurocentric. Furthermore, it offers what PC thought cannot: an integrative vision that, while allowing each expression its own free space, points to a "better" state of affairs: namely, the supreme identity. It thus has inherent in it a genuine liberal agenda: increasing freedom on both an individual and societal level.

That image since childhood of expanding, my molecules eventually mixing with the entire universe, is a kind of guiding symbol for my life. It's the only thing that really moves me, that brings tears to my eyes, my desire to follow a spiritual path, to find oneness with everything, to make my life's work further that for myself and others. I think one of the reasons that I get so restless with counseling and school is that my real interest lies within. I quickly become bored with things. I think that's partly because the only things that really interest me are the inner spiritual questions and when I keep trying to direct them outward, as in counseling, I lose interest.

I need to hear that inner voice, that inner guidance, to strengthen it, to nourish it, to contact it, to invest it with power . . . only then will I be able to hear it in a way that can give my life direction and guidance. I find my heart swelling at the thought, the possibility, typing with my eyes closed to feel indeed that inner feeling, the expansion, the longing. This has been the main theme/thread of my life. That feeling of expansion must come first, and be deepened, and later it just naturally overflows into a grounded, enlightened concern with all those issues of our humanness, which is to say, our godliness. In truth, what I ultimately yearn for is that absolutely egoless state, free of separate self. . . .

And in truth, that is exactly the goal and purpose of meditation.

"Treya, really, sweetie, that's not funny. Just get the tea and come back here, would you?" The fire has died out, leaving the air faintly singed.

"This is extremely unfunny. I'm coming out there."

But there is no there; *I really can't see anything. The only sensory experience I have is of coldness.*

"OK, you really got me. Left shoulder and all that. Ripens to their ruin. Very good, very good. Look, could we just talk a minute?"

6

BODYMIND
DROPPED!

❧❧❧

S ITTING quietly, sensing my breath moving throughout my body, legs crossed in a half lotus. I hear the low murmur of the waves beyond, water moving in to caress the shore, sink into the sand, then a slow reluctant move back out to the depths, gathering into itself, then again the sensuous glide forward, reaching out toward the other, a kind of longing and daring in that movement out from oneself. In out, withdrawing meeting, safety risking. Like the breath moving through my body, bringing the other inside my body like water mingling with sand, two different elements mixing, borrowing, giving life to each other. And I send the spent breath out again, back into the ocean of air all around to be recharged, just as the sea withdraws to its own depths before again gliding forward to caress and sink into the sand. Together they glisten and shimmer in the morning sunshine; the constant low murmur of their meeting and parting, meeting and parting fills my being.

Treya returned from the meditation retreat rejuvenated. Construction had been delayed on the Tahoe house, so we were still in our place at Muir Beach. Treya walked in the front door, and she looked radiant, almost transparent. She also looked very strong, very secure, very solid. She said that, on the one hand, she had continued to have very disturbing images of a recurrence; on the other, she wasn't afraid of it. She felt she had turned a corner in dealing with her fear of a recurrence.

So what did I do on the retreat? I was told to spend ten to eleven hours a day focusing on my breath moving in and out of my nostrils, just my breath. To notice when my mind strayed and bring it back to the breath. To notice what came up, the thoughts and the emotions, and once I was aware of a thought or emotion to again bring my attention back to my breath. Patiently, persistently, diligently. To practice, to discipline my awareness.

Then I was taught to bring this now somewhat disciplined awareness to bear on my body. To focus on the sensation around my nose and later to focus on the sensations in different parts of my body. To sweep with my awareness down and up, down and up the body. To notice the sensations, focus on blind spots, notice the pains, return when I wandered, all with poise and calm and equanimity. Rather than focusing on something external to myself, my body became the laboratory for experiments in training my attention. This was my fifth ten-day retreat with Goenka, so I was getting somewhat proficient at the practice.

What happened as I meditated on my body, on these physical sensations, some pleasurable, some painful? For the first several days I obsessed about eye pains and headaches that frightened me. Images of cancer recurrence surfaced all the time, fears of leaving Ken, of what might happen. Every painful sensation in my body, no matter how slight, triggered images of a possible recurrence, with tremendous fear around each image.

It was a difficult struggle, but by the fifth day I could just witness the sensations without judging them. I could be aware of the fearful images without reacting to them, without becoming afraid of them, or afraid of fear itself. I became acutely aware of my awareness, of my capacity simply to be aware, and of the tendency for this awareness to wander, to be captured by events or thoughts on its periphery. This focal awareness began to seem like a kind of flashlight, a beam of light which I could direct. Wherever I directed it, I became consciously aware of what was happening there. If it was the constant play of sensation on the top of my head, or the pain in my eyes, or the recurring headache, then that is what I was consciously aware of, without judging it, or moving away from it, or fearing it.

I also became more aware of the always existent background of this focal awareness, the things that moved and changed in the dimmer light at the edge of the flashlight's beam. These I was vaguely aware of but not consciously so until I directed the flashlight toward them. They were the background of my awareness. Thus I became aware of the figure-ground relationship between my focal awareness and my diffuse awareness, coexisting and shifting as I shifted my attention or as my attention shifted randomly.

I became aware of the powerful role my attention played in determining my state of consciousness. I could simply witness my sensations, in which case I felt calm, balanced, in equanimity. Or I could judge and fear my sensations, in which case I felt anxiety and sometimes panic.

As I focused within this body, I became aware of things I had never been aware of before. Aware of thoughts—ideas, concepts, words, images, stray sensations, random bits of stories, chatting voices inside filling up any empty space, odd little unfinished combinations of events emerging into and fading from my awareness. I became aware of habits—the habit of telling these inner dreamlike stories, of automatically wanting to move whenever my position grew the least bit uncomfortable, of restlessness, of continually planning ahead, the habit of a constantly wandering attention. I became aware of the passing flow of my emotions—irritation at physical pain, fear that I would not be able to last the ten days, fear of cancer, craving for special kinds of food, desire to progress in the technique, love of Ken, anger when my attention would wander, more fear of cancer, pleasure at certain waves of sensation.

I learned gradually, according to instructions, to simply watch all of this inner activity with more and more balance, with equanimity, without craving and aversion. To watch the thoughts, the habits, and even the emotions calmly. I would succeed one moment, then slip immediately into desiring for the success to continue. I would watch the pain in my eye openly for a moment, then feel the tension rise as I slipped into wanting to get rid of it. I noticed how these emotions blocked sensations, blocked progress. It was tricky to walk the razor's edge of willful effort with no attachment to results.

As the thoughts and emotions quieted and my attention sharpened I became more and more aware of a wide range of physical sensations. A tickle or an itch or a vibration appeared where before I felt nothing, then it passed away. Something new and unexpected would appear, and as quickly pass away. Then there were moments when my entire body seemed nothing but vibration. The temptation was always to think about it, to conceptualize what was happening, to talk to myself inwardly, to respond emotionally, to ponder the possible significance of an event, rather than to simply, barely notice in the moment. To notice when something changed, to notice when it went away, to notice when my attention wandered, to notice the constant change, the ceaseless flux, diligently, patiently, in ever finer detail in ever finer moments.

The first few days were spent almost entirely obsessing. What does this twinge mean? And that ache? Ken used to try to shake me out of this—"It hurts there, right there, on your toe? You mean you have big toe cancer?" But it's frightening. I find myself having several inner conversations with God, bargaining: Please just let me have ten years to spend with Ken, how happy I'd be to reach fifty even—and that sounds so young!

Suddenly, on the second day, I notice that my arm [from which the lymph nodes were removed] is swollen! Damn! What does that mean? Was never swollen after the operation, why suddenly now? This really scares me. Stray thought that maybe it would be better for Ken if I go sooner, he'll be less dependent on me. I realize I also am not paying attention to my breath!

There's a trickster in my mind. When I'm finally fully concentrated on my breath, after struggling with distracting thoughts, the danger comes when I notice my hard-won concentration. The trickster steps in. "Just checking," it says. "Well done. A little test won't hurt, though," and then it offers up some choice, tasty morsel like will that carpet color work against the table colors or could we possibly get another closet in the bedroom? "Oh yummy," goes the rest of my mind. "I'd like to chew on that one for a while." And there goes my attention, out the window once again.

By the third day there are periods of calm and quiet that break through the chattering thoughts and emotions. Arm still swollen, but it doesn't freak me out; I simply notice the sensation. I love the sense of peace and inner quiet. Thought of leaving Ken unbearable; I cry through the evening session.

On day five I find I can almost completely let go and simply witness whatever comes up, without judging it, without pushing it or pulling it.

Whatever comes, comes; whatever happens, happens. I find again the freedom of simply watching in the moment, simply sitting, without a subtle desire for repetition of a previous experience and without wishing for something new. Just being with what is, not what should be. A kind of rhythm develops in my meditation, a sense of simply being with it, of not fighting. The emotions and thoughts are still there but I am aware of them, I am not caught in them, not swept away by them—I have somehow learned to step back and just watch.

On day seven I notice that my entire body feels like a single, whole being. I feel no difference between my arms and legs and trunk, no separation or conflict between any parts. Those strong, pleasurable, almost painfully blissful energy currents are back, the same currents I felt with Ken that first night. I seem to be becoming more aware of my whole body. Sometimes it happens, comes over me, in a kind of rush, sometimes more quietly. I can travel through my body with ease; my body feels like one piece rather than a collection of parts. If I breathe very slowly and calmly, or rather when my breath slows of its own accord, I can feel where all the subtle tensions are remaining in my body, and somehow I am learning to let go of them, again and again, and then I feel the energy throughout my body in a more even way. Dissolving those areas of holding, of resistance, of separation.

On day nine I notice that whenever a cancer image comes up, I don't react to it at all; it doesn't frighten me. Or if some fear comes up, I just witness it. Equanimity, free flow, clear observation. This holds through day ten. I find a strong choiceless, effortless awareness, witnessing with equanimity, with evenness. The whole process has changed; my attention is sharp but light. I don't lead, I follow. Goenka: You cannot invent sensations, you cannot choose sensations, you cannot create sensations (wonder what the makers of Häagen-Dazs would say to that). You just witness. Not holding on but moving on, knowing things will change, the truth of impermanence. Very quiet, very peaceful. I wonder how this will hold up in the real world?

On the morning of November 21, while Treya was taking a shower, she noticed two small bumps under her right breast. As Treya and I looked more closely at them, we saw what might be two or three other small bumps. They looked just like ant bites, but they didn't itch. The good news was, they didn't much look like cancer. The bad news was, there wasn't much else they could be. And Treya and I both knew it.

95

We saw Peter Richards that afternoon. The same pained expression, the same (understandably) noncommittal attitude. "They could be insect bites, they could be something, but we better have them removed." We arranged to be in emergency surgery the morning after next, and then we drove home to Muir Beach.

Treya's equanimity was astonishing. At most she seemed slightly annoyed. We talked briefly about the possibility of its being cancer, but Treya didn't want to dwell on it. "If it's cancer, it's cancer," she finally said, and that was that. What she really wanted to talk about was meditation and the experiences she was having. Just two days earlier I had finished work on *Transformations of Consciousness*, and Treya was eager to compare notes.

"I keep having the experience of just expanding outwardly. I start out just witnessing my mind and body, or just paying bare attention to my thoughts and sensations, but then my mind and body seem to disappear, and I'm one with, I don't know, God, or the universe, or my higher Self, or something. It's wonderful!"

"I don't really care what we call it—God, universe, Self. Dogen Zenji [a famous Japanese Zen Master] got his enlightenment when his teacher whispered in his ear: 'Bodymind dropped!' Like you say, that's what it feels like, identification with the separate bodymind just drops away. That's happened to me a few times, and I think it's very real. I think, by comparison, the ego is very unreal."

"I agree. It feels like that expanded state is more real, more alive. It's just like waking up—everything else seems dreamlike. So you're convinced these experiences are real?" she asked.

When I heard Treya say that, I knew she wanted to play "professor." I knew she was going to pick my mind for hours—it had happened often before. I also knew that she had probably already made up her mind, and she just wanted to see if I'd get it right. And I realized that both of us would rather do this than obsess about those damn bumps. . . .

"We're in the same position as any scientist. All we have to go on is experiential evidence. And sooner or later we have to trust our own experience, because that's all we really have. Otherwise it's a vicious circle. If I fundamentally distrust my experience, then I must distrust even my capacity to distrust, since that is also an experience. So sooner or later I have no choice but to trust, trust my experience, trust that the universe is not fundamentally and persistently going to lie to me. Of course we can be mistaken, and sometimes experiences are misleading, but on balance we have no choice but to follow them. It's a type of phenomenological imperative. And especially mystical experiences—if anything, as you say, they are more real, not less real, than other experiences."

I was thinking of Hegel's critique of Kant: you can't question awareness since the only tool you have *is* awareness. Trying to do so, Hegel said, is like trying to go swimming without getting wet. We are drenched in awareness, in experience, and have no choice but to go with it on some profound level.

Treya continued. "The Tibetans have a phrase I always liked: 'mind is all space.' That's what it feels like for me. Of course, this experience only lasts a few seconds, then bam! it's the same old Terry again."

"I like that phrase too. You were doing vipassana meditation, where you keep your mind focused on your breath or some other sensation. But the Tibetans have a practice where, on the outbreath, you are actually supposed to 'mix the mind with all space' or 'mix the mind and sky.' This means, when you breathe out, you simply feel your separate identity going out with the breath and then dissolving into the sky in front of you— dissolving, in other words, into the entire universe. It's very powerful."

"I've actually started doing that," she said, "but almost spontaneously. And recently there's been a real change in my meditation. I start out very focused and very willful, concentrating on the breath, then carefully sweeping down and up the body. But then I experience moments when there seems to be a sudden abrupt shift of awareness. Then, instead of directing my attention somewhere, I just sit and don't pay attention to anything, really. It seems much closer to something like complete self-surrender, just *surrendering* to the divine will, letting go and letting God. Everything is sacrificed, everything is exposed. This seems much more powerful."

"My own experience is that either way will work, you just have to be consistent." I thought for a while. "You know, you're actually describing perfectly what the Japanese Buddhists call 'self-power' versus 'other-power.' All meditation breaks down into those two types. Self-power is epitomized by Zen, by vipassana, by jnana yoga. Here, one relies strictly on one's own powers of concentration and awareness in order to break through the ego to a larger identity. In other-power, one relies on the power of the guru, or on God, or simply on complete surrender."

"And you think they both come to the same end?" Treya looked unconvinced.

"I do. Remember even Ramana Maharshi [generally regarded as India's

97

greatest modern sage] said that there are two ways to enlightenment: either inquire, 'Who am I?,' which undermines the ego completely, or surrender to the guru or God and let God strike down the ego. Either way the ego is undone and the Self shines forth. Personally I'm hooked on the self-inquiry 'Who am I?,' which is also a famous Zen koan. But I'm convinced they both work."

Treya and I shifted to the kitchen to get some tea. The topic of cancer hadn't come up.

Knock, knock.
"Who's there?"
Knock, knock.
"Who's there?" Very cold, very silent. Three hallways, one door.
Knock, knock. "I said, who's there? damn it. What is this, a 'knock-knock' joke?" It's too dark to move easily or quickly, so rather haltingly I fumble toward the door and in anger fling it open.

"I'm curious how they could both work," Treya said. "They feel so different. In vipassana you strive so hard, at least at first, but in self-surrender there's no effort at all."

"Well, I'm no guru, I can only give you my beginner's understanding. But it seems to me that what they both have in common—well, actually, what virtually all forms of meditation have in common—is that they break the ego by strengthening the Witness, strengthening your innate capacity to simply witness phenomena."

"But how is that different from my ego? I tend to think that the ego can witness, or can be aware." Treya screwed up her nose, sipped her tea.

"But that's the point. The ego is not a real subject; the ego is just another *object*. In other words, you can be aware of your ego, you can see your ego. Even if parts of the ego are unconscious, all the parts can at least theoretically become objects of awareness. The ego, in other words, can be seen, it can be known. And therefore it is not the Seer, not the Knower, not the Witness. The ego is just a bunch of mental objects, mental ideas and symbols and images and concepts, that we have identified with. We identify with these objects and then use those objects as something with which we look at and thus distort the world."

Treya picked up the theme immediately. Most of these ideas were already familiar to both of us; we were just thinking out loud, reaffirming our understanding. And I, at any rate, was avoiding another topic.

"In other words," she said, "we identify with those objects in here, mental objects in our head, and that keeps us separated from the world out there. So it's self versus other, subject versus object. I remember Krishnamurti saying once, 'In the gap between the subject and the object lies the whole misery of mankind.'"

"And the odd point is that the ego isn't even a real subject, a real capital S Self; it's just a series of conscious or unconscious objects. And so the way you start to break this case of mistaken identity is to start to look at all the contents and objects of the mind, you start observing the mind, just like in vipassana or in Zen. You exhaustively look at the mental-egoic world, you . . ."

"In other words," Treya jumped in, "you take the position of the Witness instead of the ego. You just objectively and impartially witness all mental objects, thoughts, sensations, images, emotions, and so on, without identifying with them or judging them."

"Yes, to the point that it starts to dawn on you: since you can *see* all these thoughts and images, they cannot be the real Seer, capital S, the real Witness. Your identity starts to shift from the personal ego, which is just another object, to the impersonal Witness, which is the real Subject or the real Self, capital S, capital S."

"Right," Treya said. "And it's the Witness or big Self that is one with God, or one with Spirit. That's why, even if I start out with individual effort, trying to witness my own mind and body, I end up with my identity shifting outward, becoming one with all space. And that's the same place I end up if I also begin by surrendering to God, to the universe. I also end up in that larger Self or larger awareness. Well, a few times I end up there; mostly I end up Terry!"

"Yeah, I think that's why St. Clement said, 'He who knows his Self knows God.' There is only one Witness in each of us, one Spirit looking out through different eyes, talking with different voices, walking with different legs. But the mystics say it's the same Witness, one and the same. There's only one God, one Self, one Witness, all capitals."

"OK, by witnessing the ego, observing all aspects of the body and mind, I disidentify with those objects, and identify instead with the true Self, the Witness. And the Witness is Spirit, Brahman."

"According to the perennial philosophy, yes, definitely."

Treya began making another batch of tea. "Did you put any of this into *Transformations of Consciousness?*"

"Some of it, yeah. But mostly I centered on the development of the

99

Witness, on the stages of mistaken identity that the Witness goes through before it awakens to its own true nature. I also centered on the types of neuroses or pathologies that can occur at each of these developmental stages, and the types of treatment that seem best suited for each stage." I was proud of that book; it was the last thing I would write for almost four years.

"Have I heard any of that before? Sounds new."

"Most of it is new. I'll give you the Reader's Digest version. You know the Great Chain of Being. . . ."

"Sure, the various levels of existence."

"Yeah. According to the perennial philosophy, reality consists of several different levels or dimensions, from the least real to the most real. This is the Great Chain of Being, reaching from matter to body to mind to soul to spirit. Matter, body, mind, soul, spirit—those are five levels or dimensions. Some traditions have seven levels—the seven chakras, for example. Some traditions just have three levels—body, mind, and spirit. Some traditions have literally dozens of levels. As you know, in my own writing I tend to use about two dozen levels.

"Anyway, the simpler version of matter, body, mind, soul, and spirit will do. The point is that in human growth and development, the Witness, or real Self capital S, starts out identified with the material self, then the bodily self, then the mental self, then the soul self, and finally reverts to, or awakens to, its own true nature as spirit. Each stage includes the previous stage, and then adds its own unique aspects in order to form a larger union, until there is ultimately a union with the All. In the book I try to show how the various developmental psychologists, East and West, from Freud to Jung to Buddha to Plotinus, were all describing various aspects of this same sequence, this same developmental sequence that is basically just the Great Chain of Being."

"So it's kind of like plugging all of modern psychology into the perennial philosophy."

"Yes, that's right. We get a synthesis that way. The thing is, it works, it really works. I think." We started laughing. The sun was just setting on the beach. Treya seemed genuinely at ease, relaxed, smiling. As usual, we managed somehow to have at least one point of physical contact, one point of grounding between us. By this time we were lying on the carpeted floor, on our backs, at right angles to each other, my right foot lightly touching her left knee.

"So," Treya summarized, "development proceeds up the Great Chain of Being, level by level."

"Well, more or less, yes. The point about meditation is that it is simply a way to carry on development. Meditation is how you continue to grow and develop beyond the mind into the levels of soul and spirit. And you do that in essentially the same way that you developed through the first three levels: the Witness in you disidentifies with the lower level in order to find a larger and more inclusive identity with the next higher level, and this process continues until the Witness reverts to, and rediscovers, its own true nature as Spirit itself."

"I see," Treya said, warming to the topic. "So that's why awareness meditation works. By looking at my mind, or practicing bare attention to all mental events, I eventually transcend the mind, or disidentify with it, and move up the Great Chain to the levels of soul and then spirit. It's basically an extended view of evolution, like Teilhard de Chardin or Aurobindo."

"Yes, I think so. The body is aware of matter, the mind is aware of the body, the soul is aware of the mind, and spirit is aware of the soul. Each step up is an increase in awareness, a discovery of a larger and wider identity, until there is nothing but the supreme identity and a universal awareness, so-called 'cosmic consciousness.' All of that sounds pretty dry and abstract, but as you know, the actual process, or the actual mystical state, is incredibly simple and obvious." The setting sunlight was playing off the roof and walls.

"Want to get something to eat?" I said. "I could make spaghetti."

"One last thing. You said that you tied these developmental stages in with various types of neuroses or emotional problems in general. In school they tell us that most psychiatrists now break these problems down into three general categories: psychoses, like schizophrenia; the borderline conditions, like narcissism; and general neuroses. How does that fit in? Or do you agree with those categories at all?"

"Oh, I agree with them, with those three main categories, but they just don't go far enough. They only cover the first three of the five levels. If something goes wrong at level one, you get psychoses; at level two, the borderline syndromes; at level three, the neuroses. To put it rather simplistically."

"I see. So that covers the three major orthodox categories. But psychiatry ignores the higher levels of development, denies the soul and spirit, and so that's what you are trying to redress in *Transformations*, right?" It was getting dark now, and, with a full moon already out, Muir Beach began to shimmer in the dimness.

"That's right. The soul, as I am using the term, is a sort of halfway house, halfway between the personal ego-mind and the impersonal or transpersonal Spirit. The soul is the Witness as it shines forth in you and nobody else. The soul is the home of the Witness in that sense. Once you are established on the soul level, then you are established as the Witness, as the real Self. Once you push through the soul level, then the Witness itself collapses into everything witnessed, or you become one with every- thing you are aware of. You don't witness the clouds, you are the clouds. That's Spirit."

"So . . ." Treya paused. "It seems like there is sort of good news and bad news about the soul."

"Well, in a sense the soul or the Witness in you is the highest pointer toward Spirit and the last barrier to Spirit. It's only from the position of the Witness that you can jump into Spirit, so to speak. But the Witness itself eventually has to dissolve or die. Even your own soul has to be sacrificed and released and let go of, or died to, in order for your ultimate identity with Spirit to radiate forth. Because ultimately the soul is just the final contraction in awareness, the subtlest knot restricting universal Spirit, the last and subtlest form of the separate-self sense, and that final knot has to be undone. That's the last death, as it were. First we die to the material self—that is, disidentify with it—then we die to an exclusive identity with the bodily self, then to the mental self, and then finally to the soul. The last one is what Zen calls the Great Death. We make steppingstones out of all our dead selves. Each death to a lower level is a rebirth on a higher level, until the ultimate rebirth, liberation, or enlightenment."

"Wait. Why exactly is the soul the final knot? If the soul is the home of the Witness, why is that a knot? The Witness is not identified with any particular object, it is just impartially aware of all objects."

"Well, that's the point. It's true that the Witness is not identified with the ego or with any other mental object, it just impartially witnesses all objects. But that's just it: the Witness is still separate from all the objects that it witnesses. In other words, there is still a very subtle form of the subject/object dualism. The Witness is a huge step forward, and it is a necessary and important step in meditation, but it is not ultimate. When the Witness or the soul is finally undone, then the Witness dissolves into everything that is witnessed. The subject/object duality collapses and there is only pure nondual awareness, which is very simple, very obvious. Like a famous Zen Master said when he got his enlightenment, 'When I heard the bell ring, suddenly there was no "I" and no "bell," just the ringing.' Everything continues to arise, moment to moment, but there's nobody divorced or alienated from it. What you are looking out of is what you are looking at. There's no separation or fragmentation between subject and object, there is just the ongoing stream of experience, perfectly clear and luminous and open. What I am is now everything that is arising. Remember that great quote from Dogen: 'To study mysticism is to study the self; to study the self is to forget the self; to forget the self is to be one with, and enlightened by, all things.' "

"I do remember that, it's my favorite. The mystics sometimes call this ultimate state the One Self, or One Mind, but the point is that the Self at that point is one with everything, so it's really not a 'self' in that sense at all."

"Yeah. The real self *is* the real world, no separation, so sometimes the mystics will also say there is no self, no world. But that's all they mean, no separate self, no separate world. Eckhart called it fusion without confusion." I *knew* that world, on occasion well, and yet all I could feel now was fusion with confusion, a good definition of being damn near nuts.

I stood up and turned on the lights. "Let's eat, honey, really."

Treya was silent, and the unspoken topic filled the air. She turned her head away, then turned and looked directly at me. "I'm determined not to let myself or anyone else make me feel guilty or embarrassed about this," she finally said.

"I know, sweetie, I know." I sat down and put my arms around her. Treya began to cry, very quietly. When she stopped, we both just sat there, silently, not a word was said. I got up and made spaghetti, and we ate it on the porch, watching the moonlight play on the small sliver of ocean we could see through a gap in the trees.

7

"MY LIFE HAD
TWISTED
SUDDENLY"

T H E quarter drops, clanking into the pay phone. My class in Professional Ethics has just ended; it is Monday afternoon, a sunny winter day in early December. I keep my mind blank as I carefully dial the number, Dr. Richards's number, but underneath the blankness I can feel the silent "Oh God, oh God, please." All around me people fill the hallway of the school, some leaving classes just ended, others gathering for the 5:45 classes. This phone is near the busiest area; I hunch over, trying to create a cocoon of privacy as I listen to the phone ring.

"Hello, Dr. Richards's office."

"Hi, this is Terry Killam Wilber. Could I speak to Dr. Richards?" I almost call him Peter; I never know quite what to say, Dr. Richards is too formal, Peter a bit too casual for our professional friendship.

"Hello, Terry. This is Dr. Richards. We got the results of the test back today and, I'm sorry to say, it is cancer. I don't quite know what to make of it; this is an unusual kind of recurrence, especially since the area where the lumps appeared was within the field that was radiated. But don't worry, I'd call this only a local recurrence. We can take care of it. When can you come in to see me?"

Oh, hell. I knew it. Those damned little bumps, just like mosquito bites except they weren't red and they didn't itch. They were just too odd and in too incriminating a location to be anything but cancer and I knew it, despite people's attempts to reassure me. Just five tiny bumps in the skin, just below the scar from the tube that drained the area of the segmental mastectomy, the tube that collected large amounts of translucent pinkish fluid while my body was healing, the tube that stayed in for a week after I left the hospital a year ago, the tube that hurt so much when Dr. Richards pulled it out. Ouch, I still remember that. It must have carried a few cancer cells on its end and left them behind in my skin. Cancer, again! Round two. Why didn't the radiation kill those cells?

I made an appointment to see Dr. Richards the next day. I walked out of the building into the sunshine, around the block to my car. I got in and drove to a counseling appointment I had in a few minutes. I remember noticing a neighborhood grocery store and an appealing array of fruit outside when I stopped at a light; the refrain in my head was "recurrence, recurrence, I've had a recurrence." I had an odd feeling of looking down on myself from above the city, driving along in my little red car. I had a sense that suddenly I was a different person. I was no longer a person who'd had cancer, emphasis on the past tense; I was a person who'd had a recurrence, and that put me in a totally different group, different peers, different statistics, a different future ahead of me, and of Ken. My life had twisted suddenly, unexpectedly. I've had a recurrence. I still have cancer. This is not over, not yet.

I park my car on a hill, carefully turning the wheels into the curb and setting the brake. This is a nice little neighborhood, tucked away between major streets. I like the trees, the odd twists in the streets, the pastel-colored houses with their small entrance gardens. My client, Jill, rents a small apartment in one of these houses. There's something especially nice about this house, about its entrance. It's painted a lovely salmon pink and the arched doorway with a wrought iron gate leads to a tiny courtyard with potted plants. It's hard to tell exactly what combination of features makes this house so nice; I am always struck by it.

Jill opens the door. I feel fine, glad I did not decide to cancel the session. It is surprisingly easy to push my personal concerns into the background for an hour. In fact, it feels good to do so. I feel it is a good session, that I am unimpaired by the recent news. I wonder if I will ever tell Jill someday that just before this particular session I discovered I still had cancer.

Recurrence, recurrence, I've had a recurrence. I drive toward home in my little red mountain car, turn right on 19th Street, through the tunnel, beside the army houses with their screened-in porches. It is early evening, the time of transition I love so much, my favorite time to go running, when the air is soft and the light changes from moment to moment, the sky is pink along the horizon, and above this band of soft light an aqua blue moves into the deeper cobalt blue of the approaching night. Lights begin to appear in houses, in the buildings that are the skyline of San Francisco, lights shining from the pastel buildings, lights bright against the deepening night.

Recurrence. I've had a recurrence. This refrain sounds in my head as I drive, savoring the approach of night, the changing light. Recurrence. Recurrence. It becomes almost a mantra as I drive, half-hypnotized by its repetition in my mind. Recurrence. Recurrence. I believe it; I don't believe it. Perhaps this repetition will convince me, will allow me to accept what I do not want to accept, what I do not want to believe. The repetition too is a defense; I do not want to think of what this means. Recurrence. Up until now something I've only read about in medical journals, heard from my doctors. Up until now something that had not touched me. Now, here it is. A part of my life. A shaper of my life to come. Something I must deal with.

Damn little bumps. I discovered them on a Tuesday. The day before Thanksgiving. Almost a year exactly since our wedding. We celebrated Thanksgiving with my sister Kati, who flew up from L.A. On Friday Ken took me to the emergency room at 8:00 A.M., Kati along for support. I lay there prepped and waiting, alone with my thoughts and fears. Dr. Richards arrived—how nice to have a doctor you like and trust—and the procedure was over in a few minutes. Soon I was walking down Union Street with Ken and Kati, doing our Christmas shopping together, a few new stitches in my side and instructions to call on Monday for the results. Christmas all around us, one of the busiest shopping days of the year, excitement, anticipation, and me thinking of the pain in my side.

A question now answered, I think, guiding my little red car around the curves of Star Route 1, a meditation itself, this sinuous glide down to the sea, to the Pacific. Night had almost settled. A faint glow along the horizon, the sweep of the Pacific Ocean spread before me, flanked by hills on either side, my home among the lights scattered to the left, my husband waiting for the news I bear, his arms ready to enfold me.

Thus began what I came to think of as "Round Two." The blade I had for so long imagined poised above me, that ominous threat of recurrence, had dropped. Ken and I comforted each other. I cried. We called my parents. We called Ken's parents. We called Dr. Richards. We called Dr. Cantril. We called M. D. Anderson. A strange kind of recurrence, everyone agreed. A recurrence, but within the radiated area. Dr. Cantril checked that, yes, definitely within the radiated area. I had ruined his record of no recurrences, it seemed. No one quite understood how this could have happened. We called experts in other parts of the country. A strange case, they all agreed. Probably only a 5% chance of something like this happening. I imagined the statistical expert on the other end of the phone line stretched across the country scratching his head, puzzled. Everyone seemed puzzled. A difficult situation to interpret. Was this a local recurrence, treatable by surgery? Or a sign of disseminated [metastatic] disease, which would require chemotherapy? A strange situation. No one had seen a case quite like this.

No one could say how it happened. "Could it be," I asked Dr. Richards, Ken looking on with a very intense expression, "that some cancer cells from the tumor got caught on the end of the drainage tube and, when it was pulled out, caught in the skin and got left behind?" "Yes," he said, "that must be what happened, one or two cells were left behind." "Not one or two," I reminded him. "It was at least five cells and probably more, because some were killed by the radiation." I could tell he felt bad about the situation.

Even as others commented on the oddity of the recurrence, they reassured me of their complete confidence in both Dr. Richards and Dr. Cantril. I believed them. I had complete confidence in them too. Whatever had happened was just the sort of thing that was bound to happen sometimes. I just happened to be the person lying on that particular table on that particular day when the odds caught up with the surgeons.

Ken and I meet with Dr. Richards. My options? (1) A mastectomy. (Should I have had that in the first place? If I had done that perhaps none of this would be happening now.) (2) Reexcision of the tumor site, the drainage area, and the area where the bumps appeared; if more cancer cells were found in this tissue, perhaps some more radiation to the area. That had its drawbacks, however, because of the radiation I had already received. There was no way of predicting how the tissue would react to more radiation. (3) Excision of the area around the drainage tube exit and, since we could not know for sure if there were more cells left behind in the breast, more radiation to the breast. Again, this had drawbacks because of the previous radiation dose. In addition, since these cells were not killed by radiation, there was a possibility that any other cells that might still be in the breast were also resistant to radiation.

It seemed pretty clear to me. There was no way to know if there were more cancer cells along the path of the drainage tube or within the breast; if there were they might also be resistant to radiation; my breast tissue might be damaged by more radiation anyway. A mastectomy seemed the only choice. I was too frightened to take the risk of leaving more of these grade four cancer cells inside my body.

Treya and I were still intensively investigating (and practicing) alternative and holistic treatments, as I will shortly explain. But the problem, again, was the viciousness of the grade four cells found in her body. There was still no credible evidence whatsoever that *any* alternative treatment had a significantly higher cure rate against grade four cells than random or spontaneous remissions—no higher, in other words, than chance. I think if Treya had even a grade three tumor—and certainly a grade one or two—she would have opted much more heavily for alternative treatments and bypassed some (but by no means all) of white man's medicine. But the sheer viciousness of the tumor brought her back again, and yet again, to the one medicine capable of being just as vicious. "Iron Maiden doesn't fit? Not to worry, pretty little lady. We can always find something special just for you. Now you just wait right here."

Ken and I check into Children's Hospital. It is December 6, 1984. My surgery will take place on December 7—"Pearl Harbor Day," Ken mutters to no one in particular—a year and a day after my first surgery. Children's is all too familiar. I remember too well coming here every day for five and a half weeks for radiation treatments. Coming every month after that for follow-up. Coming only days ago to have the bumps removed.

I remember how my clothes were lost last year, how they were found and returned to me two months later. I take that as an omen. This time I have brought clothes I intend to leave behind, just as I intend to leave the cancer behind. Everything I wear into this hospital I will leave behind, even my shoes, underwear, and earrings. In a few days most of my underwear won't fit me anyway, not the bras. At the same time that Dr. Richards is removing my right breast, Dr. Harvey will be reducing my left breast in size. It seems time for that, finally. I could not imagine going through life with one breast a size 34DD; imagine the size of the prosthesis I would need. Imagine how lopsided I would feel. Two size 34DD breasts were problem enough; one would be an even greater problem.

When I finally ask Ken what he thinks about my losing a breast, he is great about it, though it can't be easy for him either. "Sweetheart, of course I'm going to miss your breast. But that doesn't matter. It's you I'm in love with, not some body part. This doesn't change a damn thing." He is so obviously sincere about it, it makes me feel wonderful.

Mom and Dad have flown in from Texas for the operation, as they did last time. I tried to tell them it was unnecessary, but in truth I am glad to have them here. I always feel more hopeful with my parents around, more optimistic that things will turn out well. I am glad I have a big family. I always delight in my family, in spending time with them, with any one of them. I am glad I have been able to enlarge Ken's family with people he, too, truly enjoys.

Ken and I move into our room. One like all the others, white walls, the adjustable bed, the television hanging from the wall above, the blood pressure equipment hanging from the wall behind, the closet to one side (the closet where I intend to leave my clothes), the white bathroom, the window looking out across the courtyard to rooms on the other side. Once again, Ken gets a cot; he will stay with me.

Ken and I sit down, and hold hands lightly. He can tell what I'm still thinking, what I'm still worried about. Will I be attractive to him? When I'm deformed, scarred? Lopsided? He has to walk such a fine line between trying to sympathize with me and trying to cheer me up. The same old double bind—I want him to sympathize with the loss of my breast but if he does so it will seem he really regrets it and doesn't want me without it! He's already reassured me so much, this time he sidesteps it with humor. "I really don't mind, honey. The way I look at it is, every man is given so many breast-inches per lifetime that he's allowed to grope his way through. In just one year with your double-

D's, I've already used up my quota." In the tension of the situation, we both start laughing hysterically. Ken goes on like this for fifteen minutes, everything from the sublime to the crude. "Wouldn't you know it, I'm an ass man, myself. As long as they don't figure out how to give rumpectomies in this place, we've got it made." Tears are running down our faces. But that's sort of the way it is with cancer: laugh so hard you cry, cry so hard you laugh.

I unpack, arranging all the belongings I will leave behind, stepping from them into a white gown, hopeful that I am thereby moving toward health and away from this cancer. I could almost perform a ritual of some sort, say some incantation, wave a cross around the room, whatever, anything that will help. Instead I keep the ritual inside, say my prayers internally.

My blood pressure is taken, questions asked and answered. The anesthesiologist checks in to say hello and explain the procedure. I assume it will be the same as last time and, since I had no trouble then, do not worry. Dr. Richards checks in. The procedure is simple, a simple mastectomy [as opposed to a radical or modified radical mastectomy, where much underlying muscle tissue is also removed]. Surgically, the operation I had last year was more difficult and required a longer recovery time because of the removal of the lymph nodes. I tell Dr. Richards, "I talked to M. D. Anderson about the recurrence, and they all seemed to feel it was an unusual kind of recurrence, but that this kind of thing does happen on occasion." "Yes," Dr. Richards says. "But I'm certain they're each glad it didn't happen to them." I appreciate his being honest enough to show me even this much of how bad he feels. I remember to weigh myself. All my life I've wondered how much my breasts weigh—an odd way to find out!

Dr. Harvey arrives. We have not had a chance to discuss this sculpting of my remaining breast yet. He brings pictures of breast reductions he has done. I look through them, trying to find a shape I think appropriate for me. I wish he did not have to move the nipple up, since I know that will reduce sensation. Apparently it has to be done, but it can be done in my case, since my breasts do not sag much, without severing the connection to the milk ducts. The breast will still be functional, if I should ever have a child. I already understand the procedure, where the incisions are made, what is removed, how the skin is sewn back together to make a smaller breast. Dr. Harvey measures and marks my breast. He measures and marks the circumference of the nipple, he measures and marks the inch that the nipple will be moved up, he measures and marks where the incisions will be made and what skin will be removed.

Soon after Dr. Harvey leaves, my parents come in. I show them the marks and explain the procedure. I am very matter-of-fact about it, but also aware that this is probably the first time my father has ever seen my breasts. And, of course, the last time he or anyone else will see them as they are tonight!

Ken crawls in my bed and we snuggle. He stays there as various personnel crawl over us. Neither the nurses nor the doctors complain. "You get away with murder in these hospitals, you know that?" I say. Ken makes a fierce face—"It's because I'm one tough macho animal," he says. "It's because you smile beamingly at everyone who comes in and you get flowers for all the nurses," I point out. We laugh, but mostly I feel a kind of sadness, sadness I think for a breast I am about to lose.

It is morning, early. I suppose I slept. I am much less afraid this time. I have much more equanimity, no doubt due to meditation. And cancer has become a fact of life during this past year, a constant companion. I am aware, too, of the effort I put into getting through this, into suspending my doubts, my questions, my fears, my thoughts of the future. I intentionally put blinders on, I look only straight ahead, I ignore the paths to my right and my left, the roads not taken. The research is done, the decisions made. Now is not the time for questions. Now is the time to get through what lies ahead. I am aware that I have turned off parts of myself to do this. I have turned off my worrier, my questioner. I feel relaxed and confident. Ken holds my hand, Mom and Dad wait with us. Once again, like last year, the surgery is delayed. I think of all the surgeons busily at work, both here in Children's and elsewhere around the country, around the world. Of the residents, the nurses, the hospital support personnel, the tools and equipment and complicated machines, all aligned to combat disease. The Valium and Demerol are starting to take hold. They wheel me into the surgery.

I don't know why, but I didn't want Treya to see me cry. I'm not ashamed of crying, it's just that, for some reason, at that particular point I didn't want *anybody* to see me cry. Perhaps I was afraid that if I started crying I would break down completely. Perhaps I was afraid to be weak at this point where my strength was needed. I found an empty room, closed the door, sat down, and started crying. It finally dawned on me: I am not crying because I pity Treya or feel sorry for her; I am crying because I admire her bravery so much. She simply marches through this, refusing to let it get her down, and her courage in the face of this demeaning, senseless, fucking cruelty makes me cry.

When I wake up I am back in my room. Ken smiles at me. Sunlight comes through the window and I can see pastel houses on the San Francisco hills beyond. Ken holds my hand. I raise my other hand to my right chest. Bandages. Nothing under the bandages. I am again flat-chested as I was as a child. I breathe in deeply. It is done. No turning back. A pang of fear, of doubt shoots through me. Should I have tried to keep my breast, risked just having the area resected? Has my fear pushed me into something unnecessary? The questions I would not allow last night or this morning rush in. Was this necessary? Did I do the right thing? No matter. It is done.

I look up at Ken. I can feel my lip quivering, my eyes begin to water. He reaches down to hold me, a careful embrace since bandages cover stitches only hours old all over my chest. "Sweetheart, I'm so sorry, I'm so sorry," we say to each other.

Later that afternoon my sister Kati arrives from L. A. It feels good to have the room filled with family, with support. It must be difficult for them, it is so hard to know what you can do to help at times like this. There's not much to do, really, I just like having them all around me, I like having them here. Then Daddy asks everyone to leave; he wants to talk to Ken and me. Dear Daddy, he is very serious, he takes these things hard, he worries so much about the people close to him. I remember him pacing the hospital corridor when Mother had her operation fifteen years ago, lines of worry creasing his face, his hair turning grayer almost before our eyes. This time, he turns to Ken and me and says, with great emotion, "These times I know are very difficult for you. But you can give thanks for one blessing, that you have each other and that, now especially, you know how very much you mean to each other." I could see the tears forming in his eyes as he turned to walk out; I'm sure he didn't want us to see him cry. Ken, very moved, went to the door and watched my father walk down the hospital corridor, head bowed, hands clasped behind him, not looking back. I love how much he loves my father.

"My Life Had Twisted Suddenly"

I fling open the door. I am very angry. There is nobody there. "I suppose if I say Who's there? it's not going to matter, right? Christ."

I leave the door open and, with my left hand, begin to follow the wall back toward the hallways leading off the main room. There are five rooms back there; Treya must be in one of them. As I trace my way back, I notice the wall has a strange, almost moist, feel to it. I keep thinking, is this trip really necessary?

Ken and I walk up and down the long hallways, once in the morning and once in the afternoon. I like this walk. I especially like walking by the room where the tiny babies are. I like looking at the little ones, wrapped in their blankets, at their tiny faces and clenched fists and closed eyes. I worry about them, too. These are the premature babies, and some of them are in incubators. Still, it makes me happy to see them, to stop and watch them, to imagine their parents and their futures.

Later we discover that a friend is in the hospital. Dulce Murphy is seven months pregnant and was moved into the hospital when she began bleeding. Ken and I go to visit her. She is happy, confident, but hooked up to a machine that monitors her heartbeat and that of the baby and told to lie flat on her back. She is given medications to stop a miscarriage; this medicine usually raises the mother's heartbeat but since she is a marathon runner it only raises her heartbeat into the normal range. Her husband, Michael Murphy, is there. Michael, the cofounder of Esalen Institute, is an old friend of Ken's, and mine, and we all drink champagne together and talk excitedly about the baby.

That night Ken has a dream about this baby, who, throughout the pregnancy, had seemed ambivalent about being born. He dreams he sees him in the bardo realm, the realm that souls inhabit before they are born. He asks him, "Mac, why don't you want to be born? Why are you reluctant?" Mac replies that he likes it here in the bardo, he may want to stay here. Ken tells him that's not possible, the bardo realm is nice but you're not meant to stay there. If you try to, it won't be so nice anymore. It's probably best that you choose to come to earth, to be born. Besides, Ken says, there are a lot of people down here who love you and want you to be born. Mac answers, "If so many people love me, then where is my teddy bear?"

The next day we go to visit them again. Ken brings a teddy bear. It has a tartan plaid necktie, for "Mac Murphy." Ken leans over and says in a loud voice to Dulce's stomach, "Yo, Mac . . . teddy bear." This turns out to be the first of many, many tartan teddy bears to be given to Mac, who arrives three weeks later, perfectly healthy and with no need for an incubator.

After three days in the hospital, Treya and I returned to Muir Beach. The doctors seemed fairly unanimous: the recurrence was almost certainly in the breast tissue only, and not in the chest wall. The distinction was crucial: if it were a local recurrence, then the cancer would be confined to the same type of tissue (breast). If, however, it had jumped to the chest wall, that meant the cancer had "learned" how to invade a different type of tissue—it would now be metastatic cancer. And once breast cancer learns how to jump to a different tissue, it may very quickly invade lung, bone, and brain.

If Treya's recurrence was local, then she had already taken the necessary course of action: remove the rest of the local tissue. No other follow-up— no radiation, no chemotherapy—would be needed or recommended. If, however, the recurrence was in the chest wall, that meant Treya would have a stage four, grade four cancer, absolutely the worst diagnosis one can receive. (The "stage" of a cancer is determined by the size and spread of the tumor—from stage one, which is less than a centimeter, to stage four, which is spread throughout the body. The "grade" of a cancer represents how mean it is, from grade one to grade four. Treya's original tumor was stage two, grade four. A chest wall recurrence would be stage four, grade four.) Were this the case, extremely aggressive chemotherapy would be the only course recommended to us.

Dr. Richards and Dr. Cantril think that the cancer is now gone, that surgery removed it. Neither recommends chemotherapy. Dr. Richards says even if there are any remaining cells he's not sure the chemotherapy would get them; it could miss them while hitting my stomach lining, my hair, my blood cells. I tell him that Ken and I are planning to go to San Diego to the Livingston-Wheeler Clinic, where they specialize in boosting the immune system. He feels that the immunotherapy program is fine if that's what I choose, but he doesn't put much faith in it. He says it doesn't help to gun a car that's only running on seven cylinders; that won't make the eighth cylinder start working. My immune system is missing the eighth cylinder, because it has already failed twice to recognize this particular cancer, so revving up the other seven cylinders may help a lot of other things, but probably not the cancer. But it certainly won't hurt, he says. I plan to do it; I know I need to do something, to feel I can help my recovery in some way. I can't just sit back now. I know myself too well, I would only worry. I must do something. At this point Western medicine leaves me on my own.

A few days later we returned to Children's to have the bandages removed. Treya's equanimity remained firmly in place. Her almost total lack of vanity or self-consciousness or self-pity was simply astonishing. I remember thinking, "You're a better man than I, Gunga Din."

Dr. R took off the bandages and took out the staples [used as stitches] and I got to see it—healing well but still very upsetting, to look down and see my stomach and this ugly line swelling at both ends—cried in Ken's arms. But what's done is done; what is, is. Janice called, said, "I think I was more upset over your losing your breast than you were, you were so calm." The day before, I said to Ken either losing a breast is no huge deal or it hasn't hit me yet. Probably both are true. I finally told Ken, as long as I don't have to look at it too much, I think I'll be OK.

Treya and I began to expand and intensify the alternative and holistic treatments that she had been pursuing for the past year. The basic "core curriculum" was fairly straightforward:

1. Careful diet—mostly lactovegetarian, low fat, high carbohydrate, as much raw as possible; no social drugs of any sort
2. Daily megavitamin therapy—with emphasis on the antioxidants A, E, C, B_1, B_5, B_6, the minerals zinc and selenium, the amino acids cysteine and methionine
3. Meditation—daily in the morning, often in the afternoon as well
4. Visualization and affirmations—varied daily
5. Journal keeping—including a dream journal and a daily log
6. Exercise—jogging or walking

To that core curriculum we would add, on different occasions, various electives or adjuvant treatments. At this point we were looking carefully at the Hippocrates Institute in Boston, at macrobiotics, and at Livingston-

Wheeler in San Diego. The Virginia Livingston-Wheeler Institute offered a comprehensive course of treatment based on Dr. Livingston-Wheeler's belief that a particular virus was behind all forms of cancer, since this virus can in fact be found in most tumors. They prepared a vaccine against this virus and then administered it to you, along with a rigorous dietary program. From the available evidence it was pretty clear to me that this virus was not the cause of cancer, and that it appeared in tumors as a scavenger or parasite, not a cause. But clearing out the scavengers couldn't hurt, so I was more than willing to support Treya in her decision to go to this clinic.

And so once again things began to look very bright for Treya and me. We, along with our doctors, had every reason to believe that the cancer was behind us. Our Tahoe house was almost ready. We were madly in love.

Christmas in Texas. Once again, I am recovering from surgery for cancer. It feels a bit eerie to go through this twice at exactly the same time of the year. This Christmas is easier, though. Ken and I have been married a year, an old married couple by now. And cancer has been with us for a year; by now we know a great deal about it. No more surprises, I hope. We have sailed through the surgery and are feeling good about life. Just before Christmas we went down to San Diego to the Livingston-Wheeler Clinic. We plan to return in January to do the immunotherapy program and follow the diet they advocate. We liked the feeling there, folksy, comfortable. This is our plan, to follow up the surgery with immunotherapy, diet, visualization, and meditation. I am excited about this. Ken jokingly calls it Fun with Cancer. But it definitely feels like a positive step into the future. We carefully explain this plan to each member of the family, and they all feel good about my choices.

Yes, this does feel like an exciting time ahead. Feeling like last year was my existential year, this year to come more transcendental. Is it too bold to foretell a year of transformation? Last year I confronted death, last year I was afraid, last year I worried greatly, last year I was on the defensive. All of this, even though my main memory is of being happy in my marriage. But now, as this next year prepares to begin, with my second operation but two weeks behind me, I feel different. It began with the feeling that my way of going about making decisions was too hard on me, the insight that my ego's need for control was a major factor in the wear and tear I'd experienced. Thus leading to the decision that I wanted to let go and let God more. The ego's year was one of fear and indecision and facing the abyss of death. The year I believe is ahead of me, the year of learning about surrender and true acceptance, brings a sense of peace and curiosity and discoveries-to-come.

A time of discovery and openness, dedicated to healing. No getting on my own back for not "doing-in-the-world." An adjuvant program that does not come from fear or create fear, but comes from trust and brings with it a sense of discovery and excitement and growth. Possible because of a deeper and deeper sense that somehow life and death are not all the huge issue they're cracked up to be. Somehow the line between the two has blurred for me. I don't care so much about hanging on to life, and when I have that thought I'm no longer afraid it means I've lost my will to live. The old thing about quality of life rather than quantity of life means more to me. I know I want to make choices that come from excitement and adventure rather than fear.

And I delight in having Ken to travel that path with me. At the end of January we will be starting a new life, moving to our new house in Tahoe. A new beginning in a house we have bought for our future together.

When we returned to Muir Beach from Laredo, Treya again began to confer with several doctors and specialists, just to make sure she had covered all the bases. As the number of follow-up consultations grew, a disturbing and then alarming trend emerged: the weight of opinion was that Treya had in fact had a chest wall recurrence, that Treya had metastatic cancer. The worst symbols you could ever put together on one page: grade four, stage four.

My first reaction was anger, rage! How could they say that? What if they're right? How could this be happening to me? Goddammit! Ken trying to reassure me but I don't want to be reassured, I want to be angry. The whole goddamn thing makes me angry, the possibility of it, the fact that I was mobilized for it earlier and have now let down my defenses, the fact that we're surrounded with different opinions, from the doctors advising chemotherapy to my friends suggesting all these alternative treatments that I wonder if they'd try with such glib faith if they had this wicked kind of cancer inside them. I hate the whole situation, most of all the not knowing!!! Chemotherapy's hard enough to go through when you *know* you need it—how about when you really don't know for sure, when you suspect there's nothing more going on than a few stray cells left behind during an operation. That somehow escaped radiation. How did that happen? What does that mean?

Once Treya began to consider the new evidence offered by various oncologists, it was a slow and seemingly inexorable slide to a grim conclusion. If this were in fact a chest wall recurrence, and if it weren't treated with the most aggressive chemotherapy available, the chances of Treya's having another (and probably fatal) recurrence were 50% within a mere nine months. Not years, months! From not doing chemotherapy at all, to doing a moderate course of chemo, to the most aggressive and toxic chemotherapy in existence: thus the dismal slide into yet more medieval torture. "Well what, little lady? You back again? Now you're starting to get on my nerves, little lady, you're starting to tick me off, know what I mean? Igor, would you be good enough to prepare the vat, please. . . ."

The slow movement toward chemotherapy. Thinking over Christmas we had it all handled—surgeon and radiologists didn't recommend it, the oncologist's recommendation could be written off as equivalent to asking an insurance man if you needed insurance, and we had the Livingston Clinic's approach to rely on.

Then the return to S.F. and appointments with two oncologists. They both recommended chemotherapy, one CMF and the other CMF-P [two common and fairly moderate chemotherapy regimens, both relatively easy to tolerate]. The risk factors began to weigh more heavily in my mind. Last year I had only one bad prognostic indicator, the fact that the tumor was poorly differentiated [that is, it was grade four]. The size was intermediate, just barely stage two. The other aspects—estrogen positive and twenty clean lymph nodes—were good. Very good.

But now the balance has tipped radically. Suddenly to the bad indicators are added recurrence within a year, recurrence in a radiated area, recurrence that is estrogen negative. And still the same poorly differentiated histology. Poorly differentiated, grade four histology. Slowly, ever so slowly, I am becoming convinced it would be foolish not to do chemotherapy. Especially since the CMF regimen isn't all that difficult to handle. Little or no hair loss, injections twice a month, a pill three times a day. I could carry on a fairly normal life while staying away from sources of infection and generally watching out for myself.

The wear and tear on both Ken and me is starting to show. Today I went out for a walk and while I was gone he talked to my sister and my mother and brought them up to date on what was happening. But when I got home I blew up at him; I felt he had told my story, I felt crowded out by him. Usually he doesn't get angry at my outbursts, but this time he blew up too. He said I was crazy if I thought this cancer ordeal was just my story. He was going through it too and being deeply affected by it. I felt guilty, I was being petty, but it was almost like I couldn't help it.

I want to be more sensitive to how hard this period is on Ken as well as me. To not take his support and his strength for granted. I've been doing that and it's wearing him down, I can tell. To know that he needs support from me as much as I do from him.

The wear and tear on both of us continued. Treya and I went into a frenzy of phone consultations with the finest specialists from all over the country and the world, from Bloomenschein in Texas to Bonnadonna in Italy.

Jesus, when will this all stop? Ken and I talked to five doctors on the phone today, including Dr. Bloomenschein at M. D. Anderson, who is generally regarded as the finest breast oncologist in the country. As our oncologist here in S.F. put it, "Nobody in the world can beat his numbers," which means Bloomenschein has higher success rates with chemotherapy than anybody else, anywhere.

I had decided to start with a course of CMF-P, probably getting my first injection tomorrow morning. Until Dr. Bloomenschein returned our call and my world turned upside down. Again. He strongly recommended an adriamycin regimen [generally thought to be the strongest chemotherapeutic agent around, with horrible side effects], saying it was clearly more effective than CMF. He said there was no doubt whatsoever that my recurrence was chest wall, stage four. He said recent studies showed that women who had a resection after a chest wall recurrence, which is basically what I had done, and did not have chemotherapy relapsed at the rate of 50% at nine months, 70% at three years, and 95% at five years. He said there was a 95% chance I had microscopic cancer right now, but that now was my "window of opportunity" if I acted quickly.

Fine, but adriamycin? I could see undergoing all this if I was certain that I needed it, but to lose my hair and carry a portable pump around four days and nights out of every three weeks for a year while it dripped poison into my system and my white blood cells died and my mouth developed sores and there was a danger of damage to my heart? Was that really worth it? And what about the treatment being worse than the disease?

And on the other hand, what about a 50% chance of lethal recurrence *within nine months*?

We hung up the phone, and I immediately called Peter Richards, who still maintained it was a local recurrence and chemotherapy wasn't necessary. "Just do us a favor, would you, Peter? Please call Bloomenschein and just talk to him. He scared us, I want to see if he scares you."

Peter called him, but it was a stalemate. "His figures are right if it's a chest wall recurrence, but I still think it's local."

Treya and I stared at each other blankly. "What the hell are we going to do?" she finally said.

"I have no idea."

"You tell me what to do."

"What?!" We actually both started laughing, because nobody *ever* told Treya what to do.

"I'm not even sure if I can offer you an opinion. The only way we're going to get a decision from the medical establishment is if we talk to an odd number of physicians. Otherwise these guys are splitting right down the middle. It all hinges on just what the goddamn diagnosis is. Is this chest wall or local? Nobody seems to know, or at least to agree." We sat exhausted, burned out.

"I have one last idea," I said. "Want to try it?"

"Of course. What is it?"

"What does this decision hinge on? The histology of the tumor cells, right? The pathology report, the report that decides just how poorly differentiated the cells are. And who's the one person we haven't talked to?"

"Of course! The pathologist, Dr. Lagios."

"Want me to call or you?"

Treya thought for a moment. "Doctors listen to men. You call."

I picked up the phone and rang Children's pathology department. Mike Lagios is, by all accounts, a brilliant pathologist with an international reputation as an innovative leader in the field of cancer histology. He has been the one peering down the microscope at the tissue from Treya's body, and it has been his reports that the various doctors have been reading before giving us their opinions. It was time to go to the source.

"Dr. Lagios, my name is Ken Wilber. I'm Terry Killam Wilber's husband. I realize this is very unusual, but Terry and I have to make some extremely difficult decisions, and I wondered if you could talk to me for a few minutes?"

"This is unusual, as you say. We usually don't talk to patients, I'm sure you understand."

"Dr. Lagios, our doctors—and we have now consulted ten of them—are divided precisely down the middle as to whether Terry's recurrence was local or metastatic. All I wanted to know is, just how aggressive did the cells look to you? Please."

There was silence. "All right, Mr. Wilber. I don't wish to alarm you, but since you ask, I'll tell you honestly. In my career as a pathologist, I have never seen a meaner cancer cell. I'm not exaggerating or saying that for emphasis. I'm trying to be precise. I personally have not seen a more aggressive cell."

I am looking directly at Treya as Lagios says this. I do not blink. My expression is completely blank. I feel no emotion, I feel nothing. I am frozen.

"Mr. Wilber?"

"Tell me, Dr. Lagios, if this were your wife, would you recommend to her that she do chemotherapy?"

"I'm afraid I'd have to recommend the most aggressive course of chemotherapy that could be tolerated."

"And the odds?"

There was a long pause. Although he could have rattled off statistics for an hour, he said simply, "If it were, as you say, my wife, I would want somebody to tell me that, although miracles abound, the odds are not very good."

"Thank you, Dr. Lagios."

I hung up the phone.

8

WHO AM I?

❧☙

O N the plane to Houston, Tuesday morning. There is a 50% chance that the adriamycin will permanently damage my ovaries, putting me into menopause. I am so upset at maybe not being able to have a child—not so much why me but why now, why couldn't this have happened ten years later at forty-six? Ken and I'd have been married ten years and have a child and it'd be so much easier to handle. Why now, why so young? Seems so unfair, makes me so damned angry—even a touch like committing suicide to spite life, to show it that it can't push me around like that. Fuck it all, just check out.

Of course later I think of the really young who have leukemia or Hodgkin's, who haven't even had a chance to live as much life as I have, to travel, to learn, to explore, to give, to find their partner, and I calm down. It all seems normal then—this is somehow, for some reason, life in these times. You can always think of others worse off than you, and that makes me more aware of the positive sides of my life and it makes me especially eager to help others less fortunate.

Saturday was difficult. Once I decided to go with Bloomenschein's recommendation, we decided that the best way to deliver the chemo-therapy was by implanting a Port-a-Cath catheter in my chest, and attaching to it a Travenol portable pump, which I will carry around with me for four days each month for up to a year.

For the operation [which took place at Children's before we left for

Houston]—I felt a little shaky—I asked Ken to go up with me to the prep room. He waited till I was prepped, kissed me, and left. When I met the doctor, lying there on my back draped in sheets, staring at the ceiling, in a cold hallway, he seemed so kind, a bear of a man, and his kindness and compassion made me cry. Does so even now remembering that moment. He explained the procedure to me as I lay there, tears leaking out of my eyes. The tears were because somehow this step made the decision more concrete, more irrevocable, the decision to subject myself to chemotherapy, and all that meant, especially the possibility of not having a child. Of course I couldn't tell him that at the time or I'd *really* start crying. The nurse who assisted was the same one who'd assisted when Dr. R. took out my lump over a year ago, and also assisted when Dr. R. removed my right breast while Dr. H. worked on my left. I liked her. Could talk about whatever and feel my sadness subside in the normalness of our conversation, bizarrely normal in this setting of OR #3, bright lights above, some strange x-ray machine to my right that would later check the placement of the Port-a-Cath, an IV in my left arm, a grounding pad on my left thigh, electrodes on my chest and back translating my heart beat into beeps audible to all (an odd lack of privacy, since feelings turn into public beeps). This was scary not because of the operation but because it seemed like an irreversible step. The doctor reassured me that this catheter could easily be taken out anytime, but I think he knew what I meant.

As the Demerol took welcome effect, I thought of the time last year that I got pregnant. I was sure I couldn't get pregnant, which had always worried me so much. A dreamy Demerol thought came to me: It somehow feels like a soul up there took it upon itself to have a very brief reincarnation, just to reassure me that I could get pregnant. "I love you, whoever you are." Then I began worrying about a thought I used to have when younger, more a feeling really, that I would never have a child and wouldn't live past fifty. In this context, it scared me, especially since the other premonition I had, that I wouldn't marry till I was past thirty, had come true. But now, some days later, I feel a growing resolve to turn that inside out and make it my goal—to have Ken's baby and live past fifty.

M. D. Anderson is an extraordinary and quite impressive hospital, particularly if you like white man's medicine. Walking down its enormously long and confusing corridors, I kept thinking, I better hurry or I'm going to miss my flight. When Treya and I finally found the chemotherapy unit, I discovered a strange phenomena that would follow me for the next sixth months of Treya's treatment: Because of my shaved head, everyone assumed I was the patient, assumed I was bald because of chemo. And this had the most curious, and I suppose helpful, effect on the actual chemotherapy patients: They would see me coming down the hall, looking fit and healthy, energetic, sometimes smiling, and I could almost see each of the dozens of patients thinking, "Gosh, maybe it's not so bad after all."

Sitting in the waiting room. There are dozens of women here, from all over the world, to see the famous Bloomenschein. A woman from Saudi Arabia with pure white hair, a little girl with one leg, a woman with green glasses nervously waiting for test results and trying to figure what catheter to use, a young woman with both breasts gone.

Ken and I wait three hours before we are finally admitted to a room with ten other people, sitting in chairs, all of whom have IVs in them. I am the only one with a partner, and I think how horrible it must be to do this alone. The nurse will drip three solutions into me, one at a time. First the FAC [adriamycin plus two other chemotherapeutic agents], then Reglan, a strong antinausea agent, then a large amount of Benadryl to counteract the bad effects of Reglan. The nurse calmly explains that Reglan sometimes causes violent anxiety attacks, and the Benadryl will block this. I have never had a really bad anxiety attack, so I assume everything will be OK.

The FAC goes fine, then the Reglan. Perhaps two minutes after the Reglan drip starts, I find that for no reason, I start thinking how nice suicide would be. Ken has been watching me very closely for the last few minutes, and he grabs my hand. I tell him how nice suicide would be. He whispers in my ear, "Terry, honey, the Reglan is really hitting you hard. From the way your face looks, I think you're having a bad histamine reaction. Just hold on till the Benadryl. If it gets real bad tell me and I'll have them start it now." A few minutes later I am hit by a full-blown panic attack, the first time ever. It is by far the worst feeling I can ever remember having. I want out of this body! Ken gets the Benadryl started, and a few minutes later I start to calm down, but only a little.

Treya and I had taken a room in a hotel across the street from Anderson, all graciously arranged by Rad and Sue. Her extremely strong histamine reaction to Reglan could only partially be mitigated by large doses of the antihistamine Benadryl, and so her panic and suicidal thoughts continued into the long night. And the adriamycin had not even begun to have *its* effects.

"Read me the Witness exercise from *No Boundary*, would you?" she said around 6:00 P.M.. This was a book I had written several years earlier; the Witness exercise was a summary of some of the ways that the world's greatest mystics have used in order to move beyond the body and mind and find instead the Witness. This particular version I had adapted from Roberto Assagioli, founder of Psychosynthesis, but it's a standard technique of self-inquiry—the primordial inquiry "Who am I?"—perhaps made most famous by Sri Ramana Maharshi.

"Sweetheart, as I read this, try to realize the meaning of each sentence as clearly as you can."

I *have* a body, but I am *not* my body. I can see and feel my body, and what can be seen and felt is not the true Seer. My body may be tired or excited, sick or healthy, heavy or light, anxious or calm, but that has nothing to do with my inward I, the Witness. I *have* a body, but I am *not* my body.

I *have* desires, but I am *not* my desires. I can know my desires, and what can be known is not the true Knower. Desires come and go, floating through my awareness, but they do not affect my inward I, the Witness. I *have* desires but I am *not* desires.

I *have* emotions, but I am *not* my emotions. I can feel and sense my emotions, and what can be felt and sensed is not the true Feeler. Emotions pass through me, but they do not affect my inward I, the Witness. I *have* emotions, but I am *not* emotions.

I *have* thoughts, but I am *not* my thoughts. I can see and know my thoughts, and what can be known is not the true Knower. Thoughts come to me and thoughts leave me, but they do not affect my inward I, the Witness. I *have* thoughts but I am *not* my thoughts.

Then affirm as concretely as you can: I am what remains, a pure center of awareness, an unmoved Witness of all these thoughts, emotions, feelings, and sensations.

"That really helps, but it doesn't last. This is awful. I feel like I'm jumping out of my skin. I'm not comfortable if I sit down, I'm not comfortable if I stand up. I keep thinking how sensible suicide sounds."

"Nietzsche used to say that the only way he got to sleep at night was by promising to kill himself in the morning." We both laughed at the painful, silly truthfulness of it.

"Read me more. I don't know what else to do."

"Sure." And so sitting on a tacky sofa in a large hotel room across from the Biggest White Man's Cancer Center in the Entire Fucking World, I read to dearest Treya late into the night. The poisons in her body began the medical equivalent of saturation bombing. I had never felt so helpless in my life. All I wanted to do was make her pain go away; all I had were anemic little words. And all I kept thinking was, the adriamycin hasn't even hit yet.

"OK, here's more from *No Boundary*—

"Thus, as we begin to touch the transpersonal Witness, we begin to let go of our purely personal problems, worries, and concerns. In fact, we don't even try to solve our problems or distresses. Our only concern here is to *watch* our particular distresses, to simply and innocently be aware of them, without judging them, avoiding them, dramatizing them, working on them, or resisting them. As a feeling or sensation arises, we witness it. If hatred of that feeling arises, we witness that. If hatred of the hatred arises, then we witness *that*. Nothing is to be done, but if a doing arises, we witness that. Abide as 'choiceless awareness' in the midst of all distresses. This is possible only when we understand that none of them constitute our real self, the Witness. As long as we are attached to them, there will be an effort, however subtle, to manipulate them. Every move we make to solve a distress simply reinforces the illusion that we *are* that particular distress. Thus, ultimately, to try to escape a distress merely perpetuates that distress.

"Instead of fighting a distress, then, we simply assume the innocence of a detached impartiality toward it. The mystics and sages are fond of likening this state of witnessing to a mirror. We simply reflect any sensations or thoughts that arise without clinging to them or pushing them away, just as a mirror perfectly and impartially reflects whatever passes in front of it. Says Chuang Tzu, 'The perfect man employs his mind as a mirror. It grasps nothing; it refuses nothing; it receives, but does not keep.'

"Is this helping at all?"

"Yes, a little. I know that material, I've practiced meditation for years, but it's so hard to apply it in these circumstances!"

"Oh, sweetie. You're having a really severe reaction—it's like somebody dumped four hundred pounds of adrenalin in your system; you're wired out of your skull. I'm amazed you're doing this well. Really."

"Read me some more." I couldn't put my arms around Treya because she couldn't sit still for more than a few minutes.

"To the extent that you actually realize that you are not, for example, your anxieties, then your anxieties no longer threaten you. Even if anxiety is present, it no longer overwhelms you because you are no longer exclusively tied to it. You are no longer fighting it, resisting it, or running from it. In the most radical fashion, anxiety is thoroughly accepted as it is and allowed to move as it will. You have nothing to lose, nothing to gain, by its presence or absence, for you are simply watching it pass by, as you might watch clouds pass by in the sky.

"Thus, any emotion, sensation, thought, memory, or experience that disturbs you is simply one with which you have exclusively identified yourself, identified your Witness, and the ultimate resolution of the disturbance is simply to *disidentify* with it. You cleanly let all of them drop away by realizing that they are not you—since you can see them, they cannot be the true Seer. Since they are not your real self, there is no reason whatsoever for you to identify with them, hold on to them, or allow your self to be bound by them. To witness these states is to transcend them. They no longer seize you from behind because you look at them up front.

"If you persist at such an exercise, the understanding contained in it will quicken and you might begin to notice fundamental changes in your sense of 'self.' For example, you might begin intuiting a deep inward sense of freedom, lightness, release. This source, this 'center of the cyclone,' will retain its lucid stillness even amid the raging winds of anxiety and suffering that might swirl around its center. The discovery of this witnessing center is very much like diving from the calamitous waves on the surface of a stormy ocean to the quiet and secure depths of the bottom. At first you might not get more than a few feet beneath the agitated waves of emotion, but with persistence you may gain the ability to dive fathoms into the quiet depths of your soul, and lying outstretched at the bottom, gaze up in alert but detached fashion at the turmoil on the surface.

"Treya?"

"I'm fine, I'm doing much better. Really, this helps. It reminds me of my training, reminds me of Goenka and my ten-day retreats with him. I wish I were doing that now! There's a section in *No Boundary* about how the Witness is immortal."

"Sure, sweetie." It suddenly dawned on me how utterly exhausted I was, followed by the disturbing realization that the ordeal was really just beginning. I kept reading, trying to hear my own words, the words of the wisdom seekers throughout the ages, words I had simply written down and tried to explain in a modern voice, words I needed to hear now as badly as Treya.

"Perhaps we can approach this fundamental insight of the mystics—that there is but *one* immortal Self or Witness common in and to us all—in this way. Perhaps you, like most people, feel that you are basically the same person you were yesterday. You probably also feel that you are *fundamentally* the same person you were a year ago. Indeed, you still seem to be the *same* you as far back as you can remember. Put it another way: you never remember a time when you weren't you. In other words, *something* in you seems to remain untouched by the passage of time. But surely your body is not the same as it was even a year ago. Surely also your sensations are different today than in the past. Surely, too, your memories are on the whole different today than a decade ago. Your mind, your body, your feelings—*all* have changed with time. But something has not changed, and you know that something has not changed. Something feels the same. What is that?

"This time a year ago you had different concerns and basically different problems. Your immediate experiences were different, and so were your thoughts. All of these have vanished, but something in you remains. Go one step further. What if you moved to a completely different country, with new friends, new surroundings, new experiences, new thoughts. You would still have that basic inner feeling of I-ness. Further yet, what if you right now forgot the first ten years, or fifteen years, or twenty years of your life? You would still feel that same inner I-ness, would you not? If right now you just temporarily forget *everything* that happened in your past, and just feel that pure inner I-ness—has *anything* really changed?

"There is, in short, something within you—that deep inward sense of I-ness—that is *not* memory, thoughts, mind, body, experience, surroundings, feelings, conflicts, sensations, or moods. For *all* of these have changed and can change without substantially affecting that inner I-ness. *That* is what remains untouched by the flight of time—and that is the transpersonal Witness and Self.

"Is it then so very difficult to realize that *every* conscious being has that *same* inner I-ness? And that, therefore, the overall number of transcendent I's is but *one*? We have already surmised that if you had a different body you would still basically feel the same I-ness—but that is already the very same way every other person feels right now. Isn't it just as easy to say there is but one single I-ness or Self taking on different views, different memories, different feelings and sensations?

"And not just at this time, but at all times, past and future. Since you undoubtedly feel (even though your memory, mind, and body are different) that you are the same person of twenty years ago (not the same ego or body, but the same I-ness), couldn't you also be the same I-ness of two hundred years ago? If I-ness isn't dependent upon memories, what difference would it make? In the words of physicist Schroedinger, 'It is not possible that this unity of knowledge, feeling and choice that you call *your own* should have sprung into being from nothingness at a given moment not so long ago; rather this knowledge, feeling and choice are essentially eternal and unchangeable and numerically *one* in all men, nay in all sensitive beings. The conditions for your existence are almost as old as the rocks. For thousands of years men have striven and suffered and begotten and women have brought forth in pain. A hundred years ago, perhaps, another man sat on this spot; like you he gazed with awe and yearning in his heart at the dying light on the glaciers. Like you he was begotten of man and born of woman. He felt pain and brief joy as you do. *Was* he someone else? Was it not you yourself?'

"Ah, we say, that couldn't have been me, because I can't remember what happened then. But that is to make the terrible mistake of identifying I-ness with memories, and we just saw that I-ness is not memory but the witness of memory. Besides, you probably can't even remember what happened to you last month, but you are still I-ness. So what if you can't remember what happened last century? You are still that transcendent I-ness, and that I—there is only one in the whole cosmos—is the same I which awakens in every newborn being, the same I which looked out from our ancestors and will look out from our descendants—one and the same I. We feel they are different only because we make the error of identifying the inward and transpersonal I-ness with the outward and individual memory, mind, and body, which indeed are different.

"But as for that inward I . . . indeed, what is that? It was not born with your body, nor will it perish upon death. It does not recognize time nor cater to its distresses. It is without color, without shape, without form, without size, and yet it beholds the entire majesty before your own eyes. It sees the sun, clouds, stars and moon, but cannot itself be seen. It hears the birds, the crickets, the singing waterfall, but cannot itself be heard. It grasps the fallen leaf, the crusted rock, the knotted branch, but cannot itself be grasped.

"You needn't try to see your transcendent self, which is not possible anyway. Can your eye see itself? You need only begin by persistently dropping your false identifications with your memories, mind, body, emotions, and thoughts. And this dropping entails nothing by way of super-human effort or theoretical comprehension. All that is required, primarily, is but one understanding: *whatever you can see cannot be the Seer. Everything* you know about yourself is precisely *not* your Self, the Knower, the inner I-ness that can neither be perceived, defined, or made an *object* of any sort. To the extent you contact your true Self, you don't *see* anything, you simply sense an inner expanse of freedom, of release, of openness, which is an absence of limits, absence of constraints, absence of objects. The Buddhists call it "emptiness." The true Self is not a thing but a transparent openness or emptiness free of identification with particular objects or events. Bondage is nothing but the mis-identification of the Seer with all these things that can be seen. And liberation begins with the simple reversal of this mistake.

"This is a simple but arduous practice, yet its results are said to constitute nothing less than liberation in this life, for the transcendent Self is everywhere acknowledged as a ray of the Divine. In principle, your transcendent Self is of one nature with God (however you might wish to conceive it). For it is finally, ultimately, profoundly, God alone who looks through your eyes, listens with your ears, and speaks with your tongue. How else could St. Clement maintain that he who knows himself knows God?

"This, then, is the message of the saints, sages, and mystics, whether Amerindian, Taoist, Hindu, Islamic, Buddhist, or Christian: At the bottom of your soul is the soul of humanity itself, but a divine, transcendent soul, leading from bondage to liberation, from dream to awakening, from time to eternity, from death to immortality."

"That's beautiful, honey. It takes on a really urgent meaning for me now, you know," she said. "Those are no longer just words to me."

"I know, sweetheart, I know."

I continued reading to her, sections from Sri Ramana Maharshi, from Sherlock Holmes, from the Sunday comics. Treya walked and paced, holding her sides as if trying to keep herself from jumping out of her body.

"Terry?!"

Treya had abruptly bolted into the bathroom. The Reglan, the anti-nausea agent, had worn off. Every thirty minutes, for the next nine hours, Treya vomited. She wanted to be alone; I collapsed on the sofa.

Tracing my hand along the wall, still moist, I stumble into our storage trunk and extract a small penlight. By its dim illumination, I make my way down the left hall and into the first room, a room we use for guests.

"Treya?"

As I shine the small light around the room, I am struck by the most bizarre sight: instead of the bed and table and chair I expect to see, the room is full of nothing but strange rock formations, stalactites and stalagmites, huge shining crystal formations, geometric mineral shapes of all variety, some suspended in midair, all strangely beautiful, and very alluring. A small clear water pond is on the left, and the only sound in the room is a constant "plop plop plop" of water dripping from a large stalactite into the clear pool. I sit transfixed for minutes on end, hypnotized by the puzzling beauty.

As I look closer, I realize with a shock that this landscape actually extends for what seems to be miles, maybe hundreds of miles, in all directions. In the vast distance I can see a mountain range, then another, then several, sunlight glistening off their snowcapped peaks. The closer I look, the further the vista extends.

I think, this is not my house.

Sometime during the first evening of my chemotherapy, with all the nausea and vomiting and anxiety, I reached a turning point—no longer into worrying, the chemo almost seems past even though it's just begun in time. It's part of my path, part of my journey—totally accepted. No fighting it anymore. Just watch what goes and comes. So perhaps the chemo is my way of moving beyond worry—almost like slaying the dragon of worry that has haunted me so far. Maybe it was Ken reading, maybe my meditation, maybe just luck, but I feel more ready to move into whatever comes, more fully ready for it. I also feel that something new and important is beginning for me. I don't know what, but I feel it very strongly. Perhaps a culmination of my spiritual life, perhaps a beginning.

Got a haircut in anticipation of losing my hair. Went shopping with Mom and Ken for a turban, and for an outfit that, as Ken put it, "won't clash with baldness." Mom and Dad go—I cried, sad to see them go, so touched by their care for me.

Back in Muir Beach, Treya continued to have strong feelings about reaching a turning point, about accepting chemotherapy as part of her path, about a willingness to "journey that journey."

To Suzannah's—lovely to spend the day with old Findhorn friends—seemed somehow a confirmation of the feelings that the fears of cancer are behind me, the fears (of ridicule, suspicion, whatever) of pursuing a more openly spiritual/Findhorn-style path are behind me, the judgment's behind me—I feel more back on track, borne out by my feeling of lightness and aliveness. I truly am not concerned about losing my hair. I'm into feeling good about it and moving on.

I am also surer about my work, my daemon—support Ken and do cancer work. Saw Ange [Stephens] at Suzannah's—seems we both want to work with cancer patients. And I feel a new infusion of energy and enthusiasm for it after this latest shift or passageway or graduation!

Treya would eventually take five courses or rounds of chemotherapy. We took back to San Francisco the protocol designed by Bloomenschein, and there it was administered by our local oncologist. The protocol itself was fairly straightforward: On day one of the procedure, Treya and I would go to the doctor's office or the hospital or wherever we had arranged for the treatment. The "F" and "C" chemicals of the FAC mix would be administered by IV drip (which took about an hour), along with whatever anti-nausea agent we were using at the time. Then we would hook up the portable Travenol pump to Treya's Port-a-Cath (a procedure I was taught at Anderson). The Travenol pump is an ingenious device—basically an outrageously expensive balloon—that would deliver the adriamycin over a twenty-four hour period, thus spreading out and diluting its side effects. We had three such pumps for each round of chemotherapy. Home we would go, with our pumps full of orange-colored poison, and every twenty-four hours for the next two days I would take off the empty pump and plug in a new one. Three days later the treatment would end, and Treya and I were free until the next round began, which was determined by following Treya's white blood counts.

Aside from surgery, the main forms of Western medicine's attack on cancer—chemotherapy and radiation—are based on a single principle: cancer cells are extremely fast-growing. They divide much more rapidly than any of the body's normal cells. Therefore, if you administer an agent to the body that kills cells *when they divide*, then you will kill some normal cells but many more cancer cells. This is what both radiation and chemotherapy do. Of course, the normal cells in the body that grow more rapidly than others—such as hair, stomach lining, mouth tissue—will also be killed more rapidly, hence accounting for frequent hair loss, stomach nausea, and so on. But the overall idea is simple: Since cancer cells grow twice as fast as normal cells, then at the end of a successful course of chemotherapy, the tumor is totally dead and the patient is only half-dead.

About ten days after the three-day adriamycin drip, Treya's white blood count (WBC) would drop quite low. These were some of the body's normal cells being killed. Since the white blood cells are also a major component of the body's immune system, then for the next two weeks or so, Treya would have to be extremely careful to avoid any sort of infection—stay away from crowds, practice careful dental hygiene, and so on. Sometime around three or four weeks after day one, her WBC would come back up—the body is rejuvenating itself—and then she would begin the next round.

Adriamycin is by far one of the most toxic chemotherapy agents available, notorious for its horrible side effects. I would like to emphasize that most forms of chemotherapy are nowhere near as difficult to tolerate as adria. Moreover, even adria treatments, if well managed, can be negotiated with only moderate discomfort. Treya and I were caught totally off guard on her first treatment by the unexpected allergic reaction to reglan. We adjusted her antinausea agents, first trying Compazine, which was not quite right, and then settling on THC, the active ingredient of marijuana, which worked perfectly. And the fact is, after that first night, during all of her subsequent treatments, Treya threw up not once.

Treya worked out a standard personal routine. On day one of each treatment, an hour before the first drip, she would take THC and sometimes a very small amount of Valium (1–2 mg.). Before the treatment she would usually meditate, either vipassana or self-inquiry ("Who am I?"), and during the treatment she would do visualization, picturing the chemotherapy as aggressive good guys attacking the nasties (she sometimes saw the chemo as Pac Man-type agents gobbling up the bad guys). At home she would get into bed, take an Atavan (a strong tranquilizer/ sedative), listen to music, read, and generally zone out. On the second and third day she took THC during the day, and one Atavan each night. By day four she was feeling relatively well, and we would slowly resume our "normal" schedule. In between treatments we managed, among other things, to go to L.A. one time, and on a belated honeymoon to Hawaii on another.

Physically, then, Treya managed the chemotherapy treatments fairly well, all things considered. What we overlooked, what caught us from behind, what very nearly destroyed us both, was the emotional, psychological, and spiritual devastation that the whole ordeal was having on each of us. As the months wore on, and the ordeal intensified, Treya's shadow elements surfaced and intensified, and I went into a profound depression. But in the meantime we plugged ahead, our spirits relatively high, the future relatively bright.

"Will you love me when I'm bald?"

"No, of course not."

"Look, it's starting to get thin here, and here. Let's really cut it. Sort of on the principle that you can't fire me, I quit."

I got a huge pair of scissors and we hacked away at Treya's hair until we had a perfectly far-out punk spike hairdo. She looked like she'd been run over by a lawn mower.

In the shower I reached up and a huge clump of hair came out in my hand. Then another. I didn't mind at all. I got Ken and we both stood in front of the mirror, looking at each other, both completely bald. What a sight! "My god," Ken said, "we look like the melon section in a supermarket. Promise me one thing: we'll never go bowling."

Look at my body! I have no head hair, no pubic hair, no right breast. Sort of like a plucked chicken! I have a body, but I am not my body! Thank God for small favors.

But I like finding positive role models for bald women. Like the Amazon women are a great model for not having a breast. They used to remove one breast so they could shoot a bow and arrow more effectively. Shaved black models, the shaved-headed woman in "Star Trek," the woman in *Close Encounters*, Egyptian priestess.

Everyone seems to love my bald head, very beautiful they say, though of course a part of me wonders how much of that is to make me feel better. Ken says I'm really beautiful, and the way he says it I know he really means it, which makes me feel wonderful! A small handful of our friends keep pushing Ken, they want to know (though they don't just ask) if Ken still finds me attractive. He says he feels insulted by this. "They're just scared. If they'd just ask me, I'd tell them I think you're the sexiest woman I've ever been with. If I didn't think so, I'd say so." So he usually sidesteps the issue by making an ironic joke about how *really* awful it is, and sometimes they're so bad they're funny. The other evening with Claire and George, George was sort of pushing him about how it was, and Ken said, "I've got to trade this one in on a new model. First the right bumper falls off, now the upholstery's gone. Resale value of this body is going to be nil." Afterwards he said, "But that's how they think, you know? That if a few body parts are gone the soul is somehow compromised. Of course I miss your body the way it was, but that's not the point. The point is, if I love you, I'll love your body, however it is. If I don't love you, I won't love your body, however it is. They've got it exactly backwards."

We're going to have Linda [Conger, Treya's best friend, who is an accomplished photographer] come up to Tahoe and take bald pictures of us together. Ken had the wild idea that he would wear my breast prosthesis, then Linda could shoot us nude from the waist up. We'd both be bald and we'd both have one breast. "Talk about androgyny!" he said.

I'm not sure I'll ever get up enough nerve to go around outside without my wig or turban. In the meantime, everyone thinks Ken is the patient. This was brought home to us the last time I went to the doctor's office. Ken has always come with me, and a really nice old man parks our car. We both like him a lot. This time Ken was delayed, and drove up to the office by himself. The man came over to Ken, and with a really concerned look on his face said, "Oh, you poor thing. Had to come by yourself this time?" Ken didn't know what to say, it would be too hard to explain, so he said, "Ain't that a bitch?"

The physical problems with the chemotherapy started to catch up with Treya, and we headed down to L.A., between treatments two and three, for a small vacation with sister Kati, who was a lawyer with I. Rella Minella.

I've lost my period and at some point will have to start on estrogen replacements. I've developed mouth sores that are quite painful. And bowel movements are sometimes very painful and sometimes bloody. All the fast-growing tissues in my body. Sometimes finding something to eat that tastes good is hard. But it's amazing to me what human beings can endure, can put up with. What is, is.

In L.A., stayed with Kati. Tracy came, it was wonderful. Ken really likes both my sisters, has a small crush on them. Kristen [a friend from Findhorn] and I visited the Wellness Center in Santa Monica, a cancer support network run by Harold Benjamin. I liked hearing the stories, sensing the spirit, especially of the bald women, liked that people told what illness they had right away, not shying away from it. Seemed real, earthy. And the facilitator kept things in line when word-magic got out of hand or people pushed someone else to conform or join. Like when a woman wanted to make the man with bone cancer want to live. People had jumped on him earlier for saying that part of him wanted to die. As if all he had to do was make the decision to live, as if it was not OK to want to die. But that got corrected by others—"People die here." "I wanted to die, and still do sometimes." "I've got a way to die all planned, and if it comes to that, that's OK, that's part of it."

It was a wonderful trip, but the emotional cracks—bad ones—were already starting to show.

Back at Kati's that evening, a good friend of mine called about someone who had cancer, and she wanted to talk to Ken about it. I was so upset she hadn't wanted to talk to me about it or that Ken hadn't suggested it. I got mad at him, and he blew up. First time he's ever really exploded. He grabbed my collar, said that he couldn't do anything without having to worry about how it would affect me. That for a year and a half he had submerged his own interests in favor of helping me, and that if he couldn't even take a phone call, that was it. He felt there was nowhere he could go to get solace. That really got to me. I always want him to feel that he can come to me, not that I'm not going to always criticize him. Should have realized for him to get so upset he'd been storing things and really needed to be heard. I listened but I also defended myself, which sort of pointed up what he was saying. I could have done that later. It was a big mistake on my part, I think, to attack back, because I didn't really acknowledge what he was saying. He stayed mad.

With Kati and Kristen and Ken. Talking of cancer cells and how we picture mine. Ken said that he wanted to see them as weak and confused, but that unfortunately they seemed to be strong. I said I didn't want to hear that, that I was trying to see them as weak and confused. He said there were two different things here, how he wanted to see them, which was weak and confused, versus how he unfortunately saw them, based on various reports, which was strong. I said I didn't want to hear it. He said he had a right to his opinion. I agreed, but said it was important to me how I thought of them and I'd therefore rather not hear a view that saw them as strong. Then don't ask, he said. Do you want me to tell you my true opinion, or do you want me to lie to you? he asked. Lie to me, I said. Fine, I will. He made a snide comment—"I'm going to grow my hair in so I can pull it out"—and then dropped the conversation. I know how he took it—he can't even take a phone call, he can't even express his opinion, without worrying about how it will affect "you and your cancer." "You don't realize how difficult your illness can be on the people that love you," he said. "You could have said, 'Gee, Ken, please don't say my cancer cells are strong, because that worries me.' But you just issue orders—don't do this because I say so. I'll be glad to do anything for you if you ask, but I'm tired of taking orders."

This was very difficult, one of the first times that Ken and I haven't connected. I need to feel supported, but I am starting to see that Ken needs to be supported too.

Here was the situation. In the past year and a half: Treya had one operation followed by six weeks of radiation, a recurrence, a mastectomy, and was now in the middle of chemotherapy, all the while confronted with the unrelenting possibility of an early death. In order to be with Treya twenty-four hours a day, I chose to stop writing, dropped three editorial jobs, and generally turned my life over to her fight against cancer. I had recently—big mistake—stopped meditating, because I was too exhausted. We had moved out of the Muir Beach house, but the Tahoe house still wasn't ready. We were in effect building a house while trying to do Treya's chemotherapy on the run, as if building a house or doing chemo weren't madness-enough-inducing endeavors on their own.

And *that*, we would both later realize, was the easy part. When we finally moved into the Tahoe house, the really gruesome ordeal began.

9

NARCISSUS, OR THE SELF-CONTRACTION

IT is 7:00 A.M., a bright, beautiful morning in North Lake Tahoe. Our house is situated about halfway up the mountainous hills that rise dramatically from the most beautiful lake in North America. From every window in our south-facing house you can see the entire lake, the stunning white beaches edging it, the black mountains in the background, covered with snow nearly year round. The lake itself is a color of azure-cobalt blue so intense, so deep, so electric, I wonder if there isn't some sort of huge power generator hidden somewhere in its depths: This lake doesn't look like it is just blue, it looks like a switch has been thrown and it has been turned *on*.

Treya is sleeping quietly. I take a bottle of Absolut vodka from the shelf and I very carefully pour four ounces into a cup. I drink it in one quick gulp. This will last me until exactly noon, when I will have three beers with lunch. Throughout the afternoon, I will drink beer—maybe five, maybe ten. For dinner, a bottle of wine. Brandy through the evening. I will never get drunk. I will never pass out. I will rarely even get tipsy. I will never neglect any medical problems that Treya has, nor will I shirk any fundamental responsibilities. If you meet me, you will not suspect I have been drinking. I will be alert, smiling, animated. I will do this every day, without fail, for four months. And then I will walk into Andy's Sporting Goods, on Park Street in South Lake Tahoe, to buy a gun meant to vaporize this entire state of affairs. Because, as they always say, I can simply stand it no longer.

It has been two months since Treya finished her last chemotherapy treatment. Although the treatments were physically punishing, Treya's enormous strength and courage have seen her through the worst times. Once again, she has been given a clean bill of health, although with cancer that never means anything (you are only pronounced cured of cancer when you die of something else). Once again, we have been looking forward to finally settling down, possibly even having a child, if Treya's period returns. Once again, the horizon has begun to look clear, fresh, inviting.

But something has changed this time. Both of us are exhausted. Both of us are starting to fray at the seams. It is as if we both carried a huge and heavy load up a steep mountain, carried it up quite well and set it down quite carefully—only then to completely collapse. Although the strain had been building slowly in both of us, particularly over the seven months of chemotherapy, we both came unraveled rather abruptly, as abruptly as I have introduced it in this narrative. It just seemed that one day we were fine, and then the next day life came apart at the seams like a cheap suit. It happened so suddenly it caught us both off guard.

I do not intend to dwell on this period in our lives, but neither will I gloss over it. It was, for the both of us, hell.

Incline Village is a small town of perhaps seven thousand situated on the northeast edge of Lake Tahoe, "Tahoe" being the local Indian word for "high water." (Lake Tahoe is the second largest high-altitude lake in the Western Hemisphere. It has more water than Lake Michigan, enough water, the silly tourist brochures told us, to cover all of California to a depth of fourteen inches.) In 1985 a bizarre disease blew into this village, infecting over two hundred people with a debilitating illness that seemed to resemble a mild form of multiple sclerosis. The main symptoms were low-grade chronic fever, sporadic muscle dysfunction, night sweats, sore and swollen lymph glands, and crippling exhaustion. Over thirty of the two hundred victims had to be hospitalized because they were too exhausted, literally, to stand up. CAT scans revealed numerous small lesions on the brain, not unlike MS. The especially peculiar thing about this illness was that it didn't seem to be human-to-human transmissible: husbands who had it didn't give it to their wives, wives didn't give it to their kids. Nobody seemed to know just how it was transmitted; informed opinion finally settled on some sort of environmental toxin or cofactor. Whatever it was that blew into town that year, it just as quickly blew out a year later—since 1985 there has been not one newly reported case of the disease in that area. Andromeda Strain, it seems.

This was so strange that at first the Centers for Disease Control in Atlanta denied there was any such entity. But Dr. Paul Cheney, a brilliant physician who also happened to have Ph.D. in physics, knew better, since he was getting the bulk of the cases. He collected so much incontrovertible laboratory and empirical evidence that Atlanta had to reverse itself. Disease X, whatever it was, was real.

Treya and I moved to Incline Village in 1985. I was one of the lucky two hundred.

Of those who contracted the illness, about a third seemed to keep it for around six months; about a third, for two to three years; and the remaining third have it to this day (many of whom are still hospitalized). I was one of the middle third, destined to be stuck with it for two or three years. My own symptoms included muscle spasms and almost convulsion-degree tremors, chronic fever, swollen glands, horrible night sweats, and above all debilitating exhaustion. I would get out of bed, brush my teeth, and consider it a day's work. I couldn't walk up the stairs without resting frequently.

The really difficult thing was that I had this disease and didn't know it. As disease X slowly crept over me, I got more and more exhausted, depressed, torn. I couldn't figure out why it was *that* bad. Added to this was a certain genuine or existential depression over Treya's condition and my life in general. This depression—part real, part neurotic, part disease X-induced—was interrupted only by occasional anxiety attacks, where the desperate nature of my situation jolted me out of depression and into panic. I felt I had lost all control of my life. And I saw no reason to suffer those particular slings and arrows of outrageous fortune. Off and on for months I felt suicidal.

But my central problem, the overriding problem, was simply that, in my desire to do anything to help Treya, I had for over a year completely submerged my own interests, my own work, my own needs, my own life. I voluntarily chose to do this, and I would do it again unhesitatingly under the same circumstances. But I would do it differently, with more of a support system for myself in place, and with a clearer understanding of the devastating toll that being a full-time support person can take.

Throughout Treya's illness, I learned many lessons about this difficult job. One of the main reasons I am willing to go into this extremely difficult period in my life, and in Treya's, is so that others may avoid some of the simple mistakes that I made. Indeed, as we will see, I eventually became something of a spokesman for "support people," based on lessons I learned the very hard way. When I first published an essay on the rewards and perils of being a support person, I and my publisher were taken aback by the overwhelming response the piece generated. I received hundreds of the most agonizing letters from people all over the world, people who had gone through similar circumstances and had no one with whom they could talk about the grinding nature of their roles. It is a topic I would have preferred to become an authority on by a gentler route.

In the meantime I struggled along, disease X taking its course, and my anxiety about the whole situation—Treya's illness, my predicament—slowly increasing, and a certain amount of real depression laid over the whole mess. I had not been able to do any sustained writing for over a year and a half. Up to that period, writing was my life blood. It was my daemon, my fate, my fortune. I had written a book a year for ten years; and, as men often do, I *defined* myself by my doing, by my writing, and when that suddenly stopped I was suspended in midair without a net. The landing hurt.

And most egregious of all I had stopped meditation. The strong taste I had of the Witness slowly evaporated. I no longer had easy access to the "center of the cyclone," I had only the cyclone. And it was that, more than anything else in my case, that made difficult times so hard to bear. When I lost access to pure open awareness—to the Witness, to my soul—I was left only with my self-contraction, with Narcissus, hopelessly absorbed in his own image. I had lost my soul, it seemed, as well as my daemon, and so I was left only with my ego, a frightening thought under any circumstances.

But I suppose the simplest and most crushing mistake I made I was this: I blamed Treya for my woes. I had freely and voluntarily chosen to set aside my own interests in order to help her, and then when I missed those interests—missed my writing, missed my editorial jobs, missed meditation—I just blamed Treya. Blamed her for getting cancer, blamed her for wrecking my life, blamed her for the loss of my daemon. This is what the existentialists call "bad faith"—bad in that you are not assuming responsibility for your own choices.

As I became more "depressed," it understandably hit Treya hard, especially after all she had been through. After being there for her day and night for a year and a half, I was suddenly gone, suddenly wrapped up in myself, my problems, and tired of hearing about hers. I felt I now needed a little support, and I felt she was unaccustomed or unable to give it. As I started subtly blaming Treya for much of my depression, she understandably reacted, either with guilt or anger. At the same time, exacerbated by premature menopause and mood swings caused by chemotherapy, Treya's own neurotic "stuff" was surfacing, and I reacted to *that*. We ended up in a fast-forward downward spiral of guilt and blame that led Treya to despair and me to Andy's Sporting Goods.

> Saturday. Two days ago I started writing about this and got three paragraphs into it when the electricity went off in the house. Was writing about how miserable I was then—perhaps not meant to be recorded. I'm feeling better now—Ken and I had a lovely evening together, then spent the day downtown. As I went to sleep I had the feeling of really being cared for by God, that things will all work out OK. My affirmation changed at times from "I feel the healing power of the love of God at work in every cell and atom of my body" to "I feel the healing power of God's love at work in every cell and atom of my body." A slight but telling difference. As I've said before, I know God loves me best through Ken's love, so when Ken and I really connect I connect with God too. If we don't connect, I feel cut off from everything.
>
> What led to that connection, however, was a miserable day. One of those to be noted as the depths. Ken snapped at me first thing in the morning about the work on the closet, I snapped at him later about the new computer stuff, he went out for most of the day, I sat moodily on the porch staring at the lake and trying to get through what feels like junk in my personality. We had a long talk in the evening, no real sense of movement, he said it felt like a replay.
>
> I feel lately like I'm fighting off a bad mood most of the time, quite like PMS. My period still hasn't returned; I am in effect post-menopausal. Could my moods be due to estrogen deprivation? Probably to a large degree. I started taking the [estrogen] pills a week ago, which has helped with the hot flashes some. I'm also having persistent

back pains on both sides below the waist. But somehow we got through it. Ken had a few drinks and got really sweet—turned into a lovely evening.

Today I was organizing my bathroom closet and came across some extra tampax. Wonder if I'll ever use them again?

Wednesday. Things are still pretty rocky. We arrived back from San Francisco today, the house looked nice but they'd messed up the grout color in the kitchen. It's always something. Later we went for a nice walk with a lovely view up Fairview, but I was a bit out of sorts because Ken is moping around so. His dissatisfaction with life in general comes out clearly in his voice tone towards me, and I can't help but take it personally. Sometimes when he's like this I feel like he loves me but he simply doesn't like me. He apologizes—then usually in a very sweet voice—and says he doesn't mean that. But I can't help but think sometimes that he does mean it. I tried to talk to him about it, but didn't get very far. He feels at this point that we don't do too well working things out without a third party, like Frances [Vaughan] or Seymour [Boorstein], to help us out. "Honey, we've gone over it a dozen times. I don't know why I'm so depressed, but we talk about it, you feel guilty, you get upset, I get upset, it's not working like that. I want somebody here to referee. Let's hold it till we can get somebody to help." That's hard for me, I always want things settled now. I like the air cleared so the deep love we have for each other isn't obstructed. He says we're too deep into it.

What's amazing to me is how clearly we can be in love, how solid the foundation of our connection is, and we still are going through such hard times. I doubt much of this would have come up but for every stressful event imaginable (almost) coming at once in our lives. One evening we were looking at those stress charts that measure how much stress various events in life cause. The worst, death of a spouse, was arbitrarily given one hundred points. We had three of the top five (marriage, moving, major illness). Ken had a fourth—loss of job (although voluntary). Even things like a vacation was fifteen points. Ken said, Hell, we have so many stress points already that if we take a vacation it'll kill us.

But whenever we talk about it, I keep getting the feeling that what Ken is trying to communicate is that he is really angry at me but won't say so. He feels beaten down, watched over, grounded. In a sense he's mad at me because he is not able to work. He really has given up so much to take care of me, and now he's exhausted. I feel terrible about it, I don't know what to do. Nothing seems to help.

In times like this our different styles just come to the fore. Usually they complement each other, now they just seem to grate. Me, the careful, methodical conservationist with a tendency to contract when I feel threatened, Ken the expansive, generous visionary with a tendency to not pay attention to details of daily life, and to get irritated with them.

Back in San Francisco, the next weekend, we stayed with Frances and Roger. That night Whit [Whitson] and Judith [Skutch, the publisher of A Course in Miracles] came over to celebrate the paperback publication, in England and the U.S., of the Course. We also celebrated the still-secret marriage plans of Frances and Roger. The day before, Roger and I had a nice talk about where he was with that issue. He said it was like dropping a branch—he's already let go of the branch (he knows he wants to be with Frances for the rest of his life) and now there's only the process of letting it fall to the ground. The next morning he asked Frances to marry him! Feels like it's about time . . . and very right. The wedding will be at Judith and Whit's house, the honeymoon at our Tahoe house. Ken will be Roger's best man, I'll be Frances's matron of honor. It looks like Huston Smith will do the ceremony.

At any rate, even with Roger and Frances helping, our issues were not decharged. Back in Tahoe, it's with us today in Ken's mood. He just seems stuck in it. He lies in front of the TV, not moving, for hours. My poor honey, I just don't know what to do to help. After he took care of me for so long, I just want to take care of him, but nothing seems to help. I feel absolutely terrible.

Friday. What a life! From absolute despair to one of the best days ever.

When Ken left for two days on business I fell apart. Felt awful since I was kind of weird when he left, put me back into feeling bad about the little ways I'm mean to him or try to control him. One of his main complaints is that I do try to control him, try to monopolize his time. It's true. I love him so much, I do want to be with him all the time. Some would say that my cancer was a way to have his undivided attention around the clock. There may be some truth to that, but I think I could get his attention in other ways! I do feel a bit jealous of his work, but I certainly don't want it to stop. That is by far the most painful thing to me, that his daemon is gone.

When he left I freaked out. The house felt so cold, so alone. Spent an hour on the phone crying to Kati.

After talking to him on the phone—he said he doesn't do well without me either—everything seemed good. Since his return we're both being nicer to each other, less reactive, watching out for patterns and skirting the places we get stuck, just loving each other a lot.

François and Hannah came for the weekend and Kay Lynne joined us [three friends from Findhorn]—it was a fabulous time! Sunday was one of the most perfect days ever, beginning with a drive up Mount Rose highway to show them the view, then a picnic by a waterfall, then a hike to this gorgeous lake, then dinner at the best restaurant I've ever been to, then dancing at the Hyatt. That hike was spectacular. The only way I could get Ken to go on it with us was to say, "This hike is clearly the greatest reward for the least amount of effort without mechanical assistance I've ever seen. You usually have to hike miles for this kind of view." "OK, OK, I'll go." François asked Ken, don't you like exercise? Ken said, I love exercise, in homeopathic amounts.

Treya and I were very much aware that we were starting to fall apart, both individually and as a couple. Individually, we both felt that, quite apart from circumstances, however difficult they were, we both had a fair amount of normal neurosis that was surfacing; neurosis that at some point had to be addressed anyway; neurosis that, in fact, might have remained hidden or submerged for years were it not for these pressure-cooker circumstances.

And as a couple, the same process was at work. We were forced to confront things in our relationship that most couples don't have to face for three or five or even ten years. In both cases—individually and as a couple—we had to be taken apart, as it were, in order to be reassembled in a sturdier fashion. We both had to go through the fire, and as painful as it was, we both felt, from the very beginning, that it was ultimately for the better—if we could survive it. Because what was being "burned up" in this fire was not our love for each other, but much of our "junk."

Tracy's still my biggest supporter. Last night at dinner she asked me if I was writing in my journal, encouraging me to keep it up. Said she thought the book would be a best-seller! Sometimes I too have those fantasies . . . certainly I've never found a book that contains all I intend to cover. She asked me if I was glad I'd done chemotherapy—I said,

"Ask me in six months." I feel like I'm still on it—guess that won't finish until the three-month recovery period is up and my blood is back to normal. I'm still waiting for my hair to grow back—there doesn't seem to be any sign at all of it yet. No one's specifically told me when it would start growing but I assumed it would be soon after the twenty-five-day cycle following the last treatment was up. Doesn't seem to be the case since it's two weeks since then. Ah, patience.

The other reason I don't feel done or settled about chemotherapy is my missing period. Sounds like some sort of detective novel . . . where could it be? Last week for the first time I experienced vaginal dryness during intercourse, about three-and-a-half weeks after my last (chemically induced) period. It was painful and depressing. I wish some of these male doctors had some sense of this. I've actually been in a terrible state for the last month, fits of crying and depression, with some really good days scattered in between. Not that I wasn't crying and depressed at times before, because I was, but this period (ha, great pun) seemed to start when I did Stephen Levine's self-forgiveness meditation and bumped full up against my inability to forgive myself. That was a terrible day, hay fever on top of the tears, but I managed to pull myself together enough to go into town and write the cover letter for the U.S.-U.S.S.R. Youth Exchange Funding Proposal. The next week I had a terrible night when Ken went off to San Francisco and I spent the evening crying and feeling terrible about myself. The next week is when I went to see my gynecologist, and cried most of that day too. And the next evening with Frances and Roger, talking about the part of me that feels responsible for causing so much upset and grief and inability to work in Ken's life. Seemed to start coming thicker and faster during this time. I felt upset again when it looked like Linda couldn't come, feeling so much how I wanted to be taken care of, I wanted her to love me enough to really make an effort to get there. I told her I could use someone to help cheer me up. It's actually something of a step for me to admit I need help, to let down that capable, I-can-handle-it persona. I cried again on the way to the airport to pick her up, touched by her coming, feeling simply sad about everything. A few days later, after she'd gone and after that great Findhorn Gathering weekend, I again spent the whole day crying, in the morning with Frances, in the afternoon with Dr. Cantor [a psychotherapist] and then with Hal [acupuncturist]—all my therapeutic support system. I think I finally got exhausted enough to stop, but really nothing seemed resolved. I asked Dr. Cantor if this happens to people sometimes—they carry through with the therapy really well, through all the hair loss and nausea and weakness and worry and then when it's all over they fall apart. He said, in his twenty-five years of working with cancer patients, that's more true than not. It's the same with Ken. He carried me for two years, put me down, then fell apart.

Certainly I've become aware of lots of unresolved feelings of pain and sorrow and fear and anger that I guess I felt I didn't have the strength to deal with while steeling myself for a treatment every three weeks and handling putting together this house. Now it's all coming up. I suppose it's a good thing, but it's always hard to see the good when one's in the middle of it. I can intellectually, as an abstract idea, see how it might be good, but I sure can't fully feel it yet. Again, ask me in six months.

There's a part of me that fears that falling apart now negates how well I handled all those months of therapy intertwined with the stresses of doing a house. I mentioned this to Ken and he said, "That's exactly how I feel. Mostly, I am so embarrassed by the shape I'm in." That's hard to shake. Years of being complemented for being tough, for being steady, never complemented for letting all those other feelings like fear and deep sorrow and anger come up. When they do part of me still feels they're negative and might make other people think less of me. But actually, the parts that think that have diminished in strength. Where once a lot of the clowns that together make up my personality [a reference to the movie *A Thousand Clowns*, referring to the numerous subpersonalities or "clowns" we all have within us] were afraid of showing these "negative" feelings, now there's only an occasional clown that carries that banner. That clown still gets to me, of course, but I can stay more aware of her fellows. There's even some new ones in there that encourage sometimes falling apart—perhaps in the rebuilding process some things will get left behind, new characters can enter, and the script for all these clowns gets rewritten. I get put back together differently. Reborn, as it were.

In the meantime, however, we both had to get more and more depressed, more and more taken apart, more and more smashed against circumstances and our own neurotic junk. There seemed a certain inevitability about it all, the necessary death that precedes all rebirth. And in my case, at this point, it became a question of just what kind of death.

All next day felt depressed—truly depressed, not just sad or down like I sometimes get. This was something new—and scary. Didn't feel like talking. Ken won't really answer questions anyway, dull, listless, no response to my efforts to cheer him up. Don't remember *ever* feeling like this. Silence, inability to care enough to make decisions, no energy, I answer in monosyllabic responses (if any) to questions.

The simple truth of the matter is, I'm just not happy anymore. I don't feel my own exuberance and vitality. I feel worn down by events. I'm tired, much deeper than a physical tiredness. I felt happy and generally up for the first year of cancer, so it wasn't having cancer that necessarily changed me. The shift definitely came during the chemotherapy period. Physically the chemo wasn't that bad. But I told Ken, the bad part was that it felt like it was poisoning my soul, poisoning me not just physically but emotionally, psychologically, and spiritually. I just feel shot, totally out of control.

How I do wish Ken and I had had a few years together before having to go through all this. It is so sad.

About five days ago I had two dreams. It was the night I noticed that I might be ovulating. In one dream they had to cut more out of my remaining breast and I was really upset because now it seemed too small. (Interesting that I've never dreamt about having my other breast back, actually no dreams about that breast.) In the second dream I was in my oncologist's office and asked him if I'd always be like this, meaning the lack of estrogen and vaginal dryness. He said yes and I started screaming at him, screaming and screaming, furious about not having been warned about this in the beginning, furious at all these damned doctors who seem to think those kinds of things are unimportant. They treat the body, not the person. I was absolutely, totally, uninhibitedly furious, screaming and screaming and screaming.

Daemon, daemon, daemon. Without it I felt like I had no compass, no direction, no way to find my path, my fate. It is often said that what women provide for men is grounding, what men provide for women is direction. I don't want to get involved in sexist arguments over whether that is true or not, but it does often seem to be the case. In the past Treya had offered me grounding; now I just felt grounded. As in, incapable of flight. And whereas in the past I had offered Treya direction, now I just offered her an aimless wandering in depressive circles.

Saturday started out with my feeling excited about the change in weather—lovely, bright, sunny. I suggested to Ken that we go out for brunch to our favorite restaurant. At the restaurant he was strangely morose. Still depressed, but somehow different. I asked him if anything was wrong. "It's this writing thing. I keep thinking that the desire to write will come back, but it doesn't seem to be. I know this makes you feel bad too, and I'm really sorry. It's just I can't figure it out. I don't have writer's block. That's when you want to write but can't. I just don't want to. I look inside for that crazy daemon and it just doesn't seem to be anywhere in sight. Mostly this frightens me."

I was feeling so bad for him. Ken just seems to get worse and worse, completely tired of living. That night we had some people over to the house, and Ken managed to struggle through just fine, until someone asked about his writing. This was a person whom we don't know too well but who is a great fan of Ken's work, had read everything. Ken sort of braced himself, and politely explained that he hadn't really done any extended writing for quite some time, and that he felt his writing period was over, that he had been trying to work up a desire to write for a long time, and since there didn't even seem to be a glimmer of it returning, he figured it was all over. This man got rather upset—how dare the great Ken Wilber not write? as if Ken owed him. Then the man said, "What it must be like to be called the potentially greatest philosopher of consciousness since Freud and then feel it evaporating." Everybody looked at Ken. He sat very quiet for a long time, staring directly at the man. You could hear a pin drop. He finally said, "More fun than a human should be allowed to have."

One of the main effects of my depression on Treya was that in having to deal with me, or rather with the lack of me, she had little strength and equanimity left over for her own problems. The ever-present fears of a recurrence, fears that she otherwise could handle so well, and fears that I would ordinarily have helped to absorb, now simply ran through her psyche unchecked.

Monday night. The pain is really bad. I woke up at 4:00 A.M. with pain really intense. It's been like this for a week. Very specific, definite pain. Can be ignored no longer. I think it's a recurrence—bone metastasis— what else could it be? If I could only think of something else it could be . . . but I can't. Getting worse. Thoughts of death. I might die soon.

Oh my God, how can this be? I'm only thirty-eight—it's not fair, not so soon! At least give me chance to make it up to Ken first, to heal the ravages to his own life of dealing with my cancer almost since we met. At least help me to do that. He's battle-torn and weary, the thought of yet another agonizing round on both of us is unbearable.

Oh, God, I might die in this very house. I can't even bear the thought of losing my hair again. So soon—too soon—it's only been four and a half months since my last treatment, only two months since I've had enough hair (barely) to stop wearing those damned hats. I want this to be over so I can help Ken get back on his feet, start the Cancer Support Community, get on with my life and help others. Oh God, please let this be a false alarm. Let it be anything but cancer. At least let me recover more before I get knocked down again.

As I became more and more bitter and resentful and sarcastic—and depressed and exhausted—Treya was becoming more and more defensive, obsessive, demanding, even grating. We were both terrified of what was happening; we both saw that we were contributing more or less equally to the mess; and neither of us had the strength to stop it.

A few days later, Treya hit bottom. We both did.

Last evening Ken talked about my getting out and doing things I'm interested in, distancing myself from his problems. In effect, he said save yourself, this has been going on for a long time for him and it doesn't seem to be getting any better and that does not augur well. I felt very sad that evening, even cried a bit quietly next to him but he didn't notice it. That night I couldn't sleep, kept feeling like crying. Finally got up and turned on the TV upstairs so I could cry without him hearing me. I felt terrible, like I'd ruined Ken's life, and here he was telling me to save myself, like I should jump aboard some lifeboat and leave his listing ship. I felt like everything I do hurts him, my very personality and character traits give him great pain and indeed are the main reason he's worn down so over the last year. I felt like some terrible separation was happening.

Right now I feel totally confused and helpless. Like I've fucked everything up—totally ruined my sweet Ken's life. I feel like I've done this to him—unwittingly, to be sure—and it gives me *such great pain*. I don't know how to repair it. I don't want to further burden him with my pain. I don't trust myself—I don't trust what I feel—I feel like everything I do may hurt him. Just being myself seems to hurt him, because I just seem to be too yang, too stubborn, too controlling, too insensitive, too selfish for him. Maybe I need someone simpler, less sensitive, less intelligent, so they won't be hurt by the way I am. And maybe he needs someone else, someone more gentle and feminine and sensitive. God, what pain that thought gives me.

I don't trust myself anymore. Everything I do seems to give him pain. If I share my concern, I feel perhaps I should instead be acting positive and affirmative. Even now I share my intense tears only with myself. I don't trust them. Is it just me continuing to draw attention to myself when he's the one who needs attention? Just me feeling sorry for myself, unable to really feel his needs? If I share, won't I be leaning on him, demanding something from him when he hasn't got it to give, rather than supporting and helping him? I don't even trust myself anymore. I have internal talks being mad at Ken, thinking about being alone and how simple that was. I realize how I have no one to talk to and I haven't shared any of my most scary thoughts with anyone. I used to do that with Ken all the time, but now it seems I've worn him down with my demands and complaints and stubbornness. If I can't talk to Ken about these feelings, and I've been trying hard to spare him, then I have no one right now I can be really honest with. I run through my friends and find, really, no one I can talk to like that. I'm afraid I'm ruining my marriage.

Reading that thing in the *Course in Miracles* tonight asking for God's help—just the way I feel, I can't do it myself, I fuck it up, *please* help me, show me the way, any way. Don't let Ken get hurt *any* more. When I think of what he was once like, the laughter, the wit, the charm, the love of life, the passion for his work—dear God, *please* help him.

I can never know how hard it must have been for him to stand by me through all this, our not even knowing each other for that long. He carried me on his back for so long. I can never know.

The pain for both of us was simply unendurable. The psychic anguish seemed infinite; it hurt so bad it seemed to suck your entire being back in on itself, you seemed to disappear entirely into a black hole of pain, from which nothing could escape, not even your breath.

The greater the love, the greater the pain. Our love had been enormous; the pain was proportionate. Out of that pain grew resentment, anger, bitterness, blame.

I can't help but resent how he's changed. He said he's stopped doing some of the nurturing things for me because he was exhausted. I suppose I think he stopped because he was mad at me. There are times I feel very unforgiven by him, perhaps because I haven't forgiven myself. But I'm *mad* at him, a long slow burn, mad at him for letting himself get in this shape, mad at him for his constant snideness and tone of voice—his *constant* snideness!—mad at him being so difficult at times! I worry about him leaving me, then I think I should just leave him, go it alone again, out in the country, by myself. How simple. How nice.

Neither one of us could sleep last night and so we had a talk. Talked of how I think of leaving him sometimes, often at times. How I feel I don't seem to be able to change enough to make him happy. He said he often thinks about leaving me too. Guessed he'd probably go to Boston. At one point he got out of bed—these talks get us both wired—and said you can have Tahn [our dog]. When he came back I said I didn't want Tahn, I want you. He sat down and looked at me, tears in his eyes, I started crying, but neither one of us moved. Neither one of us feels like we can go on. I want to forgive him, but maybe I can't now, maybe I'm too angry. And I know he hasn't forgiven me. I don't even think he likes me.

The next day I drove to Andy's. It seemed that everything that could go sour, had. Everything in life had gone flat; there was no taste left in any experience; there was nothing I wanted, nothing I desired, nothing I looked forward to, except getting out. It's hard to describe how utterly dark the world can look at times like that.

As I said, our own individual neuroses were surfacing, exaggerated and amplified by our fairly grisly circumstances. In my case, when I become afraid, when fear overcomes me, my ordinary lightness of outlook, which generously might be referred to as wit, degenerates into sarcasm and snideness, a biting bitterness towards those around me—not because I am snide by nature, but because I am afraid. Under these circumstances, I am no day at the beach. I end up with Oscar Wilde's epithet: "He has no enemies but is intensely disliked by all his friends."

And in Treya's case, when overcome with fear, her resilient strength would degenerate into rigidity, into a harsh stubbornness, an attempt to control and monopolize.

And indeed that is what was happening. Because I couldn't express my anger at Treya openly and directly, I constantly undercut her with sarcasm. And in her unyieldingness, she had monopolized most of the central decisions in both of our lives. I felt I had no control over my life at all, because Treya always had the trump card: "But I have cancer."

We polarized our friends, hers feeling that I was definitely the bad guy, me trying to convince mine how utterly impossible she was to live with. And we were both right. After Treya had gone to a three-day retreat with two of her best friends—during which time she made them, among other things, dress outside the room so as to give her an extra half-hour of sleep—they took me aside and said, "She's so controlling, how do you live with her all the time? We barely made it through three days." And frequently after evenings with family or friends, they would pull Treya aside and say, "How do you put up with him? He's like a coiled rattlesnake. Does he hate everybody?"

Snideness collided with unyieldingness, and the result was destroying us both. We didn't hate each other, we hated each others' neurotic clowns, which seemed locked into some sort of death spiral—the worse one of us got, the worse the other reacted.

The only way to break this dismal cycle was to break into the neurotic component. After all, there wasn't much we could do about circumstances or about our actual illnesses. And we were both therapists enough to know that the only way to crack neurotic depression is to get in touch with the rage lurking beneath its surface. But how do you get enraged at someone with cancer? And how do you get furious with a man who stood by you through thick and thin for two years?

Somehow all of this was going through my mind as I walked into Andy's. I looked at the various guns for perhaps half an hour. What would it be, handgun or shotgun? A Hemingway, I think, which will also require some strong wire. The more I walked through the store, the more agitated I got, the angrier I got. It finally dawned on me. I did indeed want to kill someone. It wasn't me.

Back at the house, it all came to a head. I had seated myself at my desk in the living room, and was working on some unavoidable business. Treya came in with a newspaper and began shuffling through it. I should point out that we had several extra rooms in the house, but in one of her frightened and monopolizing moments, Treya had wanted them for her purposes (two offices and a studio). I had blithely agreed (be nice to the cancer patient). I had the bar removed at one end of the living room and set up my office there. This was the one space in the house that I called mine—it was also the only space in my life I felt I still had control over—and since it didn't have a door, I was very territorial about who came into the living room when I was working.

"Would you mind leaving, please, that newspaper noise is driving me nuts."

"But I like to read the paper here. It's my favorite place for that. I really look forward to it."

"It's my office. You have three other rooms that are yours. Find one."

"No."

"No? No? Is that what you said? Look, nobody is allowed in this room when I'm working who doesn't have higher than a third-grade education or who can't read a goddamn newspaper without moving their lips."

"I hate it when you're snide. I'm going to read my newspaper."

I got up and walked over to her. "Get out."

"No."

We started yelling, louder and louder, screaming, red-faced and furious.

"Get out, you goddamn obnoxious bitch!"

"Get out yourself!"

I hit her. Again. And again. I kept hollering "Get out, goddamnit, get out!" I kept striking her, she kept screaming, "Stop hitting me! Stop hitting me!"

We finally collapsed on the sofa. I had never hit a woman before, and we both knew it.

"I'm leaving," I finally said. "I'm going back to San Francisco. I hate this place. I hate what we're doing to each other here. You can come or you can stay. It's up to you."

"God, it's beautiful! Look at that! It's absolutely beautiful!" I am talking to no one in particular. With my small penlight I have slowly made my way to the second room, and as I stand looking into it, I am totally captivated by what I see. The first thought that comes to mind is, Eden. This is the Garden of Eden.

Starting on the left, where a large desk should have been, and stretching out as far as I can see, is a dense jungle, lush, thick, moist, a thousand shades of richest green, wildlife roaming casually through the mists. In the center of this expansive forest is a huge tree, its uppermost branches reaching into the rain clouds above it, backlit by occasional sunlight. It is so idyllic, so peaceful, so inviting, so absolutely captivating that I . . .

"Step this way please."

"What? I beg your pardon?"
"Step this way please."
"Who are you? Don't touch me! Who are you?"
"Step this way please. I think you are lost."
"I'm not lost. Treya's lost. Look, you haven't seen a woman, have you, very beautiful, blond woman about . . ."
"If you're not lost, then where are you?"
"Well, OK, I thought I was in my house but . . ."
"Step this way please."

Looking back on it, Treya and I both felt that incident was a crucial turning point, not because striking a person is something to be proud of, but simply because it showed us how really desperate we both were. For Treya's part, she began letting up on her monopolizing tendencies, not because she thought I would hit her again, but because she began to realize how much those grasping tendencies were based on fear. For my part, I was learning the delicate task of establishing boundaries and announcing needs with someone who has a potentially terminal illness.

> He's fighting now for his own space, not being so accommodating, and it's refreshing because I don't have to expend so much energy wondering or guessing what would really make him happy and then feeling guilty if I get it wrong. As I once needed him to unconditionally support me (which he did!), I now need him to push against me, especially because I'm rather stubborn. He needs to keep pushing until I let go if it's important to him.

From that point on, things got better and better, slowly. We still had much work to do—we had both started seeing our old friend Seymour Boorstein for couples therapy, and it would be another year or so of work before things were back to normal—which meant, back to the extraordinary love that we had always had for each other, a love that had never died, but a love that had spent the better part of a year submerged in unrelenting pain.

10

A TIME TO HEAL

❦

" HELLO, Mr. Wilber?" I was sitting on the deck of our newly-rented house in Mill Valley, staring peacefully but rather blankly into the dense redwood trees, for which the area was famous.

"Yes."

"My name is Edith Zundel. I am from Bonn, West Germany. My husband, Rolf, and I are doing a book of interviews with a dozen or so avant-garde psychologists from around the world. I would like to interview you."

"I appreciate that, Edith, but I don't do interviews. But thanks, and good luck."

"I am staying with Frances Vaughan and Roger Walsh. I have come a long way and I would really like to be able to talk with you, please. It needn't take long."

Three squirrels were jumping back and forth between two enormous redwoods. I was trying to figure out if they were playing, mating, romancing, what?

"Here's the thing, Edith. I decided a long time ago not to give interviews or in any way appear in public as a teacher. The reason, other than the fact that I get nervous doing that, is that people tend to make me out as some sort of master or guru or teacher, and I'm not. In India they make a distinction between a pandit and a guru. A pandit [American "pundit"] is a simple scholar, or possibly a scholar-practitioner, a person who studies such topics as yoga, and possibly practices them as well, but who isn't enlightened. A guru is an enlightened master and teacher. I'm a pandit, not a guru. When it comes to practice, I'm a beginner like anybody else. So I've given maybe four interviews in the last fifteen years. I'll sometimes answer written questions, but that's about it."

"I can appreciate that, Mr. Wilber, but the synthesis that you have developed of Eastern and Western psychologies is uniquely yours, and I would like to talk to you as a scholar, not a guru. Your works are very influential in Germany, you know. You have had a major impact, not just on fringe areas, but in mainstream academic circles. All ten of your books have been translated into German."

The three squirrels had disappeared into the dense woods.

"Yes, my books are big hits in Germany and Japan." I decided to see if she had a sense of humor. "You know, the two peaceful countries."

Edith laughed for a long time, then said, "At least we appreciate genius when we see it."

"Mad genius, maybe. My wife and I have had some pretty rough times."

I wondered if there were such a thing as a squirrel call. Here, squirreley squirreley. . . .

"Frances and Roger told me about Terry. I'm very sorry. It seems so utterly senseless."

There was something completely endearing about Edith, even on the phone. Little did I know at the time what a crucial role she would play in our future.

"OK, Edith, come on over this afternoon. We'll talk."

Treya and I had moved back to the Bay Area, to the small town of Mill Valley, back to our friends, back to our doctors, back to our support systems. The entire Tahoe move had been a disaster, and we were both still recovering. But the corner had been turned. Even in Tahoe—once we made the decision to leave—things had begun to improve. Treya, in particular, had begun to regain her amazing equanimity and strength. She had started meditating again, and, as I said earlier, we both had started seeing Seymour for couples therapy, something we should have done on day one.

And so the simple lessons started coming home to us, beginning with acceptance and forgiveness. As the *Course in Miracles* put it:

> What could you want forgiveness cannot give? Do want peace? Forgiveness
> offers it. Do want happiness, a quiet mind, a certainty of purpose, and a

sense of worth and beauty that transcends the world? Do you want care and safety, and the warmth of sure protection always? Do you want a quietness that cannot be disturbed, a gentleness that never can be hurt, a deep abiding comfort, and a rest so perfect it can never be upset?

All this forgiveness offers you and more.

Forgiveness offers everything I want.

Today I have accepted this as true.

Today I have received the gifts of God.

I always liked the Course's reliance upon forgiveness as a way to remember the true Self. This is a somewhat unique approach, found in few of the other great wisdom traditions, which usually stress some form of awareness training or devotion. But the theory behind forgiveness is simple: The ego, the separate-self sense, is not just a cognitive construct, but also an affective one. That is, it is propped up not just by concepts but by emotions. And the primal emotion of the ego, according to this teaching, is fear followed by resentment. As the Upanishads put it, "Wherever there is other, there is fear."

In other words, whenever we split seamless awareness into a subject versus an object, into a self versus an other, then that self feels fear, simply because there are now so many "others" out there that can harm it. Out of this fear grows resentment. If we are going to insist on identifying with just the little self in here, then others are going to bruise it, insult it, injure it. The ego, then, is kept in existence by a collection of emotional insults; it carries its personal bruises as the fabric of its very existence. It actively collects hurts and insults, even while resenting them, because without its bruises, it would be, literally, nothing.

The ego's first maneuver in dealing with this resentment is to try to get others to confess their faults. "You hurt me; say you're sorry." Sometimes this makes the ego temporarily feel better, but does nothing to uproot the original cause. And, as often as not, even if the person does apologize, the likely result is now hatred of them. "I knew you did that to me; see, you just admitted it!" The fundamental mood of the ego: never forgive, never forget.

What the ego doesn't try is forgiveness, because that would undermine its very existence. To forgive others for insults, real or imagined, is to weaken the boundary between self and other, to dissolve the sense of separation between subject and object. And thus, with forgiveness, awareness tends to let go of the ego and its insults, and revert instead to the Witness, the Self, which views both subject and object equally. And thus, according to the *Course*, forgiveness is the way I let go of my self and remember my Self.

I found this practice extremely useful, especially when I didn't have the energy to meditate. My ego was so bruised, so injured—I had collected so many insults (real or imagined)—that forgiveness alone could begin to uncoil the pain of my own self-contraction. The more I got "hurt," the more contracted I got, which made the existence of "others" all the more painful, which made bruises all the more likely. And if I felt I couldn't forgive others for their "insensitivity" (in other words, the pain caused by my own self-contracting tendencies) then I used another affirmation from the *Course*: "God is the love with which I forgive."

And as for Treya, she began a profound psychological shift, an inner shift that began to resolve what she felt was the most central and difficult issue in her life, a shift that would reach fruition about a year later when she changed her name from Terry to Treya, a shift that for her meant: from doing to being.

Hooray! my period returned. Maybe I can have Ken's child after all! Things are certainly starting to look up. My energy's back to where I feel like running again. The moments of real exuberance and joy seem to come more often, more like before, but at the same time I also feel myself to be much calmer than before and particularly much less reactive to general situations. Life seems to be evening out. . . .

Of all things. Turns out Ken has some sort of viral infection that he probably caught last year in Incline. Dr. Belknap discovered it in an extensive blood panel—the same doctor that discovered my lump. Ken was skeptical—he thought it was major depression—so he had two other doctors check it out, and they all came up with the same diagnosis. Ken stopped interpreting his exhaustion as depression, and almost overnight his outlook changed, as you can imagine! He still has some anxiety—he's pretty burned by the whole ordeal—but the major depression just disappeared with the correct diagnosis. He still has the virus—apparently it's not contagious—but he's learning how to manage it, so his energy's coming back. God what he must have gone through, having that thing and not knowing it! Told me how he came close to suicide, which really scared me. The only reason I have ever been afraid of cancer is that I don't want to leave Ken. If he had done that, I don't know what I would have done. Maybe followed suit, that's how I felt at the time.

One of the good things that has come out of last year is that I find my perfectionism has died down considerably. It's a clown that has given me a lot of trouble and plays a large role in my scorpion of self-criticism. I'm always working on myself—a "gaining" idea that certainly implies I'm not all right the way I am. Somehow seeing that aspect of myself at work in the material world—like doing the Tahoe house, all the little details that had to be "just right"—and seeing how much trouble it's given me has helped diminish that self-destructive drive. I'm much more willing now to accept things as they are. All the grief I've gone through because of my rigidity, the idea that things should be just right, just so. So, so what? Life in this material world, not to mention the psychological, is fraught with difficulties. If we can get things to be OK, then that's enough. Perfect only leads to problems. If we tried to make everything perfect, then very little would be done. We'd spend all our time on details (one of my propensities) and lose sight of the broader picture, the meaning of it all. So I strive less for perfection, more at seeing how I can help things work out to be OK, and more for acceptance and forgiveness.

I'm also feeling more humility lately. I'm seeing more clearly how the things I'm dealing with in my life, the problems that come up in my friendships and in my marriage, my interpersonal problems, my doubts and fears, problems with money, questions over how to contribute to the world, uncertainty over what my calling is, wanting to find meaning in all the pain we go through . . . how all of that stuff is almost exactly like the things everyone else is working with. I think there's always been a part of me that felt like the little girl in the white house on the hill, that somehow the rules weren't meant for me, that I was different. What I'm discovering through all this is how I'm not different, how my issues are archetypal issues that other humans have been working with for centuries. And the feeling that comes from that is a new kind of humility, a new level of acceptance of things as they are, a new sense of okayness about things being as they are. And—which is nice—a greater sense of connectedness with others, like we're all parts of one being working on these issues and growing through that process. Like I'm not different also means I'm not separate.

It's like my focus has narrowed in some sense to just living for now. I feel more relaxed about doing what I'm doing, even if it doesn't satisfy my achiever subpersonality. I'm getting into simply doing what there is to do. Just letting some of that impatience drop away and chopping the particular stack of wood that's in front of me, not chasing after another one, and carrying water from the stream nearby, not traveling in search of another. Giving myself time to heal. Letting an open, quiet space develop and seeing what might eventually emerge from that.

Going for walks and hikes has been important—anything that's put me back in touch with my strength, has challenged me physically, and reminded me of the delicate beauty of sunsets or the soothing sound of the breeze in the trees or the satisfaction of watching the sun glint through drops of water.

Lately, putting in my garden has been the healthiest thing I've done. I've been out there almost every day, double digging the beds (which means digging out all kinds of rocks), planting lettuce and cauliflower and peas and spinach and carrots and radishes and cucumbers and tomatoes. Each seed looks so different, some are so tiny it's hard to believe there's so much genetic information in them, some are such odd shapes it's hard to believe they're seeds. The planting has been spread out over weeks—some things I've probably put in too late to get much in the way of a harvest—but I don't even care what it produces (did I say that! me the producer!), it's just a delight to watch seed leaves begin to poke their way through the carefully prepared soil, and then to watch the next set of leaves that proclaims the plant's identity, and to watch as each plant becomes so specifically itself. The peas with their little curling tendrils attaching themselves to the chicken wire—that may be my favorite plant to watch. Granted all the double digging was hard on my back, but the satisfaction of preparing good soil for the plants and then seeing them respond is incredibly healing. I feel back in touch with life through the garden, and it feels good to be taking care of the plants instead of needing such taking care of myself. It's good to be able to give instead of needing to receive. To see the fruits of my labors appear externally instead of being the one labored on. To start to take care of Ken, instead of needing so much care.

I remember all my years of trying to create purpose in my life, searching for that, thirsting for that. The effort of it, the strong desire. The image that comes up is of me reaching out, stretching, grasping, desiring. And the lesson of that, for me, was that it did not bring me peace or wisdom or happiness. I believe that's my lesson. Thus my path for now is predominantly Buddhist in flavor (but I'll study anybody). But I am not searching for enlightenment. I would not join a full moon group, which consists of people who have made the commitment to reach full enlightenment in this lifetime. I know that that kind of commitment is dangerous for me; it is either too soon or not the path for me at all. I need to learn how to not want to get anywhere. How to chop wood and carry water in fullness. Not grasping for more, craving for more, not desiring purpose. Just to live, and to allow.

I find that lately I am meditating regularly, for the first time in a while. And I think it is because of a change in approach. When I sit now I do not secretly wonder if I will have an interesting experience, if I will see light, if I will feel that rush of energy through my body. I do not sit with the purpose of "progressing" in my practice. I do not hunger for something to happen. Well, that is not entirely true. For the hunger and the desire do at times arise. But I notice them, release them, and return again to my current focus. When I wonder why I sit—and of course this question comes up regularly—I say to myself that I sit to express myself as I am in this moment. I sit because there is something in me that wants to give this quiet time of discipline as a kind of offering of myself. It is even a kind of affirmation, rather than a kind of seeking. Perhaps later purpose will come clear, free of the grasping I use to experience. Perhaps purpose is already here, unfolding as I let go.

With Kay Lynne that evening. Kay Lynne was saying that she sometimes feels very envious of others and doesn't quite know what to do about it. I imagine she was thinking of John, and of her brutally ended chance to share in that kind of future [John was tragically murdered the previous year by a robber]. I also imagined that seeing Ken and me together brought this up for her even more. She did mention a friend of hers who was coming to visit and noticing in herself a strong desire for a relationship, even though he's made it clear he's not interested in a committed relationship.

"This makes me really unhappy. I keep trying to make it stop but I can't. Any suggestions?"

"Ah, good old craving and aversion," I said. "Of course it makes you unhappy, it's just what the Buddhists say is the cause of all suffering. My only suggestion—and what I think works—comes straight from my vipassana meditation experiences. Just notice it, watch it, experience it fully. Right now, for example, you're aware that you're feeling that way, that you're feeling unhappy. That's good, that you notice it, that you observe it."

"That already feels better," she said. "I don't know why I have to learn that over so many times. I already feel relieved about it."

"My personal theory about this is that you don't have to make an effort to change or stop a certain behavior or thought you don't like. In fact, the effort gets in the way. The important thing is to see it clearly, to observe all its aspects, to just witness it, and every time it arises you see it, it doesn't catch you by surprise. Then I think there's some kind of mysterious something, you could call it our evolutionary impulse to grow toward our fullest potential, toward God, or whatever, but once you've cultivated awareness of the problem or defect or hangup, this mysterious something then seems able to keep us on course, to correct the defect. The change is not a question of will. Will is necessary to cultivate awareness, but it often gets in the way of that kind of subtle, profound inner change. That kind of change moves us in a direction of a way that's beyond our understanding and certainly beyond our capacity to consciously will. It's more of an allowing, an opening."

"A little like grace," she said. "I know exactly what you mean."

"Yes, that's it. Like grace. I hadn't thought of it that way before."

And I thought of the *Course in Miracles* lesson that's been sitting on my counter the last few days. The last lines are:

> By grace I live. By grace I am released.
> By grace I give. By grace I will release.

These lines never got to me before. Too much echo of the benevolent grace of a paternalistic father-figure god, forgiving his erring, sinning children. But now they made more sense. I could see grace as one way of describing what I call that mysterious something that seems to heal, to keep us heading in the right direction, to repair faults.

Treya and I were trying to allow that mysterious something to repair the faults, to heal the wounds, that we had both suffered over the last two years. We were realizing that healing occurs—and must occur—on all levels of being: physical, emotional, mental, and spiritual. And we were just beginning to realize that physical healing, although desirous, is often the least important or least indicative of genuine health, which is the health of the soul, the recovery of the soul. Treya and I were blanketing the Great Chain in our quest for healing. And we were helped in this by so many people, starting with Frances and Roger.

And then Seymour, whom we took to calling See-more. Seymour is a trained psychoanalyst who early on realized both the extreme importance of the Freudian model and its extreme limitations. He thus began to supplement his own approach with contemplative endeavors, using primarily vipassana meditation and the *Course in Miracles*. Seymour and I had known each other for almost ten years, ever since he had phoned me in Lincoln, Nebraska, to talk about some of the theoretical issues involved in trying to synthesize Eastern and Western approaches to psychotherapy. Seymour had been attracted to my work, and to my overall model of consciousness, because where others were trying to use Carl Jung as a foundation for East/West unification, I had realized early on that, although Jung had made some very important contributions to this area, he had also made some profound and very misleading errors, and that a sturdier *starting* point (but *not* end point) was Freud. This meshed with Seymour's observations, and we had become good friends.

As is so often the case in therapy—individual or couples—the really important breakthroughs are rather simple and obvious; the hard part is applying them in daily life, over and over and over again, until old habits are unlearned and gentler ones replace them. Seymour particularly helped us see that it wasn't so much what we said to each other, as how we said it.

Learning to focus more on *how* we say something, not just the content. Often each of us feels totally justified or right about the content, but we both say this "truth" in an unkind or angry or defensive or provocative way. And then we can't understand why the other reacts to the twist in the comment, not the content. The one biggest insight for me is understanding how our defensive styles interact with each other to set up a negative, downward spiral of reaction. Ken has been feeling anxiety lately, which surprises his friends (and me) because he never appears nervous. Instead, he gets angry and snide, his way of controlling anxiety. I couldn't see the anxiety, only the anger, which of course activated my fundamental fear, since childhood—that of being rejected and unloved. How do I react when I feel unloved? I withdraw, act cool, cover up, just like I used to retreat into my room to read as a little girl. My withdrawal makes Ken feel unloved, which makes him anxious, which makes him snide. I in turn become more withdrawn and rigid, and then my obsessive and controlling side takes over, I tend to issue orders, which makes Ken angry . . . and so on. I can see why at one point Ken refused to talk about any of our issues without, as he put it, someone to "referee." We could really batter each other. But when we start in this downward spiral in Seymour's office, the three of us can spot almost immediately the *first* step in this chain, and cut it off right there. The hard part, of course, is learning to do this outside of the office, but we're getting the hang of it.

After four or five months of this, Treya and I, with Seymour's ever-gentle help, had begun to turn the whole thing around. By the early summer of '86 we had reached a watershed.

It can't be June. I keep thinking it's May. It feels like it's been forever since I sat at this computer to write. I've been scribbling notes written with extra fine pens on tiny scraps of paper in ever tinier handwriting, how can I decipher these illegible signposts of moments of insight or fear or love or confusion?

But I know how I feel now. Better. Much better. Ken and I seem to have turned some kind of corner together. We don't fight now, at all, which is like it used to be, and we've learned to be more kind to each other. It takes awareness, some effort, to catch the reaction, the impulse to strike out, and learn to see underneath it the fear that fills the desire to hurt another. That's what we've been working on, what Seymour has been working with us on. And things are changing.

A good example. Taking a shower together, Ken asked me if I think we've made the right decision to move into this new house. I think so, I said, it will be good to have more room so you can get your books out, the other house was too small for Ken's library. His response was that he didn't care too much about the books now, all he was hoping was to get back into spiritual practice. I felt hurt by the whole topic, because he blamed me for not being able to write, and now he says that he doesn't care about the books. I was angry and hurt for most of the morning, but at least, thanks to Seymour, I didn't just dump this on Ken. I didn't say anything. But the first voice in my head was hurt and angry.

Then another voice within said things like wait a minute, how did this thing get started? You got defensive, didn't you? Why? Oh, you felt Ken was blaming you, you felt responsible for his not writing. You have a point, it does sound like he was blaming you. Why would he do that? Oh, he may not want to feel responsible himself, it might be easier for him to think it's your fault. What might be behind that? Maybe he's afraid it's his fault. Maybe he doesn't want to take responsibility for his not writing. Why would that come up just now? Ah, the new house with room for his books. Is he afraid that once in the house people might be expecting something from him (and they eagerly are), expecting him to write. Yes, I think that's it. He's afraid he won't live up to expectations and he defends himself against these expectations, against his fear of failure, by striking out at you.

As the second voice got closer to seeing fear at the root of our conflict, the first voice got less self-righteous. Once the fear lay exposed, I felt great compassion. Instead of a desire to defend myself in the face of Ken's "attack," I felt a desire to help him make this transition and to expect nothing from him. I could replay the scene and ask, how could I have handled this better? I could imagine myself no longer shrinking back in defeat, laying my head wearily against the shower wall, but saying—and meaning it—that would be great, honey, if you could get into meditating again in the new house. Whatever happens will be fine, and I think it's great that we're moving into a space that can help us heal.

Later that day I checked this scenario out with Ken, but very gently, no blame. He gave me a gold star, I hit it pretty close on the nose.

This feels like a real victory, and part of the other changes that are going on just now. There's some space now between my fear, the discomfort that results, and the defensive reaction. In that example I caught myself early enough in the reaction phase to back up and untangle what might have led to more conflict. I can feel more space too in my last individual session with Seymour. And more gentleness, more compassion, for others and for myself.

As important as these changes were in our relationship as a couple, the really crucial issues were being addressed on an individual level. Where I was getting a handle on my anxiety, Treya was confronting her archetypal issue: being versus doing, allowing versus controlling, trusting versus defending.

I feel more compassion for myself, more trusting. This is most noticeable in looking at my judgmentalness. In the last [individual] session with Seymour I noticed my discomfort at finally turning our attention to me, rather than to the relationship. I wanted to hide behind the relationship issues and not focus on me. So I talked about that, about my fear. It is now much easier for me to see and, especially, to acknowledge my fear. I'm less embarrassed by it. Somehow not wanting to talk about myself seemed related to something I noticed in myself years before, how difficult it is for me to acknowledge when someone says or does something that helps me understand myself. I tend to want to say something like "I already saw that" rather than, "Thanks, that helped." I think I find it hard to acknowledge help from someone because it makes me vulnerable, it puts me at their mercy in a way, that they could see me more clearly than I see myself. And even deeper than this, the important point, is the assumption that they would *judge* me for whatever they saw, they would have power over me, *not* that they would have compassion, for if I assumed that, then their insight into me could be the beginning of a deeper love connection. No, I assume that people will judge me, are judging me, always have judged me, will continue to judge me.

Because I judge myself. The old scorpion of self-criticism. And I am going to let that go, I am letting that go. Oh, I still have a way to go, but there has been a big shift within. I feel relieved. It seems it's been a long time since this process worked within me. Something has shifted, let go, opened up. I really feel I can start to trust, to allow, and not to force it, push it. And I can really let Ken's love in. It's funny, the first thing I wrote about him was "I trust him more than I trust the universe." It's true. It's been his love and trust just always being there, even in the worst times, that has helped me open up to this. Seymour says that before we can trust ourselves we have to trust somebody else.

Seymour also helped me understand my whole obsessional style better. He talked about my frittering my time away on all sorts of trivial details. That's largely at the root of my problem finding and doing what I want to do, I never seem to have the time. But the point is that that is classically the obsessive's way to keep things under control. In other words, obsessives do everything themselves. They don't trust others to do it—mistrust is at the root of the obsessional neurosis—so they try to control even the smallest details themselves. Again, trust. My big lesson.

As I said, Treya and I were covering, or at least trying to cover, all the bases—physical, emotional, mental, spiritual. On the physical level, I was learning to conserve energy and marshal my resources while the virus ran its course. Treya was exercising, jogging, going on long hikes. We both were continuing to refine our diet, based largely on general cancer-preventing measures (vegetarian, low fat, high fiber, high complex carbohydrates). I had long ago assumed the role of cook, at first out of necessity, then because I became rather good at it. At this point we were on a Pritikin-based diet, which I labored mightily to make palatable. And of course the megavitamins. On the emotional and mental levels, we were doing therapy, learning to digest and integrate various unresolved issues, and learning to rewrite our bruised scripts. And on the spiritual level, we were practicing acceptance and forgiveness, and attempting, in various ways, to reestablish the Witness, that calm center of equanimity in the midst of life's unending turmoils.

Although I had not yet started meditating again, both Treya and I had begun the search for a teacher we could both embrace. Treya's essential path was vipassana, the basic and core path of all forms of Buddhism, although she was also very fond of Christian mysticism and practiced the *Course in Miracles* daily for about two years. Although I was sympathetic to virtually any school of mysticism, East or West, I found the most powerful and profound form of mysticism to be Buddhist, and so my own practice had been, for fifteen years, Zen, the quintessential Buddhist path. But I was always attracted to Vajrayana Buddhism, the Tibetan form of tantric Buddhism, which is by far the most complete and well-rounded spiritual system to be found anywhere in the world. I was also drawn to several individual teachers who, although schooled in a particular tradition, transcended any categorization: Krishnamurti, Sri Ramana Maharshi, and Da Free John.

But Treya and I could never quite agree on a teacher, not one we could both follow wholeheartedly. I liked Goenka very much, but found vipassana to be much too narrow and limited for an overall approach. Treya liked Trungpa and Free John, but found their paths a bit too wild and crazy. We would finally find "our" teacher in Kalu Rinpoche, a Tibetan master of the highest accomplishment. In fact, it would be at an empowerment given by Kalu that Treya would have the stunning dream that made it clear to her that she had to change her name. In the meantime we continued the search, visiting, seeing, hanging out with, practicing with, the wildest assortment of teachers one could imagine: Father Bede Griffiths, Kobun Chino Roshi, Tai Situpa, Jamgon Kontrul, Trungpa Rinpoche, Da Free John, Katagiri Roshi, Pir Vilayat Khan, Father Thomas Keating. . . .

On Sunday we go to Green Gulch [of the San Francisco Zen Center], the first time in a long time. When we arrive there are lots of cars, so we know someone important is speaking. Turns out it's Katagiri Roshi, one of Ken's old Zen masters. We stand near the entrance of the overflowing zendo. I like Katagiri, he seems very direct and somehow there. Even though I can't understand everything he says. Even at that distance I can see how when he smiles his whole face smiles, every corner, every crevice, all of him. The Zen of smiling: when smiling, just smile! His head, of course, is shaved, an interesting, odd shape. I've never seen a head quite like this. Such a new-found interest in the shapes of peoples' heads underneath the hair.

Later, during the question and answer period after tea on the deck, someone asks him a question. I'm struck by his answer.

"If Buddha were to come to America today, which of his teachings do you think he would emphasize?"

"To be human, I think," Katagiri says. "Not to be an American, or Japanese, or whatever, but to be human. To be truly human. That is most important."

It strikes me at that point how appropriate it is for Americans to be so interested in spiritual teachers from other cultures. Certainly I've wondered about that, especially after having met so many from Tibet recently. I used to feel some sympathy with the criticism that we should look to our own culture, revive our own traditions, rather than naively and perhaps wrongly elevate exotic religions from elsewhere. But at this point I suddenly feel there's a certain rightness in this trend, and it has to do with being truly human. Studying a spiritual discipline with a man who speaks halting English with a thick Japanese accent (or Indian, or Tibetan) can be an experience, not of cultural differences, but of how we are all working simply toward becoming more fully human. And thus also more divine, perhaps.

That evening Ken and I have dinner with Katagiri and David [Chadwick] in the Lindisfarne Center. Bill [William Irwin] Thompson, director of Lindisfarne and married to a friend of mine from Findhorn, took me on a tour of it a few years ago when it was almost finished. Small world it is. Ken and Katagiri reminisce about a sesshin [Zen intensive practice session] that Ken did with him in Lincoln, almost ten years ago, when Ken had a satori experience—"real little one," Ken added—which happened when Katigiri said, "The Witness is the last stand of the ego." They talked about this and laughed and laughed. Some sort of Zen joke, I thought. Seems there are a few pretty crazy spiritual seekers out there on the plains they both know.

Katagiri is very unassuming and somehow warms my heart. Some feel he's the true successor to Suzuki Roshi. I feel interested in studying with him and meditating at the Zen Center and seeing where that might lead. I'm no longer looking for perfection on the spiritual path either. It would be lovely to find a teacher I fall in love with, but that may take time and it makes no sense to wait for that. Perhaps, who knows, he's sitting in front of me at the moment only I just don't know it yet.

The next night we're having dinner with some friends who are members of the Johanine Daist Community and devotees of Da Free John. Ken had written an introduction to one of Free John's books and has just given a strong endorsement of his latest, *The Dawn Horse Testament*. Great people. I always look at a teacher's senior students to see what the teacher is really like, and these people are about as great as you get. We're watching a videotape of Free John, and I find I like him more than I expected. I think the path of the devotee, even the word devotee, has put me off. In the video he says the process first involves studying his written teachings (there's a lot of them!). Then, when that is understood, and if you feel the pull, one moves into closer relationship with him. It sounds like your life is totally controlled by him and his teachings once you are a devotee, and I have to admit I resist that. It's probably the very neurosis I most need to deal with, but only when I'm ready.

Later I find, reading *The Dawn Horse Testament*, that he outlines two clear paths. One is that of the devotee, the other is that of inquiry. This is exactly what Ken is talking about with other-power and self-power. I like what he says in this book, especially about relationship, about how the ego is nothing but the contraction or avoidance of relationship. I certainly recognize in myself when he describes the ego as reactive and contracting away from relationship. I recognize myself as often feeling rejected and then engaging in the "egoic ritual" of defending myself against what I see as insults or hurts. When I'm reacting in a hurt way—which means withdrawing, avoiding, usually through defending myself—to what I see as rejection, it helps to think of his teaching that I must stop dramatizing the situation as being betrayed, stop reacting, stop rejecting and punishing others when I feel rejected. I must not withhold love, dissociate myself, but instead be vulnerable and suffer myself to be wounded. "Practice the wound of love," he says, you can't help but be wounded, just notice it, don't contract, and continue to love. "If you are merely hurt, you will still know the need for love, and you will still know the need to love."

"Step this way please."

I can't make out the Figure next to me at all. Something is gently pulling at my elbow. I would strike out, or yank back, if I could even vaguely see what it is that I might react against. I slowly point the penlight in the direction of the Figure, but the light just seems to disappear, to enter this thing and not come out. It has a definite shape, however, because it is much darker than the surroundings, which are already rather black. Then it dawns on me. This Figure isn't dark, it is the absence of either light or dark. It's there, but it is not.

"Look, I don't know who you are, but this is my house and I'll thank you to leave." I start laughing nervously. *"Or I'll call the cops."* I laugh because, the cops?

"Step this way please."

I decided to move off the porch and back into the house. Edith, I supposed, would be over in about an hour and I needed to get some lunch. The squirrels were gone for good, anyway. Treya was in Tahoe, finishing up some of her things in order to move more permanently to the new Mill Valley house.

All in all, things were going quite well; or at least, improving rapidly. As Treya told Seymour, she thought a corner had been turned; several corners, actually, and I agreed.

I got a sandwich and a Coke and sat back down on the porch. The sun was just starting to rise above the gigantic redwoods, so tall they hid the light every day until almost noon. I always looked forward to that, to the sun hitting me on the face and reminding me that there are always new beginnings.

I thought of Treya. Her beauty, her integrity, her honesty, her pure spirit, her enormous love of life, her astonishing strength. The Good, the True, and the Beautiful. God I love that woman! How could I have ever blamed her for my ordeals? Caused her such pain? The best thing that had ever happened to me! I knew from the moment I had met her that I would do anything, go anywhere, suffer any pain, to be with her, help her, hold her. That was a profound decision I had made, on the very deepest level of my being—and then to forget that decision, blame someone else!—no wonder I felt I had lost my soul. I had. By my own hand.

I had forgiven Treya. I was in the much slower process of forgiving myself.

I thought of Treya's courage. She simply refused, absolutely refused, to let this ordeal get her down. Life knocked her down, she got right back up. Life knocked her down, she got right back up. If anything the events of the last year had increased her enormous resiliency. I turned my face to warm the other side. It always felt like the sun was energizing my brain, pouring light into my brain. Probably, I thought, during the first part of Treya's life, her strength came from her being able to fight. Now, I thought, it started to come from her being able to surrender. Where before she would square off and take the world on, now she opened up and let it all come pouring through. But it was the same strength, backed by one overwhelming factor: an absolutely uncompromising honesty. Even in the worst of times, there is one thing I had never seen her do: I had never seen her lie.

The phone rang. I decided to let the answering machine record the message. "Hello, Terry, this is Dr. Belknap's office. Could you please come in and see the doctor?"

I raced to the phone and yanked it up. "Hello? This is Ken. What's up?"

"The doctor would like to discuss some test results with Terry."

"Nothing's wrong, is there?"

"The doctor will explain."

"Come on, ma'am."

"The doctor will explain."

11

PSYCHOTHERAPY AND SPIRITUALITY

"Hi, Edith, come on in. Give me a few minutes, would you? Just got a weird call. I'll be right back." I went in the bathroom, splashed water on my face, and looked in the mirror. I don't remember what went through my mind. But then, as so often happens to people in these circumstances, I simply dissociated: the whole nightmare that was surely awaiting us in the doctor's office I simply sealed out of awareness. A blanket denial settled on my soul, which allowed me to put on my professor's persona for the interview, and out I walked, with a plaster smile, to meet Edith.

What was it about Edith that was so likable? She was in her early fifties, I guessed, with a bright and open face, almost transparent at times, but nonetheless very strong and firm and sure. Somehow, within just a few minutes, her presence seemed to announce loyalty, seemed to say that she would do literally anything for a friend, and do so gladly. She smiled most of the time, and it was in no way forced, nor did it seem to hide or deny the pain of being human. That was part of it: a very strong and yet very vulnerable person, who smiled in the midst of angst.

As my mind continued to seal off the probable future, I was struck, for the first time really, by the strange aura that had developed around me due to my refusal, for the past fifteen years, to give interviews or appear in public. A simple decision it was for me, and yet it had generated rather intense speculation, usually centering on the question, did I even exist? For the first fifteen minutes, my "invisibility" is all Edith wanted to discuss, and when her article appeared in Die Zeit, this is exactly how it started:

He is a hermit, I heard of Ken Wilber, one can't interview him. It made me still more curious than I was anyhow. So far I knew him just from reading, which indicated that he possessed encyclopedic knowledge, an open mind for very divergent paradigms, a precise style full of powerful pictures, unusual combinatory vision and rare clarity of thinking.

I wrote to him. When I got no answer I flew to Japan, to a congress of the International Transpersonal Association. According to the program, Wilber was one of the speakers. Japan in the spring was very beautiful, the encounter with Japanese cultural and religious traditions unforgettable, but Ken Wilber was not there. In spite of that he was "present": many hopes were projected on him. To be invisible is not a bad public relations technique—if your name is Ken Wilber.

I asked who knew him. The President of the Association, Cecil Burney: "We are friends. He is sociable and quite unpretentious." How did he manage—born 1949, 37 years young—to have written ten books already? "He is working very hard and he is a genius," came the laconic reply.

With the help of friends and his German publishing houses I later tried again to get an interview. Already in San Francisco I still had no definite assent. And then, suddenly, he is on the phone: "Sure, come on over." We meet in his house. The living room is furnished with garden table and chairs, through a half-open door one sees a mattress on the floor. Ken Wilber, barefoot, his shirt open—it is a warm summer day—puts a glass of juice on the table for me and laughs: "I do exist."

"You see, Edith, I do exist," I laughed as we sat down. The whole thing was enormously funny to me, and I thought of Garry Trudeau's line: "I am trying to cultivate a life-style that does not require my presence."

"What can I do for you, Edith?"

"Why don't you give interviews?"

And I told her all my reasons—mostly that I find them too distracting, and that anyway all I really wanted to do was write. Edith listened intently, and smiled, and I could feel her warmly reaching out. There was something very motherly in her way, and the kindness in her voice, for some reason, made it all the harder for me to forget the background dread that every few minutes attempted to surface.

We talked for hours, ranging over an enormous number of topics, which Edith discussed with ease and intelligence. As she moved to the main topic of the interview, she switched on her tape recorder.

EZ: Rolf and I, and our readers, are particularly interested in the interface between psychotherapy and religion.

KW: And by religion you mean what? Fundamentalism? Mysticism? Exoteric? Esoteric?

EZ: Well, that's a good place to start. In *A Sociable God* you give, I believe, eleven different definitions of religion, or eleven different ways the word religion is used.

KW: Yes, well, my point was that we really can't talk about science and religion or psychotherapy and religion or philosophy and religion until we decide just what it is we mean by the word religion. And for our purposes right now I think we must at least distinguish between what is known as exoteric religion and esoteric religion. Exoteric or "outer" religion is mythic religion, religion that is terribly concrete and literal, that really believes, for example, that Moses parted the Red Sea, that Christ was born from a virgin, that the world was created in six days, that manna once literally rained down from heaven, and so on. Exoteric religions the world over consist of those types of beliefs. The Hindus believe that the earth, since it needs to be supported, is sitting on an elephant which, since it needs to be supported, is sitting on a tortoise which in turn is sitting on a serpent. And to the question, "On what, then, is the serpent sitting?" the answer is given, "Let us now change the subject." Lao Tzu was nine hundred years old when he was born, Krishna made love to four thousand cow maidens, Brahma was born from a crack in a cosmic egg, and so on. That's exoteric religion, a series of belief structures that attempt to explain the mysteries of the world in mythic terms rather than direct experiential or evidential terms.

EZ: So exoteric or outer religion is basically a matter of belief, not evidence.

KW: Yes. If you believe all the myths, you are saved; if not, you go to Hell—no discussion. Now you find that type of religion the world over—fundamentalism. I have no quarrel with that; it's just that that type of religion, exoteric religion, has nothing to do with mystical religion or esoteric religion or experiential religion, which is the type of religion or spirituality that I'm interested in.

EZ: Esoteric means what?

KW: Inner or hidden. The reason that esoteric or mystical religion is hidden is not that it is secret or anything, but that it is a matter of direct experience and personal awareness. Esoteric religion asks you to believe nothing on faith or obediently swallow any dogma. Rather, esoteric religion is a set of personal experiments that you conduct scientifically in the laboratory of your own awareness. Like all good science, it is based on direct experience, not mere belief or wish, and it is publicly checked or validated by a peer group of those who have also performed the experiment. The experiment is meditation.

EZ: But meditation is private.

KW: No it isn't. Not any more so than, say, mathematics. There is no external proof, for example, that negative one squared equals one; there is no sensory or empirical proof for that. That happens to be true, but it is proven to be true only by an internal logic. You can't find negative one in the external world; you find it only in your mind. But that doesn't mean it isn't true, that doesn't mean it is only private knowledge that can't be publicly validated. That only means that its truth is validated by a community of trained mathematicians, by those who know how to internally run the logical experiment that will decide whether it is true or not. Just so, meditative knowledge is internal knowledge, but knowledge that can be publicly validated by a community of trained meditators, those who know the internal logic of the contemplative experience. We don't let anybody vote on the truth of the Pythagorean theorem; we let trained mathematicians vote on that truth. Likewise, meditative spirituality makes certain claims—for example, that the inward sense of the self is, if you look at it closely, one with the feeling of the external world—but that is a truth to be checked experimentally and experientially by you and anybody else who cares to try the experiment. And after something like six thousand years of this experiment, we are perfectly justified in making certain conclusions, making certain spiritual theorems, as it were. And those spiritual theorems are the core of the perennial wisdom traditions.

EZ: But why is it called "hidden"?

KW: Because if you don't perform the experiment, then you don't know what's going on, you are not allowed to vote, just as if you don't learn mathematics you are not allowed to vote on the truth of the Pythagorean theorem. I mean, you can form opinions about it, but mysticism is not interested in opinions but in knowledge. Esoteric religion or mysticism is hidden to the mind that won't perform the experiment; that's all it means.

EZ: But religions vary so much from each other.

KW: Exoteric religions vary tremendously from each other; esoteric religions the world over are virtually identical. Mysticism or esotericism is, in the broad sense of the word, scientific, as we have seen, and just as you don't have German chemistry versus American chemistry, you don't have Hindu mystical science versus Muslim mystical science. Rather, they are in fundamental agreement as to the nature of the soul, the nature of Spirit, and the nature of their supreme identity, among many other things. This is what scholars mean by "the transcendental unity of the world's religions"—they mean esoteric religions. Of course, their surface structures vary tremendously, but their deep structures are virtually identical, reflecting the unanimity of the human spirit and its phenomenologically disclosed laws.

EZ: This is very important, then: I take it that you do not believe, as Joseph Campbell does, that mythic religions carry any valid spiritual knowledge.

KW: You are free to interpret exoteric religious myths any way you like. You are free, as Campbell does, to interpret myths as being allegories or metaphors for transcendental truths. Free, for example, to interpret the virgin birth as meaning that Christ operated spontaneously from his true Self, capital S. I happen to believe that. The problem is, mythic believers do not believe that. They believe, as a test of their faith, that Mary really was a biological virgin when she got pregnant. Mythic believers do *not* interpret their myths allegorically, they interpret them literally and concretely. Joseph Campbell violates the fabric of mythic beliefs in his very attempt to salvage them. This is unacceptable scholarship. It says to the mythic believer, "I know what you *really* mean by that." But the problem is, that is *not* what *they* mean by that. His approach is fundamentally wrong right at the start, in my opinion.

These types of myths are very common in the six- to eleven-year-old; they are produced naturally and easily by the level of mind that Piaget calls concrete operational. Virtually all of the fundamentals of the world's great exoteric myths can be culled from the spontaneous productions of today's seven-year-olds, as Campbell himself acknowledges. But once the next structure of consciousness—called formal operational or rational—emerges, the mythic productions are abandoned by the child himself. He himself no longer believes them, unless he is in a society that rewards such beliefs. But by and large the rational and reflexive mind finds myths to be just that, myths. Once useful and necessary, but no longer sustainable. They do not carry the evidential knowledge that they claim to carry, and thus, once they are actually or scientifically checked, they fall apart. The rational mind looks at, say, the virgin birth and just grins. This woman gets pregnant, goes to her husband and says, "Look, I'm pregnant, but don't worry, I didn't sleep with another man. The real father is not from this planet."

EZ: [Laughing] But some followers of mythic religions do in fact interpret their myths allegorically or metaphorically.

KW: Yes, and they are the mystics. In other words, the mystics are the ones who give an esoteric or "hidden" meaning to the myths, and those meanings are discovered in the direct interior and contemplative experience of the soul, not in some outward belief system or symbol or myth. In other words, they aren't mythic believers at all, but contemplative phenomenologists, contemplative mystics, contemplative scientists. This is why historically, as Alfred North Whitehead pointed out, mysticism has always allied itself with science as against the Church, because both mysticism and science depend on direct consensual evidence. Newton was a great scientist; he was also a profound mystic, and there was, is, no conflict there whatsoever. You cannot, on the other hand, be a great scientist and a great mythic believer at the same time.

Moreover, they, the mystics, are the ones who agree that their religion is basically identical in essence to other mystical religions, that "they call Him many who is really One." Now you will not find a mythic believer, say a fundamentalist Protestant, saying that Buddhism is also a way to perfect salvation. Mythic believers maintain that they have the only way, because they base their religion on outward myths, which are everywhere different, so they don't realize the inner unity hidden in the outer symbols. The mystics do.

EZ: Yes, I see. So you do not agree with Carl Jung that myths carry archetypal and in that sense mystical or transcendental importance?

It has to be cancer, is all I thought at that moment. What else could it be? The doctor will explain. The doctor will explain. The doctor . . . can go jump in the lake. Damn! Damn! Damn! Where was the denial and repression when I really needed it?

But in a sense, denial and repression is what Edith was here to talk about. We were to discuss, principally, the relation between psychotherapy and spirituality. And we were to do this by going into the general model that I had developed which related these two most important attempts at human understanding.

This was no mere academic concern for me, or for Treya. We were both deeply involved in our own therapy, with Seymour and others, and we had both been long-term meditators. And how did the two relate to each other? This was a constant topic of conversation between Treya and me, and our friends. I think one of the reasons I had agreed to talk with Edith was exactly that this issue was now central to my life, in both a theoretical and a very practical sense.

But, as Edith's question came floating back into my mind, I realized that we had reached a formidable obstacle to our discussion: Carl Gustav Jung.

I figured this question would come up. Then, as now, the towering figure of Carl Jung—Campbell is but one of his many followers—utterly dominates the field of the psychology of religion. When I first began in this field, I, like most, was a strong believer in Jung's central concepts and in the pioneering efforts he had made in this area. But over the years I had come to believe that Jung had made some profound errors, and these errors were now the single greatest obstacle within the field of transpersonal psychology, made all the worse by the fact that they were so widespread and so apparently unchallenged. No conversation about psychology and religion could really even get started until this difficult and delicate topic was addressed, and so for the next half hour or so Edith and I went into it. Did I, in fact, disagree with Jung that myths were archetypal and therefore mystical?

KW: Jung found that modern men and women can spontaneously produce virtually all of the main themes of the world's mythic religions; they do so in dreams, in active imagination, in free association, and so on. From this he deduced that the basic mythic forms, which he called archetypes, are common in all people, are inherited by all people, and are carried in what he called the collective unconscious. He then made the claim that, and I quote, "mysticism is experience of the archetypes."

In my opinion there are several crucial errors in that view. One, it is definitely true that the mind, even the modern mind, can spontaneously produce mythic forms that are essentially similar to the forms found in mythic religions. As I said, the preformal stages of the mind's development, particularly preoperational and concrete operational thought, are myth-producing by their very nature. Since all modern men and women pass through those stages of development in childhood, of course all men and women have spontaneous access to that type of mythic thought-producing structure, especially in dreams, where primitive levels of the psyche can more easily surface.

But there's nothing mystical about that. Archetypes, according to Jung, are basic mythic *forms* devoid of content; mysticism is *formless* awareness. There's no point of contact.

Second, there is Jung's whole use of the word "archetype," a notion he borrowed from the great mystics, such as Plato and Augustine. But the way Jung uses the term is *not* the way those mystics use the term, nor in fact the way mystics the world over use that concept. For the mystics—Shankara, Plato, Augustine, Eckhart, Garab Dorje, and so on—archetypes are the first subtle forms that appear as the world manifests out of formless and unmanifest Spirit. They are the patterns upon which all other patterns of manifestation are based. From the Greek *arche typon*, original pattern. Subtle, transcendental forms that are the first forms of manifestation, whether that manifestation is physical, biological, mental, whatever. And in most forms of mysticism, these archetypes are nothing but radiant patterns or points of light, audible illuminations, brilliantly colored shapes and luminosities, rainbows of light and sound and vibration—out of which, in manifestation, the material world condenses, so to speak.

But Jung uses the term as certain basic mythic structures that are collective to human experience, like the trickster, the shadow, the Wise Old Man, the ego, the persona, the Great Mother, the anima, the animus, and so on. These are not so much transcendental as they are existential. They are simply facets of experience that are common to the *everyday* human condition. I agree that those mythic forms are collectively inherited in the psyche. And I agree entirely with Jung that it is very important to come to terms with those mythic "archetypes."

If, for example, I am having psychological trouble with my mother, if I have a so-called mother complex, it is important to realize that much of that emotional charge comes not just from my individual mother but from the Great Mother, a powerful image in my collective unconscious that is in essence the distillation of mothers everywhere. That is, the psyche comes with the image of the Great Mother embedded in it, just as the psyche comes already equipped with the rudimentary forms of language and of perception and of various instinctual patterns. If the Great Mother image is activated, I am not dealing with just my individual mother, but with thousands of years of the human experience with mothering in general, so the Great Mother image carries a charge and has an impact far beyond what anything my own mother could possibly do on her own. Coming to terms with the Great Mother, through a study of the world's myths, is a good way to deal with that mythic form, to make it conscious and thus differentiate from it. I agree *entirely* with Jung on that matter. But those mythic forms have nothing to do with mysticism, with genuine transcendental awareness.

Let me explain it more simply. Jung's major mistake, in my opinion, was to confuse collective with transpersonal (or mystical). Just because my mind inherits certain collective forms does not mean those forms are mystical or transpersonal. We all collectively inherit ten toes, for example, but if I experience my toes I am not having a mystical experience! Jung's "archetypes" have virtually nothing to do with genuinely spiritual, transcendental, mystical, transpersonal awareness; rather, they are collectively inherited forms that distill some of the very basic, everyday, existential encounters of the human condition—life, death, birth, mother, father, shadow, ego, and so on. Nothing mystical about it. Collective, yes; transpersonal, no.

There are collective prepersonal, collective personal, and collective transpersonal elements; and Jung does not differentiate these with anything near the clarity that they demand, and this skews his entire understanding of the spiritual process, in my opinion.

So I agree with Jung that it is very important to come to terms with the forms in both the personal and the collective mythic unconscious; but neither one of those has much to do with real mysticism, which is first, finding the light beyond form, then, finding the formless beyond the light.

EZ: But coming across archetypal material in the psyche can be a very powerful, sometimes overwhelming experience.

KW: Yes, because they are collective; their power is way beyond the individual; they have the power of a million years of evolution behind them. But collective is not transpersonal. The power of the "real archetypes," the transpersonal archetypes, comes directly from being the first forms of timeless Spirit; the power of the Jungian archetype comes from being the oldest forms in temporal history.

As even Jung realized, it is necessary to move away from the archetypes, to differentiate from them, to be free of their power. This process he called individuation. And again, I agree entirely with him on that issue. One must differentiate from the Jungian archetype.

But one must *move toward* the real archetypes, the transpersonal archetypes, ultimately to have one's identity shift entirely to that transpersonal form. Big difference. The only Jungian archetype that is genuinely transpersonal is the Self, but even his discussion of that is weakened, in my opinion, by failing to sufficiently emphasize its ultimately nondual character. So . . .

EZ: OK, I think that's very clear. So now I believe we can return to our original topic. I guess I would ask . . .

Edith's enthusiasm was infectious. Her smile lit up from question to question, she never seemed to tire. And it was her enthusiasm more than anything that helped keep my mind off that background dread that was menacing in its caress. I got Edith some more juice.

EZ: I guess I would ask, what is the relation between esoteric religion and psychotherapy? In other words, what is the relation between meditation and psychotherapy, since both claim to change consciousness, to heal the soul? You address this issue very carefully in *Transformations of Consciousness*. Perhaps you could just summarize that statement.

KW: All right. I suppose the easiest way is for me to explain the diagram in *Transformations* (see p. 184). The overall idea is simple: Growth and development occur through a series of stages or levels, from the least developed and least integrated to the most developed and most integrated. There are probably dozens of different levels and types of levels of growth; I have selected nine of the most important. These are listed in column one, "basic structures of consciousness."

Now, as the self develops at each stage, things can go either relatively well or relatively poorly. If things go well, the self develops normally and moves on to the next stage in a relatively well-functioning way. But if things go persistently badly at a given stage, then various pathologies can develop, and the type of pathology, the type of neurosis, depends precisely on the stage or level at which the problem occurs.

In other words, at each stage or level of development, the self is faced with certain tasks. How it negotiates those tasks determines whether it winds up relatively healthy or relatively disturbed. First and foremost, at each stage of development, the self starts out identified with that stage, and it must accomplish the tasks appropriate to that stage, whether learning toilet training or learning language. But in order for development to continue, the self has to let go of that stage, or disidentify with it, in order to make room for the new and higher stage. In other words, it has to *differentiate* from the lower stage, *identify* with the higher stage, and then *integrate* the higher with the lower.

This task of differentiation and then integration is called a "fulcrum"—it just means a major turning point or a major step in development. So in column two, labeled "corresponding fulcrums," we have the nine major fulcrums or turning points that correspond to the nine major levels or stages of consciousness development. If anything goes persistently wrong at a given fulcrum, then you get a specific and characteristic pathology. These nine major pathologies are listed in column three, "characteristic pathologies." Here you find things like psychoses, neuroses, existential crises, and so on.

Finally, different treatment methods have evolved over the years to treat these various pathologies, and I've listed those treatments in column four, "treatment modalities," the treatments that I think have been demonstrated to be the best or more appropriate for each particular problem. And this is exactly where the relation of psychotherapy and meditation comes in, as I guess we'll see.

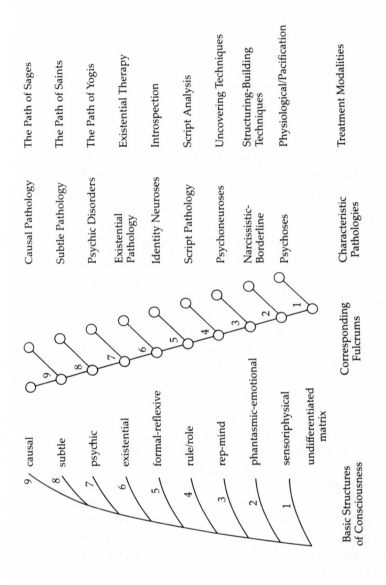

Basic Structures of Consciousness	Corresponding Fulcrums	Characteristic Pathologies	Treatment Modalities
9 causal	9	Causal Pathology	The Path of Sages
8 subtle	8	Subtle Pathology	The Path of Saints
7 psychic	7	Psychic Disorders	The Path of Yogis
6 existential	6	Existential Pathology	Existential Therapy
5 formal-reflexive	5	Identity Neuroses	Introspection
4 rule/role	4	Script Pathology	Script Analysis
3 rep-mind	3	Psychoneuroses	Uncovering Techniques
2 phantasmic-emotional	2	Narcissistic-Borderline	Structuring-Building Techniques
1 sensoriphysical	1	Psychoses	Physiological/Pacification
undifferentiated matrix			

CORRELATION OF STRUCTURES, FULCRUMS, PSYCHOPATHOLO-
GIES, AND TREATMENTS

Reprinted from Ken Wilber, Jack Engler, and Daniel P. Brown, *Transformations of Consciousness: Conventional and Contemplative Perspectives on Development* (Boston & Shaftesbury: Shambhala Publications, 1986), p. 145. Diagram copyright © 1986 by Ken Wilber.

EZ: There is a tremendous amount of information packed into that simple diagram. Why don't we go over each of its points in a little more detail. Start with a brief explanation of the basic structures of consciousness.

KW: Basic structures are the fundamental building blocks of awareness, things like sensations, images, impulses, concepts, and so on. I have listed nine major basic structures, which are just an expanded version of what is known in the perennial philosophy as the Great Chain of Being: matter, body, mind, soul, and spirit. In ascending order, the nine levels are:

One, the sensoriphysical structures—these include the material components of the body plus sensation and perception. This is what Piaget called sensorimotor intelligence; what Aurobindo called the physical-sensory; what Vedanta calls the *annamaya-kosha*, and so on.

Two, the phantasmic-emotional—this is the emotional-sexual level, the level of impulse, of libido, élan vital, bioenergy, *prana*. Plus the level of images, the first mental forms. Images—what Arieti calls the "phantasmic level"—start to emerge in the infant around seven months or so.

Three, the representational mind, or rep-mind for short—what Piaget called preoperational thinking. It consists of symbols, which emerge between the ages of two and four years, and then concepts, which emerge between the ages of four and seven.

EZ: What is the difference between images, symbols, and concepts?

KW: An image represents a thing by looking like that thing. It's fairly simple. The image of a tree, for example, looks more or less like a real tree. A symbol represents a thing but it doesn't look like that thing, which is a much harder and higher task. For example, the word "Fido" represents your dog, but it doesn't look like the real dog at all, and so it's harder to hold in mind. That's why words emerge only after images. Finally, a concept represents a *class* of things. The concept of "dog" means all possible dogs, not just Fido. A harder task still. A symbol denotes, a concept connotes. But symbols and concepts together we refer to as the preoperational or representational mind.

EZ: And next, the rule/role mind?

KW: Level four, the rule/role mind, develops between the ages of seven and eleven or so, what Piaget called concrete operational thinking. The Buddhists call it the *manovijñana*, the mind concretely operating on sensory experience. I call it rule/role, because it is the first structure that can perform rule-dominated thinking, like multiplication or division, and it is the first structure that can take the role of other, or actually assume a perspective different from its own. It's a very important structure. Piaget calls it *concrete* operational because, although it can perform complex operations, it does so in a very concrete and literal way. This is the structure, for example, that thinks that myths are concretely true, literally true. I would like to emphasize that.

Level five, which I call formal-reflexive, is the first structure that can not only think but think about thinking. It is thus highly introspective, and it is capable of hypothetical reasoning, or testing propositions against evidence. What Piaget called formal operational thinking. It typically emerges in adolescence, and is responsible for the burgeoning self-consciousness and wild idealism of that period. Aurobindo refers to this as the "reasoning mind"; Vedanta calls it the *manomaya-kosha*.

Level six is existential, or vision-logic, a logic which is not divisive but inclusive, integrating, networking, joining. What Aurobindo called the "higher mind"; in Buddhism, the *manas*. It is a very integrative structure. Particularly, it is capable of integrating the mind and body into a higher-order union, which I call the "centaur," symbolizing mind-body union (not identity).

Level seven is called psychic, which doesn't mean psychic capacities per se, although these might begin to develop here. But basically it just means the beginning stages of transpersonal, spiritual, or contemplative development. What Aurobindo called the "illumined mind."

Level eight is called the subtle, or the intermediate stage of spiritual development, the home of various luminous forms, divine forms or Deity forms, known as *yidam* in Buddhism and *ishtadeva* in Hinduism (not to be confused with the collective mythic forms of levels three and four). The home of a personal God, the home of the "real" transpersonal archetypes and supra-individual forms. Aurobindo's "intuitive mind"; *vijñanamaya-kosha* in Vedanta; in Buddhism, the *alaya-vijñana*.

Level nine is the causal, or the pure unmanifest source of all the other and lower levels. The home, not of a personal God, but of a formless Godhead or Abyss. Aurobindo's "overmind"; in Vedanta, the *anandamaya-kosha*, the bliss body.

Finally, the paper on which the entire diagram is drawn represents ultimate reality, or absolute Spirit, which is not a level among other levels but the Ground and Reality of all levels. Aurobindo's "super-mind"; in Buddhism, the pure *alaya*; in Vedanta, *turiya*.

EZ: So level one is matter, level two is body, levels three, four, and five are mind.

KW: That's right. And level six is an integration of the mind and body, what I call the centaur, levels seven and eight are soul, and level nine plus the paper are Spirit. As I said, it's just an elaboration on matter, body, mind, soul, and spirit, but done in a way that can tie it up with psychological research in the West.

EZ: So at each of the nine levels of consciousness growth, the self is faced with various tasks.

KW: Yes. The infant starts out at stage one, which is basically the material or physical level. Its emotions—level two—are very crude and undeveloped, and it has no capacity for symbols, concepts, rules, and so forth. It is basically a physiological self. Moreover, it is undifferentiated from the mothering one and the material world around it, so-called adualism or oceanic or protoplasmic awareness.

EZ: Many theorists maintain that this oceanic or undifferentiated state is a type of proto-mystical state, since the subject and object are one. That this state is the unity state that is regained in mysticism. Do you agree with that?

The squirrels were back! In and out of the giant redwood trees, playing in the bliss of ignorance. I wondered if you could sell your soul, not to the Devil but a squirrel.

When Edith brought up the subject of the infantile fusion state being something of a prototype of mysticism, she had hit upon the most hotly debated issue in transpersonal circles. Many theorists, following Jung, maintained that since mysticism is a subject/object union, then this early undifferentiated fusion state must be what is somehow *recaptured* in mystical unity. Being an earlier follower of Jung, I had agreed with that position, and had indeed written several essays explaining it. But as with so much of Jung, it was now a position I found completely untenable. And more than that, annoying, because it unmistakably meant that mysticism is a regressive state of some sort or another. This was, as they say, a real sore spot with me.

KW: Just because the infant can't tell the difference between subject and object, theorists think that state is some sort of mystical union. It's nothing of the sort. The infant doesn't transcend subject and object, the infant just can't differentiate them in the first place. Mystics are perfectly aware of the conventional difference between subject and object, they are simply also aware of the larger background identity that unites them.

Moreover, the mystical union is a union with *all* levels of existence, physical, biological, mental, and spiritual. The infantile fusion state is an identity with *just* the physical or sensorimotor level. As Piaget said, "The self is here material, so to speak." That's not a union with the All, there's nothing mystical about it.

EZ: But in the infantile fusion state there is a union of subject and object.

KW: It's not a union, it's an indissociation. A union is two separate things brought together in a higher integration. In infantile fusion, there are not two things to begin with, just a global undifferentiation. You cannot integrate that which is not first differentiated. Besides, even *if* we say that this infantile state is a union of subject and object, let me repeat that the *subject* here is merely a *sensorimotor* subject undifferentiated from a sensorimotor world, it is *not* a total integrated subject of *all* levels united with *all* higher worlds. In other words, it isn't even a prototype of mystical union, it is rather the precise *opposite* of the mystical state. The infantile fusion state is the greatest point of alienation or separation from all of the higher levels and higher worlds whose total integration or union constitutes mysticism.

This, incidentally, is why the Christian mystics maintain that you are *born* in sin or separation or alientation; it's not something that you *do* after you are born, but something that you are from birth or conception, and something that can only be overcome through growth and development and evolution, from matter to mind to spirit. The infantile material fusion state is the *start* and lowest point of that growth, not some sort of mystical prefiguration of its end.

EZ: That's related to what you call the "pre/trans fallacy."

KW: Yes. The early developmental stages are prepersonal, in that a separate and individuated personal ego has not yet emerged. The middle stages of growth are personal or egoic. And the highest stages are transpersonal or transegoic.

My point is that people tend to confuse the "pre" states with the "trans" states because they superficially look alike. Once you have equated the infantile fusion state—which is prepersonal—with the mystical union—which is transpersonal—then one of two things happens. You either elevate that infantile state to a mystical union it does not possess, or you negate all genuine mysticism by claiming it is nothing but a regression to infantile narcissism and oceanic adualism. Jung and the Romantic movement in general do the first—they elevate pre-egoic and prerational states to transegoic and transrational glory. They're "elevationists." And Freud and his followers do just the opposite: they reduce all transrational, transegoic, genuinely mystical states to prerational, pre-egoic, infantile states. They're "reductionists." Both camps are half right, half wrong. Neither camp can tell the difference between "pre" and "trans." Genuine mysticism does exist, and there's precisely nothing infantile about it at all. Saying otherwise is like confusing preschool with postgraduate school; it's kind of crazy, and totally confuses the situation.

The squirrels were now frantic in their play. Edith kept smiling and gently asking questions. I wondered if any of my anger at the "mysticism-is-regression" notion showed through.

EZ: Okay, so we can now return to the original topic. The infant is basically at stage one, at the sensoriperceptual level, which we may grant is not mystical. And if something goes wrong at this stage of development?

KW: Since this level is so primitive, disturbances here are very grave. If the infant fails to differentiate itself from the environment, then its ego boundaries remain completely permeable and diffuse. The individual can't tell where his or her body stops and the chair begins. There is a hallucinatory blurring of boundaries between inside and outside, between dream and reality. This is, of course, adualism, one of the defining characteristics of psychoses. It's a severe pathology affecting the most primitive and basic level of existence, the material self. In infancy this disturbance leads to autism and symbiotic psychoses; if it persists to any large degree in adulthood, it contributes to depressive psychoses and most adult schizophrenias.

I have listed the treatment modality as "physiological/pacification," since unfortunately the only treatments that seem to really work are pharmacological or custodial.

EZ: So as the next level, level two, emerges?

KW: As the emotional-phantasmic level emerges, particularly during the first to the third years, the self has to differentiate itself from the material world and identify instead with the biological world of its separate and feeling body, and then integrate the physical world in its perception. In other words, the self must break its exclusive identity with the material self and the material world and establish a higher-order identity with the body, the body as a separate and distinct entity in the world. This is fulcrum two, which researchers such as Margaret Mahler call the "separation-individuation" phase of development. The bodyself has to separate and individuate from the mother and from the physical world at large.

EZ: And if difficulties occur at that stage?

KW: Then the boundaries of the self remain vague, fluid, confused. The world seems to "emotionally flood" the self, the self is very volatile and unstable. This is the so-called borderline syndromes, "borderline" because it is borderline between the psychoses of the previous level and the neuroses of the subsequent level. Related to this, but slightly more primitive, are the narcissistic disorders, where the self, precisely because it has not fully differentiated itself from the world, treats the world like its oyster and people as mere extensions of itself. Completely self-centered, in other words, since world and self are the same.

EZ: And the treatment for these disorders?

KW: It used to be thought that these disorders were untreatable because they were so primitive. But recently, spurred by the work of Mahler, Kohut, Kernberg, and others, a series of treatments known as "structure-building techniques" have been developed that are fairly successful. Since the main problem with the borderline disorders is that the self boundaries are not yet firm, the structure-building techniques do just that: they build structures, they build boundaries, ego boundaries. They help the person differentiate self and other, by basically explaining to the person, and showing the person, that what happens to the other does not necessarily happen to the self. You can disagree with your mother, for example, and it won't kill you. This is not obvious to someone who hasn't completed separation-individuation.

Now it's important to realize that with these borderline syndromes, psychotherapy is not attempting to dig something up from the unconscious. That doesn't happen until the next level, level three. In the borderline conditions, the problem is *not* that a strong ego barrier is repressing some emotion or drive; the problem is that there isn't a strong ego barrier or boundary in the first place. There is no repression barrier, and so there is no dynamic unconscious, and so there is nothing to dig up, as it were. In fact, the goal of the structure-building techniques is to get the person "up" to the level where they can repress! At this level, the self just isn't strong enough to forcefully repress anything.

EZ: So that, I take it, occurs at the next level, level three.

KW: Yes, that's right. Level three, or the representational mind, begins to emerge around age two or so and dominates awareness until around age seven. Symbols and concepts, language itself, emerges, and this allows the child to switch its identity from a merely body-based self to a mental or egoic self. The child is no longer just a body dominated by present feelings and impulses, he or she is also a mental self, with a name, with an identity, with hopes and wishes extended through *time*. Language is the vehicle of time; it is in language that the child can think of yesterday and dream of tomorrow, and therefore regret the past and feel guilt, and worry about the future and feel anxiety.

Thus guilt and anxiety emerge at this stage, and if the anxiety is too great, then the self can and will *repress* any thoughts or emotions that cause anxiety. These repressed thoughts and emotions, particularly sex, aggression, and power, constitute the dynamically repressed unconscious, what I call (after Jung) the shadow. If the shadow becomes too much, too overloaded, too full as it were, then it erupts in a whole series of painful symptoms known as the psychoneuroses, or neuroses for short.

So, at level three the mental-egoic self emerges, assisted by language, and learns to differentiate itself from the body. But if that *differentiation* goes too far, the result is *dissociation*, repression. The ego doesn't transcend the body, it alienates it, casts it out. But that only means that aspects of the body and its wishes remain as the shadow, painfully sabotaging the ego in the form of neurotic conflict.

EZ: And so treatment for the neuroses means contacting the shadow and reintegrating it.

KW: Yes, that's right. These treatments are called "uncovering techniques," because they attempt to uncover the shadow, bring it to the surface, and then reintegrate it, as you say. To do so, the repression barrier, created by language and sustained by anxiety and guilt, has to be lifted or relaxed. The person, for example, might be encouraged to say whatever comes into his mind without censoring it. But whatever the technique, the goal is essentially the same: befriend and reown the shadow.

EZ: The next stage?

KW: Level four, the rule/role mind—which typically reigns between the ages of seven and eleven—marks some very profound shifts in consciousness. If you take a child at level three, preoperational thought, and show the child a ball colored red on one side and green on the other, then place the red side toward the child and the green side toward you, and then ask the child what color *you* are looking at, the child will say red. In other words, he or she cannot take your perspective, cannot take the role of other. With the emergence of concrete operational thinking, the child will correctly say green. He or she can take the role of other. Also, the child at this stage can start to perform rule-governed operations, like class inclusion, multiplication, hierarchization, and so on.

The child, in other words, increasingly inhabits a world of roles and of rules. His or her behavior is governed by scripts, by linguistic rules that govern behavior and roles. We see this particularly with a child's *moral sense*, as outlined by Piaget, Kohlberg, and Carol Gilligan. In the previous stages, stages one through three, the child's moral sense is called preconventional, because it is based, not on mental and social rules, but on mere bodily reward and punishment, pleasure and pain—it's self-centric or narcissistic, as we would expect. But with the emergence of the rule/role mind, the child's moral sense shifts from preconventional to conventional modes—it goes from self-centric to sociocentric.

And this is very important: because the conventional or rule/role mind cannot yet *introspect* with any degree of strength, the rules and roles the young child learns are for all purposes set in concrete. The child accepts these rules and roles in an unquestioning fashion— what researchers call the conformist stage. Lacking introspection, the child cannot independently *judge* them, and so follows them unreflexively.

Now, most of these rules and roles are necessary and beneficial, at least for this stage, but some of them may be false or contradictory or misleading. A lot of our scripts, the scripts we live by, the scripts we got from our parents, our society, whatever, are simply myths, they aren't true, they are misleading. But the child at this stage cannot judge that! The child at this stage takes so many things literally and concretely, and if these mistaken beliefs persist in adulthood, you have a script pathology. You might tell yourself that you're no good, that you're rotten to the core, that God will punish you for thinking bad thoughts, that you are unlovable, that you are a wretched sinner, and so on.

Treatment here—particularly the treatment known as cognitive therapy—tries to uproot these myths and expose them to the light of reason and evidence. This is called script rewriting, and it's very powerful, very effective therapy, especially in cases of depression and low self-esteem.

EZ: I think that's clear. What about level five?

KW: With the emergence of formal operational thinking, usually between the ages of eleven and fifteen, another quite extraordinary transformation occurs. With formal operational thought, the individual can *reflect* on the norms and rules of society and thus judge for him- or herself whether they are worthy or not. This ushers in what Kohlberg and Gilligan call postconventional morality. It is no longer bound to conformist social norms, no longer bound to the tribe or the group or the particular society, but rather judges actions according to more universal standards—what is right, or fair, not just for my group, but for persons at large. This makes sense, of course, because higher development always means the possibility of higher or more universal integration—in this case, from self-centric to sociocentric to world-centric—on the way, I would add, to theo-centric.

At this stage, too, the person develops the capacity for strong and sustained introspection. "Who am I?" becomes for the first time a burning issue. No longer protected by, and embedded in, the con-formist rules and roles of the preceding stage, individuals here have to fashion their own identity, so to speak. If there are problems here, the person develops what Erikson called an *identity crisis.* And the only treatment for that is more introspection. The therapist here becomes something of a philosopher, and engages the client in a Socratic dialogue that helps them . . .

EZ: Helps them ferret out for themselves just who they are, who they want to be, the type of person they can be.

KW: Yes, that's right. It's not a great mystical quest at this point, it's not looking for the transcendental Self, capital S, that is one and the same in all people. It's looking for an appropriate self, small s, not the absolute Self, big S. It's *Catcher in the Rye.*

EZ: The existential level?

KW: John Broughton, Jane Loevinger, and several other researchers have pointed out that if psychological growth continues, people can develop a highly integrated personal self, where, and these are Loevinger's words, "mind and body are both experiences of an inte-grated self." This mind-body integration I call the centaur. Problems at the centaur level are existential problems, problems inherent in manifest existence itself, like mortality, finititude, integrity, authen-ticity, meaning in life. Not that these don't come up at other stages, only that they come to the fore here, they dominate. And therapies that address these concerns are the humanistic and existential thera-pies, the so-called Third Force (after the First Force of psycho-analysis and the Second Force of behaviorism).

EZ: OK, so now we come to the higher levels of development, starting with the psychic.

KW: Yes. As you continue to grow and evolve into the transpersonal levels, levels seven through nine, your identity continues to expand, first moving beyond the separate bodymind into the wider spiritual and transcendental dimensions of existence, finally culminating in the widest identity possible—the supreme identity, the identity of your awareness and the universe at large—not just the *physical* universe, but the multidimensioned, divine universe, theocentric.

The psychic level is simply the beginning of this process, the beginning of the transpersonal stages. You might experience flashes of so-called cosmic consciousness, you might develop certain psychic capacities, you might develop a keen and penetrating intuition. But mostly you simply realize that your own awareness is not confined to the individual bodymind. You begin to intuit that your own awareness somehow goes beyond, or survives, the individual organism. You start to be able to merely witness the events of the individual bodymind, because you are no longer exclusively identified with them or bound to them, and so you develop a measure of equanimity. You are *starting* to contact or intuit your transcendental soul, the Witness, which ultimately can lead, at the causal level, to a direct identity with Spirit.

EZ: You call the techniques of this level the path of yogis.

KW: Yes. Following Da Free John, I divide the great mystical traditions into three classes, namely, yogis, saints, and sages. These address, respectively, the psychic, subtle, and causal levels. The yogi harnesses the energies of the individual bodymind in order to go beyond the bodymind. As the bodymind, including many of its otherwise involuntary processes, is brought under rigorous control, attention is freed from the bodymind itself and thus tends to revert to its transpersonal ground.

EZ: This process, I take it, continues into the subtle level.

KW: Yes. As attention is progressively freed from the outer world of the external environment and the inner world of the bodymind, awareness starts to transcend the subject/object duality altogether. The illusory world of duality starts to appear as it is in reality—namely, as nothing but a manifestation of Spirit itself. The outer world starts to look divine, the inner world starts to look divine. That is, consciousness itself starts to become luminous, light-filled, numinous, and it seems to directly touch, even unite with, Divinity itself.

This is the path of the saints. Notice how saints, in both the East and West, are usually depicted with halos of light around their heads?

That is symbolic of the inner Light of the illumined and intuitive mind. At the psychic level you start to commune with Divinity or Spirit. But at the subtle, you find a union with Spirit, the *unio mystica*. Not just communion, union.

EZ: And in the causal?

KW: The process is complete, the soul or pure Witness dissolves in its Source, and the *union* with God gives way to an *identity* with Godhead, or the unmanifest Ground of all being. This is, of course, what the Sufis call the Supreme Identity. You have realized your fundamental identity with the Condition of all conditions and the Nature of all natures and the Being of all beings. Since Spirit is the suchness or condition of all things, it is perfectly compatible with all things. It is even nothing special. It is chop wood, carry water. For this reason, individuals who reach this stage are often depicted as very ordinary people, nothing special about them. This is the path of sages, of the wise men and women who are so wise you can't even spot it. They fit in, and go about their business. In the Ten Zen OxHerding Pictures, which depict the stages on the path to enlightenment, the very last picture shows an ordinary person entering the marketplace. The caption says: They enter the marketplace with open hands. That's all it says.

EZ: Fascinating. And each of these three higher stages has its own possible pathologies?

KW: Yes, that's right. I won't go into each of them, since it's a very long topic. I'll just say that at each stage you can become attached or fixated to the experiences of that stage—as you can at any stage—and this causes various developmental arrests and pathologies at that level. And there are, of course, specific treatments for each. I try to outline all this in *Transformations*.

EZ: So, in a sense, you have already answered my question about the relation of psychotherapy and meditation. By outlining the whole spectrum of consciousness, you have in effect placed each according to its role.

KW: In a sense, yes. Let me just add a few points. Point number one, meditation is *not* an uncovering technique, like psychoanalysis. Its primary aim is not to lift the repression barrier and allow the shadow to surface. Now it *may* do that, which I'll explain, but the point is that it may not. Its primary aim is to suspend mental-egoic activity in general and thus allow transegoic or transpersonal awareness to develop, leading eventually to the discovery of the Witness or the Self.

In other words, meditation and psychotherapy generally aim at quite different levels of the psyche. Zen will not necessarily, nor was it designed to, eliminate psychoneuroses. Moreover, you can develop a fairly strong sense of the Witness and still be quite neurotic. You just learn to witness your neurosis, which helps you live with the neurosis quite easily, but does nothing to uproot the neurosis itself. If you have a broken bone, Zen won't mend it; if you have a broken emotional life, Zen won't fundamentally fix that either. It's not supposed to. I can tell you from rather bitter personal experience that Zen has done much to let me live with my neuroses, and not much at all for getting rid of them.

EZ: That's the job of uncovering techniques.

KW: Exactly. There is virtually nothing in the massive amount of the world's great mystical and contemplative literature about the dynamic unconscious, the repressed unconscious. This is a rather unique discovery and contribution of modern Europe.

EZ: But when somebody takes up meditation, sometimes repressed material does erupt.

KW: Indeed. As I said, that might happen; the point is, it might not. This is what takes place, in my opinion: Let's take a meditation that aims at the causal level, the level of the pure Witness (which eventually itself dissolves into pure nondual spirit). An example of this would be Zen, vipassana, or self-inquiry (of the form "Who am I?" or "Avoiding relationship?"). Now, if you start Zen meditation, and if you have a severe neuroses, say a fulcrum three depression due to severe repression of anger, this is what happens: As you begin to merely witness the ego-mind and its contents, instead of identifying with them and getting caught up in them and carried away by them, then the machinations of the ego start to wind down. The ego starts to relax, and when it relaxes sufficiently, it suddenly "drops"—you are suddenly free as the Witness beyond the ego—or, at any rate, you suddenly glimpse it. Now, for this to happen it is not necessary that all parts of the ego relax. It is only necessary for your general hold on the ego to let go long enough for the Witness to shine through. Now the repression barrier might be part of what relaxes; if so, you are going to derepress, you are going to have shadow elements, in this case rage, erupt rather dramatically in awareness. This happens fairly often. But sometimes it happens not at all. The repression barrier is simply bypassed, left largely intact. You relax your general hold on the ego long enough to temporarily drop the ego altogether, but not long enough to relax all parts of the ego itself, such as the repression barrier. And since the repression barrier is often bypassed, and can be bypassed, then the actual mechanism of Zen has to be explained as something other than a mere uncovering technique. That is completely incidental and nonmandatory.

Likewise, you can use uncovering techniques all you want, and you won't get enlightened, you won't end up as the supreme identity. Freud was not Buddha; Buddha was not Freud. Trust me.

EZ: [Laughing] I see. So your recommendation is that, what, people use psychotherapy and meditation in a complementary fashion, letting each do its respective job?

KW: Yes, that's exactly right. They are both powerful and effective techniques that fundamentally aim at different levels of the spectrum of consciousness. This is not to say that they don't overlap, or that they don't share some things in common, because they do. Even psychoanalysis, for example, trains to some degree the capacity for witnessing, since keeping "evenly hovering attention" is a prerequisite for free association. But beyond that type of similarity, the two techniques diverge rapidly, addressing very different dimensions of awareness. Meditation can help psychotherapy, in that it helps establish witnessing consciousness, and it can assist in the repair of some problems. And psychotherapy can help meditation, in that it frees up consciousness from its repressions and entanglements in the lower levels. But beyond that, the aims, goals, methods, and dynamics differ dramatically.

EZ: One last question.

Edith asked the question, and I didn't hear it. I was watching the squirrels, who disappeared once again into the deeper recesses of the forest. Why had my own ability to stand as the Witness so thoroughly departed me? Fifteen years of meditation, during which I had had several

unmistakable "kensho" experiences, fully confirmed by my teachers—
how had this all left me? Where are the squirrels of yesteryear?

In part, of course, it was exactly what I was telling Edith. Meditation
does not necessarily cure the shadow. I had, too often, simply used
meditation to bypass the emotional work I needed to complete. I had used
zazen to bypass neurosis, and that it will not do. And that I was now in the
process of redressing. . . .

EZ: You have said that each level of the spectrum of consciousness has
   inherent in it a particular worldview. Could you briefly explain what
   you mean by that?

KW: The idea is this: What would the world look like if you *only* have
   the cognitive structures of any given level? The worldviews from the
   nine levels are called, respectively, archaic, magic, mythic, mythic-
   rational, rational, existential, psychic, subtle, and causal. I'll
   quickly run through them.

   If you have *only* the structures of level one, the world looks fairly
   undifferentiated, a world of *participation mystique*, global fusion,
   adualism. I call it archaic simply because of its primitive nature.

   As level two emerges, and images develop, along with early symbols, the self differentiates from the world but is still tied to the world
   very closely, in a quasi-fused state, and so it thinks it can magically
   influence the world by merely thinking or wishing. A good example
   of this is voodoo. If I make an image of you and then stick a pin in
   the image, I believe it will actually hurt *you*. This is because the
   image and its object are not clearly differentiated. This worldview is
   called magic or magical.

   As level three emerges, self and other are fully differentiated, and
   so magical beliefs die down, to be replaced by mythic beliefs. I can
   no longer order the world around, as in magic, but God can, if I
   know how to please God. If I want my personal wishes to be fulfilled,
   I must make certain pleas or prayers to God, and then God will
   intervene on my behalf and suspend the laws of nature through
   miracles. This is the mythic worldview.

   As level four emerges, with its capacity for concrete operations or
   rituals, and I realize that my prayers are not always being answered, I
   then try to manipulate nature in order to please the gods, who will
   then mythically intervene on my behalf. To prayers I add elaborate

rituals, all carefully designed to get God to step in. Historically, the main ritual that emerged at this stage was human sacrifice, which, as Campbell himself pointed out, beset every single major civilization the world over at this stage of development. As gruesome as that is, the thinking behind it is more complex and complicated than simple myth, so it is referred to as mythic-rational.

With the emergence of formal operational thought, level five, I realize that the belief in a personal God who caters to my egoic whims is probably just not true, there isn't any credible evidence for it, and anyway it doesn't reliably work. If I want something from nature—food for example—I'll skip the prayers, skip the rituals, skip the human sacrifices, and approach nature itself directly. With hypothetico-deductive reasoning—that is, with science—I'll go directly after what I need. This is a big advance, but it also has its downside. The world starts to look like a meaningless collection of material bits and pieces, with no value, no meaning, at all. This is the rational worldview, often called scientific materialism.

As vision-logic emerges, level six, I see that there are more things in heaven and earth than are dreamt of in my rationalistic philosophy. By integrating the body, the world becomes "reenchanted," to use Berman's phrase. This is the humanistic-existential worldview.

When level seven, the psychic level, emerges, I begin to realize that there are *really* more things in heaven and earth than I have dreamt of. I begin to sense a single Divinity lying behind the surface appearances of manifestation, and I commune with that Divinity— not as a mythic belief but an interior experience. This is the general psychic worldview. At the subtle level, I directly know that Divinity, and find a union with it. But I maintain that the soul and God are two distinct ontological entities. This is the subtle worldview—that there is a soul, there is a transpersonal God, but the two are subtly divorced. At the causal level that divorce breaks down, and the supreme identity is realized. This is the causal worldview, the worldview of *tat tvam asi*, you are That. Pure nondual Spirit, which, being compatible with all, is nothing special.

EZ: Now I see why, in your books, you have always maintained that the modern rise of rationality, which has usually spent so much time trashing religion, is actually in itself a very spiritual movement.

KW: Yes, I seem to be alone among the sociologists of religion in this regard. In my opinion, these scholars do not have a detailed cartography of the whole spectrum of consciousness. They then naturally lament the rise of modern rationality and science, because modern rationality and science—level five—definitely transcends and dismantles the archaic, magic, and mythic worldviews. Most scholars therefore seem to think that science is killing spirituality *in general,* killing *all* religion, because they don't seem to understand mystical religion very well, and so they fervently wish for the good old mythic days, before science, the good old prerational days, which they think was "real" religion. But mysticism is transrational and thus lies in our collective future, not our collective past. Mysticism is evolutionary and progressive, not devolutionary and regressive, as Aurobindo and Teilhard de Chardin realized. And science, in my opinion, is stripping us of our infantile and adolescent views of spirit, it is stripping us of our prerational views, in order to make room for the genuinely transrational insights of the higher stages of development, the transpersonal stages of genuine mystical or contemplative development. It is stripping magic and mythic in order to make room for psychic and subtle. In that sense science (and rationality) is a very healthy, very evolutionary, very necessary step toward real spiritual maturity. Rationality is a movement *of* spirit *toward* spirit.

And that, again, is why so many great scientists have been great mystics. It's a natural wedding. The science of the external world joined with the science of the internal world, the real meeting of East and West.

EZ: That's a perfect place to end.

I said goodbye to Edith, wishing that she could meet Treya, thinking I would unfortunately never see her again, unaware that she would re-enter our lives during a desperate time when a true friend was sorely needed.

Dreams are so strange, I think, as I am gently pulled down the long hall corridor toward the third room. Toward the third room, good title for a novel. Dreams can seem so real, that's it. Dreams can seem so real. Then I think of that line from Blade Runner—*"Wake up, time to die."*
And then I think, If that's so, do I want to wake up or not?
"Say, you don't happen to have a name, do you?"

Treya returned home the next day. I had set up an appointment with Dr. Belknap's office for that afternoon.

"Terry," he said as we sat down in his homey office, "I'm afraid you have diabetes. Of course, we'll want to do more tests, but the urinalysis was pretty clear."

When Dr. B told me and Ken that my urinalysis indicated diabetes, what went through my mind was that line from the movie *Out of Africa*, when she discovers that she has syphilis. Very calmly she says, "This is not what I had expected would happen to me next." Same here. In my wildest dreams or nightmares, this is not what I had expected would happen to me next.

12

IN A DIFFERENT
VOICE

❧❧❧

T H E number three killer of adult Americans. Most people don't give diabetes that much attention; the big two, heart disease and cancer, grab the headlines. But in addition to being the number three killer, it is also the leading cause of adult blindness and amputation. It meant another radical life-style change for the both of us, but for Treya especially— insulin injections, painfully strict diet, always checking blood glucose levels, always carrying that little bit of sugar in case of insulin shock. One more wave to learn to surf. I couldn't help but think of Job, the answer to whose perennial question "Why me?" seems to have been, "Why not?"

I have diabetes, I have diabetes. Jesus, when will all of this ever end?
Just last week I asked Dr. Rosenbaum [our local oncologist] if he would take the Port-a-Cath out, since I didn't think I would need it anymore. He hesitated, said we should leave it in. That means he thinks there is a significant chance of a recurrence. Just when I am starting to feel good, feel confident. Just when I am starting to think that maybe I will live awhile. Maybe I will even live a long time. Maybe I will have a full life. Maybe Ken and I will get to grow old together. We might even have a child. I might be able to make some kind of contribution to the world. Then the weight of cancer comes

crashing back down on me. The doctor won't take the port-o-cath out. Suddenly I'm back in it again. It's inescapable. Cancer is a chronic disease.

In the office I overhear a nurse talking with a cancer patient. "I've never had cancer myself, so perhaps this is presumptuous of me to say, but there are worse things than cancer if you catch it early."

I jumped in, very interested. "Like what for example?"

"Oh, glaucoma or diabetes. They create so many really bad chronic problems. I remember when I was diagnosed with glaucoma . . ."

Well, now on top of everything else, I have diabetes. I can't believe it. I feel crushed, absolutely crushed. What can I do but cry? Despair, anger, shock, fear of this disease I do not understand, they all come out in my salty tears. I remember an incident a few days ago. Ken and I had spent the weekend after New Year's up in Tahoe with some friends (we're still getting ready to put it on the market), and I had noticed that I seemed unusually thirsty. When we got back home to Mill Valley I mentioned this to Ken. He looked up from his desk and said, "That can be a sign of diabetes." I said, "Oh, interesting," he went back to his work, and neither of us thought any more about it.

What would I do without Ken? What if he'd been out or away at work when this news came? He holds and consoles me. He seems to soak up so much of my own pain. We left the doctor's office with me crying. Another disease to learn about, another disease to have to cope with, another disease to limit and threaten my life. I feel very, very sorry for myself and angry at the entire setup.

I hardly even remember what Dr. Belknap and the nurse told us. I sat there crying the whole time. We will see if my diabetes responds to glyburide, an oral medication developed in Europe. If not, I will have to go on insulin. In the meantime, I am to have a blood test every morning, including Saturday and Sunday, so we can see how much of the oral medication I need. The nurse reviewed all of this with us; I hoped Ken was listening more carefully than I was. I was feeling an odd combination of rebellious and angry while at the same time sad and defeated; it did sound like this would be with me for life. The nurse gave us a food exchange diet to follow; I would become very familiar with this. Twelve hundred calories of a diet balanced between milk exchanges, starch exchanges, fruit exchanges, meat exchanges, and fat exchanges. Thank God for the free foods—radishes, Chinese cabbage, cucumbers, pickles.

Our first stop, food exchange list in hand, is the supermarket. I still feel glum, but for the moment lose myself in the fascination of reading food labels and finding sugar, sugar everywhere, hidden in breads, hidden in peanut butter, hidden in salad dressings, hidden in prepared foods, hidden in mixes, hidden in spaghetti sauce, hidden in canned vegetables, everywhere, everywhere! Ken and I roam the aisles, calling out to each other with an especially outrageous find—"Sugar in baby food, aisle seven!" Ken yells—or when we stumble on something I can actually eat—"Potting soil, aisle four, no sugar." There are a lot of new things in the cart when we reach the checkout stand, things like Equal and diet sodas and a measuring scale and new measuring cups and measuring spoons. This food exchange diet depends on measurement, I am to learn.

Each morning before breakfast I drive to the lab for a blood test. On Saturday and Sunday I have to go to Marin General Hospital, where I acquire yet another hospital ID card to add to my collection. At the hospital they are experts at drawing blood; it hardly hurts as the needle enters the vein. At the clinic during the week, however, each time I cross my fingers and hope for the kindly white-haired woman, who also has the magic touch, not for the nurse who somehow manages to make it hurt each time and occasionally needs two tries to get it right. This is especially important to me because all of this poking is happening on one arm only; because of my previous breast and lymph surgery I am supposed to always have blood drawn from my left arm. It looks more and more like the arm of a drug addict.

And each morning I take my pill, 5 mg. of glyburide, one of the "second generation" of diabetes medication. And each afternoon, around five, I take my second pill. I may have to get a wristwatch with an alarm on it to remind me of this late afternoon routine.

And each day I begin by examining the Food Exchange Diet taped on the refrigerator door. I consider: Can I trade a milk exchange for more peanut butter? Can I trade a starch exchange for more vegetables? Or for more fish at dinner? I measure out my cup of cereal, my cup of milk, my two teaspoons of raisins, my 1/4 cup of cottage cheese. I prepare my lunch, a container of free salad foods seasoned with vinegar, a peanut butter (2 tablespoons) and banana (1/2 small) sandwich, and 1/2 cup of a vegetable. Dinner too is considered and measured, 3 oz. of fish, 1 cup of whole wheat pasta, 1/2 cup of vegetables, which Ken will probably think of some clever way to cook. Then an evening snack of ¹/₂ cup milk and 2 crackers.

And each day I test my urine for sugar four times—when I wake up, before lunch, before dinner, and at night before my required evening snack. I watch those damned sticks turn brown before my eyes four times a day. I watch that clear aqua color begin to turn green, then brown around the edges, I watch it as the brown turns deeper and darker. It is this process, watching those damned strips turn brown before my eyes, again and again, that finally convinces me. I have diabetes. I am a diabetic. I have diabetes.

Over the weeks, Treya's diabetes responded slowly to the glyburide and the strict diet, but it did so only with the maximum dose of the medication, indicating that she would almost certainly have to go on insulin, maybe in a few months, maybe in a few years, but inevitably.

Insulin. That means insulin shots. How well I remember visiting my grandfather. We all—my two sisters and my brother—loved visiting Pop in his magical house with the white columns in front and the wide porches and the green lawns and the wonderful trees to climb and hide in. I remember well watching him give himself his shots; the white skin exposed, gathering the skin together, all of us wide-eyed as he guided the needle into his skin. Later we'd clamber all over him in his beautifully carved wooden bed then trundle off to our own bedrooms. We all loved Pop. Everyone loved Pop. He was a large, jovial, barrel-chested man who lived life to the fullest. When he came to visit he'd hide candy and gifts and, our favorite, comic books in his pockets and jacket. We'd climb all over him to ferret out the treats, then sit happily on his lap. My grandmother died when I was very young; I feel blessed to have known Pop until I was almost twelve and even so I still miss him. I wish he were around, I wish he were in my life, I wish Ken could have known him.

Pop had diabetes. He died of cancer of the pancreas, in fact, but he was eighty-three and had lived a full, active life. Now I understood the care with food at his house, the fresh unsalted butter, the fresh eggs from the chickenhouse, the whole grains and legumes. I remember that Pop paid more attention to good food than anyone else I knew, but only now did I understand why. My father's brother, Hank, also had diabetes as an adult. Adult onset diabetes has a strong genetic connection, unlike juvenile onset diabetes. Children who get diabetes often have no relatives with diabetes; there is speculation that the disease is triggered by some viral infection, but basically no one knows what causes diabetes. Or how to cure it.

Insulin. Damn, damn, damn. I was hoping my blood sugar would come down more easily and that ultimately I could control it with diet and exercise. That's still a possibility, I guess, but it's more remote after this news. I'm a bit numb by now. I don't really want to let it in. It frightens me. It angers me.

A friend congratulated me on how well I was handling it. That made me feel weird. I'm certainly doing what I need to do to control it, but I'm angry and disbelieving. I make bad, bitter jokes about it. I complain about having to control my diet so tightly. I'm sure all this will be good for me, thank you, but I don't think it's any fun at all. I'll do what I need to do, but I don't like it one bit. The only part of this acknowledgement I could accept was the part about being authentic. I am being authentic. I am being authentically pissed. I trust my anger, it feels healthy and appropriate. I'm not going to falsely put on a happy face about this. I suppose my feeling is that will come more completely and more deeply later if I go through the anger; or I may stay somewhat angry always about it. I don't know what will happen, but I do know that I need to stay with the anger for now and let it evolve.

Earlier today I was thinking how ironic it all is. Talking with a friend only a few days ago about how in growing older one becomes less anxious about achieving major victories in life, and of the need to cultivate pleasure in the small victories of day-to-day life. This diabetes is certainly making me pay more attention to the small pleasures of a few bites of food, since that's all I get. You can't imagine how tasty the meager amount of two tablespoons of peanut butter can be when you thought you might never get it again! I open the refrigerator door and see all those good things in there and realize how long it will take, with my one- and two-ounce portions, to eat it all! I buy a health-food, no-sugar, cakelike thing as a special treat and it takes me a week to eat the whole thing as I dole it out in small portions.

And I suppose I have feeling better to look forward to. I imagine the effects of the diabetes have been puttering along on a low level for some time now. I hope at least that my family and friends will notice and cherish their own good health more as a result of hearing what I'm going through.

It turns out that Treya's diabetes was almost certainly triggered by chemotherapy, a not uncommon occurrence. With adult onset diabetes, genetics loads the gun but stress pulls the trigger. The stress of chemotherapy, in this case.

As diabetes begins to take its toll on the unsuspecting victim, several unpleasant things happen. Since the pancreas is not producing enough insulin, the body cannot utilize blood glucose. This sugar accumulates in the blood, causing it, in effect, to become dense and honeylike. Some of this sugar spills into the urine—the Romans used to test for diabetes by putting urine next to honey bees, who would swarm around the urine if the person was diabetic. Because the blood has become "thick" with sugar, the blood tends to suck up water from the surrounding tissues. Hence the person stays rather chronically thirsty, drinks fluids all the time, and urinates frequently. Also, the thick density of the blood, for the same reason, can cause small capillaries to collapse. This means that areas of the body served most by small capillaries, like the extremities, the kidneys, and the retinas in the eyes, are slowly damaged, which accounts for the blindness, the kidney troubles, the amputations. And for the same reason, the brain becomes dehydrated, which results in dramatic mood swings, lack of concentration, depression. Along with everything else—the artificial menopause, the aftereffects of chemo, the general difficulties we were both going through—this almost certainly had contributed to Treya's overall depression and her black moods. Her eyesight had already begun to deteriorate, though we didn't then know why; she had to wear glasses all the time.

"Why, exactly, is it so dark in here?" Even a short distance walked in the dark seems unending, and I am disoriented enough. We must be approaching the third room, but I don't remember the hallway being nearly this long.

"Why exactly is it so dark in here, please?"

The hallway wall abruptly gives way to an opening, the door I suppose, and there we both stand, this Figure and I.

"What do you see?" The strange voice simply floats out of the absence that seems to be its source.

"When I look at you, nothing."

"In there."

I look in the room. Is this handwriting, hieroglyphics, symbols, what?

"Look, fascinating, really, but I have to go now, I'm looking for someone, I'm sure you understand."

"What do you see?"

As in the other rooms, this one seems to stretch out in all directions for as far as I can see. The closer I look at any particular point in the room, the more it expands away. If I look intently at a point two feet from me, it begins stretching out for miles, hundreds then thousands of miles, it seems. Suspended in this expanding universe are symbols, maybe millions of them, some of which I recognize, most of which I do not. They are not written on anything, but simply suspended there. And with a luminous edge to them all, as if painted by some crazed god on magic mushrooms. I have the strangest sensation that these symbols are actually alive, and that they are looking at me, too.

As Treya began to get her blood sugar under control, her mood improved dramatically, her depression virtually disappeared. But these were secondary, in a sense, to that inner shift that was now occurring at full speed, and that would very soon make its first dramatic announcement. This profound shift was beginning to affect not just her personal life, but her spirituality, her work in the world, and what she saw as her calling, her daemon, which—after all these years!—was on the verge of erupting into consciousness.

I watched all of this with a mixture of admiration, amazement, and envy. It would have been so easy for her to stay bitter, self-pitying, jaded. But instead she seemed to become more open, more loving, more forgiving, more compassionate. And she got stronger by the day, apparently along the lines of Nietzsche: "That which does not destroy me makes me stronger." I don't know what "lessons" Treya was learning from cancer and diabetes, but for me, the lesson was turning out to be Treya.

I have diabetes. I am a diabetic. What's the best way to say it? One sounds like I have a disease that comes from outside myself, that might be catching. The other makes it sound like something intrinsic to my character, to my bodily being. This body whose resale value now is, as Ken says, nil. I always thought I'd donate my organs when I died, but nobody would want them now. At least I get to be buried in one piece, or have my ashes scattered over Conundrum peak.

Ken's been wonderful, going with me to the doctor, making jokes and keeping my spirits up, taking me each morning for my blood test, helping me figure out all the food exchanges, doing all the cooking. But the best part is how good I'm feeling. I felt wonderful yesterday, and came home to hear the doctor's report of 115 [glucose blood level], almost normal, since it started out at 322. I suppose I've been feeling not quite right for a while, with the most obvious symptom my failing eyesight. No wonder I didn't feel like exercising much. No wonder I had such trouble concentrating. No wonder I had such mood swings. Now I'm remembering what it feels like to feel good. I have so much more energy, a much more positive outlook on things, lots more buoyancy and bounce. I'm sure I'm easier to get along with, too. Poor Ken, having to put up with me while I was subtly but surely going downhill, and neither of us really knowing it. It feels great to have my energy and spirit and excitement about life back again!

Part of this comes from new feelings about work, about my profession, my calling, that same issue that I've been bugging myself about for so long. Lots of influences at work in this inner shift. Work with Seymour, my meditation, giving up my perfectionism, learning to be and to not just mindlessly do. I still want to do, I still want to contribute, but I want my doing suffused with being. This is also a shift in my feelings about my femininity that opens up new possibilities, possibilities I once condemned. I am realizing more and more how much I adopted my father's values—production and contributing and all that—and I see now that his shoes don't actually fit me too well, much as I admire them. This combines with the new direction I feel feminism taking, away from imitating men or proving we can do what they can do, toward valuing, defining, bringing forth, making visible the special kinds of work that women do. The invisible work. The work that doesn't have a title or a hierarchy of professional advancement. Amorphous work. Work that has to do with creating a mood or a setting or an atmosphere, whether in a meeting or in a family or in a community, where other kinds of more visible work flourish.

A group of us had a lovely discussion the other day about women's spirituality that helped crystalize these thoughts. A few notes:

- The whole area of women's spirituality is blank. Much of nuns' writings lost. Women don't write much about the spiritual search anyway. Women kept out of important positions in most established religions.
- Women's spirituality looks different from men's. Less goal-oriented. Might change our notions about what enlightenment is. More encompassing, embracing; again, more amorphous.

- Women's spirituality hard to see, hard to define. What are the stages, the steps, the training? Is crocheting or knitting as good as meditating to train attention and quiet the mind?
- A continuum, with men's spiritual development on one extreme and women's on the other. Men's has been defined, women's not. Lots of variations in between. Are there parallel but different/separate tracks, à la Carol Gilligan?
- Long discussion on Gilligan and her book *In a Different Voice*. She was a student of Lawrence Kohlberg, a moral theorist who first codified three broad stages of moral development that people go through—the preconventional stages, where a person thinks that what is right is whatever they want; the conventional stages, where people base their decisions on what society wants; and the postconventional stages, where moral decisions are based on universal principles of moral reasoning. These stages have been verified in numerous cross-cultural tests. But women seemed consistently to score lower than men on these tests. Gilligan found that women go through these same three hierarchical stages, from preconventional to conventional to postconventional, but the reasoning they use is quite different from men's. Men base their decisions on ideas of rules, laws, judgments, and rights, where women tend to value feelings, linkings, relationship. Looked at this way, women do not score lower, only different.

  My favorite Gilligan example: a young boy and girl are playing together. The boy wants to play "pirate," the girl wants to play "house." So the girl says, "OK, you play the pirate who lives next door." The linking, the relationship.

  Another favorite: when young boys are playing baseball, and a boy strikes out and starts crying, a girl will say, "Give him another chance"; the boys say, "No, rules are rules, he's out." Gilligan's point: boys will override feelings to save the rules, girls will override rules to save the feelings. Both are important in the real world, but very different, and we need to honor those differences and learn from them.
- Ken has incorporated much of Kohlberg and Gilligan into his model, but says he has no idea how this would affect women's spirituality, because there has been almost nothing written on the subject. "The whole field is blank. We need a lot of help here."
- Women who have gained enlightenment—did they get it through

following traditional male paths, models? Did they get it through following their own way? How did they find that? What kind of conflict, self-doubt, etc., did they go through to find their own way?

- Findhorn the closest model. A very feminine, mothering place. Each to find their own way—a feminine ideal? No need to adhere to a strict, already defined way, within a supportive community/family context. Problems of this approach. Slower, more organic? More easily sidetracked? Less visible sense of movement, accomplishment, because no outer awards, degrees, definite stages to mark progress.
- Goddess more of a descent, God more of an ascent. Both necessary, both important. But little work done on the descent of the Goddess. Some exceptions: Aurobindo, tantra, Free John.
- I talked of moving out of the sphere of identifying with my father and masculine values and moving into my power as a woman, how I could become a teacher to Ken once I did that. Then I realized it wasn't so much a moving away from—all those abilities I developed are good, not to be left behind. It's more adding something—and the image of ever larger circles came to mind. Both/and, not either/or.

During this discussion I suddenly felt that part of my problem, if I still want to define it as such, might have to do with my womanhood. Certainly I've thought this before, but more on the level of how hard it is for a woman to fit into a male-defined world. The new feeling this time had to do with a sense that perhaps the reason I've failed to find my niche had to do with my incorporating male values too much, so I was going the wrong way. Perhaps the reason I've failed to find my niche had to do with some inner way of being true to myself, my special talents and interests as a woman. So rather than seeing myself as a failure, I can see this period of searching as a time I needed to bring myself to this realization. Time I needed to uncover and learn to value and learn to simply see the more female values deep within me.

Suddenly it seems OK to be what I am. To have an amorphous professional life. To get involved in various projects that move me and inspire me. To learn more about creating environments in which things can happen. To bring people together, to network. To communicate, to make ideas known. To let it unfold and not try to force myself into a form, a structure, a profession with titles.

What a sense of relief and freedom! Just living is OK! Being is OK, doing isn't necessarily necessary. It's a kind of allowing. Of letting go of this society's overly masculine and hyper-doing values. To work on the whole issue of women's spirituality, the feminine faces of God. To settle down, to till the soil in one place and see what will grow there.

The first thing that grew there was the Cancer Support Community (CSC), an organization that would eventually offer support services and education, free of charge, to over three hundred and fifty cancer patients a week, along with their families and support people.

It was right after Treya's mastectomy that we first met Vicky Wells. I was walking out of Treya's room and down the hospital corridor when a rather striking-looking woman walked past. She was tall, statuesque, good-looking, with black hair, red lipstick, a red dress, and black high heels. She looked like an American version of a French fashion model, which confused me. Until I found out that Vicky had spent several years in France with her best friend at the time, Anna Karina, then wife of the French director Jean-Luc Godard. I don't think she ever recovered from the Parisian thrill.

But Vicky was far from all pretty face. Back in the States she had worked as a private detective in a ghetto, an alcohol- and drug-abuse counselor, and an activist for poor people caught in the criminal justice system—all of which she did for over a decade—only to discover she had breast cancer. A mastectomy, chemotherapy, and several reconstructive surgeries had all left her with a painful realization of how pitiful the support services were for cancer patients and their families and friends.

So Vicky had begun volunteer work with several organizations, such as Reach for Recovery, but she found even those services less than adequate. She had a vague, somewhat amorphous notion of starting the type of center that would meet her vision, and that is when she met Treya.

They would eventually spend hours, weeks, months—in fact, two years—brainstorming about the support center they wanted to start. They interviewed dozens and dozens of doctors, patients, nurses, support people—praying all the while to the "CSC angel" for help. They were initially joined by Shannon McGowan, another cancer patient, who had once worked with Harold Benjamin in creating the Wellness

Community in Santa Monica, a pioneering center that was one of the first to offer free support services for cancer patients and their families. This is the center that Kristen had taken Treya to when we were staying with Kati in Los Angeles between Treya's second and third chemotherapy treatments.

In October of 1985, Vicky, Shannon, Treya, and I visited the Wellness Community. The question was whether to start a branch of the Wellness Community in San Francisco or to start up a completely separate center. Although we were all very impressed with Harold and the work he was doing, Vicky and Treya felt that perhaps a different approach could also be useful. And this was related *directly* to the issue of being versus doing. It all came to a head during a discussion with Naomi Remen, a medical therapist working in Sausalito.

Our talk with Naomi was quite stimulating and exciting. I completely lost track of time and was late to my next appointment—something that is now a problem because of my diabetes (scheduling food right on time!). Naomi said she felt quite in tune with me and Vicky, but when she received the materials on the Wellness Community she felt something was off, something was wrong, something was out of sync with who we were.

I told her we were aware of that, aware we had a somewhat different emphasis than Harold's. Ours felt like a more feminine approach, with less emphasis on fighting cancer or on recovering from cancer, and more emphasis on overall quality of life during the whole process. We didn't want to set it up so people felt they failed or lost somehow if the cancer remained, which seems to be the drawback of Harold's approach. When Vicky showed the materials to her friends at the Stephen Levine retreat, all of whom have recurring and metastatic cancer, their general comments were things like "I'm not sure I like the tone of this," "Could I come if my cancer didn't go away?," "What if I felt I'd accepted my cancer and wasn't into fighting it, would I fit in there?" Naomi said the feeling she'd gotten from his materials was that disease is something bad, something to be fought, and that you failed if you didn't win that fight. For her—and she's had Crohn's disease since childhood—disease has been something to learn to live with and to learn from.

Certainly as a cancer patient, I've become aware that although cancer is often seen as a chronic disease—witness the confusion over

Treya (*foreground*) and Kati at Pop's ranch, July 4, 1951.

Rad and Treya at "Fiesta," San Antonio, 1967. *Photo: Billo Smith.*

Working at Windstar in Aspen, August 1975.

Winter 1981. Treya had just moved to San Francisco.

At our wedding, San Francisco, November 26, 1983. (*Below*) Dancing with Radcliffe. *Photos: Kathy Thurmond.*

A "bald picture" taken by Linda Conger at Tahoe, spring 1985, right before the really difficult times.

(*Above*) At the Mill Valley house—"a time for healing." (*Left*) At the Janker Klinik in Bonn with Vicky, after the first round of "killer chemo."

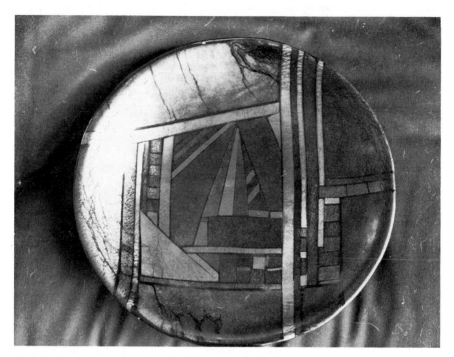

(*Above*) Fused glass—"the woman who works with her hands." (*Below*) One of almost one hundred spontaneous line drawings.

how or when you call someone cured—other people, people who are not doctors and people who don't have cancer themselves, want to hear you say that you're cured. They don't want to hear you talk in the same careful and measured way your doctors talk, that there's no sign of it now and the tests are clear but, of course, with cancer one can never be sure, one can only hope. No, they want to hear it's over and done with, that you're fine and they can go on about their lives and not worry about you, no ogres are lurking behind bushes or around corners. That could be part of what's going on with Harold's approach, and the difference between his attitude and ours, that of former cancer patients who know how tricky this disease can be. Our center, we decided, would not be affiliated with Harold's, much as we really wished him well.

The talk with Naomi triggered some other thoughts I didn't realize at the time. They arose out of a strange combination of seeing her—so beautiful and active and healthy, yet knowing she has a serious illness— and working with the women in a Monday-night breast cancer group I was attending. I've felt quite hesitant about committing myself to work with cancer patients, partly from fear of being constantly reminded of the future possibilities out there for all cancer patients, but also from a fear of them simply having cancer, of that too much always in front of me, too much always on my mind.

Over a few days I realized that that fear came out of letting the disease and its possibly awful consequences overshadow the human being there in front of me. It hit me the evening of my last session with the group. These were people first and foremost. We sometimes spent a whole session not even talking about cancer; it was only an incidental presence among us. These were people involved in their lives, their pains, their triumphs, their loves, their children, and only incidentally at this point with their cancer. It came to me that I had hesitated because on some level I thought I'd be working with cancer patients who were people, rather than with people who were often only incidentally cancer patients. I suppose this is part of my own evolution away from cancer and back, gradually and step by step, into my own life. I want to work with people who are moving toward life, even in the midst of cancer. Again, it all seems part of that shift, of being able to just *be* with cancer, even while you are trying to *do* something about it, important as that is. And just being with cancer patients as people, not as a collection of parts that need to have something done to them.

That shift came to its first dramatic head late one night in early summer. We were visiting the Tahoe house; Treya couldn't sleep. And then all the pieces began to fall into place. She was vibrant with the discovery. According to Treya, it was nothing less than her long-sought daemon! Not born fully fledged, but nonetheless loudly announcing its presence—but in a different voice, a voice she had too long suppressed.

Earlier in Tahoe. One night I lay awake, unable to sleep. I could see the burnished silver of the moonlight on the lake outside my window, ringed by the dark shapes of the pine trees around the house and far away by the dark shapes of the mountains of Desolation Wilderness. Such a bleak name, such a beautiful place.

Images of glass, deep red, iridescent white, cobalt blue, float through my head. I feel so excited, I simply can't sleep. Is it the tea I had earlier? Partly, maybe. But something else is happening, something inside me has been stirred up, reawakened. Glass, light, forms, shapes, flowing lines, fitting things together, watching a vision emerge from nothingness, watching beauty take shape in this world of form. How very exciting! I lie there, aware of energy swirling through my body. Is this it? Is this what I am to do, or at least an important part of it? Is this a critical piece I have been missing? A piece of myself I had lost?

I think so. I have found a part of myself missing lo these many years. *The woman who works with her hands.* The artist, the craftsperson, the maker. Not the doer or the knower, but the maker. The maker of things of beauty, who finds as much joy in the process as the end product.

The next day I felt like I had experienced a small epiphany. It felt like a moment of important insight into myself and into my future. I remembered that the times I felt most involved in my work, most excited about what I was doing, were times of making and crafting . . . drawing a richly textured map for my final project in cartography . . . making vibrant pen and ink drawings on Iona . . . crafting candles and flowing pots at Findhorn . . . creating beautiful shapes from nothingness . . . crafting words in written notes, journals that I showed no one. Those were the times I was unaware of time, totally involved, in a sort of meditative state of absolute concentration and self-forgetfulness.

I began to feel, the following day, that I had rediscovered an important part of myself. That perhaps *my* path was emerging from the undergrowth and thick tangle of shoulds and desire to adopt the masculine cultural values emphasizing the life of the mind. School emphasized knowledge, facts, content, thinking, analysis. I discovered I was good at that. It was a way to excel, to win praise and attention. What else was there, really? So I walked that road, clearly marked and smoothly paved.

Only it has never felt quite right. Why did I not go on to get my Ph.D. and teach somewhere? I thought about it, but something inside kept pulling me aside from that paved road. I had the ability for it, but not really the heart for it. And yet I criticized myself for not following through, thought I was weak, accepted criticisms that I was trivializing my life by not focusing on a doing career.

But now I see that the reason the paved road wasn't right for me is that I am more of a maker than a knower or a doer. That perhaps the reason I was so happy at Findhorn had more to do with all the time I spent in the candle studio and the pottery studio than I had suspected. That I have always loved making things since early childhood, but accepted the prevailing view that such work was frivolous, superficial, unimportant, unnecessary, not a true contribution, fit only for spare time as a hobby. That by doing so I cut off, stopped up a major source of joy and life energy and vitality in myself. Well, no more!

What's stirring in me is the emergence of a new standard by which to choose what I do. I hear myself talking about possibly, just possibly, doing the kinds of things I've always wanted to do, not felt I should do, even if I haven't the vaguest idea of what their outcome will be or if I'll be making a needed contribution or if I'd even be any good at it.

So what are these things I feel drawn to? All things I've discovered by accident, that have come bubbling up out of me, so to speak. Never planned or discovered through thought. Makes me nervous even to write them down. One is hand-built pottery, the kind of things I did at Findhorn. This is exciting, engaging, satisfying. I can picture myself looking at the world differently, always thinking of shapes, designs, forms, whether inspired by art or the natural world. I can picture myself going to art shows and craft shows and being fully engaged in looking, appreciating, coming up with new approaches. It feels very stimulating, very enlivening, exciting. I've always loved doing things with my hands, crafting things. I feel like this would bring me out of my head, out of ideas so much, to become more engaged in the world out there.

Another thing I am going to pursue is stained glass. I've wanted to do this for years and never have, I guess because I thought it was unimportant relative to everything else. Writing all this, I can just feel the artist within straining to get out! I want to pursue those line drawings of mine—again, they bubbled up spontaneously, beginning with my doodles and evolving into real pictures. And seeing what kind of a base for stained glass they would make. And remember all the needlepoint designs I used to do? Again something I just started doing spontaneously, no one taught me how or suggested it.

Another thing is writing, crafting words, an early love quelled, pure and simple, by fear. This one is still the scariest of them all, the most public, revealing the inner workings of my mind and soul, afraid I'll be judged superficial, juvenile, boring, etc., etc. But I'm determined to write this book, even if it never gets anywhere near being published. I will come back to that delight in words, in their beauty and power and capacity to surprise. I still remember vividly that paper I wrote in junior high school about what it felt like to sit in bed late at night and read. I described my feelings, the warmth of the light bulb, the bugs attracted to the light, the feel of the sheets on my legs, the quiet late night sounds, the feel of the pages as they turned, the subtle sounds of the pages and the spine of the book cracking ever so slightly. And I remember my love of certain turns of phrase, especially reading Lawrence Durrell. I would copy out short phrases, even single words, that I liked in the back of those books, savoring each one. It was almost like eating candy, the pleasure I took in the feel of those phrases.

Another thing I've always loved is working with groups, as at Findhorn. I don't think I want to go back to school and study theories anymore. I'm interested—this is pretty much a feminine way, I think—in practical approaches that will help people. Cancer Support Community—that's it.

All these things! The love of which has always come to me spontaneously, never planned. Where did all this go? How did it get lost? I'm not sure. But whatever happened, it seems to all have come back again. The simple pleasure of being and making, not knowing and doing. It feels like coming home! Is this what Ken talks about when he said he discovered his daemon? Mine is not flashy, not of the mind, not of the incredible feats he seems to accomplish. But that's the point, I now see—mine is quieter, more amorphous, more gentle, I think. More background, more feminine, more invisible. More of the body. More of the Earth. And more real for me!

"And so that's what went on last night," she said as she finished relating the story. I caught her excitement, it was so obviously genuine. And the funny thing is, everyone who met Treya was invariably impressed with her mind; she was easily one of the most intellectually acute people I had ever met. When Treya wrapped her mind around a topic, pity that topic. But she was discovering that her ability to do this wasn't deeply satisfying to her. She said she'd been listening to the wrong voice.

Directly related to this shift in voice was the increasingly insistent issue of whether we make ourselves sick—the whole new age notion that people bring on their illness either by their own thoughts or as some sort of megalesson they need to learn (as opposed to simply learning from illness, whatever its cause). The whole issue erupted again with Treya's having diabetes. She was simply assaulted by well-meaning people who were going to help her see why she gave herself diabetes. To the theoretical reasons that this idea is very lopsided, partial, and dangerous—reasons I will return to in a later chapter—Treya added another: the whole approach is too masculine, too controlling, too aggressive, too violating. And indeed, Treya would very soon become a national spokesperson for a more compassionate view of illness. How do I know this? Why, by the only really viable academic test in America: "The Oprah Winfrey Show" called and asked her to appear opposite Bernie Siegel.

This whole issue of whether or not I caused my disease(s) is up for me again. Because the person who is theorized about or who theorizes about him- or herself often sees this question of responsibility in the light of blame. "What did I do to deserve this?" "Why me?" "What did I do wrong that this should happen to me?" "No wonder I got cancer. I gave it to myself." That kind of thinking.

I've imposed this "logic" on myself at times. My friends have done it to me. I did it to my mother when she had cancer eighteen years ago, and I imagine she too felt violated in some way—and rightly so. For even though I think there is some truth in the idea that something I might have done once, or certain habitual modes of behavior, or certain ways of relating to the world and dealing with stress might have contributed to my developing cancer and diabetes, I don't believe that is the whole picture. I've reacted to the natural human desire to find a simple and clear cause for diseases that are frightening. It's been a natural and understandable defense against the fear of the unknown.

Thus I've been careful to explain that I believe disease has many causes—genetic, hereditary, diet, environment, life-style, personality. But saying that one of these causes is the only cause, that personality alone brings on disease, overlooks the fact that while we can control how we respond to what happens to us, we can't control everything that happens to us. This illusion of being in control, that we can control everything that happens to us, is so destructive, so aggressive.

The point, however, lies more with the question of guilt. If someone develops cancer, theorizes that they brought it on themselves, then feels guilty or wrong or bad because of that, the guilt itself becomes a problem that might even interfere with how well they cope with the disease and move forward toward health or better quality of life. That's why this is such a sensitive issue. That's why the whole issue of responsibility needs to be dealt with sensitively. That's why it's important to make careful distinctions about causation and not impute unconscious motives to others. It's difficult to deny unconscious or subconscious motives. For me, having people theorize about me on that level is what makes me feel violated and sometimes quite helpless. We all know how frustrating it can be to feel unjustly accused by another of acting on some unconscious motive and then have them interpret all our protestations as simply denial and further proof that they were right in the first place about us! Psychology at its cruelest.

Most people who are ill are undergoing a great deal of stress dealing with it, whether or not they are involved in these complex questions of psychological factors and causation. They may be undergoing even more stress if they do get involved in these issues of being responsible for their illness. Their needs should be respected, the limits they suggest should at least be considered. Not that I don't believe in healthy confrontation at the right moment, for I certainly do. What I object to is people theorizing about me and not bothering to ask me what my thoughts on myself and this illness are. I don't like someone saying to me, "X says cancer is caused by resentment," especially if this is said in a way that makes it sound like they believe that was the cause of my developing cancer. Or "Diabetes is caused by lack of love." Who really knows? But I don't mind them saying to me, "X says cancer is caused by resentment; what do you think? Is that true in any way for you?"

I do believe that we can use the crises in our lives for healing. I believe that absolutely. I know that there are times in my life I have felt resentment, and while I do not know if that played any role in my developing cancer, I do believe it can be very helpful to become aware of that possibility and choose to use this crisis to heal myself of resentment, to practice forgiveness and develop compassion.

I suppose a summary of all this would read something like this:

I have had cancer. I feel bad enough about this, about the threat to my life, about the surgery and treatments I have had to undergo. It has been frightening. I have felt guilty for getting cancer. I have asked myself what I might have done to bring this on myself. I have been unkind to myself in asking some of these questions. Please help. I do not need you to be unkind to me too. I need you to understand, to be gentle, to help me wrestle with these questions. I do not need you to theorize about me behind my back, so to speak. I need you to ask me, not to tell me. I need you to try to understand what this must feel like, just a little, to put yourself in my place and hopefully treat me more kindly than I sometimes treat myself.

In March Treya and I journeyed to the Joslin Clinic in Boston, famous for its treatment of diabetes, in an attempt to get a better handle on this new illness. We combined this with a business trip to Shambhala, which meant seeing Sam.

Sammy! What a sweetie. Such a brilliant businessman, yet so loving and open. I love the way he and Ken love each other, how they always tease each other. In Shambhala's office, they read some recent reviews of Ken's books. Seems they're having a big impact, not just in America. Sam said Ken is a big cult in Japan, but he's thought of as "new age," which freaks Ken out. In Germany he is a real mainstream hit, big academic phenomenon. We made jokes about Wilberians which soon degenerated into Wilberries. Everybody commented on how Ken seems to be changing, more vulnerable, more approachable, less caustic and distant and arrogant, sweeter.

We had lunch with Emily Hilburn Sell, the editor at Shambhala. I like her a lot, trust her judgment. I told her about the book I was working on—cancer, psychotherapy, spirituality—and asked her if she would edit it for me. I'd love to, she said, which makes me even more determined to see this project through!

Later that day we found ourselves standing in the Children's Section at the Joslin Diabetes Clinic, waiting for the teaching nurse. The bulletin board was filled with newspaper articles, announcements, posters, children's drawings. One headline read "Life is a Balancing Act for a 10-Year-Old." There was a quote from the ten-year-old kid in large type about how most kids, when they first learn they have diabetes, are simply angry and want it to not be true; they don't want to have to do anything about it. There was a poster next to this clipping that said, "Do you know someone who wants to have a baby and has diabetes?" with the face of a small child peering out at me. There was another clipping about a four-year-old with diabetes, another poster about helping children overcome their fear of hospitals. Tears welled up inside and dampened my eyes. These poor kids and what they have to deal with, so young. It seemed so very, very sad. There were a number of drawings in bright crayon about a Dr. Brink, but one especially pulled at my heart. It said, "Dr. Brink and diabetes go together like . . ." and then there was a drawing below of a soda plus a banana split plus chocolate chip cookies—all the things the kid who made the drawing must have loved and now could no longer have. He chose them, those forbidden goodies, to make his point.

The next day, Easter Sunday at Trinity Church, built in 1834, a congregation since 1795. Fabulous church, Romanesque feel to the arches, gold-leaf decorations within, warm colors of deep green and reddish terra-cotta. The church was overflowing this Easter Sunday. As we entered we saw tables filled with geraniums, later to learn it is a church tradition to give one to each child in the congregation that day. It was a bit of a surprise to me, a reminder that this is basically a Christian country when I didn't even realize I'd forgotten that fact. All these people dressed in their Easter Sunday finery. As we walked to church it looked like a coat and tie were required to be out on the sidewalks this morning, Boston's dress code run rampant.

We squeezed in among all the special suits and coordinated outfits and Easter hats, finally arriving at a perfect vantage point, looking down on the altar from behind one of the trumpeters announcing the triumph of Easter. Looking down on the gray and brown and blond and bald, hatted, unhatted, and some thinning heads below. All of us elevated, reminded of our status as sons and daughters of God, by the gold gilt around us, the soaring arches above us, the handsome crucifix over the central sanctum before us.

I liked the sermon. It was very short and cultured, with references to Joyce's *Ulysses* as well as to the Bible. Leave it to the Episcopalians. The pastor spoke of the suffering in our world, of the old belief that those who suffer in some way deserve it, and asked, "Can we not give up that ancient superstition that those who suffer deserve their suffering? Every night two-thirds on this earth go to bed ill-clothed, ill-housed, and ill-fed." He commented on Jesus' suffering as having to do with the human condition. I've never heard it described as part of his simply being human, part of his humanness rather than his saintly mission. The pastor also spoke of our need for meaning, and prayed for us to find meaning in the ordinary and meaning in the heroic. God knows that speaks to me, with my constant hunger for meaning.

And yet, even as I heard that, I felt a shift has occurred. The word "meaning" doesn't have quite the same bite for me as it once did, not quite the same ability to make me unhappy and dissatisfied and restless and searching still. I believe perhaps I am being more compassionate with myself. More gentle with life, with what it is to be human. Part of the move toward wisdom that I was talking to Ken about. But sometimes when I talk to others about changes I believe are happening within I'm not quite certain if it's true; am I bragging, am I only hoping this is true, am I affirming something I want to be true but which is not yet so? The ring of truth, the feeling that I am actually not pretending, comes more when I begin to write or talk about things that used to bother me as if they still do, but the complaint, the edge, the bitterness simply isn't there with its old force. I'm not trying to convince anyone of my progress, I'm simply being my old cantankerous self, complaining, self-pitying, going over the same old territory, and yet the complaints are weak, my heart isn't in them anymore, I feel a bit bored with what I'm saying. That's when I feel confident that I am indeed moving on, leaving that particular thing behind after so many months or years I've lived with it.

Then over to Old South Church—the enclosed, separate boxes with high walls for each family. Because this religion (Protestant) was a private experience, between man and his God, rather than an essentially communal one? A very different feel from Trinity Church, where one can see the whole congregation. A pastor was there, wanting to know if he could help us. He showed us the box at the front where the governor—the governor when Massachusetts was still under England—sat and told us Queen Elizabeth sat there on her visit. He said he imagined they would put Dukakis there when he came. Short circuit—who is he, the present governor perhaps?

We wandered in the memorial garden afterwards, enclosed by a high brick wall with plaques commemorating the man who put in the bells used by Paul Revere on the one-if-by-land, two-if-by-sea night, commemorating George Washington, commemorating some person who in 1798 proved to the satisfaction of many who saw him that he could fly from the belfry tower. Ken joking that "they should have put the plaque down here where the grease spot still is." All around, the brick walls glowed in the spring sunshine, in places thickly covered with the bare stems of ivy plants, overlapping, interweaving, layer upon layer of these stems delicately intertwining, each thin branch catching the light just so, so that the sunlight itself seemed interwoven and textured. I felt so blessed, and do so now just thinking of it.

June 2, back in San Francisco—a red-banner day. The doctors have decided Treya can have her Port-a-Cath removed. Hallelujah! This means they think that her chances of a recurrence are slim enough that she needn't leave it in. We are ecstatic. After the Port-a-Cath is removed, we go out for a big celebration on the town, diet be damned! Treya is alive, glowing, radiant. For the first time in a very long while I feel I can breathe, actually breathe.

Exactly two weeks later, to the day, Treya discovered a lump on her chest. The lump was removed. The lump was cancer.

13

ESTRELLA

☙§§☙

I WAS lying in bed next to Treya the morning she discovered the lump.

"Honey, look. Right here." Sure enough, a small, rock-hard bump under her right arm.

Very calmly she said, "It's probably cancer, you know."

"I suppose so."

What else could it be? And worse, a recurrence at this point would be extremely serious. It would mean, among other things, that the chance of a really gruesome metastasis—to the bone, brain, or lung—would now be very, very high. And we both knew it.

But what amazed me so, and what continued to amaze me in the coming days and weeks and months, was Treya's reaction: little or no alarm, no fear, no anger, not even tears, not even once. Tears were *always* a giveaway for Treya; if something was wrong, her tears told. No tears. And it wasn't that she was simply resigned or defeated. Treya seemed to be genuinely at peace with herself and with the situation, relaxed, open. What is, is. No judgment, no avoidance, no grasping, no aversion—or at any rate, incredibly modest amounts. Her meditative equanimity seemed to be unshakable. I myself would not have believed it had I not witnessed it in person, carefully, closely, over a long period of time. It was unmistakable, and not just to me.

Something was definitely going on, something was happening to her. Treya herself described it as the culmination of that inner shift, in so many of its facets—from doing to being, from knowing to making, from obsessive to trusting, from masculine to feminine, and, most of all, from controlling to accepting. It just all seemed to come together in a very simple, very direct, very concrete way.

Treya had indeed changed over the last three years, and if anything she openly expressed gratitude for this recurrence because it showed her, proved to her, as nothing else really could, just how profound that inner shift was. She felt that her old self, Terry, had died, and a new self, Treya, was born. She herself described it as a rebirth, and Treya was not given to hyperbole.

And how do I feel now? This moment? Basically I feel fine. A nice Sufi class tonight, a feeling that I like that practice and would like to continue it. Ken and I are going for a drive tomorrow along the coast and we'll spend the night wherever we find ourselves. That feels good.

And yet just this afternoon I talked to Peter Richards and discovered that, again, I have a recurrence. Treatment failure, I think they call it. That sounds so big, so ominous. I feel fine, and yet at the same time there's a voice, not very loud, that says you should be worried, why are you taking this so calmly, is this denial, don't you know what fearsome things probably lie ahead of you? This voice is present, but it doesn't have much power. I think it's the same part of me that freaked out when I first learned I had cancer, that woke in the middle of the night full of fear. It is an ignorant voice; at that time it knew so little it couldn't paint fearsome pictures of what having the big C might mean other than the obvious, death. But it had picked up on the general tone around cancer out there and played those ominous notes loudly in my ear.

Now it knows more. I've read a lot about how really terrible cancer and its treatments can be, really horrific accounts like A *Mortal Condition* and *Life and Death on 10 West*, scenes that used to give me nightmares. But now they're rather pale. Not full of horror as they once were.

When I first found the bump, except for catching my breath that first moment, I didn't feel particularly afraid, though I recognized what it meant. I didn't panic, I didn't cry, I didn't feel I was fighting back tears. It was more of an oh, this again? kind of reaction.

To Peter's office, an examination, of course it has to come out. We had a good time, I showed him the bald pictures, he was in a good mood as was I. The next day as he cut it out, while Ken and Vicky waited, he told me the story of how one of the doctors had finally married a woman that he [the doctor] had dated for a long time after she issued an ultimatum—either you marry me or I won't go out with you anymore. Classic male-female tale, and I could tell the nurse with us enjoyed hearing the inside story.

Ken is wonderful. We'll go through this thing together, he says. I feel at peace with it all. If it's my karma, my lot in life to go through this, then I accept it. No use agonizing over it. No use thinking of frightening future possibilities. If this is the way my life is, then this is the way my life is, and I'll live it well. A kind of curiosity, a calmness. For now I feel great. My diet is great, my exercise is regular, I feel energetic and excited about life again.

In meditation tonight, it feels like I am no longer avoiding relationship, no longer resisting life and all it means. To open up to life in all its aspects. To take risks, to completely trust. To stop using my mental sharpness as justification for my defenses, my avoidances. To follow my intuition, that gut feeling that something is right, and to move away from those things that feel wrong even when I can support them with reasons upon reasons. To eat fully of life, of experience. To no longer taste and then reject. To embrace, enfold, include. All feminine qualities, I noticed. To stop trying to be a man and rejoice in becoming a woman.

And immediately it came up for me. To stop trying to be a man. To stop calling myself Terry. To become Treya. Treya Wilber. To let go of being the eldest son. I had a dream that night, full of wonder and excitement; the only line I can remember from it is: "Hello, my name is Treya."

The next morning Terry asked me to start calling her "Treya," which I did. Treya, Treya, Treya. At that point I, and many of her friends, couldn't help but worry that perhaps Treya was indeed, to some degree, caught in denial—she was so calm, so quietly joyous, so open and accepting. But that, I would learn, was simply to underestimate Treya. She had, in fact, changed; it was very genuine, very real, very deep.

It seems appropriate that as I begin to write specifically about how different I feel now, after this most recent recurrence, that the diskette I've been working on for the last six months is now full. I begin anew, on a blank disk.

This does feel like a new beginning, a rebirth as it were. I have changed, in some deep and profound way. It's easy to think you're unafraid of something that hasn't happened and that you don't think will happen, but you never know for sure, not until the fearful thing actually occurs. Only then do you know if you are afraid or not afraid.

And this time, I am unafraid. Oh sure, there are still parts of me that are afraid; I am still human, after all. There are still a few fearful clowns, but they don't even have bit parts. They're stagehands, and happy to get even that job!

And I never would have known that this shift had taken place internally without the recurrence. When I say I'm grateful for this recurrence, I mean it. Something wonderful has happened. A great load of fear I have been carrying around has left me, silently, sometime in the night, I do not know exactly when or how.

I am much less afraid, too, of the future, of possible recurrences that might lead to one of those grim cancer deaths I've read too much about. When I look up that particular alley there are still bogeymen hiding in corners, but this shift has given me faith that even if I must travel that alley I can now travel quite lightly. Ken's favorite line: "To be the Witness of fate, not its victim." I simply notice, with bare attention, and quiet joy and calm walk with me down that alley. That boulder I have been carrying with me ever since my shock and fear at the first announcement is gone. If I am tempted to pick up pebbles along the way, I think I can also put them back where they belong.

How do I feel about it? Oddly excited. Like it is a wonderful opportunity. Here is the perfect impetus to explore other modes of cancer treatment, a kind of postgraduate course in experimental therapies. I intend to explore alternatives ranging from metabolic therapies to low-fat, raw-food diets to immune-system stimulation to psychic healers to Chinese herbs. I have looked at my life, at what I enjoy that has been missing, and now have a real commitment to reintroduce things I have left out. To pursue my daemon of artisanship, the woman who works with her hands. To continue meditation. To continue looking into the psychological component that is 20% (or whatever it is) of disease genesis. I am no longer afraid of being blamed or feeling guilty. I no longer want to be right. I no longer want to defend myself. I am simply interested in life, terribly interested. I can expand into life, just like my childhood vision, mixing with the universe.

The only treatment the doctors could offer Treya was more radiation to the general area, a treatment that Treya rejected immediately for the obvious reason that the earlier recurrence, the five bumps, had already demonstrated that this cancer was resistant to radiation. That left her free to explore any and all alternatives, since white man's medicine had been exhausted. Terry might have listened to the doctors' pleas—they have to offer something, they have to treat the sickness if they can't treat the illness—but Treya wasn't buying.

And so began what was by far the most entertaining leg of our journey through the mad world of cancer cures. On the road again, we headed down to Los Angeles, to see first a very competent physician who specialized in immune-system stimulation, and then down to Del Mar, where we spent an entire week with the wild, fabulous, insane, lovable, sometimes effective, wacked-out psychic healer Chris Habib.

Whatever Chris Habib did in terms of actual healing, I won't say now. But I will tell you that she did one incredibly important thing: She completed the transformation from Terry to Treya by injecting the new Treya with an irreversible shot of humor.

Nomads we have been, these last few days. One night in a Holiday Inn on the fifth floor, windows won't open and the air conditioner doesn't work, but the furnishings are plush. Another night in a Mission Inn, all one level, cozy, with a very popular coffee shop-bakery attached, always full of families eating good old American food and pies and cakes. Another night in a Budget Motel where the carpet doesn't feel quite clean and you can hear the people on the third floor, just above, as they unpack and pack, and there's a sign in the bathroom saying you'll be charged for any missing towels. Fabulous dinner that night, in a place called the Five-Foot restaurant. It is, of all things, a European gourmet establishment run entirely by Chinese. What does the name mean? Nobody knows. Ken's guess: the average height of the waiters.

Del Mar—this place is so lovely, so washed with waves and sunshine, so relaxed (how does anybody work here?) that we decided to make a holiday of it and splurge on a motel right on the beach. So the trip has turned from a have-to-be-headquartered-in-a-budget-motel to an adventure in beach life and quiet dining and a sleep lulled by the sound of waves. When we came in after dinner and window-shopping and provisioning our tiny refrigerator with vegetables and fresh fish, the wide beach where the river empties into the sea had large bonfires licking the edges of the night, shadowy figures moving on the edge of the golden light, and I imagined I could smell hotdogs and marsh-mallows in the soft evening air. I imagine them out there now, the wives and husbands and lovers, the embers still golden, small against the vastness of the night sky.

What did I do this afternoon? Why, I went to see a psychic healer. When the session was over I wrote her a check for $375 for a week of treatment, and felt better about spending that money than most of the money spent on my cancer care. Only I don't dare tell my orthodox doctors I'm doing this. To choose a psychic healer over radiation? How subversive. And yet it feels like a fully healthy and life-affirming decision for me, made in full awareness of the options and the alterna-tives. Everyone agrees that belief in the efficacy of a treatment is critically important, and I no longer believe in radiation or chemo-therapy to deal with the kind of disease I have left. They were OK for me then, but no longer. Not now.

Now I am ready for something different. With this healer, I will simply see what happens, without judgment.

At 3:00 P.M., while Ken is setting up our headquarters, I walk into the Holistic Health Center and find my way up the stairs to the reception area. A nice-looking young man—clear blue eyes, blond hair, a nice openness to his face—offers to show me the way. He is Dr. George Rawls, he tells me, the director of the Center. We walk into Chris's treatment room, through a waiting room. An older man is lying on the treatment table and Chris is working on him. Her young son is also in the room, and a man who is observing and, he says, learning from her. George sits down. Conversation flows easily while Chris continues to work, a very relaxed and casual atmosphere. The older man, Bill, has an inoperable brain tumor. He had two tumors earlier which Chris treated and which shriveled, apparently, but later another tumor came back. He was wheeled in on a gurney from the local hospital last week. Now he's walking around, and in the coming days Chris would often send him out to get coffee for us. At times she talks about him as if he's not there, and later his brother enters and joins the talk. She works with her left hand behind his head, her right hand on the side of his head. At one point she says she feels a spot of cold there, still, a small one. He agrees, he feels it too. She chides him gently, you're supposed to tell me these things, do you want me to guess it all myself? George explains that Chris's casual way of working isn't typical of the Center, just her way.

Then it is my turn to lie on the couch. George leaves, after saying he would love to meet Ken. He thinks highly of *Up from Eden* and of Ken's writings in general. First she works on my left side. I feel a coolness on the side of my breast where her right hand is; she tells me to be sure and tell her if I ever feel anything really cold. Then her hands move and I feel a coolness in my rib area, just below my breast. Then she works for several minutes on my abdomen. Something's going on in the pancreas, she says. "Oh, I forgot to tell you, I also have diabetes." Interesting. She works there for maybe twenty minutes more, moving her left hand to the center just under my breastbone and keeping the right over the ribs, where I continue to feel coolness. She talks a bit about cancer being caused by a virus, how the virus may still be there, hiding, when medical doctors say it is gone. What she is doing now is keeping it from moving to another place, she says. She has one hand in the center of my chest, just below the sternum, and the other still over my rib and my pancreas. One place feels cool, the other does not. When she moves to the left side of my body I still feel some coolness over the pancreas and remember that my grandfather died of cancer of the pancreas.

On my right side she puts her left hand under me and her right along my side just where the recurrences have been. I couldn't feel any coolness or cold, I told her. After a while she moves her right hand up, over the top of my prosthesis. I offer to remove it, but she says it's not necessary, her energy can travel through it easily. All of this, of course, with her son and the man looking on.

I find that she had cancer when she was twenty-three, a lump in her breast that in three years had spread through her body. She tells me that was the beginning of her work, that she went to all kinds of doctors and healers. For a while she studied with a biochemist in Italy, but somewhere in there she was arrested for healing a child with leukemia. Can you imagine, she says, if that's a crime . . . This biochemist was a believer in unusual approaches, and told her that he had known from the moment he met her that she could heal.

Her dream is to go to a Third World country and teach others how to heal. She says her method is very mathematical and teachable, though certainly some have more talent for it than others. There are ten levels that disease can exist on, she says, and cancer is a fifth level disease. Diabetes is a fourth level disease. To heal, you have to raise your vibrations to just the right level and then tailor it to the type of cancer and learn to exert just the right amount of pressure in your brain. For example just now, she says, I'm exerting about thirteen units of pressure. I usually work between ten and twenty-five. She needs a Third World country, she says, because this sort of thing isn't allowed in the U.S.

Next day, back to Chris. Ken is staying away until the end, so any of his skepticism won't rain on my parade. I find I like her so much, what is it about her? Today she tells me that she had cancer seven times (and three heart attacks) and two of those times was pronounced terminal. Her husband—she was married at age fifteen—walked in one day when she was thirty and said he was leaving her. For his secretary, whom he had hired a month earlier. That was it, no other explanation, no previous problems, things had seemed fine. At that time they had three children and two adopted children. Within a month, she said, she had cancer all through her. The reason it kept coming back was that she had a broken heart and was empty; she hadn't learned to meet her own needs. Her stepfather left the family when she was eight and she, being the eldest child, took care of everyone, including her mother— who had nineteen heart attacks over the years. She also had a retarded sister a year younger whom she took care of. This type of situation: her stepfather, who was a carpenter, came in one day with his guts hanging out; he had split himself open on a circular saw. He told her mother to call an ambulance, her mother fainted, so Chris called the ambulance and helped her father lie down and hold himself together. She had to learn to take care of herself, she says, before she could really be cured.

She talks about chasing a virus around my body, making sure it doesn't hide out anywhere else. When she applies energy, if there is any virus the area gets cold. The cold is how she knows the virus is there. The cold is also what kills the virus, they don't like the cold, she says. So as she works on me she's moving her hands to different places; sometimes she'll ask me if I feel cold somewhere or if I feel a flow from one place to another, sometimes she'll say she feels something in a particular place and ask me if I do. When I feel the cold it's more a coolness and usually not too deep. Good, she says, it's good you're not feeling a sharp cold or we'd have a lot of work to do. I ask her if it makes it harder to work with people who can't feel in certain areas because of surgery or radiation. She says no, not really, because she can feel it. But it does seem important for people's healing for them to be able to feel it and see it, so they know something is happening. When she put her hand down where it was cool she said, we don't want this virus hiding out anywhere else, do we?

While the treatment was going on she had two stones placed on me, one a strange fluorite crystal down on my abdomen and another, a beautiful smooth metallic stone, on my heart. Can't say I clearly felt anything from either of them, but the whole time I was there I was aware of a lot of energy moving in my body, especially in my legs and in my feet.

That day she talked a lot—we were alone for this session—about how difficult it is to work in the U.S. An inspector came by recently, for example, looked around, couldn't see any instruments in her office. He wanted to make sure all she was doing was laying on hands, which she assured him was all. She invited him to stay, but he couldn't. Apparently she's watched off and on a lot.

Once, she said, people brought her a little girl with leukemia. They had tried everything, all the doctors, all the treatments, and Chris was their last hope, they said. When they brought the little girl in they had suitcases full of vitamins and herbs and special foods. Chris laughed, told them to go out and get the girl a McDonald's burger. The little girl was delighted, the others horrified, but they did it. The little girl was cured after only four sessions, Chris said. She loves working with children, they are easy, they don't have all the adult stuff in the way.

She said her eighteen-year-old son gave her a lecture this morning. Mom, he said, you've got to dress more professionally and clean up your language. But Chris feels she has to do it her way, and she's just as likely to come up with a dirty joke as some soothing, healing statement. After all, she says, most of the time I'm trying to get my patients to lighten up about life. People get so serious about this stuff, and the jokes help. I've been around so much illness and suffering and death all my life I don't take it seriously anymore, and that helps the people who come in here. They're usually too serious. My homework: come in with a joke the next day.

Why is she so very likable? Why do I like her so much? I trust her openness about what she does and her desire to teach it. She's not greedy, that's for sure. I like being around her, look forward to coming back. Definitely a strong, nurturing, mothering energy she has. I hope she has learned to take care of herself; I can still hear her saying how all those years she was giving and taking care of others she was empty inside, she didn't know how to give to herself.

Chris Habib was something else. She was really quite beautiful, in a slightly broken-down kind of way. Of course, if you believed the seven bouts of self-cured cancer, the broken-down part was easy to understand. But it was just this type of skepticism that Treya wanted me to keep to myself, thank you very much. The atmosphere had gotten rather bad between us—something fairly rare by then—and we had run to our respective friends with tales of woe and remorse. We finally had it out that evening, the gentle sound of the waves standing in sharp contrast to the heat of the discussion.

"Look," I began, "I'm not skeptical about faith healing in general or the laying on of hands in particular. I happen to believe that both of those are sometimes very real phenomena."

Treya interrupted. "You know as well as I do the theory behind it. There are subtle energy currents in the human body—prana, chi, ki—the same energies used in acupuncture, the same energies manipulated in kundalini yoga. And I do believe that some people, the so-called healers, can intentionally manipulate those energies in themselves and in others."

"So do I, so do I." Those energies, in fact, were level two in the model I had outlined to Edith Zundel, the emotional-bioenergy level, the level that forms the crucial link between the physical body—and its diseases—and the mental and spiritual levels. I personally believe that manipulating those energies, whether through yoga, exercise, acupuncture, or laying on of hands, can be an important and sometimes crucial factor in the healing of physical illness, since each higher level has a profound impact on its lower level(s). So-called "downward causation."

"Then why the skepticism about Chris? I can tell by your snide tone that you don't approve."

"No, it's not that at all. It's just that, in my experience, healers or psychics don't always understand exactly what it is they are doing or even how they do it. And yet it does sometimes work. So they tend to make up stories or theories about it, about what they do. I don't question that the energy is there, that this can sometimes work very well. I question their stories, their theories. I don't question what they do, I question what they *say* about what they do. Sometimes the stories are really funny, and they are usually bolstered with some half-baked theories from physics. I can't help but react to that stuff."

I had, late that afternoon, stepped in to watch Chris work. And it was as I said: I didn't doubt that something genuine was going on—she was definitely moving energy—but I believed hardly a word of what she said. I had never heard so many tall tales in my life. She was spinning them out with an ease that would shame the brothers Grimm. But that was exactly her charm, that was what I found so endearing about her. Like Treya, I found her enormously likable. You just wanted to hang out with her, get caught up in her magical stories. That, I came to see, was exactly a crucial part of whatever it was she was doing. But that didn't mean I had to believe her tales, not literally. Plato said that at least one-third of what a good doctor has to do is provide what he called "charm," and by that criterion alone, Chris was a fabulous doctor.

But Treya took my skepticism about Chris's stories for a skepticism about Chris's efficacy, and she wanted none of that. "I just don't need that now," she kept saying. What I was still learning, and still learning the hard way, was just how to be a good support person. My lesson here: if you are genuinely skeptical about a particular treatment, voice that skepticism during the period that the person is trying to decide whether or not to do the treatment. That's being honest and helpful. But if the person decides to do the treatment, then shelve your skepticism and get behind them 100%. At that point your skepticism is cruel and unfair and undermining.

And anyway, Chris's charm was having a wonderful effect on Treya. It's this "charm" that is so missing in white man's medicine, where its effects, if any, are dismissed with the decontaminated term "placebo." But would you rather be cured by a "real" medicine or a "charmed" medicine? Do you really care?

In the past, while Treya had always depended on me to keep up a certain humor about the situation, she sometimes found my humor inappropriate. But Chris made me look anemic by comparison. There was nothing she wouldn't make fun of, there was nothing sacred, nothing off-limits, nothing that couldn't be laughed at. And this, if anything, was what Treya and I took away from crazy Chris Habib: lighten up, kids. It's all a joke anyway.

Running along the beach, now in the dimmer twilight and on my home stretch returning to the motel, I thought of how I want myself to change, to change even more. I want to hold things more lightly, not see everything as so very, very serious. I want to laugh more and play more and not think of things as always in crisis. I want to take the pressure off of myself, and off of others. To hold life lightly, my new motto.

Fourth treatment. "A lot of people don't want to learn to heal themselves," she says. "They want someone else to do it, to turn it over to someone else. Sometimes I have to be a love object to them too. There was one man I worked with—the kind of handsome man that everyone falls in love with right away—ran five businesses, had a couple of Corvettes, had paid for seventeen abortions with seventeen different women. He came to me at thirty-two with cancer. He fell in love with me. He would come back all the time, and always tell me he loved me. You don't love me, I said, you love the energy. And you have it in yourself, you can heal yourself. Why don't you get yourself a crystal and I'll program it for you. Then you won't have to keep coming back all the time. So he got a crystal and found he could use it to handle the cold when something happened. I saw him yesterday for the first time in eight months. Whenever he feels something is going wrong, he uses the crystal. He says he has only felt a little bit of cold lately, and he feels he can handle it."

Ken came in at that point. We're doing much better after we had it out over his skepticism. It's his turn on the table. He really likes Chris, thinks she's a kick. She works her hands over his body, says she doesn't feel any coldness anywhere. Does he? Nope. Then she starts working on his head. This is strange, she says. Each side of the brain has ten channels. In most people, only two or three channels are open. Four at most. She says in her brain both sides are open to ten, but that was only after many great healers had worked on her. Only once every two thousand years does that happen, she says, do both sides open up to ten. The last person before her was the Buddha. But she says Ken is open to ten on one side and to seven on the other. She's never seen that before. Since his brain is already so open, she says she thinks she can open the seven side all the way to ten. She works on him for about thirty minutes, all the time asking him questions, particularly if he can smell anything strange. "I smell smoke." "Good." "Now it smells like mildew." She finally says that both sides of his brain are open to ten. There goes that theory, she says. Only supposed to be one person like this every two thousand years, and there are two of them in this room! Ken starts laughing hysterically—he doesn't buy any of this—and I don't know whether to be happy for him or angry at him!

Chris asks me if I want to learn how to heal myself. I say definitely. So she gives me the exercise. Ken seems quite interested in this. "Imagine you are weighing yourself, only you are weighing your etheric body. Picture yourself standing on the scale and the dial reads from 1 to 10. Now this 1 to 10 scale is not the same as the ten channels in the brain. This is an entirely different scale. See where the needle stops." I visualize this. First there is a flash of two, but that is more a thought, not a picture. I try to keep my mind on the picture, and I see the needle wavering between 4.5 and 5. I tell her this. "Good," she says. "Five means you are in balance. Take the needle and move it toward five and hold it there awhile. Now, take the needle and move it toward ten, and watch what happens in your mind as you do this." I visualize the movement. Inwardly I feel resistance, I have to push the needle over. I tell her this. "And what did you feel happening in your mind, did the energy move to one side?" Yes, it did. And she tells me now to move the energy to one and watch what happens. My attention then moves to the left side of my head, of my brain. "What I want you to do from now on is practice holding the needle steady on five. When you can hold it there for thirty-five minutes, you are on track. Just check every so often and see if the needle is on five; if it is not, move it there and hold it there."

During the rest of the session I check every now and then. The needle stays fairly steady at five for this time, with a slight tendency to move down toward 4.5. Good, she says. I can't find any more cold in your body. The virus is gone, you'll be just fine.

She charges a beautiful crystal and gives it to me. If I ever feel any coldness in my body, put that crystal on it until the cold disappears. And, she says, looking at Ken, he can now do anything I can, so if you need healing he can do it.

"Can you do it?" she asked, as soon as we stepped out of the Holistic Health Center. "And why did you start laughing?"

"I couldn't help it, honey. I'm no Buddha. You know it, I know it. I wish I could move energy like she does, but I can't."

"Could you feel anything while she was working on you?"

"I could definitely feel the energy moving, but what was most bizarre, I was definitely smelling odd smells way before she even asked me about it. As I told you, I think something actually does happen with gifted healers. I just don't buy their interpretations."

But the net effect was charm. Chris had definitely moved a lot of energy around in both of us. We both felt vitalized, alert, happy. And the constant stream of outrageous tales made both Treya and I hold everything more lightly: Around Chris, truth lost all meaning—everything was equally true or equally false, equally a tall tale, it didn't matter. Everything started looking humorous. Treya being sick, me being a Buddha—they were both a joke. And that, I think, was the only point Chris wanted us to get.

"What do you see?" The voice is unwavering.

I decide not to fight it, since it makes no sense anyway. I start reading out loud what few words and symbols and sentences I can understand, from the millions that seem to open up in front of my eyes, me looking at them, them looking at me.

"Thus we cannot escape the fact that the world we know is constructed in order (and thus in such a way as to be able) to see itself. But in order to do so, evidently it must first cut itself up into at least one state which sees, and at least one other state which is seen. In this severed and mutilated condition, whatever it sees is only partially itself. In any attempt to see itself as an object, it must, equally undoubtedly, act so as to make itself distinct from, and therefore false to, itself. In this condition it will always partially elude itself."

"Keep reading," says the voice, and I find another paragraph floating by.

"Everything that from eternity has happened in heaven and earth, the life of God and all the deeds of time simply are the struggles for Spirit to know itself, to find itself, be for itself, and finally unite itself to itself; it is alienated and divided, but only so as to be able thus to find itself and return to itself."

"Again."

"It does not emphasize the ruling Caesar, or the ruthless moralist, or the unmoved mover. It dwells upon the tender elements in the world, which slowly and in quietness operate by love; and it finds purpose in the present immediacy of a kingdom not of this world. In this way, the insistent craving is justified—the insistent craving that zest for existence be refreshed by the ever-present, unfading importance of our immediate actions, which perish and yet live for evermore."

"Do you know what all that means?" the voice from the absence says.

On the long drive back to the Bay Area, Treya read aloud to me sections of *The Causes and Prevention of Cancer*, by the psychoanalyst Frederick Levenson, which was one of the few books that she felt dealt adequately with the psychological components of cancer, at least in her case. She was now working hard on that psychogenic slice of the cancer pie, a slice we both figured was about 20% of the picture. Not the whole picture, but a crucially important segment.

"His theory is that people are more prone to cancer if, as adults, they have a hard time bonding with other people. Rather, they tend to be hyperindividualistic, overly self-contained, never asking for help, always trying to do it themselves. Because of this, all the stress that they accumulate can't be discharged easily by bonding with others, or by asking others for help, or allowing themselves to depend on anybody. This built-up stress thus has nowhere to go, and if they are genetically primed for cancer, this stress can trigger it."

"And you feel that applies to you?" I asked.

"Definitely. My favorite lines, throughout my life, have been things like, 'Oh, no thanks, I can handle it,' 'I can do it on my own,' 'Oh, don't bother, I can do it.' It's extremely hard for me to ask for help."

"Maybe that was part of being the eldest son, being the tough guy."

"I think so. It embarrasses me to think of how often I've said these things. Over and over again, throughout my life. I can do it on my own. I can handle it. No, thanks.

"And I know what's beneath it. Fear. Fear of being dependent. Fear of being rebuffed if I were to ask. Fear of being turned down if I showed my need. Fear of being needy. I remember how quiet I was as a child, how easy, how undemanding, how uncomplaining. I didn't ask for much. I didn't tell anybody about my problems in school. I went to my room, where I read books, alone. Very quiet, very self-contained, holding myself still. Shy, reserved, afraid of criticism, imagining negative judgments everywhere. Even when I played with my brother and sisters, I often felt alone.

"Here's Levenson's point," she continued. "I'll read this: 'The precancerous individual, lacking emotional entropy, will be unable to fuse with anyone else as a means of dissipating irritation. He will most likely be able to experience intimacy only when he is caring for someone else. This is safe. To be loved and cared for, however, results in emotional discomfort, an uneasiness that is easily detected.'

"That's me. You're the first person I've really been able to fuse with. Remember that list I made on what I thought caused my cancer, and one of the items was 'not meeting Ken sooner'? Looks like Levenson would agree with that. He says that 'Do it yourself is a carcinogenic concept. Well, I've had it all my life, and I don't think anybody gave it to me, I think I came born with it. It feels like some deep karmic trend of mine. It wasn't just wanting to be the eldest son. I've had it forever, it seems like."

"Then ditch it, right? You're Treya now, not Terry. The corner has already been turned, right? It's obvious in everything about you. So let's hear it for fusing, which means major cuddle time for me, which I can definitely handle."

"I guess I'm just kicking myself for not starting it earlier."

"No kicking allowed in this here car."

"OK. And you? What's your major issue? Mine is trying to let love in, to not do it myself or control it myself, to come to terms with the fact that there are people out there that *love* me. What's yours?"

"To come to terms with the fact that there are people out there that *don't* love me. I tend to make the opposite mistake. I think everybody should love me, and when someone doesn't, I get nervous. So, as I child, I overcompensated like crazy. Class president, valedictorian, even captain of the football team. A frantic dance for acceptance, an attempt to have *everybody* love me.

"Underneath this was the same fear as yours—fear of rejection. But where you closed down and became too inner-directed, I opened up and became too other-directed. All of it was driven by anxiety, by an attempt to please and to perform. Classic anxiety neurosis."

"What you call F3 pathology."

"Fulcrum three pathology, yes. I've had that anxiety most of my life. It's what I've been working on with Roger, with Frances, with Seymour. It's pretty recalcitrant; or I should say, I am. But I don't think that's my main problem. I mean, it is a problem, I definitely have it, but I've always had it and I've always handled it. What I can't handle is not being true to my daemon, my own inner voice. When I abandon that, I get in real trouble."

"And you abandon that when you don't write?"

"No, I abandon that when I don't write and then blame the not-writing on someone else. That's the lie. And that comes from your soul, not your body. F3 anxiety is just some lower bodily energy, usually aggression, that you won't let *come up*. Your daemon is some higher psychic or subtle energy that you won't let *come down*. And it's the blocking of that coming-down energy that causes the anxiety that I can't handle, the anxiety that just wipes me out. So if I'm being true to my daemon, I can handle F3 anxiety. But if I'm not, then I get an F7 or F8 pathology, a soul pathology, and the two of them together wipe me out. That's what happened in Tahoe. God, I'm really sorry I blamed you for all that shit."

"That's OK, sweetheart, we both have a lot to forgive."

That was the first time I had admitted, in a free and open way, that I had blamed her for so much of my own woes, though we both had known it for some time. It was good to clear the air on that difficult issue, especially since, on the way down to Del Mar, we were not getting along well at all. Ever since we had been seeing Seymour, we had virtually ceased fighting (we both credited Seymour with very probably saving the marriage). But, fueled by my skepticism over her latest treatment choice, we were going at each other with an aggressiveness that only married couples can muster, an aggressiveness that neither of us had displayed in some time. At first we both thought this meant the beginning of a new and difficult round of fighting. But it was just the opposite—it was marital aggression's last major stand, although it was a good one. From that point on, we simply ceased fighting, at least to the point of flying apart. Perhaps, from Chris, we got the joke.

Back in San Francisco, we heard that the Venerable Kalu Rinpoche would be giving the Kalachakra empowerment in Boulder, Colorado. Sam was going to be there, and he encouraged us to come. We agreed, and, a few months later, found ourselves in the auditorium of the University of Colorado, along with sixteen hundred other people to participate in this, the very highest of Buddhist ceremonies, stretching over four days. And although we didn't know it at the time, this ceremony would mark the final emergence of "Treya," an emergence that she would officially announce a month later on her fortieth birthday. This was altogether appropriate since, after taking one look at Kalu, Treya and I knew that we had found our teacher.

November 25, 1986

Hello, friends. November 16 was my fortieth birthday and on that day I changed my name to Treya. Henceforth I will no longer be known as Terry Killam or Terry Killam-Wilber but as Treya Wilber or Treya Killam Wilber.

Seven years ago while I was living at the Findhorn Community in Scotland I had a dream, one of those very clear ones that somehow feel significant. I dreamt that my name should be Estrella, which is Spanish for "star." When I woke and thought about it I felt the name should be shortened to Treya (most people wouldn't know that "ll" in Spanish is pronounced "y" anyway). But . . . I never got around to it. I'd always been suspicious of people who change their names anyway, and judgmental of people who choose names like Diamond and Angel Ecstasy. At that time, I would have been embarrassed to change my name; my own judgment blocked me from "following that dream."

Or perhaps it just wasn't time yet. Perhaps I needed seven years to grow into that name. Without a doubt, these last years have been the most dramatic and challenging years of my life. Especially the last three, beginning with meeting Ken Wilber, marrying him four months later, and ten days after our wedding discovering I had breast cancer. Surgery and radiation, a recurrence eight months later, more surgery, six months of chemotherapy and baldness, eight months later diabetes, and, just this June, another recurrence.

My reaction to the most recent recurrence surprised me. With the two preceding bouts with cancer, my predominant response was fear, but this time I felt quite calm. There was some fear, of course—after all this time I am certainly not naive about cancer—but the degree of calmness and matter-of-factness I felt showed me that my relationship to this disease had changed profoundly. If I had not had the recurrence, I would never have fully recognized this inner shift.

One evening soon after receiving the biopsy results, I wrote in my journal about this recurrence, letting thoughts spill out about what this meant to me and how it felt in a stream-of-consciousness way. Without realizing where I was heading, I found myself writing about the new balance I felt between my masculine and feminine sides and how I felt I could now stop trying to be my father's eldest son. I found myself saying "Treya . . . my name should be Treya now. Terry is a masculine, independent, no-nonsense kind of name, no frills, very straightforward—the way I've always tried to be. Treya is softer, more feminine, kinder, more subtle, with a bit of mystery to it—the person I feel I'm becoming. More myself."

But I waffled about the name. How silly, to change one's name! Yes, that would have been Terry's attitude; what nonsense. But Treya, Treya would understand, Treya would encourage and support the change. I had two more dreams last summer, and one with the recurrence, each with the flavor of "Come on now, stop messing around. It's time to change your name. Your name is Treya."

Then last month Ken and I did a four-day Kalachakra empowerment with Kalu Rinpoche. On Saturday night everyone is supposed to sleep on pieces of kushi grass (Buddha was seated on a mat of this grass when he reached enlightenment) and remember their dreams; these dreams are thought to be particularly important and auspicious. That night I dreamt that Ken and I were looking for a place to live—the sense was that this was about "coming home." At a house by the ocean I saw a big black fountain pen lying on the ground and picked it up. I wanted to see how it felt to write with it, so I took the top off and wrote, as clear as day, "Treya."

And so, I decided to change my name on my fortieth birthday; not only that, my fortieth birthday was a full moon. Very Goddess-like!

Other ways I've changed, besides my name? I'm doing something I really love to do, fused-glass art work, something I can't wait to get back to, something I dream about. Something totally new, that doesn't come from my past, from anything anybody encouraged me to do. A real break with the past. And yet something I've always been intrigued by, interested in; something that was somehow innately there, inside me, all along only I never saw it through the filters I was wearing then.

I'm less critical of others. I don't hold them to the standards of conventional or "doing" success. I have a good friend who is a weaver; her husband is a political activist. I no longer think her work is unimportant compared to his. I'm not only more tolerant of but genuinely interested in the various ways people choose to shape their lives, and a quick judgment isn't waiting in the wings, ready to pop on stage at any time. I see all of life as more of a game, not quite so totally loaded with importance. It's more fun, easier. I hold life more lightly.

My own schoolmarmish attitude, the tendency to proofread others' lives, is lessening. I don't have to have it my way so much, control so much, and I assume less and less that there is a "correct" or accurate grammar for peoples' lives. I am therefore less quick to anger, to react. I try to simply witness, without judgment, myself and others.

I trust myself more. I'm kinder to myself. I believe there is a wisdom guiding my life and that my life doesn't have to look like anyone's else to feel good and fulfilling and, yes, even successful.

And it does feel amazing that all these changes are coming together, snowballing, gaining momentum, becoming really integrated on this, my birthday, in so many ways. I am, in some sense, being reborn. Shedding my past and moving into a future that is really mine, not shackled and conditioned so heavily by my past, rather guided and strengthened by my past but with a direction that is truly my own.

So, with congratulations to all of you who have also changed your names, my name is now Treya Killam Wilber.

Love,
Treya

14

WHAT KIND OF
HELP REALLY
HELPS?

K ALU R I N P O C H E was an altogether extraordinary teacher, generally
thought to be one of Tibet's very greatest modern masters. As a young
man, Kalu decided to pursue wholeheartedly the path of enlightenment,
and so he abandoned ordinary life and began meditating, alone, in
various caves throughout mountainous Tibet. He spent an incredible
thirteen years in solitary meditation. Word of an extraordinary saint began
to circulate throughout Tibet; pious laypeople brought him food, and set
it outside of whatever cave he was meditating in at the time. Finally the
Karmapa, who might be thought of as the "Pope" of Kalu's tradition,
sought him out, tested his realization, and announced that Kalu's meditative attainment was equal to that of Milarepa, Tibet's greatest yogi and
sage. He charged Kalu with taking the Buddhadharma to the West, and
Kalu reluctantly gave up his solitary life and began establishing meditation centers in the West. By the time he died, in 1989, he had founded
over three hundred meditation centers throughout the world, and had
single-handedly initiated more Westerners into the Dharma than any
man in history.

During the Kalachakra empowerment, on the same night that Treya had her "Treya" dream, I dreamt Kalu had given me a magical book, a book that somehow contained all the secrets of the universe. Shortly after the Kalachakra, Treya and I went to a ten-day Transmission of Wisdom retreat given by Kalu at Big Bear, right outside of Los Angeles.

As I've said, I do not think that Buddhism is the best way or the only way. And I would not especially call myself a Buddhist; I have too many affinities with Vedanta Hinduism and Christian mysticism, among many others. But one has to choose a particular path if one is to actually *practice*, and my path has been Buddhist. So I have ended up with Chesterton's quip: "All religions are the same, especially Buddhism."

Where I do think Buddhism excels is in its completeness. It has specific practices that address all of the higher stages of development—psychic, subtle, causal, and ultimate. And it has a graded system of practice that leads you, step by developmental step, through each of these stages, limited only by your own capacity for growth and transcendence.

The Transmission of Wisdom retreat was an introduction to all of these practices and stages. This retreat was particularly important for Treya, because it marked a major change in the type of meditation practice she would henceforth do.

Tibetan Buddhism divides the overall spiritual path into three broad stages (each with several substages): the Hinayana, the Mahayana, and the Vajrayana.

The Hinayana is the foundation practice, the basic and core practice found in all schools of Buddhism. Central to this stage is the practice of vipassana, or insight meditation, the type of meditation that Treya had been practicing for almost ten years. In vipassana, one simply sits in a comfortable position (lotus or half-lotus if possible, cross-legged if not), and one gives "bare attention" to whatever is arising, externally and internally, without judging it, condemning it, following after it, avoiding it, or desiring it. One simply *witnesses* it, impartially, and then lets it go. The aim of this practice is to see that the separate ego is not a real and substantial entity, but just a series of fleeting and impermanent sensations like anything else. When one realizes just how "empty" the ego is, one ceases identifying with it, defending it, worrying about it, and this in turn releases one from the chronic suffering and unhappiness that comes from defending something that isn't there. As Wei Wu Wei put it:

What Kind of Help Really Helps?

Why are you unhappy?
Because 99.9% of everything you think,
And everything you do,
Is for your self,
And there isn't one.

The first several days of the Transmission of Wisdom retreat were devoted to this fundamental practice. Everybody there, of course, had already practiced it extensively, but Kalu gave his own extra instructions.

As profound as this practice is, it is still not complete, because there is still a subtle dualism contained in pure witnessing awareness itself. There are many technical ways to explain this, but the simplest is: the Hinayana level aims at enlightenment for oneself but neglects the enlightenment of others. And doesn't that show that there is some trace of ego left, getting yours and neglecting others?

And so where the Hinayana teachings stress individual enlightenment, the Mahayana teachings go one step further and also stress the enlightenment of all beings. It is thus the path, first and foremost, of compassion, and this is meant not just in a theoretical sense; there are actual practices for developing compassion in your own mind and heart.

Foremost among these practices is the one known as *tonglen*, which means "taking and sending." After one has developed a strong foundation practice in vipassana, one moves on to the practice of tonglen. This practice is so powerful and so transformative it was kept largely secret until just recently in Tibet. And it was this practice that Treya took to heart. The practice is as follows:

In meditation, picture or visualize someone you know and love who is going through much suffering—an illness, a loss, depression, pain, anxiety, fear. As you breathe in, imagine all of that person's suffering—in the form of dark, black, smokelike, tarlike, thick, and heavy clouds—entering your nostrils and traveling down into your heart. Hold that suffering in your heart. Then, on the outbreath, take all of your peace, freedom, health, goodness, and virtue, and send it out to the person in the form of healing, liberating light. Imagine they take it all in, and feel completely free, released, and happy. Do that for several breaths. Then imagine the town that person is in, and, on the inbreath, take in all of the suffering of that town, and send back all of your health and happiness to everyone in it. Then do that for the entire state, then the entire country, the entire planet, the universe. You are taking in all the suffering of beings everywhere and sending them back health and happiness and virtue.

When people are first introduced to this practice, their reactions are usually strong, visceral, and negative. Mine were. Take that black tar into me? Are you kidding? What if I actually get sick? This is insane, dangerous! When Kalu first gave us these tonglen instructions, the practice of which occupied the middle portion of the retreat, a woman stood up in the audience of about one hundred people and said what virtually everybody there was thinking:

"But what if I am doing this with someone who is really sick, and I start to get that sickness myself?"

Without hesitating Kalu said, "You should think, Oh good! It's working!"

That was the entire point. It caught all of us "selfless Buddhists" with our egos hanging out. We would practice to get our own enlightenment, to reduce our own suffering, but take on the suffering of others, even in imagination? No way.

Tonglen is designed exactly to cut that egoic self-concern, self-promotion, and self-defense. It exchanges self for other, and thus it profoundly undercuts the subject/object dualism. It asks us to undermine the self/other dualism at exactly the point we are most afraid: getting hurt ourselves. Not just talking about having compassion for others' suffering, but being willing to take it into our own heart and release them in exchange. This is true compassion, the path of the Mahayana. In a sense it is the Buddhist equivalent of what Christ did: be willing to take on the sins of the world, and thus transform them (and you).

The point is fairly simple: For the true Self, or the one Self, self and other can be easily exchanged, since both are equal, it makes no difference to the only Self. Conversely, if we cannot exchange self for other, then we are locked out of one-Self awareness, locked out of pure nondual awareness. Our unwillingness to take on the suffering of others locks us into our own suffering, with no escape, because it locks us into our self, period. As William Blake put it, "Lest the Last Judgment come and find me unannihilate, and I be seized and given unto the hands of my own selfhood."

A strange thing begins to happen when one practices tonglen for any length of time. First of all, nobody actually gets sick. I know of no bona fide cases of anyone getting ill because of tonglen, although a lot of us have used that fear as an excuse not to practice it. Rather, you find that you stop recoiling in the face of suffering, both yours and others'. You stop running from pain, and instead find that you can begin to transform it by simply being willing to take it into yourself and then release it. The real changes start to happen in *you*, by the simple willingness to get your ego-protecting tendencies out of the way. You begin to relax the self/other tension, realizing that there is only one Self feeling all pain or enjoying all success. Why get envious of others, when there is only one Self enjoying the success? This is why the "positive" side of tonglen is expressed in the saying: I rejoice in the merit of others. It's the same as mine, in nondual awareness. A great "equality consciousness" develops, which undercuts pride and arrogance on the one hand, and fear and envy on the other.

When the Mahayana path of compassion is established, when the exchangeability of self and other is realized, at least to some degree, then one is ready for the Vajrayana path. The Vajrayana is based on one uncompromising principle: There is only Spirit. As one continues to undercut the subject/object duality in all its forms, it increasingly becomes obvious that all things, high or low, sacred or profane, are fully and equally perfect manifestations or ornaments of Spirit, of Buddhamind. The entire manifest universe is recognized as a play of one's own awareness, empty, luminous, clear, radiant, unobstructed, spontaneous. One learns not so much to seek awareness as to delight in it, play with it, since there is *only* awareness. Vajrayana is the path of playing with awareness, with energy, with luminosity, reflecting the perennial wisdom that the universe is a play of the Divine, and you (and all sentient beings as such) *are* the Divine.

The Vajrayana path therefore has three main divisions. In the first (the outer tantras) you visualize Deity in front of you or on top of your head, and you imagine healing energy and light raining down and into you, conferring blessings and wisdom. This is, of course, the psychic level, level six, where one first establishes a communion with Deity.

In the second division (the lower inner tantras), you visualize yourself *as* the Deity and you repeat certain syllables or mantras that represent divine speech. This is the subtle level, level seven, the level of establishing union with Divinity. And then finally, in the third division (the higher inner tantras, *mahamudra* and *maha-ati*), one dissolves both self and Deity in pure unmanifest emptiness, the causal level of the supreme identity. At this point, the practice no longer involves visualization or mantra recitation or concentration, but rather the realization that your own awareness, just as it is, is always already enlightened. Since all things are *already*

Spirit, there is no way to *reach* Spirit. There is *only* Spirit in all directions, and so one simply rests in the spontaneous nature of the mind itself, effortlessly embracing all that arises as ornaments of your own primordial experience. The unmanifest and the manifest, or emptiness and form, unite in the pure nondual play of your own awareness—generally regarded as the ultimate state that is no state in particular.

Translating for Kalu Rinpoche at the retreat (and at the Kalachakra empowerment) was Ken McLeod, a brilliant senior student of Kalu, with whom Treya and I became friends. Ken, incidentally, translated a key Tibetan text on the practice of tonglen—*The Great Path of Awakening* (Shambhala)—that I highly recommend if you are interested in this practice.

Treya, then, under Kalu's guidance, and with Ken's help, expanded her practice to include not just vipassana, but also tonglen and Deity yoga (visualizing herself as Chenrezi, the Buddha of compassion). I did the same. She began her tonglen practice by taking in my pain and suffering from the year in Tahoe; I did the same with her. Then we expanded that to eventually include all sentient beings. It was this path, more than any other, that Treya and I would practice in the coming years.

And it was this tonglen practice, more than any other, that so deepened Treya's compassion for all those suffering. She talked of the deep connection she felt with all beings, simply because all beings suffer. And doing tonglen allowed her, in a special sense, to redeem her own suffering, her own ordeal with cancer. Once you are proficient in tonglen, you find that every time you have pain or anxiety or depression, on the inbreath you almost spontaneously think, "May I take all such suffering into me," and on the outbreath you release it. The effect of this is that you befriend your own suffering, you step into it. You don't recoil in the face of suffering, but rather use it as a way to connect with all beings who are suffering. You embrace it and then transform it by giving it a universal context. It's no longer just you and your isolated pain, but rather a chance to establish a connection with all others who are hurting, a chance to realize that "inasmuch as you do this to the least of my brethren, you do this to me." In the simple practice of tonglen, of compassionate exchange, Treya found much of her own suffering redeemed, given meaning, given context, given connection; it took her out of her "own" isolated woes and into the texture of humanity on the whole, where she was not alone.

And most importantly, it helped her (and me) stop judging illness or suffering, whether ours or others'. With tonglen, you don't distance your-self from suffering (yours or others'); you relate to it in a simple and direct and compassionate way. You don't stand back from it and weave pet theories about what caused it or why the person "brought it on themselves" or what it really "means." That is not a helpful way to relate to a person's suffering; that is a way to distance yourself from them. No matter how "helpful" you might think your theorizing is, it is ultimately just a way to say, "Don't touch me."

It was directly from this practice of tonglen, this practice of relating to suffering with compassion, as taught to us by Kalu, that Treya wrote "What Kind of Help Really Helps?" It was published by the *Journal of Transpersonal Psychology* and then picked up by *New Age* magazine, where it got one of the largest reader responses in the magazine's history. And it was this piece that brought her to the attention of the *"Oprah Winfrey Show."* (Treya politely declined—"They just want me to argue with Bernie [Siegel].") The editors of *New Age* called it a "more compassionate view of illness," more compassionate, that is, than the prevalent new age notion that you cause your own illness. Here are some highlights:*

WHAT KIND OF HELP REALLY HELPS?

Five years ago I was sitting at my kitchen table having tea with an old friend, who told me that some months earlier he learned he had thyroid cancer. I told him about my mother, who had surgery for colon cancer fifteen years ago and has been fine ever since. I then described the various theories my sisters and I came up with to explain why she had gotten cancer. We had a number of them; probably our favorite was that she had been too much my father's wife and not enough herself. We speculated that if she had not married a cattleman she might have become a vege-tarian and avoided the fats implicated in causing colon cancer. Our other pet theory was that her side of the family's acknowledged difficulty expres-sing emotions may have contributed to her getting cancer. Over the years we had become quite comfortable with our theories and stories about this traumatic event. My friend, who obviously had thought deeply about cancer, then said something that shook me deeply.

*A copy of the complete essay can be obtained from the Cancer Support Community. Please see page 421 for details.

"Don't you see what you're doing?" he asked. "You're treating your mother like an object, spinning theories about her. Other people's theories about you can feel like a violation. I know, because in my case the ideas my friends have come up with about my having cancer have felt like an imposition and a burden. It doesn't feel like they're coming primarily from concern for me, and they certainly did not honor me at a difficult time. I felt their 'theories' as something done *to* me, not something done to *help* me. The thought of my having cancer must have frightened them so much they needed to find a reason, an explanation, a meaning for it. The theories were to help them, not to help me, and they caused me a lot of pain."

I was shocked. I had never looked at what was behind my theorizing, never speculated about what my theories might feel like to my mother. Even though none of us ever told her about our ideas I'm quite certain she felt it in the air. That kind of climate wouldn't encourage trust or openness or asking for help, I realized. I suddenly saw that I had made myself largely unavailable to my mother during the greatest crisis of her life.

That incident with my friend opened a door. It was the beginning of a shift toward my becoming more compassionate toward people who are sick, more respectful of their integrity, more kindly in my approach—and more humble about my own ideas. I began to see the judgment only partly hidden behind my theorizing and to recognize the un-acknowledged fear that lay deeper still. The implicit message behind such theories began to emerge. Instead of saying, "I care about you; what can I do to help?," I was actually saying, "What did you do wrong? Where did you make your mistake? How did you fail?" And, not incidentally, "How can I protect myself?"

I saw fear—unacknowledged, hidden fear—as what motivated me, what compelled me to come up with stories that told me the universe made this kind of sense, that it was ordered in a way I could control. . . .

Over the years I've talked to a lot of people who have cancer, many who have recently been diagnosed. At first I wasn't sure what to say. It was easiest to talk about my own experiences as a cancer patient, but I soon saw that often that was not what a particular person needed to hear. The only way I could discover how to help someone was by listening. Only when I heard what they were trying to say could I get a sense of what they needed, of the issues they were confronting at that time, of the kind of help that would really help at that specific moment. Since people go through many different phases during the course of an illness that can be as persistent and unpredictable as cancer, learning to listen to what they need is especially important.

At times, especially when decisions about treatment options loom ahead of them, people want information. They may want me to tell them about alternatives or help them research conventional therapies. Once they've chosen their treatment plan, however, they usually don't need more information, even though it may be the easiest and least threatening thing for me to give. Now they need support. They don't need to hear about the dangers of the radiation or chemotherapy or Mexican clinic they've chosen, a choice usually made with great difficulty after long deliberation. My coming to them at this point with new suggestions about healers or techniques or therapies might only throw them back into confusion, might make them feel I doubt the path they've chosen and thus fuel their own doubts. . . .

The decisions I made [about my own cancer treatments] were not easy; I know that the decisions everyone has to make in this kind of situation are some of the toughest they'll ever confront. I have learned that I can never know in advance what choice I would make when in someone else's place. This knowledge helps me feel genuinely supportive of the choices others make. A dear friend of mine, who made me feel beautiful even when my hair fell out, recently said, "You didn't choose what I would have chosen, but that didn't matter." I appreciated her for not letting that come between us then, clearly the most difficult time of my life. Then I said, "But you can't know what you would have chosen; I didn't choose what you *think* you would have chosen. I didn't choose what *I* thought I would have chosen either."

I never thought I would agree to chemotherapy. I had tremendous fears about putting poisons into my body and fears about long-term effects on my immune system. I resisted it until the very end but ultimately decided that, despite its many drawbacks, chemotherapy was my best chance for a cure. . . .

I'm certain that I played a role in my becoming ill, a role that was mostly unconscious and unintentional, and I know that I play a large role, this one very conscious and intentional, in getting well and staying well. I try to focus on what I can do now; unraveling the past too easily degenerates into a kind of self-blame which makes it harder, not easier, to make healthy, conscious choices in the present. I am also very aware of the many other factors which are largely beyond my conscious or unconscious control. We are all, thankfully, part of a much larger whole. I like being aware of this, even though it means I have less control. We are all too interconnected, both with each other and with our environment—life is too wonderfully complex—for a simple statement like "you create your own reality" to be simply true. A belief that I control or create my own reality actually attempts to rip me out of the rich, complex, mysterious, and supportive context of my life. It attempts, in the name of control, to deny the web of relationships which nurtures me and each of us daily.

As a correction to the belief that we are at the mercy of larger forces or that illness is due to external agents only, this idea that we create our own reality and therefore our own illnesses is important and necessary. But it goes too far. It is an overreaction, based on an oversimplification. I have come to feel that the extreme form of this belief negates what is helpful about it, that it is too often used in a narrow-minded, narcissistic, divisive, and dangerous way. I think we are ready for a more mature approach to this idea. As Stephen Levine says, this statement is a half-truth dangerous in its incompleteness. It is more accurate to say we *affect* our reality. This is closer to the whole truth; it leaves room both for effective personal action and for the wondrous rich mysteriousness of life. . . .

If someone asks me a question like, "Why did you choose to give yourself cancer?," it often feels like they're coming from a self-righteous place, a place of separation where they are well and I am sick. This question does not invite constructive introspection. People sensitive to the complexity of the situation might ask a more helpful question, something like, "How are you choosing to use this cancer?" For me this question is exciting; it helps me look at what I can do now, helps me feel empowered and supported and challenged in a positive way. Someone who asks this kind of question conveys that they see my illness not as a punishment for something I did wrong but as a difficult and challenging situation also potentially full of opportunities for growth, which naturally helps me approach it in the same way.

In our Judeo-Christian culture, with its pervasive emphasis on sin and guilt, illness is too easily seen as punishment for wrongdoing. I prefer a more Buddhist approach where everything that happens is taken as an opportunity to increase compassion, to serve others. I can look at "bad" things that happen to me not as punishment for past actions but as my chance to now work through the karma of the past, to cleanse the slate, to be done with it. This approach helps me focus on working with the situation in the present.

I find this very helpful. From a new age perspective I might be tempted to ask someone who's ill, "What did you do wrong?" But from a Buddhist perspective, I'm more likely to approach someone with a life-threatening illness, even someone working with it in a way I think I would not choose, and say something that conveys the thought: "Congratulations, you obviously have the courage to take this one on, the willingness to work this through. I admire you for that."

When I talk to someone who's been newly diagnosed with cancer or who has had a recurrence or who is growing tired after years of dealing with cancer, I remind myself that I don't have to give concrete ideas or advice to be of help. Listening is helping. Listening is giving. I try to be emotionally accessible to them, to reach through my own fears and touch them, to maintain human contact. I find there are many fearful things we can laugh at together once we've allowed ourselves to be truly afraid. I try to steer clear of the temptations to define imperatives for others, even imperatives such as fight for your life, change yourself, or die consciously. I try not to push people to move in directions I have chosen or think I might chose for myself. I try to stay in touch with my own fear that I might one day find myself in the same situation they are in. I must constantly learn how to make friends with illness, to not see it as failure. I try to use my own setbacks and weaknesses and illnesses to develop compassion for others and for myself, while remembering to not take serious things too seriously. I try to stay aware of the opportunities for psychological and spiritual healing all around me in the very real pain and suffering that ask for our compassion.

15

THE NEW AGE

❧§❧

T REYA and I liked Boulder so much we decided to move there. In the summer of that year (1987), Treya began having a series of menacing dreams. This was disturbing because it was the very first time, in all three years of dealing with cancer, that she had ever had ominous and foreboding dreams about her physical health. Although it had been nine months since the last recurrence, and although medical tests at that time showed no signs of illness, her dreams seemed to be saying differently. Two dreams were particularly vivid and charged.

> In the first I dreamt there was a porcupine attached to the left side of my body, but it was also like a manta ray, a flat, dark black figure stuck to me from about midcalf to shoulder height. Kati helped me peel it off and take out a few quills. There were hooks on the ends of the quills. And the feeling was that it had left some kind of poison inside me, and the poison was still there.
>
> In the second dream, I was seeing a woman doctor and she was very concerned over how the skin was changing where the mastectomy and radiation were. She said it was a very bad sign of something going on inside. She didn't say cancer, but of course that was the implication.

Although I agree that dreams are a road to the submerged unconscious—usually the magic and mythic *past* (individual and collective)—and although I think dreams can sometimes point to the *future*—psychic and subtle—I usually don't put much emphasis on them in daily life, simply because interpretation is so tricky. Yet both of us couldn't help but be struck by the foreboding portent of these powerful dreams.

But since all other signs were clear, there was nothing we could do but continue with her program: meditation, visualization, strict diet, exercise, immunostimulation (for example, thymus extract), megavitamins, journal-keeping. We were, on the whole, convinced that Treya was on the road to recovery, and in that happy light we spent a glorious summer, the first time in three years that, instead of everything seeming to go wrong, everything seemed to go right.

Treya threw herself into her art work, particularly fused glass, with joyful abandon, and began producing her own designs that seemed to stun people with their beauty and originality. I had seen nothing even remotely of that caliber in fused glass; nobody else had either. We showed them to several professionals in the area. "These are exquisite. You must have been doing this for years." "A few months, actually."

I began writing! In a month and a half, working feverishly day and night, I turned out an eight-hundred-page book, tentatively titled *The Great Chain of Being: A Modern Introduction to the Perennial Philosophy and the World's Great Mystical Traditions.* My good old daemon, after three years of confinement in the prison of my lie—the lie of blaming Treya—burst forth on the scene full of energy and drive. God, I was ecstatic! Treya helped enormously with the book, reading each chapter hot off the computer printer, and giving invaluable feedback, often suggesting I redo entire sections. In our off-hours we would sit around and dream up silly titles for the book, like *Who Is This God Person, Anyway?*

I decided that I did, after all, want a child, maybe two, which totally flabbergasted Treya. But I had realized that not wanting a child was simply based on my own recoil from life, from relationship. I had felt so wounded over the last few years that, instead of opening up into life, I retreated into myself, a bad plan under the best of circumstances. We spent a wonderful month in Aspen, where Treya was actively involved with Windstar and the Rocky Mountain Institute. We were visited there by John Brockman and Katinka Matson, Patricia and Daniel Ellsberg, and Mitch and Ellen Kapor and their young son Adam. Mitch, the founder of Lotus, was an old friend of mine; he had visited me back in the Lincoln days to discuss my books. It was watching Mitch and Adam that first got me thinking about having kids. Further talks with Sam and with Jack Crittenden convinced me.

But it wasn't that, really. It was that Treya and I had finally reconnected, on all levels it seemed, after so much hardship. It was just like at the beginning; maybe better.

And Ken? For the first time *ever* since we've been married he seems to want to have a child! The time he spent with Jackson and Mitch and Sam has really affected him. Apparently he asked them about having children (Sam has two, Jack three, Mitch one). They all said, without question, don't hesitate, don't think about it, just do it. It's the most wonderful experience ever. Your life will be totally changed, they'll jerk you around in more ways than you can imagine, and it's wonderful. Do it. Have a child. So all we have to do now is watch my health for a year!

Yet even before he decided he wanted children, Ken seemed to have changed so much. He is being so wonderful, so sweet, so loving. He's so cute sitting there in front of his computer working, so cute as he experiments with spices and comes up with these wonderful gourmet meals—and on my diet no less! Is this what he was like before we went through our hard times? He's even more wonderful than I remember!

I remember that period I was going through, when I was bald, when I wondered if we were ever going to get back to where we had been. That seemed very important to me then. I think I meant by that the kind of closeness and hunger for each other, especially me for him, we started out with. Well, I think we're back there, but of course in a different way. It seems perhaps pretentious to call it a higher rung of the spiral, but that may be the closest I can get. What's different is the intensity of the need, the attachment, and although I miss that, I also think its lack indicates I've grown. I remember the feeling as being a kind of barnacle attached to him; he satisfied such a deep, old, empty need that I only wanted to be with him. I still far prefer to be with him than anything else, but the intensity of that need is gone, those holes have largely been filled. What's back is the sheer pleasure of being together, the small delights in the small unique things he does, how noticing those moments brightens up the day. What's back is our being kind and gentle and playful with each other, a return of the lightness and joyfulness in being with each other. What's added to this is a more mature awareness of each other's sensitive spots and a willingness to humor and care for those sore points. I've learned to encourage him, give him positive feedback, something that wasn't my family's way. He's learned, I think, that being snide really hurts me. We've both learned to sense a problem coming and either back off or work with it in a gentle way. Things are in general much softer, much kinder around our house, in our relationship. I delight in the sensitive interplay of it all.

Another lovely thing is happening as Ken writes his new book. The really nice part, aside from the great pleasure I get in seeing his ideas put forward in a clear, readily accessible way (this is another book I can give my mother's friends!) is that Ken is giving me each chapter as it comes off the printer and asking for my comments. Which he really seems to value and has in many cases incorporated. It's nice to see so many of our past conversations get into print, for example all our talks about male-female differences. And it's nice to be able to contribute, to be able to help shape his ideas. Whatever the actual comments, the main thing is that I feel like a real participant in this project. And it's a project I feel really behind because it's so accessible to people. Just reading about the transition from existential to soul [from level 6 to level 7/8] has answered so many questions in my own life now. I am delighted he is doing this book!

And I love doing my art work! I create my own designs, based on the abstract drawings I make, and transfer these to carefully cut glass pieces that I then assemble three and four levels deep. I put the total piece in a kiln and fire it. I've seen this done in books, but nothing like my designs. People seem to really love them, and I don't think they're saying that just to be nice. I love doing it!!!!! I think about it constantly, dream about it, can't wait to get back to it.

And CSC in San Francisco is going strong. We received a $25,000 grant from a major foundation and people are knocking at our doors. From what I hear—and I'm sad I can't be there more for this fun part—people are benefiting tremendously from being in the groups. One man with metastatic cancer said it's his only support system and he no longer feels so afraid. One older woman in the breast cancer group who lives far away from her daughters now feels that she has four new daughters (the younger women in the group). People have told their doctors that even one or two group meetings have helped tremendously, they no longer feel so alone or so afraid. Vicky is now running it, and she is doing a fabulous job! Yesterday I wrote this to Vicky's mother:

"I'd like to share with you one aspect of CSC which I think is very special. I've only become aware of it by seeing CSC in contrast to both the Wellness Community, which as you know was our original model, and now Qualife, which is a group doing similar work in Denver. I highly value the work both of these groups are doing, and I see that CSC is different mainly because it was begun by people who had themselves had cancer. The other groups, though similarly motivated to help people during an incredibly difficult time, are more focused on techniques, on results, on making a point. The Wellness Community, for example, talks about "Let's Fight Cancer Together" in their brochures. These groups feel they have something concrete to teach, like visualization or whatever, and they want to show that it makes a difference.

"CSC, on the other hand, seems to come from a softer 'we're in this together' kind of place. Yes, we believe these techniques can help but we're much more interested in meeting people where they are and giving them what they ask for than in proving a point. In fact, I've often said that in one sense all the things we do—the support groups, the classes, the social events—are merely excuses to bring people together, structures in which that can happen. When I had cancer I found that it was difficult to be with my friends. I had to expend a lot of energy taking care of them, explaining things, dealing with their fears for me, with their often unexpressed fears for themselves. I discovered that being with other people who had cancer felt like a big relief. I realized that I had become a member of another family, the family of people who know about cancer from personal experience. And I believe that much of what CSC does is to provide a place and a way for members of that family to come together and support each other. Support each other through friendship, through sharing information, through sharing fears, through being able to discuss things like suicide and leaving your children and pain and fear of pain or death and what it's like to be bald and so on.

"We have to be compassionate with each other, yes. We know we shouldn't introduce someone who's just been diagnosed with cancer to someone with their same type of cancer who has metastases, for example (other places mix people who are at various stages without preparing them for the shock). We know how important it is to stress a larger definition of health than simple physical health, for we believe the true test of success in facing cancer is how you live your life. We know—I hope—how to suggest things to people, how to open doors for them, in such a way that they know whatever their choice, if they turn down the suggestions or choose not to walk through the door, we'll still be there for them. We know these things because we've been there. And that's what's different about the Cancer Support Community."

It's strange, just reading that. I love that Ken wants to have children. But who knows what my health will allow? But whatever happens, I suppose I will always consider things like CSC as my child. It's so special, and like any doting parent I'm so proud of it. For the first time I feel some peace about this question of having a child.

In the meantime, I plugged away on the book. One of its chapters, "Health, Wholeness, and Healing,"* was published in *New Age* alongside Treya's piece, with the new title, "Do We Make Ourselves Sick?" I won't repeat the entire piece here, but I will briefly outline its major points, since it represented a culmination of my thoughts on this difficult issue that Treya and I had wrestled with for the past three years.

1. The standard argument from the perennial philosophy is that men and women are grounded in the Great Chain of Being. That is, we have within us matter, body, mind, soul, and spirit.

2. In any disease, it is extremely important to try to determine on which level or levels the disease primarily originates—physical, emotional, mental, or spiritual.

3. It is most important to use a "same-level" procedure for the primary (but not necessarily sole) course of treatment. Use physical intervention for physical diseases, use emotional therapy for emotional disturbances, use spiritual methods for spiritual crises, and so on. If a mixture of causes, then use a mixture of appropriate-level treatments.

4. This is especially important because if you misdiagnose the disease by thinking it originates on a level higher than it in fact does, then you will generate *guilt*; if on a level lower, you will generate *despair*. Either way, the treatment will be less than effective, and will have the added disadvantage of burdening the patient with guilt or despair caused solely by the misdiagnosis.

For example, if you get hit by a bus and break a leg, that's a physical illness with physical remedies: you set the leg and plaster it. That's a

---

* A copy of the complete essay can be obtained from the Cancer Support Community. See page 421 for details.

"same-level" intervention. You don't sit in the street and visualize your leg mending. That's a mental-level technique that isn't effective in this physical-level problem. Moreover, if you are told by those around you that your thoughts alone caused this accident, and that you should be able to mend the leg yourself with your thoughts, then all that is going to happen is that you will feel guilt, self-blame, and low self-esteem. It's a complete mismatch of levels and treatments.

On the other hand, if you do happen to suffer from, say, low self-esteem, because of certain scripts that you have internalized about how rotten or incompetent you are, that is a mental-level problem that responds well to a mental-level intervention such as visualization or affirmations (script rewriting, which is exactly what cognitive therapy does). Using physical-level interventions—taking megavitamins, say, or changing your diet—is not going to have much effect (unless you actually have a vitamin imbalance contributing to the problem). And if you only try to use physical-level treatments, you are going to end up in some form of despair, because the treatments are from the wrong level and they just don't work very well.

So the general approach to any disease, in my opinion, is to start at the bottom and work up. First, look for physical causes. Exhaust those to the best of your ability. Then move up to any possible emotional causes, and exhaust those. Then mental, then spiritual.

This is particularly important, because so many diseases that were once thought to have a purely spiritual or psychological origin, we now know have major physical or genetic components. Asthma was once thought to be caused by a "smothering mother." It is now known to be largely biophysical in cause and emergence. Tuberculosis was caused by a "consumptive personality"; gout, by moral weakness. There was a widely believed "arthritis-prone personality" that has simply not stood the test of time. All these notions did was instill guilt in their victims; the cures didn't work at all because they were from the wrong level.

Now this is not to say that treatments from other levels can't be very important in a supporting or adjuvant fashion. They most definitely can. In the simple example of the broken leg, relaxation techniques, visualization, affirmations, meditation, psychotherapy if you need it—all of those can contribute to a more balanced atmosphere in which physical healing can more easily and perhaps readily occur.

What is not helpful is taking the fact that these psychological and spiritual aspects can be very useful, and then saying that the reason you broke your leg is that you lacked these psychological and spiritual facets in the first place. A person suffering any major illness may make significant and profound changes in the face of that illness; it does not follow that they got the illness because they lacked the changes. That would be like saying, if you have a fever and you take aspirin the fever goes down; therefore having a fever is due to an aspirin deficiency.

Now most diseases, of course, don't originate from a single and isolated level. Whatever happens on one level or dimension of being affects all the other levels to a greater or lesser degree. One's emotional, mental, and spiritual makeup can most definitely influence physical illness and physical healing, just as a physical illness can have strong repercussions on the higher levels. Break your leg, and it will probably have emotional and psychological effects. In systems theory this is called "upward causation"—a lower level is causing certain events in a higher level. And the reverse, "downward causation," is when a higher level has a causal effect or influence on the lower.

The question, then, is just how much "downward causation" does the mind—do our thoughts and emotions—have on physical illness? And the answer seems to be: much more than was once thought, not nearly as much as new agers believe.

The new school of psychoneuroimmunology (PNI) has found convincing evidence that our thoughts and emotions can have a direct influence on the immune system. The effect is not large, but it is detectable. This, of course, is what we would expect from the axiom that all levels affect all other levels to some degree, however minor. But since medicine started out as a purely physical-level science, and disregarded the influence of the higher levels on physical-level illness ("the ghost in the machine"), PNI has provided a necessary correction, offering a more balanced view. The mind can affect the body to a small but not insignificant degree.

In particular, imagery and visualization have been found to be perhaps the most important ingredients in the "small but not insignificant" influence of the mind on the body and the immune system. Why images? If we look at the extended version of the Great Chain, notice where images occur: matter, sensation, perception, impulse, image, symbol, concept, and so on. Image is the lowest and most primitive part of the mind, putting it directly in touch with the highest part of the body. Image, in other words, is the mind's direct connection with the body—its moods, its impulses, its bioenergy. Our higher thoughts and concepts, then, can translate downward into simple images, and these apparently have a modest but direct influence on bodily systems (via affect or impulse, the next lower dimension).

All things considered, then, psychological mood plays some part in every illness. *And that component should be exercised to the maximum*, I agree entirely. In a close election, that component may be enough to tip the scales in favor of health or illness, but it does not single-handedly stuff ballot boxes.

Thus, as Steven Locke and Douglas Colligan write in *The Healer Within*, every illness in effect has a psychological component, and every healing process is affected by psychology. But, the authors continue, the problem is that people have confused the terms *psychosomatic*, which means that a physical disease process can be affected by psychological factors, and *psychogenic*, which means that the illness is caused solely by psychological factors. The authors state: "In the correct sense of the word, every illness can be said to be psychosomatic; it may be time to retire the term psychosomatic altogether. [Because] both the public and some physicians have used the terms psychosomatic (meaning that the mind can influence the health of the body) and psychogenic (meaning that the mind can cause diseases in the body) interchangeably. They have lost sight of the true meaning of psychosomatic disease. As Robert Ader suggests, 'We're not talking about the causation of disease, but the interaction between psychosocial events, coping and the preexisting biological conditions.'"

The authors themselves mention heredity, life-style, drugs, location, occupation, age, and personality. It's the interaction of all these factors—I would add existential and spiritual factors—from *all* the levels that together seem to influence the cause and course of a physical illness. Singling out any one of these factors and ignoring the others is thus a wild oversimplification.

So where did this new age idea that your mind *alone* causes and cures all physical illness come from? It claims, after all, to have a firm foundation in the world's great mystical, spiritual, and transcendental traditions. And here they are on very shaky ground, I believe. Jeanne Achterberg, author of *Imagery in Healing* (which I highly recommend) believes that the notion can historically be traced back to the New Thought or Metaphysical Thought schools that grew up based on a (distorted) reading of the New England Transcendentalists, Emerson and Thoreau, who based much of their work on Eastern mysticism. The New Thought schools, of which Christian Science is the most famous, mistake the correct notion

"Godhead creates all," with the notion, "Since I am one with God, I create all."

That position makes two mistakes, I believe, which both Emerson and Thoreau would have strongly disagreed with. One, that God is an intervening parent for the universe, instead of its impartial Reality or Suchness or Condition. And two, that your ego is one with that parental God, and therefore can intervene and order the universe around. I have found no support for that notion in the mystical traditions at all.

Advocates of the new age themselves claim that they are basing this idea on the principle of karma, which says that your present life circumstances are the results of thoughts and actions from a previous lifetime. According to Hinduism and Buddhism, that is partially true. But even if it were totally true, which it isn't, the new agers have, I believe, overlooked one crucial fact: According to these traditions, your present circumstances are the results of thoughts and actions from a *previous* life, and your present thoughts and actions will affect, not your present life, but your *next* life, your next incarnation. The Buddhists say that in your present life you are simply reading a book that you wrote in the previous life; and what you are doing now will not come to fruition until your *next* life. In neither case does your present thought create your present reality.

Now I personally don't happen to believe that particular view of karma. It's a rather primitive notion subsequently refined (and largely abandoned) by the higher schools of Buddhism, where it was recognized that not *everything* that happens to you is the result of your own past actions. As Namkhai Norbu, master of Dzogchen Buddhism (generally regarded as the pinnacle of Buddhist teaching), explains: "There are illnesses produced due to karma, or the previous conditions of the individual. But there are also illnesses generated by energies that come from others, from the outside. And there are illnesses that are provoked by provisional causes, such as food or other combinations of circumstances. And there are illnesses generated by accident. Then there are all kinds of illnesses linked with the environment." My point is that *neither* the primitive version of karma nor the more evolved teachings lend any support to the new age notion.

And so where does that notion itself come from? Here I am going to part ways with Treya and spin out my own pet theories on the people that hold these beliefs. I am not going to relate compassionately to the suffering these notions cause. I am going to try to pigeonhole them, categorize them, spin theories about them, because I think the ideas are dangerous and need to be pigeonholed, if for no other reason than to prevent further suffering. And my comments are not addressed to the large number of people who believe these ideas in a rather innocent and naive and harmless way. I have in mind more the national leaders of this movement, individuals who give seminars on creating your own reality; who give workshops that teach, for example, that cancer is caused solely by resentment; who teach that poverty is your own doing and oppression something you brought on yourself. These are perhaps well-intentioned but nonetheless dangerous people, in my opinion, because they divert attention away from the real levels—physical, environmental, legal, moral, and socioeconomic, for example—where so much work desperately needs to be done.

In my opinion, these beliefs—particularly the belief that you create your own reality—are level two beliefs. They have all the hallmarks of the infantile and magical worldview of the narcissistic personality disorders, including grandiosity, omnipotence, and narcissism. The idea that thoughts don't just influence reality but create reality is the direct result, in my opinion, of the incomplete differentiation of the ego boundary that so defines level two. Thoughts and objects aren't clearly separated, and thus to manipulate the thought is to omnipotently and magically manipulate the object.

I believe the hyperindividualistic culture in America, which reached its zenith in the "me decade," fostered regression to magical and narcissistic levels. I believe (with Robert Bellah and Dick Anthony) that the breakdown of more socially cohesive structures turned individuals back on their own resources, and this also helped reactivate narcissistic tendencies. And I believe, with clinical psychologists, that lurking right beneath the surface of narcissism is rage, particularly but not solely expressed in the belief: "I don't want to hurt you, I love you; but disagree with me and you will get an illness that will kill you. Agree with me, agree that you can create your own reality, and you will get better, you will live." This has no basis in the world's great mystical traditions; it has its basis in narcissistic and borderline pathology.

While much of the mail and response to the original *New Age* piece shared my sense of moral outrage at what these ideas were doing to so many innocent people, the hard-core new agers reacted with rage, saying things like, if Treya and I thought that, she deserved to get cancer. She was bringing it on herself with these thoughts.

This is not a blanket condemnation of the *entire* new age movement.

There are aspects of that movement—it's a large and varied beast, after all—that are indeed based on some genuinely mystical and transpersonal principles (such as the importance of intuition and the existence of universal consciousness). It's just that any genuinely *trans*personal movement always attracts a very large number of *pre*personal elements, simply because both are *non*personal, and it is exactly this confusion between "pre" and "trans" that is one of the major problems with the new age movement, in my opinion.

Here's a concrete example based on empirical research. During the Berkeley riots protesting the war in Vietnam, a team of researchers gave a representative sample of the students the Kohlberg test of moral development. The students, after all, claimed that their major objection to the war was that it was *immoral*. And so what stages of moral development were the students themselves operating from?

What the researchers found was that a small percentage of the students, something like 20%, were indeed operating from the *post*conventional stages (or the "trans"-conventional stages). That is, their objections were based on universal principles of right and wrong, they were not based on any particular society's standards or on individual whim. Their beliefs about the war might have been right, they might have been wrong, but their moral reasoning was quite highly developed. On the other hand, the vast majority of the protesters—around 80%—were found to be *pre*conventional, which means their moral reasoning was based on personal and rather selfish motives. They didn't want to fight, not because the war was immoral, not because they were actually concerned with the Vietnamese people, but because they didn't want anybody telling them what to do. Their motives weren't universal or even social, but purely selfish. And, as we would expect, there were almost no students at the conventional level, the level of "my country right or wrong" (since these students would not have seen any reason to protest in the first place). In other words, a small number of truly post- or transconventional students attracted a very large number of preconventional types, because what they both had in common was being nonconventional.

Just so, in the new age movement, I believe, a small percentage of genuinely mystical or transpersonal or transrational elements and principles (levels seven through nine) have attracted a huge number of prepersonal, magical, and prerational elements (levels one through four), simply because both are nonrational, nonconventional, nonorthodox (levels five and six). And these prepersonal and prerational elements then claim, as the preconventional students did, that they have the authority and the backing of a "higher" state, when all they are doing, I'm afraid I have to conclude, is rationalizing their own self-involved stance. As Jack Engler pointed out, they are drawn to transpersonal mysticism as a way to rationalize prepersonal inclinations. It's a classic "pre/trans fallacy."

I would also conclude, with William Irwin Thompson, that about 20% of the new age movement is transpersonal (transcendental and genuinely mystical); about 80%, prepersonal (magical and narcissistic). You can usually find the transpersonal elements because they don't like to be called "new age." There's nothing "new" about them; they are perennial.

In the field of transpersonal psychology, we are constantly having to deal as delicately and as gently as we can with the prepersonal trends, because they give the entire field a "flaky" or "goofy" reputation. We are not against prepersonal beliefs; we just have trouble when we ourselves are asked to embrace these beliefs as if they were transpersonal.

Our "flakier" friends get rather mad at us, because they tend to think that there are only two camps in the world: rational and nonrational, and so we should join with them *against* the rationalistic camp. But there are in fact *three* camps: prerational, rational, and transrational. We're actually closer to the rationalists than to the prerationalists. The higher levels transcend but *include* the lower. Spirit is translogic, not antilogic; it embraces logic and then goes beyond, it doesn't simply reject logic in the first place. Every transpersonal tenet has to stand the test of logic, and then, but only then, move beyond it with its added insights. Buddhism is an extremely rational system that then supplements rationality with intuitive awareness. Some of the "flaky" trends, I'm afraid, are not beyond logic but beneath it.

So what we are trying to do is tease apart the genuine, universal, "laboratory-tested" elements of mystical development from the more idiosyncratic, magical, and narcissistic tendencies. This is a difficult and tricky task, and we don't always get it right. Leaders in this area are Jack Engler, Daniel Brown, Roger Walsh, William Irwin Thompson, and Jeremy Hayward.

But let me end this discussion by reaffirming my original point: in treating any disease, make every effort to determine just which levels the various components of the disease are coming from, and use same-level treatments to deal with them. If you get the levels more or less right, you will generate action that has the highest chance of being curative; if you get them wrong, you will generate only guilt or despair.

"They're really quite beautiful, aren't they? I mean those images, those ideas. They seem to be alive, aware. Are they?" I am actually asking the Figure a question.

"Step this way please."

"Wait a minute. Couldn't I just go in there? This is bizarre, but, I don't know, it seems that all the answers to all the questions I've ever had are in that room. I mean, look at them, all those ideas alive. Come on, I'm a philosopher." I am aware how utterly silly that sounds.

"Well, anyway," I continue, "this is a once-in-a-lifetime opportunity. If I'm going to get lost in a dream, you might as well let me play it out." I am actually saying that? Go in there? And yet there they are, those ideas, so alluring, so willing to cooperate. You must admit, I think to myself, you don't find ideas like that just anywhere.

"You are looking for Estrella, are you not?"

"Treya? What do you know about Treya? Have you seen her?"

"Step this way please."

"I'm not going anywhere in this stupid place until you tell me what's going on."

"Please, you must come with me. Please."

As the time approached for Treya's next complete physical, I think we were both slightly apprehensive, mostly because of those ominous dreams. Treya had a bone scan, and . . . all clear!

> I got the results of my one-year tests, the first time I've gone a year without a recurrence! I am delighted! At the same time, I am not going to focus on just the physical level, because if I define health that way, what happens if a recurrence does happen? Am I then a failure?
>
> The fact is, my life feels whole and healthy anyway. I feel so blessed. Hanging out with Ken, reconnecting with the earth, working in my small garden, creating in glass—the purity of the newly born, the part I most delight in, the Treya, the artist, peaceful, of the earth. My roots go deep now. . . .
>
> I continue to do my circle of love visualization, sometimes several times a day, in which I imagine myself surrounded by people who love me, breathing in their love. At first this was hard for me, but it has become easier and easier. And just two nights ago I had a dream, by far the most positive self-image dream I've ever had. I dreamt some friends gave me a big party and everyone was telling me how wonderful I was. I

seemed to have no trouble letting all this in, no protestations of modesty, no inner barriers saying even if they think this is so I don't. No, I heard it all and let it all into my heart. The most positive dream I remember ever having.

Sometimes in my circle of love visualization I imagine the love around me as a golden light. Once, I was imagining a very rich, very golden light around me, then I saw a thin blue line close around my body and realized that blue light was my sadness about some of the hard times Ken and I have had to go through. Suddenly the two lights mixed and created a very bright light, green, vibrant, electric, very powerful. Felt bathed in that healing light, felt love's presence inside me rather than outside. Felt that would be with me forever.

I have several affirmations. My present one is: "The universe is unfolding perfectly." Trust is always my issue, and control. This affirmation also helps because it even lets me off the hook for the things I didn't do, because I've learned from them in a way I'll never forget.

I call all of this the immune system of spirit. The T and B and white cells of this system are positive thinking, meditation, affirmations, sangha, dharma, compassion, and kindness. If these factors are worth 20% of the physical disease process, I want all 20%!

The other meditation I do now is tonglen. When I first started doing this almost a year ago, the first thing that came up with that was with Ken and Tahoe. I expected to feel sad or angry or bitter; instead, I felt only compassion. Compassion for all that Ken and I went through during that time, for our fights, our struggles, our fearfulness. It surprised me to feel that compassion, that softness for those two wounded, hurting, frightened people, doing the best they knew how. Tonglen seemed to have cleaned all of the bitterness out. Now when I practice it, it gives me a sense of deep connection with all beings. I no longer feel singled out, I no longer feel alone. Fear is replaced with a deep peace and calm.

And sometimes I just sit, like in Zen, with a sense of openness and spaciousness, into the sky. I always come back to Suzuki Roshi's approach—that I feel drawn to meditate as a way of expressing something inside me, something that feels affirmed by my making an offering of my time and my attention. It feels like a gift I give to some greater power. So I sit with that attitude of making an offering that both satisfies and affirms some mysterious part of myself that I cannot describe. Any changes that come are not sought after, not looked for. If nothing changes, fine. The offering remains, and a sense of peace comes with making that offering.

So, how do I feel about cancer? I still have occasional flashes of what it would be like to be in a hospital again, thoughts of "would I do chemo again if it came to that?," but I'm not obsessing about it at all. Cancer has become more of a background presence. But I don't read any of that as a "sign," one way or the other. I've heard too many stories of people who've made it past five years, who thought they were cured, and who then discovered something like bone metastases. Still, it's nice that it's no longer a looming, ominous presence.

In the immediate months after the physical, Treya and I began, for the first time in three years, to feel that our life might actually return to something resembling normal. We were very happy about this, we let our hopes rise up gently to face the future. In addition to writing, I had begun meditating again, combining my Zen training with the tonglen and Deity yoga given by Kalu Rinpoche.

Particularly due to the tonglen, I began to stop being afraid of my fear, of my anxiety, of my depression. Each time a painful or fearful state arose, I would breathe in deeply with the thought, "May I take all such fear into myself," and then I would release it on the outbreath. I began to step into my own states, and not always recoil from them in fear or anger or annoyance. I was, in effect, digesting my own painful experiences, experiences from the last three years that at the time I could not or would not digest.

Treya and I spent Christmas in Laredo, as we had for the last four years. It was a lovely time, everybody making New Year's resolutions with the happy thought of Treya's clear health in mind.

When Treya and I returned to Boulder, she noticed that a particularly annoying waviness in her left visual field would not go away. She had been noticing this on and off for a month or so, but it became more and more insistent.

We saw our oncologist in Denver, who arranged for her to have a high-density CAT scan of the brain. I was sitting in the waiting room when the doctor came in and pulled me aside.

"It looks like there are two or three tumors in her brain. One of them is quite large, perhaps three centimeters. We're going to scan her lungs as well."

"Have you told Treya yet?" The shock has not set in. I am discussing somebody else, not Treya.

"No, I haven't. Let's wait till the lung pictures come up."

I sit down and stare blankly into space. Brain tumors? *Brain* tumors? Brain tumors . . . are . . . serious.

"She has tumors throughout both lungs, possibly a dozen altogether. I'm as shocked by this as you are. I think it would be best to tell her in my office tomorrow morning. Please don't say anything to her now. I want to have all the information ready for her."

I am so shocked, so frostbitten, that I don't think to say, "Hey wait a minute, we don't do it like that. I'm going to tell her right now. We *never* do that kind of bullshit." No, I numbly nod my head and say, "What? Oh, yeah, sure, OK."

The drive home is horrendous.

"I really don't think it's anything. I feel clear; I feel quite good, really. It's probably just related to the diabetes. We're going to have a good life together, honey, don't look so worried. What do you think?"

What I think is that I am going to kill that doctor. I want to tell Treya, but now it's gone too far. I am physically nauseated at what this means for her, at what she will have to endure. God, if only tonglen really worked! I would close my eyes and breathe her likely death into me with such force I would vanish on the spot, taking that damn disease with me into the cosmic void. Both my love for Treya and my hatred of that doctor went to infinite proportions simultaneously. I kept muttering things like, "I'm sure everything will be fine."

When we got home, I went in the bathroom and threw up. That evening we went to see a movie—of all things, *Fatal Attraction*. When we got back, Treya called the doctor and got the news.

My first reaction was rage! Absolute, total, complete, overwhelming rage! And totally shocked! How could this happen! I've done everything right! How could this happen! Damn! Damn! Damn! Damn! Damn! I didn't feel fear. I wasn't particularly afraid of what this meant. I was simply furious. I began kicking kitchen cabinets, throwing things, yelling. Enraged, outraged. I was not about to let go of my anger. It was the right response. I'm pissed at this, I want to fight! In my visualizations, the white knights turned into furious piranhas.

We called family and friends, and then the next day Treya and I began a furious and intensive search for any treatments, anywhere, that had any chance of handling a case this aggressive and this advanced. Treya seriously considered almost two dozen approaches, including Burzynski, Revici, Burton, the Janker Klinik (Germany), Kelley/Gonzales, American Biologics, Livingston-Wheeler, Hans Nieper (Germany), the Steiner Lucas Clinic (Switzerland), Gerson (Mexico).

> After the anger, I went through a period of a few days of resignation and sadness. I would sob uncontrollably in Ken's arms, for hours on end. I felt like I was totally falling apart, something I hadn't felt for years. Regret, self-blame, I could have done more, did I do enough? I thought of things I would miss: art, skiing, growing old with family and friends, Ken, Ken's child. I want so much to grow old with all my wonderful friends. I don't even like to write this down—I'll never be able to have Ken's child. Ken—I want to be with him in life, I don't want to desert him. I want to cuddle with him for years. He'll be alone; will he find somebody? He may go into Kalu's three-year retreat; that makes me feel good.
>
> I feel like I have just been born, and now I am not supposed to be here.

The choices narrowed down to a few: standard American treatment, which was more adriamycin; aggressive American treatment, recommended by Bloomenschein; and extremely aggressive treatment, offered by the Janker Klinik in Germany. The first option was outlined by Dr. Dick Cohen, a good friend of Vicky and CSC, who recommended a program that included low-dose, long-term adriamycin with an average treatment failure of fourteen months. But Treya simply did not want to do more adria, not because she couldn't handle it, but because, for personal reasons, she felt it wasn't effective against her cancer.

The Janker Klinik is world famous for its short-term, high-dose chemotherapy, which is so aggressive that people sometimes have to be kept on life-support systems. The Klinik gets in the news every now and then for treating people like Bob Marley and Yul Brynner. Published (but nonscientific) reports give the Janker an incredible 70% remission rate, all the more amazing in that most people go there as a last resort. American doctors claim that the remissions are extremely short-lived, and that when the cancer returns it is quickly fatal.

Bloomenschein gave Treya a series of recommendations that, basically, any Central American dictator would consider cruel and unusual. He ended by saying, "I beg you, dear, don't go to Germany." But he was only giving us the grim statistics for a case like Treya's: maybe a year, maybe with luck.

16

BUT LISTEN TO THOSE BIRDS SING!

❧❦❧

"EDITH. Hi, it's Ken Wilber."

"Ken! How are you? It is so good to hear your voice."

"Edith, I'm sorry to say we've had some bad news. Treya has had a very bad recurrence, this time to the lungs and to the brain."

"Oh, how awful. Oh, I am so, so sorry."

"Edith, you're never going to guess where I'm calling from. And Edith, we could use some help."

Well, I can't believe I've been in the hospital ten days and I still haven't started chemotherapy. We arrived in Bonn on Monday, went out to dinner Monday night, and Tuesday morning I started feeling strange, checked into the Klinik Tuesday afternoon. By then I had a terrible, terrible chest cold, with a temperature of 103.6. I'm still not quite over it, and they can't start chemotherapy until I am, because of risk of pneumonia, and so this has meant a delay of almost two weeks.

My first night here, I was in a room with two other women, both German. Very nice ladies, neither spoke English. But one of them snored all night, and the other lady seemed to think that if she just spoke *more* German I might understand, so she kept throwing all these German words at me, chattering away constantly; she even talked to herself, on and off all night.

Somehow Dr. Scheef, the head of the Klinik, managed to find a single room for me (there are only two or three in the entire Klinik), and I have been in seventh heaven ever since. It's small, it's absolutely tiny [8′ × 14′], but it's wonderful.

I've been surprised that so few of the nurses speak any English. A few speak some English; none are fluent; most speak no English whatsoever. I'm a little ashamed I don't speak German; I explain to people that I speak French and Spanish as a way of apologizing for my total lack of German.

The first evening I was here the talkative German lady took Ken and me down to the cafeteria; dinner is served from 4:45 to 5:30. The food is atrocious. Most of the time, breakfast and dinner, they serve cold cuts—slices of cheese, slices of ham, slices of meat, slices of sausage, plus various wheat breads, which are off-limits because of diabetes. Occasionally for lunch they serve hot, cooked meat and potatoes. That's the extent of the variety here. With my diet, I am allowed none of it. What is it about hospital food the world over? Ken wondered aloud just who kills more people, hospital doctors or hospital cooks?

That first evening in the cafeteria there was an attractive younger woman who had a really nice wig on with a lovely cap over it. She spoke a little English, so I asked her about her wig, knowing I would soon need one myself. I also asked her the German name for cancer, because I hadn't been able to communicate even that little bit. She told me it was *Mütze*. So then I asked her, does everyone here have Mütze? And she said yes, gesturing to all the other people in the dining room. I asked her, what kind of Mütze do you have? And she said, I have a white one and a blue one. I sat there, stunned, didn't say anything, could not figure this one out. It wasn't until the next day that I discovered that Mütze is the word for hat or cap. The word for cancer is *Krebs*.

Both Treya and I had expected, from an article we had read, that Bonn would be dreary, grimy, industrial. But the only thing gloomy about Bonn was the weather. Otherwise it is a lovely and in many ways quite beautiful city—Germany's diplomatic center, with a spectacular *Dom* or cathedral, built in 1728, an imposing and impressive university, a huge *Zentrum* or downtown mall, stretching perhaps thirty blocks (all off-limits to cars), and the magnificent Rhine just a short walk away.

The railway station or *Hauptbahnhof* was one block from the Klinik, which was one block from the Hotel Kurfürstenhof, where I stayed, which was right on the edge of the Zentrum. A large and gorgeous park ridged the whole town. In the center of the Zentrum was the *Marktplatz*, where each day the local farmers brought the most magnificent variety of fresh fruits and vegetables and displayed them for sale in a large, open, brick-covered area that was perhaps four square blocks in size. At one end of the Zentrum was the house, built in 1720, where Beethoven was born. At the other end was the Hauptbahnhof, the Klinik, and the Kurfürstenhof. In between was every imaginable kind of shop—restaurants, bars, health food stores, department stores a block long and four stories high, sporting good stores, museums, clothing stores, art galleries, drug stores, and sex shops (German pornography being the envy of Europe). Everything, in other words, from the Rhine to the hotel, within walking distance, or, at any rate, hiking distance.

I would spend the next four months walking the brick-paved paths and roads of the Zentrum, getting to know any cabbie, waitress, or merchant who spoke English. They all began to follow Treya's story, asking after her any time I saw them—"Undt how iss dear Trey-yah?"—many coming to visit her in the Klinik with flowers or candies. Treya said she had the feeling that half of Bonn was following her progress.

And it was in Bonn that I would have my final crisis of acceptance of Treya's situation and of my role as a support person. I had labored hard—from Seymour to tonglen—to digest and work through and accept the difficult times that we had both endured. But I still had a few deeply unresolved issues, issues about my own choices and my own bad faith, and issues (no longer deniable) about Treya's possible death. It all came to a head in a three-day period during which I seemed to crack wide open. My heart just broke, broke for Treya, broke for me.

In the meantime, we set up shop. Our immediate problem was Treya's chest cold, which was severely complicating the situation. The Klinik specializes in giving radiation and chemotherapy concurrently, believing that it delivers a double knockout punch. The chest cold prevented the administration of chemotherapy because of likely pneumonia. In the States, Treya had been told that the brain tumor, untreated, would kill her in six months. The Klinik had to do something, and do it very quickly, and

276

so they proceeded with radiation alone, waiting for her temperature to drop and her white blood counts to rise.

I wandered around in a bit of a daze for the next three days because my temperature was so high. They had started me on sulfamide, but it was slow to work. Ken helped me walk up and down the hallways, and cooked for me in my room, and ran interference. He shopped for fresh vegetables in the Marktplatz each morning. He got a hot plate, a coffee pot (to make soup), and, best of all, an exercise bike (for my diabetes). He brought me little plants, and flowers, and crosses for my shrine. With the food and flowers and shrine and bike, my room was full! All and all I was weak and dizzy, but relatively contented.

We gleaned from Scheef that I will continue the hyperthermia and radiation to the brain, which is painless and takes about a half hour each day. Once we start the high-dose chemotherapy, about which we have heard so much (none of it pleasant), the treatments will last for five days. On day eight or nine my body will reach its low point. If my blood count is under 1000, I need to be in the Klinik; if it's under 100, I'll need bone marrow injections. On day fifteen, they'll check the brain tumor and the lung tumors with a CAT scan or NMR to see the results. I'll have two to three weeks off between treatments, of which there will be three.

Under the stress of the high fever and chest infection, Treya's pancreas ceased producing any insulin at all.

Ken and I are walking so slowly down the hall because I am feeling so dizzy and so sick. My temperature is high and my blood sugar is soaring. I spent about five days, over Ken's nagging objections, trying to handle my blood sugar with exercise on the bike. But even the bike didn't do the trick. I lost eight pounds, eight pounds I could ill afford to lose. Lying on my side was painful because my hip pushed through my skin. This freaked me out. Things don't always move fast around here. Ken made some very big waves, and they finally put me on insulin. I started eating, trying to gain this weight back.

As I was trying to adjust my insulin dose, I had my first insulin reaction. My heart started pounding, my body was shaking, and when I checked my blood it was 50. Insulin blackout or convulsions can set in at 25. Ken thank God was there, and since we can't really communicate with the nurses, he ran down to the cafeteria and got some sugar cubes. I checked my blood again, it was 33. But twenty minutes later it was up to 50, then 97. Ah, the ups and downs of life in room 228. . . .

The days dragged on and on and on, waiting for the infection to subside. And in the background constantly was the thought of the notorious "killer chemotherapy" lying yet ahead, the whole thing made all the more ominous by not being able to face it except in imagination, a strange H. P. Lovecraft atmosphere where the monster is always mentioned, never seen. Kati arrived just in time to take up some of the tension, and proved an absolute godsend. With Kati's help, both Treya and I returned to a measure of equanimity and even humor. Sorely needed!

And then there was Edith. I met her on the steps of the Klinik and took her up to room 228. It was love at first sight, I think, something even I had not been accorded. They immediately latched on to each other, as if a tight friendship had already been sealed. But I had seen this happen so often in the past. More than once I had found myself almost instantly in the background, as *my* good friends fell in love with Treya. "Like, I'm her husband, I'm a good friend of hers, you know, honest. I can arrange dinner with her if you like."

We would spend many a delightful occasion with Edith and her husband Rolf, a rather famous political theorist to whom I took an immediate liking. Rolf was everything I admired in the best of the "European" man: cultured, witty, brilliant, widely read in all fields, very powerful in his knowledge, very gentle in his being. But most of all it was Edith's presence that made things so much better, and all of our family and friends who met her immediately relaxed and stopped worrying about us kids lost in Germany—Edith was there!

As I am being gently pulled down the hall toward the fourth room, I wonder how this Figure can seem to be tugging at my arm, since in every other way it seems to be only an absence, a nothing. How does a nothing pull at a something? Unless—and the thought startles me—

"What do you see?"

"What? Me? What do I see?" I slowly peer into the room. I already know I will see something weird. But what I see is not so much weird as breathtaking, absolutely breathtaking. I stand for minutes in sheer child-like wonder.

"And now we will go in, yes?"

278

Still no chemotherapy, but really it's odd. Here I am just lying in the hospital waiting and I don't seem to have enough time to do anything! Write letters, read novels, read my spiritual books—right now it's Stephen Levine's *Healing into Life and Death*—do my meditation, do my bicycling, answer mail, write in my journal, visit with Ken and Kati and Edith, visit with the other Americans, do my art work. It's kind of ridiculous. Just proves that there's never enough time. Which gives me a kind of funny feeling when I think of that, because certainly I'm not going to have enough time in this life. I feel very positive at times, and then at other times I feel quite frightened that this could be it, I could die within the year.

I just walked out of my room and came across a bunch of people who were all teary-eyed and crying. Who knows what kind of bad news they got, about their relative or friend. It just seems so sad. One young man embracing a woman who could have been his wife or girlfriend, both with red swollen eyes. Another woman over by the table embracing a woman in a green robe, maybe she's the one who's sick, both of them crying. Three other people sitting around the table, all with red swollen eyes. The first noble truth: there is suffering.

I finished reading that *Newsweek* issue on the right to die. It's been something that's interested me for a long time, even before I got cancer. Because of all the time, expense, and suffering—real suffering—involved in keeping people alive with heroic measures, keeping them alive but not living in a way that makes life worth living. I do hope when my time comes that I can die in the hospice way without incredible life-support measures and with the pain under control. I was saying to Ken the other day that I might ask Scheef for some pills just to have around, just to know they're there.

I want my will to live to be strong, I want to get as much time out of this as I can, and so I need to work at that with complete focus and dedication and clarity and concentration and right effort, and yet at the same time be completely unattached to the results either way. Pain is not punishment, death is not a failure, life is not a reward.

Got a nice letter from Lydia. She said something that really touched me. "If the Lord calls you, if you are meant to do that, I know you will do that also with grace." If I don't make it, I will do that with grace. I do hope so. Again, I sometimes feel that those around me will judge my success or failure depending on how long I live, rather than on how I live. Of course I want to live a long time, but if it's short, I don't want to be judged a failure. So it was really nice that she said that.

I've started a program of meditation at least twice a day, vipassana in the morning and tonglen/Chenrezi in the afternoon. I'm trying to do visualization three times a day. Right now, I'm doing this just to prove to myself that I'm not too lazy to do something that might help. It strengthens my conviction that I'm in this for the long haul—but again, hopefully without attachment to results. To simply strengthen my own faith in myself, to honor my own spirit, to make an offering.

As difficult as the circumstances were, within a week of our arrival in Bonn, Treya had once again regained her steady and even joyful equanimity, which was frequently commented on by the doctors and nurses and her various visitors. People began hanging out in her room, just to be around the delight she seemed to generate. It was sometimes hard to find time to be alone with her!

It's amazing to me how quickly I bounce back from bad news, how ready I am to be with what is. The meditation, no doubt. The first week after I got the bad news I just fell apart. I let everything come up that wanted to come up—anger, fear, rage, sadness. It all seemed to wash through me and then out of me, and I returned to simply being with what is. If this is what is, then this is what is. It feels like acceptance, not resignation, but who can know for sure? Am I kidding myself? That same small voice saying, Treya, you should be worried. But it's a pale voice, it seems. It's there, but it's having a hard time getting an audience.

And the fact is, I feel so incredibly blessed—blessed with my family, blessed with my husband, blessed with my wonderful friends. I just can't believe how perfect my life is! Except for this damn cancer.

I told Ken that I can't understand it myself, but my mood is excellent, my spirits are good, I'm enjoying life, I like hearing the birds sing outside my window, I love visiting with all the people in the Klinik. I don't have enough time to do everything. I look forward to the day, I don't want it to end. I don't understand it! I know I may not live out the year. But just listen to those birds sing!

Finally we got word that the chemotherapy would begin on Monday. On the day of the treatment, I sat awkwardly on the exercise bike, Kati in the corner. Treya was quite relaxed. The yellow fluid began to drip slowly into her arm. Ten minutes passed. Nothing. Twenty minutes. Nothing. Thirty minutes. Nothing. I don't know what we expected, maybe that she would explode or something, so horrifying were the stories we had been fed in the States. Just the week before people had begun calling with "goodbye" wishes, all convinced the treatment would kill her. And in fact, this *was* a very aggressive and powerful treatment; peoples' white blood counts sometimes go to zero! But the Klinik has developed equally powerful "rescue" drugs that mitigate most of the problems. This, of course, our American doctors neglected to tell us. Treya decided it was a piece of cake and began calmly eating her lunch.

Well, it's now some hours after the first treatment, and I feel fine! I feel a little sleepy because of the antinausea medication, but I cannot believe how much easier it is than adriamycin. I was eating while the chemotherapy was dripping into me. . . .

I had my second treatment today and once again I feel absolutely fine. Began exercising fifty minutes on my bike. I think they've got this rescue-drug routine down pat. Bravo for them. Bravo! Bravo! Bravo! But I am *pissed* at all the American doctors who, without knowing anything about this treatment, filled our heads with sadistic images. Oh well, all's well that ends well, I suppose. And the fact is, I feel quite normal, quite healthy. This is a cinch!

Janker Klinik
March 26, 1988

Dear friends,

I cannot thank each of you enough for your wonderful and inventive cards and letters and phone calls . . . it feels wonderful to feel so supported, sort of like floating in a deliciously warm, soothing, caressing ocean. Each card and each call adds to the warmth and buoyancy of the ocean.

I have many major sources of support in this lovely ocean. One is Ken, who has been the Perfect Support Person—never an easy task and often insufficiently acknowledged. He runs errands for me, holds my hand, entertains me, we have great talks, and are simply as in love as ever these days. The other is my family, who have been beyond compare in their love and support. My mother and father met us in San Francisco when I had the bone marrow harvest before coming to Germany (just in case I needed it for future treatments), my sister Kati was just here for ten days and helped us get over the initial adjustment, my parents are here now in Germany and planning a driving trip when my counts rise enough, and my other sister, Tracy, and her husband, Michael, will meet us in Paris and come back to Bonn for the beginning of the second treatment. Not to mention Ken's wonderful family, Ken and Lucy, who are so supportive and loving. Then there's all the special people at the Cancer Support Community, most especially Vicky, who has been instrumental in setting up the bone marrow harvest and gathering information on all fronts. Then there's my wonderful friends in Aspen and Boulder and my special Findhorn friends scattered all over. . . . I feel very, very blessed.

We had a bit of a rough beginning on arrival. I caught a cold which unfortunately lasted for three weeks. I was in the hospital during that time doing radiation daily, afraid to give up my room because there might not be one available when it came time to start. My sister came over which helped us through that difficult time. Now we're off and running and I have complete confidence in Herr Professor Doktor Scheef, the man who runs the Janker Klinik. He is full of energy and vitality and jolliness; I liken him to a younger Santa Claus (salt-and-pepper beard) who has a bulging red bag full of anticancer presents. Unlike most doctors in the U.S., whose bag is smaller due to the FDA and what sometimes seems like an almost professionally mandated too-limited interest in the full range of treatments available. For example, the main drug that Dr. Scheef is using for me is called ifosfamide; it's a cousin of cytoxan, or cyclofosfamide, one of the main chemotherapy drugs used in the U.S. and a drug which Scheef himself first developed. He's been using ifosfamide for ten years and it was just approved last year by the FDA for use in the U.S.—but only against sarcomas (it's effective against a wide range of cancers) and only at doses well below what Dr. Scheef thinks should be used. So I could not have been treated with this drug in the U.S.

After consultation with many doctors in January and February, all they had to offer me was the same drug I had before, adriamycin, basically on a program that meant I'd take it until I died (or the drug killed me through complications, as it recently did a friend of mine). The average time before treatment failure on this drug is fourteen months, and that's counting from when they give you the first treatment. I couldn't see that this was really buying me any time at all, and I well knew the kind of misery it would buy me. When my sister asked me what it was like on adria and I began to list the symptoms, I realized it didn't sound all that terrible. Then I remembered what I used to say to Ken while on the drug: you know, I don't feel that bad, I can get around and do things, but the terrible part about this drug is that it poisons the soul, I feel like it's poisoning my soul. So you can imagine that I was less than thrilled about having that kind of chemotherapy again, and less than thrilled about the figures the doctors gave me. When I pinned them down about how much extra time would I actually get, they said if I got a partial response (to be expected since I had already "failed" on this drug), I had a 25–30% chance of getting an extra six to twelve months. Chickenfeed I said, rather indignantly, and went looking elsewhere!

I've known for quite a while (though at times conveniently forgotten!) that because of the type of cancer cell I had (the worst grade) and the two recurrences I had so soon after the first surgery, my chances of a metastatic recurrence were very, very high. Since getting the news of my situation on January 19 I've moved through a lot of different spaces about it—starting with extreme anger that this sort of thing happened to me and that it has to happen to anyone at all. My fighting spirit was definitely aroused, and actually my spirits have been pretty good throughout. Even better once I discovered this Klinik. . . . Clearly the very hardest period was trying to choose a treatment.

In addition to the anger I was often extremely upset, though too busy and frantic to have time to get depressed (I must have set a record for number of phone calls while trying to decide what to do). I had several days at first when I felt incredibly shaky, crying a lot, very agitated, close to falling apart, dwelling on fears of pain and thoughts of death . . . and then would come thoughts of all who are suffering on this planet at this moment, of all who have suffered in the past, and I would immediately feel a wave of peace and calm pass through me. I no longer felt alone, I no longer felt singled out; instead I felt an incredible connection with all these people, like we were part of the same huge family. I thought of all the children who have cancer, I thought of the people who die unexpectedly at young ages in traffic accidents, I thought of those who suffer from mental illness, I thought of the starving in the Third World, of children who will always be handicapped by malnutrition even if they survive. I thought of parents who must endure the death of a child, of all those who died in Vietnam when they were only half my age, of those who are victims of torture. My heart went out to them all as members of my family and I felt comforted by remembering the first noble truth, the noble truth of suffering. There is suffering in this world, no way around that one, always has been.

I feel very thankful for my Buddhist training in the midst of all this, particularly vipassana and tonglen. I am also feeling drawn to Christianity again, the music and the rituals and the magnificent cathedrals, not the theology. They move me in a way that Buddhist ritual does not. It feels like a blending of the two is happening for me, Christianity with its emphasis on the vertical dimension or the divine and Buddhism with its calm acceptance of what is and its straightforward path that leads to the extinction of suffering.

A group of nurses came in a little after I arrived and set up shop in my room to ask me, rather shyly and tentatively, "What religion are you?" I don't blame them for being confused! I have a lovely shrine set up on the one table in my room. There's a beautiful statue of the healing Buddha and another of Mary which Ken gave me; a striking round quartz crystal from my friends in Sunshine Canyon; a lovely statue of the Madonna and Child from my sister-in-law; a statue of St. Anne from Vicky that once helped her heal; a delicate picture of Kwan Yin from Ange; a small thangka of Green Tara from Ken; a lovely saying painted by my sister Tracy in an old frame; salt that Trungpa Rinpoche's body was packed in from his successor, the Regent (and other relics which I wear most gratefully); a picture of Kalu Rinpoche, whom I've studied with, and of Trungpa Rinpoche and the Regent; other pictures, sent to me by various people, of Ramana Maharshi, Sai Baba, and the Pope; an old Mexican painting on metal of a healing figure; a lovely cross from a relative and an old prayer book from my aunt; a prayer from Eileen Caddy, cofounder of Findhorn; touching gifts from friends at the Cancer Support Community; a rosary and a mala from a Wisdom Retreat with Kalu Rinpoche . . . no wonder they're confused! But it feels very right to me. I've always been an ecumenist at heart, now it's made concrete in my shrine!

Although I have philosophical problems with both Christianity and Buddhism, at a time like this those fade into insignificance. When I get caught in trying to puzzle it out, I remember the Buddha's warning against philosophizing about things we cannot find answers for. So I make no effort at all to try and reconcile the two—an impossible task to be sure!—but I do notice that in a situation like mine Christian philosophy seems to lead to unhelpful kinds of approaches and questions: why did this happen to me, why does it happen to anyone, is "God" punishing me, did I do something wrong, what can I do to make it all right again, it's unfair that children have to get this terrible disease, why do bad things happen to good people, why does God let these things happen in the world? But the stillness of a cathedral and hymns that soar over organ music and the simple peaceful joyousness of Christmas carols all move me deeply.

Buddhism, on the other hand, is a real source of comfort when things are bad. Instead of leading me to rant and rave about the state of things or start a crusade to correct them, it helps me accept the way things are. But this doesn't lead to passivity since the emphasis is always on right effort while freeing oneself from craving and from aversion. In fact, for me effort becomes easier, almost paradoxically, because I find myself less attached to results, more involved in investigating what's happening than in setting goals, striving to reach them, and being disappointed if I don't.

For example, I still have waviness in my left eye—this is the symptom that led to the discovery of the brain tumor (in my right occipital lobe) and then the lung tumors. I had completed the radiation treatments to my brain and was hoping to see some change, so every time I noticed the waviness I felt a small reaction—revulsion, fear, disappointment, all of that. Suddenly, everything shifted for me. The waviness became something to notice, to investigate, to witness. There it is, and all the reacting in the world won't change the truth of that present moment. With this approach my level of fear subsided dramatically, and even when the fear comes up I can simply witness it instead of piling fear on fear. I find this incredibly helpful whenever fear arises, like when my WBC [white blood count] is low or my temperature goes up a few tenths of a degree. This is what is, this is what is happening, I can watch it, watch my reactions, watch my fear, and as they subside feel myself gently move back toward equanimity.

So, to return to the treatment. I'm being treated with two drugs, ifosfamide and BCNU. The treatment is five days, with ifosfamide being given every day IV and BCNU on days 1, 3, and 5. They have developed a number of rescue drugs and supportive things that make the treatment side effects, both short- and long-term, relatively minor. One drug, mesna, is given four times each day of treatment and protects the kidneys. There's another drug they call "antifungal" which is given during and after treatment, a double dose while the WBC is below 1000. Their antinausea drugs, both mixed in the chemo and given by suppository, work extremely well with no side effects for me except a little sleepiness. They have stronger ones in reserve if needed. When I remember how doped up (literally—one drug I took was THC in capsule form) I had to get to simply endure the adria treatments and even then how awful that first eight hours was . . . not a pleasant memory. This was so much easier I simply couldn't believe it! When I commented to Dr. Scheef how easy it was in comparison he said, "Ah, and it's much, much stronger!"

Not only that, but there's none of this stuff about being on chemotherapy for years. This is high-dose, short-term chemotherapy, only three treatments, approximately one a month. The rough outline (this all depends on blood counts, of course) is five days of chemotherapy followed by ten to fourteen days in the hospital while your [white blood] counts go down (one American here had his counts down to 200) and then up. All the time they're giving you supportive medication, following your temperature, reminding you to brush and rinse with a terrible tasting antibiotic mouthwash every time you eat. You can leave the hospital when your counts reach 1500 and leave on a trip between treatments when they reach 1800. You get usually two weeks off between treatments, but often if you ask for three that's OK too. They want your WBC between 2,500 and 3,000 before beginning the next treatment.

The one thing I miss here is the valuable information you usually get from other patients. I speak no German, and there's only one other American patient here now. He's a young man by the name of Bob Doty; he and Ken have become fast friends. He's on treatment #2 (eight to ten days of chemotherapy for a relatively rare sarcoma) and I've learned a lot from him. The nurses don't speak much English, so I'm putting together a letter for future English-speaking patients about procedures, what to expect, menus, how to convert Celsius to Fahrenheit (for your temperature) and kilograms to pounds, the scientific and U.S. names of drugs they use, how to schedule your breaks, the general menu here, etc.

Two of my favorite people in the world to hang out with are my Mom and Dad; fortunately, Ken feels the same way! We're spending our two week break with them, driving through Germany, Switzerland, and France, ending up in Paris and spending five days there. My favorite times with my parents have been two other driving trips in Europe, so I'm really looking forward to this. And it will be extra special because this is Ken's first trip to Europe! So far all he's seen is Bonn and its surroundings . . .

but I can't wait to show him Paris! He's a city boy, while I most look forward simply to the drive, to the landscape unfolding before me, the open hills, the narrow valleys and high mountains, to the lakes, the fields, the small villages, the rivers, the changing vegetation and geography—there's something about the land that brings a deep delight for me. Kati and Ken and I took a drive on the Sunday before I began treatment and I was reminded of how it soothes my soul, of how my spiritual roots lie in a deep love of the land.

I hope I don't get too attached to the side benefits of being sick! It's been quite an experience for a do-it-myself type to let everyone else do for me. A real letting go . . . allowing myself to feel worth it, not keeping any kind of I'll-pay-you-back internal ledger, sort of like learning to let compliments in instead of shrugging them off. I sit here in my hospital bed while Ken and whoever else is here at the time buys me food and runs errands and brings me magazines and sometimes cooks for me.

Ah, the weather. The only uniformity to it is that on average it's bad, wet, overcast, dreary. The sleet/snow that greeted our arrival has changed to rain. The sun does come out, but only for ten minutes or so at a time. The rain, however, lasts longer. The Rhine is now at the highest flood stage in eight years because of the rain. It doesn't bother me much, queen of room 228; I haven't been out of the hospital since the beginning of treatment, thirteen days ago. It's good weather to take naps to!

There's a cute young girl who teaches art classes here twice a week. She's got me started on acrylics, which is a shift from my pencil drawings and the glasswork. I'm just fooling around with it, mainly learning how to mix colors and how to construct a picture from the background to the highlights (with pencils I work the other way around, beginning with the highlights). It seems hard to believe that I'm actually enjoying myself sitting here in this room for so long, but it's true.

As for Dr. Scheef, I'm afraid I've joined the ranks of those who think he walks on water. Ken thinks Scheef has one of the "finest, fastest" minds he's ever seen. His Tuesday rounds are breezy and too quick, so I've learned to make appointments to see him every so often. Each time we have had to wait an incredibly long time, from two to four hours, before being ushered into his office.

Once inside, however, he's ours. I have started tape-recording these meetings, because my pen can't keep up with his facts and stories and opinions and laughter! Turns out he has read two of Ken's books in German, and he said he was delighted to "be treating such famous people." We've seen books on Issels's therapy, Burzynski, Gerson, and Kelley on his bookshelves; would I find those in an American doctor's office? It increases my confidence to know that Dr. Scheef has taken the trouble to inform himself thoroughly about a wide range of options and that he's tried a number of them himself. He has incredible energy and vitality and I have tremendous confidence in him. He's on top of all the latest research and has access to the latest techniques, from interferon to enzymes. Not only do I trust his judgment on choosing among them, I feel confident that if he thinks they would work better in my situation he would certainly recommend them. To me, that's a pretty amazing thing to say about a doctor, and a tremendously comforting way to feel about the doctor who is treating me.

I will finish this letter after our conference on Monday with Dr. Scheef, when we'll get the results of the CAT scan and find out how the brain tumor is. I'll work on my equanimity over the weekend in preparation for Monday's results. . . .

"Do you like licorice?" was the first thing he ever said to me.

"Licorice? It's my favorite." Thereafter, our meetings with Scheef always began with a handout of the best licorice I had ever tasted.

But it wasn't even the licorice. It was the beer. Scheef had put a beer dispensing machine—two Kolsch beers for 5 marks—in the Klinik. The day I left Tahoe I quit drinking vodka, but allowed myself beer. Scheef himself used to drink ten or fifteen beers a day—Germans have the highest per capita consumption of beer in the world—but he was now diabetic and had only, as a poor substitute, his licorice. I became good friends with that machine. "Beer," Scheef would encourage me, "is the only alcohol that puts more into your body than it takes out," and it was openly available to all his patients.

At one point I asked him, as I often did doctors, would you recommend this particular treatment for your wife? "Never ask a doctor if he would recommend something for his wife. You don't know how they're getting along. Ask him if he would do it for his daughter!" he said with a laugh.

"Well, for your daughter?" Treya asked. She had in mind adrenal suppression for breast cancer.

"We don't do it because the quality of life is so much lower. You must never forget," he said, "around the tumor is a human being." *That's* when I fell in love with Scheef.

We asked him about another treatment that was popular in the States. "No, we don't do that." "Why?" "Because," he said directly, "it damages the soul." Here was the man famous for the most aggressive chemotherapy in the world, but there were things he simply would not do because they damaged the soul.

How about the widespread belief that psychological factors alone cause cancer, that cancer is psychogenic?

"Some say breast cancer is a psychological problem: problems with your husband, problems with your children, problems with your dog. But during the war and the concentration camps, where there were many problems and enormous stress, there was the lowest rate of breast cancer. It's because there was no fat in their diets. Between 1940 and 1951 there was the lowest cancer incidence in Germany, but the highest stress. Where were the cancers caused by psychological problems?"

"How about vitamins?" I asked. "I'm a biochemist by training, and from the studies I've seen, not only can megavitamins help against cancer, some of them are powerful enough to deactivate chemotherapy agents. Our American doctors disagree with both."

"No, you are right. Vitamin C in particular has anticancer properties, but if you give it at the same time with chemotherapy, it will deactivate ifosfamide and most other chemotherapy agents. There was a doctor here in Germany who announced he could give chemotherapy and the patients' hair wouldn't fall out. He also gave his patients massive doses of vitamin C at the same time, so of course their hair didn't go away. Neither did the cancer. To prove this"—and here you have to understand the European tradition of the Herr Professor: try it on yourself first—"to prove this, I gave myself a lethal injection of ifosfamide, in the presence of the doctors of course, plus twenty grams of vitamin C. I am obviously still here. So this doctor wasn't giving ifosfamide IV, he was giving it OTW—out the window."

Treya talked to a German woman whose son lived in Los Angeles. She had just contracted severe ovarian cancer, and, worried that she might die, wanted to visit her son. But she had no money and she couldn't get a visa. Scheef got her a plane ticket and a visa, and told her simply, "First we take care of the cancer, then you will see your son."

If Scheef is what you were supposed to be like when you left medical school, I would never have left Duke. Most American medical schools, alas, teach you only to put a plaque on your desk that faces the patients and says, "Death does not remove your obligation to pay."

I met Scheef on the sidewalk one day. "Where on earth is a good restaurant around here?"

He laughed. "Two hundred miles in that direction, right across the French border."

April 1

We met with Dr. Scheef on Tuesday, after having a brain CAT scan on Monday. He said the results were "amazing, excellent" . . . the large brain tumor is almost all gone, just a bit of the outside left, sort of like a crescent moon. Actually the radiation keeps on working and of course there are two more chemotherapy treatments to go, so I still have a chance for a complete remission. Hooray! (They won't check my lungs until before the next treatment.) This is very encouraging, and both Mom and Dad, who were with us, felt much reassured.

The only disappointment has been that my blood counts have not gone up yet, although this is temporary. They have to reach 1500 before I can leave on the trip with Mom and Dad and Ken. The white blood cell count has hovered between 400 and 600 for seven days now, and the hemoglobin is still low. It's not exactly a surprise, however, since I had that bone marrow harvest before coming over here and half of my bone marrow was removed. That means, said Dr. Scheef, that I have fewer "mother cells" and in general a young population of cells in the marrow. Once they mature enough, though, my counts will go up "exponentially." Bob Doty had his counts go to 200, up to 400, back down to 200 but once they reached 800 they went the next day to 1300 and the next day to 2000.

That's the kind of progress I'm awaiting . . . as the days we'd planned to spend with my parents in Paris diminish the longer I'm confined to the hospital. But my sister and her husband are meeting us in Paris so we'll travel back with them, which will be fun.

They weren't planning to test my WBC today since it's a holiday (today is Good Friday). If they don't test, I can't leave. Ken went out and made a few waves, he says everyone is angry with him now, but the blood test is underway. I'm glad there's that study out saying that difficult, i.e. demanding, cancer patients do better. My parents said the doctors they talk to at M. D. Anderson agree with that; they don't want passive patients since the others do better. I keep hoping the nurses here have read the same studies! Whatever part of me might feel guilty at asking for what I want or afraid of angering others by being demanding is assuaged by these studies. Funny the effect the studies have—in this case I get permission to not be "good" or "nice" but ask for what I want, while another study might make me wonder if I should be acting differently. For example, as I have reconnected with my Buddhist training and pondered on right effort and acceptance and simply being with what is, I have felt the fight and the anger and the "I'll beat this cancer back" attitude melt away. This shift felt right for me, but a small part also remembered the studies showing that angry patients with a fighting spirit did better and wondered. Am I losing my "fighting spirit"? Is this bad? The same old paradox, being and doing.

Only last night I read a New York Times article by Daniel Goleman (September 17, 1987). A Dr. Sandra Levy studied this contrast between angry, fighting spirit cancer patients and those who were passive and "good" in a group of thirty-six women with advanced breast cancer. Here are the results:

> After seven years, 24 of the 36 women had died. To her surprise, Dr. Levy found that, after the first year, anger made no difference in survival. The only psychological factor that mattered for survival within seven years seemed to be a sense of joy in life.
>
> The primary factor that predicted survival, she found, was already well established in oncology: the length of time the patients remained disease free after first being treated. . . . But the second strongest factor was having a high score on "joy" on a standard paper-and-pencil test measuring mood. Test evidence of joy was statistically more significant as a predictor of survival than was the number of sites of metastases once the cancer spread. That a joyous state of mind should be so powerful a predictor of survival was completely unexpected.

That was nice to hear, especially since I've been feeling so happy lately in spite of being confined to the hospital. I'll gladly trade in my anger for joy, thank you! Now I wonder how this study will make me feel when I'm feeling depressed and unjoyful. . . . The possibility of endless bouts of this kind of yo-yo reaction to new articles, new studies, new test results, new prognoses, on and on, is exactly why cultivating equanimity, being with what is, observing without trying to change or make "better" helps me so much.

Today is Good Friday. The hospital is quiet, not much activity. The birds are singing outside my window. There's one that sings a trilling kind of song, which forms a background to the other song, which is just one note, insistent, one two three four, pause, one two three four, pause. Nectar of the gods.

Interwoven with the bird songs, which I wake up to, are the church bells from the Bonn Cathedral, only six blocks away. They chime on and off all day, a beautiful accompaniment to the birds. Ken goes there each morning to light a candle, and sometimes, as he says, to have a "little cry." He took Mom and Dad there the other day and they all lit a candle for me.

My window looks out on a lovely open space ringed by other buildings. The trees haven't started leafing out yet, but I'm sure that I will be here when they do. That will be wonderful to watch.

And now tomorrow is Easter Sunday. This morning I was awakened by the sun. This is the sunniest day we've had since we've been here. As I was sitting here later in the morning, eating my breakfast, I was thinking again how much I enjoy the bird songs, and suddenly a smooth redheaded bird landed on my window sill. There's a rye cracker that's been out there for days. I've been watching it get rained on and crinkle up as it dries out and get rained on again. No bird has ever been close to it when I've been in the room, which is most of the time. Suddenly this morning there's the smooth redheaded bird, eyeing me; I'm trying to stay still so I don't scare it away. Then another one, with spotted head, lands, and after a few minutes of watching me and pecking at the cracker, off they go with it. It's sort of like the communion wafer. They accepted my accidental offering!

Much, much love to each of you. I feel your love and your support quite palpably and it makes a tremendous difference. It's like the water and the fertilizer I give to the plants that line my window ledge; your love and support nourishes my spirit and helps keep my joy strong and vital. I feel incredibly blessed to have the family and husband and friends I do, a very strong Circle of Love!

Love,
Treya

P.S. My white count went up to 1000, so it looks like we might make it to Paris after all!

17

"SPRING IS NOW MY FAVORITE SEASON"

❧❀❧

"Don't let that accident put you off, Ken. Paris is a beautiful city."

Radcliffe had just rear-ended a car in a small village outside of Paris—the first time in his 77-year life that he had caused an accident. He had been driving for days, me sitting shotgun with numerous maps, playing navigator, and Sue and Treya riding in back. It was a fabulous drive, through Germany and Switzerland and now France, Treya soaking up the countryside after being confined in the tiniest of rooms for over a month.

At this particular moment, we were moving fairly slowly, entering the lineup of cars all headed for Paris. Rad looked in back for just a moment, hit the car in front of him, which then hit the car in front of it. Nobody was hurt, though it was rather colorful; and the locals, not one of whom spoke even the slightest English, all came out for the show, excitedly gesturing and jabbering. Treya, fortunately, spoke fluent French, and for the next three hours she patiently and calmly negotiated with the involved parties, standing there with her Mütze on to cover her now perfectly bald head, and finally gained our release.

The day we left Bonn, Easter Sunday, was brilliantly sunny and crisp—the first day like this since our arrival in late February. We drove and drove, Dad at the wheel and Ken navigating us onto the smallest, most scenic roads. As we drove through different towns we watched people coming out of churches dressed for Easter, fathers leading daughters by the hand, grandparents trailing behind as they entered a restaurant, all crisp and clear in the bright sunshine with spring green all around. One town felt like a seaside resort, overflowing with celebrating people enjoying the sunshine and spring flowers. There must have been thirty restaurants with outdoor tables overlooking the river, each table completely full. The broad promenade was filled with festive folk, the park beside the river dotted with casual strollers of all ages. Everyone, it seemed, wanted to be in this town; on our way out we saw a line of traffic backed up for quite a ways.

As we drove and drove my eyes greedily drank in the sights: rolling lime-green meadows, newly leafed trees along streams and bordering fields, yellow forsythia scattered like exclamation points, the flowering cherry trees, patchwork vineyards festooning the steep hills and river banks, the land undulating and changing as we climbed from one river valley to another, as we left Germany and moved closer to Paris. My hospital-starved eyes and soul drank it all in, drank deeply and deeply yet again. I never tire of looking at the land, especially in the spring. Do you think it means anything that autumn used to be my favorite season but now spring, gentle bright spring, has taken its place?

Paris, indeed, was beautiful. And we got a once-in-a-lifetime extravagant treat: Rad and Sue put us all up in the Hotel Ritz, where a simple breakfast of croissant and coffee was a mere $40 a person. But forget the Ritz. Right around the corner was Harry's New York Bar, favorite haunt of Hemingway, Fitzgerald, and the Lost Generation, and one of the few places in Paris where people can actually speak English. Still in the downstairs room is the piano on which Gershwin composed much of *An American in Paris*. Harry's claims to have invented the Bloody Mary and the Sidecar; whether true or not, their Bloody Marys, we all agreed, were unforgettable.

But what moved Treya and me to tears, literally, was Notre Dame. One foot inside and you knew immediately you were in sacred space; the profane world of cancer, illness, poverty, hunger, and woes, all checked at the magnificent doors. The lost art of sacred geometry was everywhere apparent, inviting your awareness to assume the same divine contours. Treya and I attended Mass there one day, holding on to each other as if God Almighty, this time as a Benevolent Father figure, might actually reach down, miraculously, and strike the cancer from her body just like that, due to no other reason than that even He Himself would be compelled to act in a space that sacred, that far removed from what His children had done with the rest of His creation. The sun through the stained-glass windows alone seemed curative; we sat for hours in awe.

Tracy and Michael arrived, we said goodbye to Rad and Sue, and moved to the Left Bank. Tracy is a gifted artist, Treya an artisan, Michael and I appreciative onlookers, so we all lined up at the Musée d'Orsay to see the van Gogh exhibit. Schopenhauer had a theory of art that said, in effect: bad art copies, good art creates, great art transcends. And by "transcends," he meant "transcends the subject and object duality." What all great art has in common, he said, is its ability to pull the sensitive viewer out of him- or herself and into the art, so completely that the separate-self sense disappears entirely, and for at least a brief moment one is ushered into nondual and timeless awareness. Great art, in other words, is mystical, no matter what its actual content. I never believed art had that power until I saw van Gogh. It was simply stunning. Take your breath away, take your self away, all at once.

Then, out of Paris on the way back to Germany, Michael driving, Tracy navigating, Ken and I lounging in the rear. Back to the countryside again, always my favorite part. One night in Vittel, where the water comes from. Hard to tell if it is a town past its resort prime or simply a resort town not yet awake from winter, but I didn't care since our room looked out on a sunfilled, brilliantly green park. I pulled a chair out onto the small balcony, and I was content.

More winding, back country roads, a lovely private picnic by a stream, and then as we climbed into some higher hills a surprise . . . ski slopes, operating chair lifts, snow, and people skiing! It was already about 4:00 P.M. or I might have tried to persuade the crew to let me take a few runs—it quite tugged at my heart, how I would have loved to be out there in that sunshine on that snow, and I remembered the young boy Dr. Scheef told us about who went skiing when his WBC was only 400. He died of pneumonia, alas, but I felt the same desire that led him to take that foolhardy risk move within me.

Colmar was our favorite town. Half-timbered, crazy little houses all crowded together, companionably leaning against each other, as if holding one another upright against the pull of the centuries. Slouching, sagging, tilting, squatting, swaying, crouching, bulging—each one a unique personality. One painted a lovely weathered salmon, the next a rich mottled cream, then a weathered, streaked blue and a cracked, peeling gray next to a crumbling taupe. The streets in the old section are cobbled, narrow, and winding, only for pedestrians. The cottages lean across these narrow streets toward each other like wizened, bent neighbors gossiping over the fence year after year. Down below we tourists avidly window-shopped, lit candles in the churches, and walked and walked and walked.

A well-known altarpiece, the Retable d'Issenheim (1515), is on display in Colmar. It's a bit gruesome—life probably was a bit gruesome in those days—with Jesus portrayed on the cross not only with vivid crown of thorns and nails that drip blood but with his body covered with small red bleeding sores. Tracy pointed out that syphilis was rampant in Europe at that time and the artist depicted Jesus with this particularly striking mark of suffering. At first I react to what I see as the Christian emphasis on suffering, then I remember that Buddhist monks traditionally meditate in graveyards where the dead lie aboveground in various states of decomposition. The suffering and the pain are there—what must it have been like to live in the sixteenth century?—and this altarpiece serves as simply yet another reminder. I take a breath and watch my reaction to this particular depiction, watch the part of me that doesn't want to know this sort of thing happened and still happens, the part that sends a shiver of revulsion through my skin at the thought of that happening to me or to anyone. I watch my revulsion and take a deep breath and feel for the tendrils of mercy, friendliness, compassion that I know are also within me.

In Salzburg we drank Alsatian wine and ate frog legs and bought printed peasant tablecloths and visited the cathedral. Our jolly waitress—this was one of our best meals—said next time we went to Paris she would come with us, that too often the food in Paris was "*très cher et pas bonne,*" very expensive and not good.

Back in Germany, heading for Bonn, we stopped in Baden-Baden, one of the more famous of the spa towns. Here Treya had an experience that upset her deeply, and caused all of us to revert to magical thoughts about what it all meant.

The next day we went to the Roman-Irish bath, a very relaxing experience where you are led through ten different baths or stations, all a slightly different temperature, the whole series calculated to produce the most relaxation. But that night I suddenly discovered that my gold star necklace was gone. Gone! I couldn't believe it! We searched everywhere and asked everyone we could. My good luck charm! My namepiece! The star had been given to me by my parents in San Francisco the day before Ken and I left for Germany. It was based on a picture I had drawn and had been handmade by Russell, an old and very dear friend of the family. It meant a lot to me. A couple of times during that first dark month in Germany I had awakened from sleep to find myself clutching the star, and feeling less alone because of it. I was devastated. How could I have lost it? It made no sense, but it was gone. My superstitious side, which naturally gains power during times of crisis, frightened me with thoughts like: Is whatever good luck I've had now gone? Does this mean things will get worse? Have I lost my "star" figuratively too?

After a tearful evening, with Tracy and Michael and Ken all doing their best to console me, I suddenly thought of something. I thought of a section in the Chenrezi meditation as taught to me by Kalu Rinpoche. Here you visualize all the gods and goddesses, buddhas and bodhisattvas before you and you offer to them all that is beautiful and pleasing in the world; they are very pleased and rain down blessings in all forms to the entire universe. I also remembered the taking and sending visualization [tonglen], where you take on the sufferings and pains of others in the form of black tar and send out to them all your own merit and good karma in the form of white light.

Here was my framework, a way to work the pain of attachment, a way to turn a physical loss into a beneficial experience. I meditated on truly letting go of the gold star, both its physical being and its "good luck" qualities, and on sending these qualities out to others. As I tried this I could feel the strength of my attachments—to my parents, to the friend who made the star, to the circumstances of getting the star, to the idea of good luck, to the original significance of the estrella (Spanish for star) in my dreams years ago that led to my changing my name. Deep tendrils of attachment, of clinging, made clear by the shock of losing the physical symbol, intensified by the fact that it was also a valuable piece of jewelry.

And so I worked, over and over, to give it away. Just give it away. I would visualize the star itself in front of me, multiply it in my mind many times, then scatter all these shining, golden stars far and wide so that others benefited from their beauty, their good luck, their healing properties. Every time I felt the pain of the loss, which was often, every time I unconsciously reached for the star around my neck and found it gone, I would do this. It was not easy, but it was the only thing that helped. Sometimes in my mind I would very specifically give the star to each person in sight. Sometimes I would give it to each person in the restaurant we were in, specifically visualizing it around each person's neck. Sometimes I would visualize it shining over the heads of people on the streets. Sometimes I would visualize scattering millions of the stars all over the globe, myriads of them twinkling in the sunlight as they fell slowly to earth to bring light into others' lives.

This exercise made me more acutely aware of other forms of clinging or selfishness—like wanting the last bit of the best cheese on the picnic, or the last sip of wine, or the room with the best view. The loss of the star highlighted these tiny, moment-to-moment forms of clinging, of desire, of grasping and then, as I did with the star, I could practice letting go by making a gift of whatever it was I craved to someone else. A very interesting experience.

With this practice, I don't always like what I see in myself, I'm not always quick to notice the clinging, I am by no means always successful in letting go—nor do I expect to be, really. I feel a kind of understanding smile appear when I notice that I just grabbed for the best morsel or become aware of mean thoughts swirling in my head or hear unkind words simply pop out of my mouth in spite of my best intentions. I hope I'm learning to become aware of these moments in a way that the mercy I feel outweighs the self-judgment. I often think of the saying from St. Paul that Ken reminded me of, something like "the good that I would I do not; the evil that I would not, that I do." It reminds me that I am not alone in this struggle either and strengthens my sense of compassion for what it is to be human. . . .

I realize this may all sound a bit Pollyannaish here, but this is a challenging exercise for me and very, very helpful. By visualizing the star in this way it still existed, in all its beauty; in fact, in my mind there were myriads of them, impossible to lose. My superstitious thoughts about its physical presence or absence faded. Those tendrils of attachment grew weaker. I actually enjoyed this visualization; what fun to constantly give a gift of this kind to everyone! Every now and then there was an ache to have lost something my parents gave me, made by Russell. But I remember saying to Ken, "You know, it's only been three days, but I really think I'm almost over losing the star."

And so back to Bonn it was. In the last motel we stayed in, Michael commented that "the mattresses are as lumpy as the hills of Verdun"—the pockmarked hillsides from World War I shelling. Tracy was looking for some creme rinse, and all the stores were closed. Michael poked his head in our room.

"Hey, any of you guys got any creme rinse?"

"Just put your foot out and take one step. Everything else will follow naturally."

"But it's just empty space," I complain. Black, unending, empty space.

"Please, you must do it."

"What the hell. Dreamtime." I take a step forward and find myself falling through free space, only to alight on what appears to be a mountaintop, or perhaps a hilltop, the Figure next to me. As I look up, I see millions of stars, stars in all directions, stars lighting up the universe.

"So, the stars mean Treya, right? Estrella? That's pretty obvious, sir."

"The stars do not mean Estrella."

"No? OK, I'll bite. What do the stars mean?"

"They are not stars."

"OK, what do the whatever they are mean?"

"You don't know what they mean?"

"No. I don't know what any of this means."

"Good. This is very, very good."

Back in Bonn we said goodbye to Michael and Tracy. I was very sorry to see them go. Some rough times lay ahead, I could sense it, and their company would be missed. Scheef had been looking at Treya's recent tests and making grumbling sounds, the meaning of which we didn't yet know. And because of complications due to Treya's various illnesses—lung infection, diabetes, swollen legs, depleted bone marrow, not to mention cancer—an overall procedure that might have taken two months ended up taking four. The days dragged heavily along, boredom added to fear, a bizarre combination.

"Norbert? You around?"

"Yes, Ken, and what can I do for you?"

Norbert and his wife Ute ran the Hotel Kurfürstenhof. In the months that I would be there, Norbert became our man Friday, proving himself absolutely indispensable time and time again. He possessed a brilliant and quick intelligence, with a slightly sick sense of humor, not unlike mine (he once told me, of a doctor he thought less than competent, that "he could predict the past with 90% accuracy"); I pictured him as a lawyer, perhaps a doctor, but he seemed to love conciergedom. The first day I arrived there I had Norbert make up several 3×5 cards, all in German, that said things like, "Dr. Scheef gave me special permission to do this," cards with which I navigated fairly easily through the Klinik (the cards had allowed me, for example, to race through the cafeteria on the day of Treya's insulin reaction, grabbing anything that looked like sugar).

But more than that, Norbert was a good friend, with whom I shared some very difficult times.

"Norbert, what's the weather going to be like today?"

"Ask me tonight."

"Right. Tell you why I'm asking. Treya just had her blood checked, and it's still way too low to start the next round of chemotherapy. She's feeling a bit dejected. It's not just that she wanted to get it over with, it's that every delay, of even a day, means the therapy is less effective, and now it looks like it will be another week, at least. Last time it was delayed two weeks. This just isn't looking good, Norbert. God *damn* it. How do you say that in German?"

"Oh, Ken, I am sorry. Is there anything I can do?"

"Let's try this. I need a cute little motel, not too expensive, on the river, say thirty kilometers down. And a cab with a driver that speaks English. And directions to Königswinter. And I need the schedules of the ferries across the Rhine. And the hours of visiting Drachenfels. Oh, and in Königswinter, a restaurant with something other than meat. Can this be done?"

"It is done, Ken."

That would have taken me the better part of a day to arrange. Thirty minutes later Treya and I were headed down the Rhine, first to Bad Godesberg, then across to Königswinter and the magnificent Drachenfels, and then to the cutest little motel on the Rhine, all courtesy of Norbert.

The weather! No longer gloomy and rainy rotten but clear and sunny and gentle. Some days there's not a cloud in the sky, other days puffy white clouds come and go. They say it's an unusually lovely spring, after an unusually rainy winter. Ken and I spent a wonderful weekend in Bad Godesberg and Königswinter, surveying the view from various high points crowned with ruined castles. We stayed in a motel on the Rhine, and it was incredibly romantic. Spring is indeed my favorite season. I love watching it grow ever more robust around me. And I can take it with me back into the hospital: I can close my eyes and see before me, in crystal clarity, white cherry blossoms crisp against the sunlight, the clear green of newly unfolded leaves on forest branches all about me, the sweep of a green green meadow decorated with tiny white daisies and brave bright yellow dandelions. As clear as a well-focused slide projected on my eyelids!

Now, back in the hospital, back to the dirty business of dealing with this cancer. I started chemotherapy a week later than we had anticipated, waiting for my counts to rise. Another week making chemotherapy less effective. But the chemotherapy treatments themselves were, again, unbelievably easy. Loss of appetite, need for more sleep, need for sleeping pills, and a bit of dizziness was about it—again, so much easier than adriamycin. If a doctor ever proposed to put me on these drugs for a year, as they did with adria, I could handle it. While adria felt like it poisoned my soul, like I was always struggling to break through to some kind of happiness, I feel quite fine with this treatment, positively joyful!

Ah, the Germans. They have been extremely helpful, pleasant, and kind to us—especially to Ken, who has much more contact with them out in the world than I do. Just the other day two waitresses from a local restaurant Ken frequents brought me flowers. There are more cabbies, shop owners, waitresses following my story than you can imagine!

"The Rhine in Flames" is a big celebration which happened this weekend; all the castles are lit up and there's a big fireworks display. Vicky is visiting us, which is great, and so Ken and Vicky went to watch from the river. There's a big crowd, people six deep, all ages, lots of children, lined up and down the Rhine. It's a great display, I could see a few of the fireworks from my window. Ken and Vicky are going ooh, ahh, look at that one, when they suddenly realize that everyone around them is completely silent. You could hear a pin drop. Nothing from the children either. Very eerie, they said. Ken later asked the desk clerk what was happening, explaining that in the U.S. we go oooh and aaahh when there are great fireworks. The clerk first said, maybe you drink more beer? Ken laughed and said, impossible, you drink more beer than anybody in the world, that's not it. The clerk then said, "In Germany we don't go ooohh or aahh, we say 'shhhh.'"

Vicky and I seemed to stumble around Bonn from one hilarious situation to the next, which did all of our spirits good. At one point we sat down at a small sidewalk café, Vicky to get her cappuccino, me my Kolsch. A waiter came up to the table and said, "You're Ken Wilber, aren't you? I have a hole in my stomach and need urgent help."

A hole in his stomach? We were horrified. We figured he had stomach cancer, and that he thought because of my bald head I also had cancer, and he needed medical attention right away. Vicky looked ashen. I got up to rush him to the Klinik.

Turns out he had seen one of my books in a local bookstore window, recognized my picture, and wanted desperately to talk about all his problems, particularly about the girlfriend that had just left him. "Hole in my stomach" was his endearing attempt in English to say "emptiness in the pit of my being"—in other words, he was depressed. And so down he plopped, other customers be damned, and for over an hour explained this awful hole in his stomach.

I couldn't help but comment to Vicky and Ken that I wished I had found this place earlier. I talked a bit about the "mistakes" I felt I had made in the past—not having a mastectomy first instead of a segmental, not going on tamoxifin. This is water under the bridge, of course, and any cancer patient who has a recurrence probably always feels they did not do enough. Each of us can come up with more than one instance of something we passed up that might have helped at least delay recurrence.

The point for me is not to get lost in recrimination—although I sometimes slide down that slippery slope of regret—but to try to use the glasses of hindsight-wisdom (always in plentiful supply) to look at my current situation. What I see in many of these past points of choice is a certain laziness and a tendency to rely on the "big gun" treatments and neglect the all-important follow-up (staying on a strict diet, megavitamins, exercise, visualization, etc.). I've done that fairly well, but there are times I just let it slide. As in, I've done surgery and radiation or I've done chemotherapy, isn't that enough to pay, won't that take care of it, I want to just get back to my life and not go anywhere else or see another doctor or have to make another difficult treatment choice. I've given my pound of flesh or my year of suffering, that will take care of it, and it's too hard to decide what else to do in this murky area anyway.

I also see a natural desire to believe the best ("it's only a local recurrence") blown a bit out of proportion by the whole positive thinking movement: concentrate hard on being clear of cancer, say "I'm well" with total conviction, guard against any stray thoughts of future stays in hospitals or suspicions that cancer still lurks somewhere in your body, because these are negative thoughts that have the power to magically make them come true.

I felt some pressure from friends and family to think positively also. While it's understandable that no one, whether sick or well (i.e., potentially sick), wants to think about the worst possibilities, friends and family should remember that the fear of someone with cancer is not unrealistic, not simply negative thinking. Hopefully they can learn to become more comfortable with this fear, because in many cases it can serve a positive function; it should be listened to and worked with, not denied.

I now feel that simplistic ideas about positive thinking not only led me to deny my fear but diminished my motivation to continue with other treatments after chemotherapy. An incredibly high level of motivation is needed when the "something elses" require first making a difficult choice (nothing is clear in the field of alternative or complementary cancer treatment), then a lot of daily work, not to mention the time and expense of traveling to distant clinics and doctors. What looks like an interesting treatment on paper when you're well becomes quite a challenge to actually carry through in daily life when you're sick. And if you are just practicing positive thinking, you won't have the necessary motivation.

When I turn my attention to the present, gingerly adjusting these special wisdom-of-hindsight glasses on my nose, what do I see? Again, the bit of laziness that wants to rely on Dr. Scheef's "big guns" and let the rest slide. Again, the rather insidious belief that thinking positively will make it go away. But with the glasses these tendencies are in focus, I see them rather clearly, and because of that I am highly motivated to carry on my search for complementary, long-term therapies. Once I choose the combination that feels right to me, I know I will be highly committed to following through. I know that my laziness, my desire to lead a normal life like others, will feed on the questions and doubts about my choice that will inevitably come up as I get new recommendations or hear new stories from friends or as new results emerge. But I feel I will be able to keep the laziness and the desire to believe the best from clouding the picture. And I write about this in hopes that it will help others maintain the high level of motivation needed to deal with the constant ups and downs of living with cancer.

And then again, I remind myself that everything I do may have little or no effect on the course of disease or the outcome. I remind myself to breathe deeply, to relax. Motivation fueled by recriminations about the past only undermines me. When I feel myself begin to clutch at something, I remind myself to let go. To be gentle with myself. To stay with not knowing. Always the riddle of effortless effort, of choiceless choice, of motiveless motivation. Effort without attachment to a goal.

As Treya began her second chemotherapy treatment—which went without a glitch—the whole issue of visualization came up for her again, since one is supposed to visualize the chemotherapy attacking the cancer. Her difficulty centered around so-called active versus passive visualization. Treya would eventually come to feel that both were important—again, it is not being versus doing but the right balance of both. At this time, however, most of the visualization exercises being used by cancer patients were very active, and Treya felt they needed to be supplemented with more open and nondirected approaches. Toward this end she worked often with Edith, who was herself a transpersonal therapist with a Rogerian slant. Treya wrote up her observations in a paper that was widely circulated throughout various cancer centers in America (a copy of which may be obtained from the Cancer Support Community).*

"Ken? Ken? Are you there?"

"Oh, hi, Norbert. What's up?"

"Look at this."

"You're kidding! Where on earth did that come from? I do *not* believe this."

---

* Please see page 421 for information.

I was sitting in my room the other day, visiting with Edith, and Ken walked in. I was telling Edith about losing my star, and how I was working to just give it away, give it to everybody. I told her that I had read much significance into losing it, since it was my namesake. Ken began kidding me about this odd, superstitious side of myself. He joked that I don't put nearly as much faith in positive omens as I do in negative ones. I immediately said, "No, that's not true, the good signs are just as full of meaning." He said, "Oh good, so you do believe in positive omens. Then what do you make of this?" he asked, pulling the gold star on its chain out of his pocket. I was stunned. Where could it have come from, after all this time? Ken wouldn't tell me for the longest time. "I just want to make sure that, if you're going to read something really bad into losing it, you're going to read something equally good in its showing up."

The laundry lady at the hotel had found it in the back pocket of my pants, a pocket I had forgotten existed. At the baths, out of concern about leaving the star in a locker with my clothes, I must have buttoned it into this pocket and promptly forgotten about it. I was delighted to have the star back, comfortably around my neck, hopefully bringing me good luck. But the odd thing is that, much as I love the star, it was even more powerful for me when lost. I still practice giving it away, seeing it on other people, imaging it living in their hearts. It's a good practice, but less challenging than giving away something I still longed for but did not have. On the other hand, the practice of giving it away might have faded with time as the memory of the star faded; now the star around my neck is a constant reminder, and the practice continues.

Just the other evening, while on my hour walk in the woods behind Edith's, I had a very powerful continuation of this "giving-away." I was practicing giving away the star, and I noticed that I always feel that when I'm being good to myself it means not being nice to other people. The last bit of wine routine—if I'm being nice to myself I give the last bit of wine to me and then someone else can't have it.

I was feeling conflicted about that, and suddenly the "Who am I?" question popped up. And I began to realize that the distinction between being nice to others and being nice to myself, the conflict that I saw there, wasn't really there. And that if I work with the "Who am I?" inquiry enough, the boundaries, the distinctions, between me and others begin to fade, so that it's not a question of either/or, being nice to myself *or* being nice to someone else. The more those boundaries fade, then the more an action that I always construed as being nice to someone else is something I want to do for myself. I enjoy giving someone else the last bit of wine. Or all of it for that matter!

This was a very important issue for me. I had been working with it with the star, and before then with tonglen. This was another step along that path, using the "Who am I" question to uproot that sense of division, that sense of separateness. Every time I grab for the last bit of cheese, I ask, "Oh. Who's doing the grabbing? Who feels deprived?" And then I get as much pleasure giving it away. As Ken says, there's only one Self enjoying it all anyway. So it seems that the somewhat hard and fast distinction between self and other is what has been in my way in the past and what has kept me from actually being nice to myself as well. Locked in that distinction, if I was nice to others I felt deprived myself, and if nice to myself I felt stingy and mean. Now it's so much easier to let go of that and enjoy the giving, which benefits me *and* others. I've known this before, of course, but this was a very concrete and practical realization, and was very important to me.

While Treya was recovering from the second treatment, she developed a mild flare-up of her lung infection. Nothing serious, the doctors assured us; but, concerned with outside contamination, they asked me to curtail my visits for a few days. Treya and I checked in by phone; she was working on her art, meditating, writing letters, working with "Who am I?," writing in her journal, doing fine.

I was not. Something very bad was going on inside me, but I couldn't figure out what, exactly. I felt awful.

"Norbert, I'm going back over to Drachenfels. I'll call you from Königswinter. And you have Edith's number, right?"

"Yes, Ken. Are you OK?"

"I don't know, Norbert. I don't know."

I walked to the Rhine, took the ferry to Königswinter. From there the trolley runs all the way up to the top, to the fabulous Drachenfels, Europe's most visited mountain, site of a noble fortress that once held the Rhine for two hundred miles. Like any scenic wonder, Drachenfels is a mixture of breathtaking monument covered with rather tacky tourist attractions. But there is a tower in the fortress that not many tourists bother to walk up. It takes perhaps twenty minutes of labored climbing up steep, small, claustrophobia-inducing steps.

From the top of this tower I could see for perhaps a hundred miles in all directions. My eyes swept right: the tower at Bad Godesberg, the Bonn cathedral, the great Dom of Cologne, seventy kilometers north. I looked up: Heaven; I looked down: Earth. Heaven, Earth; Heaven, Earth. And that's what started me thinking of Treya. In the past few years she had returned to her roots in the Earth, to her love of nature, to the body, to making, to her femininity, to her grounded openness and trust and caring. While I had remained where I wanted to be, where I myself am at home—in Heaven, which, in mythology, does not mean the world of Spirit but the Apollonian world of ideas, of logic, of concepts and symbols. Heaven is of the mind, Earth is of the body. I took feelings and related them to ideas; Treya took ideas and related them to feelings. I moved from the particular to the universal, constantly; Treya moved from the universal to the concrete, always. I loved thinking, she loved making. I loved culture, she loved nature. I shut the window so I could hear Bach; she turned off Bach so she could hear the birds.

In the traditions, Spirit is found neither in Heaven nor in Earth, but in the Heart. The Heart has always been seen as the integration or the union point of Heaven and Earth, the point that Earth grounded Heaven and Heaven exalted the Earth. Neither Heaven nor Earth alone could capture Spirit; only the balance of the two found in the Heart could lead to the secret door beyond death and mortality and pain.

And that is what Treya had done for me; that is what we had done for each other: pointed the way to the Heart. When we put our arms around each other, Heaven and Earth united, Bach and the birds both started singing, happiness opened up before us as far as the eye could see. When we were first together, we were sometimes irritated by these differences, me the absent-minded professor always taking flight in ideas, spinning complex theories around the simplest of events; Treya always hugging the ground, refusing to fly without planning the schedules ahead of time.

But we soon came to see that that was the entire point, that we were different, that maybe this applied to many men and women (à la Carol Gilligan), and that, far from being whole and self-contained people, we were each half-people, one of Heaven, one of Earth, and that was exactly as we should be. We came to appreciate those differences—not just honor them, but be thankful for them. I will always be at home in ideas, Treya will always be at home in nature, but together, joined in the Heart, we were whole; we could find that primal unity which neither alone could manage. Our favorite Plato quote became: "Men and women were once whole but were torn in two, and the pursuit and desire of that whole is called love."

The union of Heaven and Earth, I kept thinking, as my eyes looked up, looked down. With Treya, I thought, I am beginning, just beginning, to find my Heart.

And Treya is going to die. And with that thought I began crying, sobbing actually; uncontrollably and very loudly. A few people speaking German asked me, I presumed, if I was all right; I wished I had my little German card that said "Dr. Scheef gave me special permission to do this."

I don't know when it was that I first realized Treya would die. Perhaps it was when that doctor told me of her brain and lung tumors, and asked me to sit on it. Perhaps it was when our American doctors gave her six months to live without treatment. Perhaps it was when I actually *saw* the CAT scans of her tumor-ridden body. But whenever it was, it all came finally crashing down on me. Thoughts that I had pushed out of my mind for years came rushing up. The brain tumor might go into remission; but even Scheef had given her only a 40% chance of lung remission, and not too many people were counting on those figures. Horrible images of her likely future ran through my mind: Treya in pain, trying to breathe, gasping for air, hooked up to a respirator, continuous morphine IV drip, family and friends pacing hospital corridors waiting for the labored breathing to come to rest. I held my sides and kept rocking back and forth, saying, "No, no, no, no, no, no, no, no. . . ."

I took the first trolley down the mountain and called Norbert from the local pub.

"Treya is fine, Ken. And you?"

"Don't wait up for me, Norbert."

I sat at the bar and started drinking vodka, lots of it. The horrible images of Treya kept going through my mind, but now I was also being swept up in seemingly unending self-pity. Poor me, poor me, as I kept throwing down *Korn*, the wretched German imitation of vodka. Even in Tahoe I had *never* gotten falling-down drunk. I proceeded to do so.

When I got back to the Kurfürstenhof, how I don't remember, Norbert poured me into bed and left a handful of vitamin B tablets on the nightstand. The next morning he sent the cleaning lady in to make sure I took them. I called Treya's room.

"Hi, honey, how you doing?"

"I'm fine, sweetheart. It's Sunday, you know, so around here nothing is happening. My fever's going down. I should be fine in a few days. We have an appointment with Scheef on Wednesday. He's going to go over the results of the last treatment."

I got violently nauseated at the thought, because I knew what he was going to say, or thought I did, which is all that mattered in my state.

"You need anything, honey?"

"Nope. I'm actually in the middle of my visualization, so I can't talk long."

"No problem. Listen, I'm going out for a ride. You need anything, you call Norbert or Edith. OK?"

"Sure. Have a good time."

I took the elevator down to the front desk. Norbert was there.

"Ken, you should not get drunk like that. You have to be strong for Treya."

"Oh God, Norbert, I'm tired of being strong. I want to be weak and spineless for a while. Suits me better."

"Don't talk like that, Ken, it does not help anything."

"Look, Norbert, I'm going out for a drive. To Bad Godesberg. I'll call and check in."

"Don't do anything stupid, Ken."

I stared at him as the cab pulled away.

Germany is closed on Sunday. I began walking the back streets of Godesberg feeling sorrier and sorrier for myself. At this point I wasn't so much thinking of Treya as I was wallowing in me. My whole fucking life is a shambles, I've given it all up for Treya, and now Treya, I'll kill her, is going to die.

As I walked and emoted, pissed that no pubs seemed to be open, I heard polka music coming from several blocks away. It must be a pub, I thought; even on Sunday you can't keep good Germans away from Kolsch and Piers. I followed the music to a cute little pub about six blocks out of town. Inside were perhaps a dozen men, all of them somewhat elderly, maybe in their late sixties, rosy cheeks from years of starting the day with Kolsch. The music was lively, not what Americans think of as polka, which is a kind of shmaltzy Lawrence Welk mush, but more like authentic German bluegrass music; I loved this music. About half of the men—there were no women, and no younger men—were dancing together in a semicircle, arms over each others' shoulders, a type of Zorba-the-Greek dance, it looked like to me, every now and then kicking their legs up in unison.

I sat down at the bar, by myself, and put my head in my arms. A Kolsch appeared in front of me, and, without wondering where it came from, I drank it at one pull. Another appeared. I drank it. I guess they think I'm running a tab, I thought.

About four beers later I started crying again, though now I try to hide it. I don't ever remember crying this much, I think. Crying for myself, anyway. I am starting to get slightly tipsy by now. A few of the men dance in my direction and gesture for me to join them. No, thank you, no, I gesture back. A few beers later they gesture again, only this time one of them takes me by the arm, in a friendly way, and tugs.

"Ich spreche kein Deutsch," I say, the one phrase I have memorized. They keep tugging and gesturing, smiling, looking concerned, looking like they want to help. I think seriously about bolting for the door, but I haven't paid for the beer. Awkwardly, very self-consciously, I join the men dancing, arms around those on both sides of me, moving back and forth, kicking our legs up every now and then. I start laughing, then I start crying, then laughing, then crying. I would like to turn away, to hide what is happening to me, but I am locked arm-and-shoulder into the semicircle. For about fifteen minutes I seem to lose all control over my emotions. Fear, panic, self-pity, laughter, joy, terror, feeling sorry for myself, feeling happy about myself—they all come rushing through me and show on my face, which embarrasses me, but the men keep nodding their heads, and smiling, as if to tell me it's all OK, young man, it's all OK. Just keep dancing, young man, just keep dancing. You see? Like this. . . .

I stayed in that pub for two hours, dancing and drinking Kolsch. I never wanted to leave. Somehow, in that short period, it all seemed to come to a head, to rise up and wash through my system, to be exposed and to be accepted. Not totally; but I did seem to come to some sort of peace about it all; enough, at any rate, to carry on. I finally got up to go, and gestured goodbye to all the men. They waved and kept dancing. Nobody ever charged me for the beer.

I later told Edith this story, and she said, "Ah, now you know what the real Germany is like."

I would like to claim that my big satori about accepting Treya's condition, that my coming to terms with her likely death, that my becoming finally responsible for my own choices about setting aside my interests and doing anything to support her—I would like to claim that all of that came from some powerful meditation session with blazing white light and spontaneous insights pouring over me, that I grabbed a handful of Zen courage and plunged back into the fight, that I reached high for some transcendental epiphany that set me straight at once. But it happened in a little pub with a bunch of kindly old men whose names I do not know and whose language I did not speak.

Back in Bonn, my worst fears, and Treya's, began to materialize. First, the brain tumor had not gone into complete remission, as it does in about 80% of similar cases. This was particularly serious, because Treya had already received the upper limits of brain radiation. Second, although the large lung tumor had shrunk, at least two new tumors showed up. And third, ultrasound turned up two spots on her liver.

We went back to her room, and Treya collapsed in tears. I put my arms around her and we gazed out the small window while she cried. I breathed in her pain and held her tightly. Somehow, I felt the tears I had already cried were tears for just this, just exactly this.

"I feel like I've received my death sentence. I'm standing here at my window, looking at the beautiful spring, my favorite, favorite season, and now I think this one will be my last."

Treya wrote to her friends, being very careful in her wording:

I've decided the only metaphor for living with metastatic cancer is riding an endless roller coaster (and how I used to love them!). I simply never know if I'm about to get good news or go off the edge of a cliff, leaving my stomach behind and feeling fear flood through my body. They did an ultrasound liver scan last week; there I lay while the technician went over and over the area from all possible angles and then called in another woman. They discussed things—in German—and then went over it again and again. By now I was completely panicked, though no one said anything to me other than "Breathe deeply—hold—normal breathing," over and over. When I got up I saw two small spots on the screen. Convinced I had liver cancer, I went up to my room and fell apart. I might not even make it through the year, I thought; I have to get ready for that possibility.

So how do I prepare myself inwardly for terrible news, which can come at any moment, while not undermining my life force, my "will to live"? How do I cultivate acceptance while also fighting for my life? I don't really know. I'm not even sure it's a valid question; there may be no opposition between the two, fundamentally. I've come to feel that perhaps the fact that sometimes my mood is more predominantly one of acceptance and at others more of a fighting attitude is the way life is, alternating between negative and positive nodes, like the necessary alternation in life between day and night, action and contemplation. Perhaps I need to practice both, perhaps some sort of interpenetration of the two is possible. Again, the conundrum of effort without attachment. I first went through incredible grief at the thought of liver cancer (we still don't know what the spots are). Then, after taking the equivalent of a number of very deep breaths, I discovered that I had now, although reluctantly, incorporated that possibility into myself. If it happens, it happens. I'll deal with it then and not dwell on it now. And I found I was still greatly enjoying life in all its details, even circumscribed by my hospital room with its flowers on the window ledge. I felt within me a surge of determination to do what I can, a recognition that even if I do have cancer in my liver it's not necessarily the beginning of the end, there are other treatments that still have a chance of working. And, always, miracles do happen.

Another dip in the roller coaster—my immune system isn't bouncing back as my doctor would like (whoops, there goes my stomach again . . .) so he's giving me a high dose of anabolic steroids (an eight-week dose in four days) to kick it into gear. And yet another stomach-wrenching dip— Dr. Scheef is disappointed that the brain tumor is not completely gone. He had expected a full remission after the radiation and the first round of chemotherapy. If it is not completely gone after the third treatment he would like to use cis-platinum—how much and for how long I don't yet know.

Ken and I have decided to go back to Boulder until time for the third treatment, since my body seems to take so long to bounce back. I simply cannot wait to be back in the States, back in the land of American accents! It takes getting out of America to put it back in perspective—we read about the primaries and the drug problems and the homeless with newly sensitized eyes from our perch here in Bonn. Amazing to hear that the number of gang-related homicides in Los Angeles last year was greater than the total number of homicides in Europe. But . . . I love it still. I want to be home.

Love and hugs to each of you!!! Once again, your letters and calls and prayers and good wishes have lightened our days immeasurably. We're in it for the long haul. How eternally grateful I am that Ken continues to recommit himself to this journey—and we both deeply appreciate your company along the way. . . .

Love,
Treya

What she did not put in the letter was more telling.

I will bring the fear into my heart. To meet the pain and the fear with openness, to embrace it, to not be afraid of it, to allow it—this is what is, this is what is happening. This is the suffering that we know all the time, constantly changing, changing. Realizing that brings wonderment at life. I definitely feel that. Just when I hear the birds outside my window, or when we drive through the countryside, it gladdens my heart and nourishes my soul. I feel such joy. I'm not trying to "beat" my sickness; I'm allowing myself into it, forgiving it. As Stephen Levine says, "Pity is the experience of meeting pain with fear. It makes one want to change the givens of the moment. . . . But when we touch the same pain with love, letting it be as it is, meeting it with mercy instead of fear and hatred, then that is compassion."

To open my heart. I've particularly been feeling a tremendous openness and lovingness to Ken lately, he's so open and present after his crisis. I guess that is the most important point of healing, whether or not I heal physically—to soften around my heart, to open my heart. This is always the issue, isn't it? This is always the issue.

Gazing out my window, I realize once again how spring is now my favorite season. I'll always love the golden fire of fall, but spring reaches deep into my heart. I suppose because I'm hoping for a new chance, a new spring in my life.

I'm still very moved to do what I have to do to get better, but not as a battle, not as an angry fight. I will go on, not with anger and bitterness, but with determination and joy.

18

BUT NOT A DEAD ONE!

❦

TREYA and I returned to Boulder, to our house, our dogs, our friends. I felt an odd type of peace with Treya's situation, if "peace" is the right word; it was more a mixture of genuine acceptance and melancholy forbearance, I think. Treya understood full well the gravity of her situation, and in spite of all that, both her equanimity and her sheer joy in life seemed to increase almost daily. Her joy was genuine—she was happy to be alive *now*! Damn tomorrow! At times her joyous mood was positively infectious, and as I watched her gleefully play with the dogs or happily put in plants in the garden or work her fused glass with a smile, I found the same type of quiet joy creeping into my own soul, joy at having *this* moment of life, a moment that seemed utterly precious. I was so happy to have this present moment—happier, in a sense, than when I had an unending series of moments before me through which I could dilute my happiness, stretching it over a lifetime instead of concentrating it into the present, a lesson taught me by Treya as she lived daily with death.

Friends and family couldn't help but notice and comment on the delight that seemed to permeate Treya's life. The Windstar Board of Directors, of which Treya was a member, held a four-day vision quest/retreat, which Treya wanted to attend but couldn't, because of that lingering cold. At one point in the retreat, each of the thirty or so members had to stand up, choose a word they thought most described themselves—anger, love, beauty, power, whatever—and then say to the group, "I am _____," using their word. If they were believable, group members would stand up; if not, they had to choose another word, and then another, until everybody was standing. It took most people several words to be convincing. People would spend five or ten agonizing minutes in front of everybody trying to come up with a word, only to blurt out things like "I am rain" or "I am turtle," which got nobody standing. Right in the middle of this process, Cathy Crum stood up and said, in effect, there is one person who can't be here, and so I am going to stand up for her. Everybody knew she meant Treya. Cathy said, "I am joy!" and it sounded so immediately right that everyone jumped up and started cheering.. They sent Treya a large scroll, with the words "I am Joy" on it, and wonderful inscriptions from everybody there.

Both Treya and I soon came to the same stance about her likely death: the realistic odds were slim that she would live out the year. We both knew that in Bonn. But after fully acknowledging that, we dropped it. Except for practical matters, like making out a will, or occasional private talks about what I would do if she died, or what she wanted me to do for her if she died, we simply let the issue go and lived pretty much moment to moment. Treya, more than ever, began to live in the present, not in the future, giving her allegiance to what is, not what might be.

Friends and family often wondered, is she being unrealistic—shouldn't she be worrying? fretting? unhappy? But the fact is, by living in the present, by refusing to live in the future, she began *exactly* to live consciously with death. Think about it: death, if anything, is the condition of *having no future*. By living in the present, as if she had no future, she was not ignoring death, she was living it. And I was trying to do the same. I thought of that beautiful quote from Emerson:

> These roses under my window make no reference to former roses or to better ones; they are for what they are; they exist with God today. There is no time for them. There is simply the rose; it is perfect in every moment of its existence. But man postpones or remembers; he does not live in the present, but with reverted eye laments the past, or heedless of the riches that surround him, stands on tiptoe to foresee the future. He cannot be happy and strong until he too lives with nature in the present, above time.

And that is exactly what Treya was doing. If and when death came, she would deal with it then, not now. There's a great Zen koan on this. A student comes to a Zen Master and asks, "What happens to us after death?" And the Zen Master says, "I don't know." The student is aghast. "You don't know!? You're a Zen Master!" "Yes, but not a dead one."

Yet this certainly did not mean we were going to give up, either. Resignation is also oriented toward the future, not the present. For now, there were all the remaining alternative treatments that Treya was considering, several of which were, and are, quite promising. Foremost was the Kelley/Gonzales enzyme program, which has shown some rather remarkable results even in cases as advanced as Treya's. We arranged to stop in New York City, where Gonzales has his practice, on the way back from Bonn after Treya's third and last treatment.

In the meantime she concentrated on getting rid of that cold.

One of my goals while home has been to get rid of the lingering remnants of the cold I caught in February, the one that delayed chemotherapy for three weeks and was still present after three months. This persistent sickness has kept me constantly on the edge of worry that it would pop back up again during [the third] chemotherapy and I wanted that stress out of my life. As I'm about to leave again [for Bonn], I find that I seem to have succeeded with a many-pronged approach. But I don't know what actually did the trick . . . or if it was simply programmed to go away by a certain time. I find it instructive to look at my thoughts about what helped, since having a cold is so much less emotionally charged or laden with cultural and new age beliefs than cancer.

I went to the acupuncturist; he treated me with needles and herbal teas and acupressure. Was that what tipped the scale toward healing? I upped my vitamin C intake tremendously to about twelve grams a day; is that what did it? I took echinacea, the herb that's supposed to boost your immune system; was this the secret? I rested as much as possible; was that the critical factor? I set aside time each day to tune in to the rough place in my chest, to simply give it attention, to dialogue with it when something came up and follow any instructions that came through; once it told me to scream and, after closing the door and turning on the shower for sound protection, I had a very satisfying but throat-tearing session of screaming. Is that what did the trick, unlocking some psychological knot? I consulted with my guides, Mary and the Old Man of the Mountains, and did what they said; was following their guidance the critical factor?

Who can say? Whether it's a cold or cancer . . . who can say with any assurance what the critical factors are? I am constantly aware that I can't know "the truth" about these situations. This is what underlies my stance of being playful with my "theories," of always holding things lightly, of realizing I favor some types of explanations over others, of remembering that I can't really know what is "true" in the entertaining and sometimes compelling stories I make up about all this.

I am now planning to see a Dr. Gonzales in New York on our way home to get started on the "metabolic ecology" program begun by a Dr. Kelley, a dentist who had pancreatic cancer. I've known about this program for years, even had two copies of his book at home, and was always somehow attracted to it. Not because the diet appeals to me; it sounds terribly rigorous, possibly every bit as rigorous as the macrobiotic diet, but also very individual, which I like. I was told that for one person the diet might be 70% raw and completely vegetarian, for another they might prescribe meat three times a day. What appeals to me is the idea that a lack of enzymes is connected with cancer; the idea is if you don't have enough pancreatic enzymes they're all used to digest food and none are left over to circulate in the bloodstream and help control cancer when it arises. Clearly, because of the diabetes that popped up after chemotherapy in '85, my pancreas isn't working properly. So, after my last chemotherapy treatment, next up: Kelley/ Gonzales!

Treya and I were both meditating, and meditating quite a bit. I had begun getting up at five in the morning so I could sit for two or three hours before starting my day as a support person—without, incidentally, any lingering bitterness or resentment. I seemed to have reached a genuine peace about all that—due to what, exactly, I don't know, except perhaps that I was beginning to realize that blaming cancer, or blaming Treya, or blaming life for my circumstances was simply bad faith. During meditation the stance of the Witness slowly but inexorably returned; and at least in those moments of profound equanimity, all manifestation—whether "good" or "bad," whether life or death, whether pleasure or pain—was equally of "one taste": perfect just as it is.

And Treya continued with her vipassana and tonglen. The latter, in particular, was becoming deeply moving and transformative; even when she wasn't doing the practice formally, she began spontaneously assuming its central message: healing makes no sense whatsoever for an isolated

person—nobody is really healed until everybody is healed—
enlightenment is for self and other, not just self.

I recently went to a healing circle for a friend who also has cancer. This
group of special women created a very rich and healing experience for
both of us. I felt more comfortable with my body as it is now, and I
acknowledged that in spite of missing a breast I like this thin, now very
fit body of mine. Ken agrees! When I was lying in the center of the
circle one of the women prayed for a complete healing for me. This felt
very daring to me, especially after hearing again and again what the
doctors have to say, especially since I've spent a lot of time trying to
prepare myself to accept the worst (alternating, of course, with hoping
and envisioning the best). I thought of the dream I had the night I got
the news of the full extent of the recurrences, a dream that ended when
I told a friend, with total conviction, "I believe in miracles!" It could
happen, I could be healed; it's very unlikely, given the statistics, but it
could happen. I felt myself take a deep breath as I let this possibility
flood through me, leaving a sense of relaxation in its wake.

And then I thought, gently, but why me? What about everyone else
who suffers? I will certainly be delighted if I am healed, or even if I live
a relatively long time, but the thought of all the others who suffer, from
cancer or whatever, flooded through me. Why should I be luckier than
my sisters and brothers? Why not healing for them too, why not all of
us? How can I ask for my suffering to end when they still suffer, these
other members of my family? Awareness of my pain keeps me aware of
their pain, keeps my heart open to suffering. The first noble truth,
"There is suffering." And tonglen: have compassion for it.

No matter what happens to me, this experience with cancer will
forever keep me aware of my kinship with those who suffer. Which
means, everybody. If I live for awhile I intend to use what I've learned to
help others through cancer, whether they move on in time to health or
to death. That's the purpose of the book I'm writing, that's why I'm so
proud of the Cancer Support Community. Sometimes life just doesn't
make sense, try as we might to make sense of it. Sometimes all we can
do is help each other out, gently, without judgment. As other friends
who are also dealing with cancer recently said to Ken and me, the
experience has taught them, so clearly, that life is simply not fair,
we're not entitled to any rewards for good behavior, these things
happen. Certain "new age" beliefs once enticed many of us with the

possibility of understanding why and how these things happen, with the hope there was some greater purpose or lesson behind each personal tragedy, but we've learned the hard way—perhaps the only way—that many times we don't understand. Nothing is simple. It's hard to live in what I call "don't know land," but here we are!

This makes me think of something I read in Ramana Maharshi's biography last night, a direct quote from one of his answers to a devotee: "God has no desire or purpose in His acts of creation, maintenance, destruction, withdrawal and salvation to which beings are subjected." That's a tough one for a life-long meaning and purpose junkie like myself, but Buddhism has been a big help in my letting go of trying to figure it all out, in my learning to let things just be. Ramana Maharshi goes on to say "As the beings reap the fruit of their actions in accordance with His laws, the responsibility is theirs, not God's." Yes, I feel responsible, in the sense of my ability to respond to the challenges in my life while recognizing the role of both my choices and the vagaries of life and chance and heredity/past lifetimes, a way that is not judgmental or heroic but understanding and merciful.

Ramana Maharshi used to say, "You thank God for the good things that happen to you, but don't thank Him for the bad things as well, and that is where you go wrong." (That, incidentally, is also exactly where the new age movement goes wrong.) The point being that God is not a mythic Parent punishing or rewarding egoic tendencies, but the impartial Reality and Suchness of *all* manifestation. As even Isaiah, in a rare moment, realized: "I make the light to fall on the good and the bad alike; I, the Lord, do all these things." As long as we are caught in the dualities of good versus bad, pleasure versus pain, health versus illness, life versus death, then we are locked out of that nondual and supreme identity with *all* of manifestation, with the entire universe of "one taste." Ramana maintained that only in befriending our suffering, our illness, our pain, could we truly find a larger and more encompassing identity with the All, with the Self, who is not the victim of life but its impartial Witness and Source. And especially, Ramana said, befriend death, the ultimate teacher.

At that healing circle one friend who has been deeply involved and supportive in the confrontations with cancer going on among her friends said her challenge was to learn to keep the kind of awareness and aliveness in her life that came from being so close to our struggles (and possible death) without having to be sick herself. I know what she means. I suddenly thought, if I do become well for long periods of time, will I lose this deliciously keen knife-edge of awareness I now have, this satisfyingly one-pointed focus? Certainly I and others have felt some inner restrictions burst and new creativity pour forth under the pressure of this illness. I would hate to lose that. . . . Then I realized, the possibility of death will never be far from me. Each month, each week, each day, each minute of however long I have left will be lived with the possibility of death never far away. A strange realization, that I will always carry with me this goad, this spur, this thorn, reminding me to *stay awake*. It's rather like carrying a meditation master around with me at all times, at any moment the roshi could unexpectedly give me a sound whack!

This reminds me of a great movie, *My Life as a Dog*. Ken and I first saw it last summer at the Aspen film festival, where I immediately said it was a perfect movie for people with cancer and CSC should have a copy. Since then it's become a huge hit, and Ken and I recently watched it again on video. It's about how this adorable twelve-year-old boy deals with the ups and downs of his life—a sick mother who eventually dies, his beloved dog taken away from him, having to leave his home. "It's not so bad," he says. "It could be worse. Like the man who got a kidney transplant, he was famous, you saw him on the news. But he died anyway." He's always thinking of Laika, the Russian space dog who starved in space: "I think it's important to have things like that to compare with," he says. "You have to compare like that all the time." There was the Tarzan movie where someone swung on a high voltage wire: "He died on the spot." "It could have been worse, you must remember that," he says as he describes a train wreck where many were killed. He scours the newspaper for reports like this. "Actually, I've been pretty lucky compared to a lot of people," he says another time. "You have to have the right perspective." There was the motorcyclist who tried to break the world record jumping over cars: "He was one car short." Then there was the guy who took a shortcut across a track field during a meet and was pierced by a javelin: "He must have been surprised," the little boy says. "You have to compare; think about Laika, for instance, they knew she was going to die, they just killed her." This is all from the mouth of a twelve-year-old, riding his "it could be worse" philosophy through the ups and downs of his tumultuous life; the realization that death is never far away makes him so aware, so alive.

But Not a Dead One!

We secured the house, and prepared for the plunge back into Bonn, where some very surprising news awaited us.

This morning I took the dogs for a final walk before Ken drops them off at the kennel. It was a stitch (Ken watched from the balcony above) because the grasshoppers were out! Kairos, our pharaoh hound, was determined to catch one and in the process executed innumerable funny stiff-legged hops and elegant points and long leaps through the grass as he puzzled over where to find them and how to catch them and how did they always manage to get away in the end? Moments of bewilderment, head high, ears cocked for the slightest sound, then nose to the ground, an eager snuffling search through the grass, all senses on red alert, then the sudden surprising pounce, near success, a last-second escape. Then his searching snout sniffing through the grasses, once again so close, almost there, almost within his grasp, almost captured . . . then gone, vanished, yet again and again. Head up, frozen in a point, a puzzled look around. Then a graceful trot along the roadside, the hunt with its contortions momentarily over when, suddenly . . . another alert, stiff attention, gravity-defying leap from a standstill into the grass—the hunt is on again! This happened over and over and over again, the funniest thing I've seen in a long, long time. A perfect going away present!

"Reach out and touch one," the Figure said.
"Touch a star? You can't touch a star."
"They are not stars. Reach out and touch one."
"How?"
"Just point with your finger at the one that most attracts you, and push with your mind."
Strange instructions, but I try it. The "star" immediately turns into a geometric five-pointed figure, which definitely looks like a star to me. Around the star is a circle. The outer rim of the circle is yellow. The inner part is blue. The center of the circle, which is also the center of the star, is purest white.
"Now push the very center, push with your mind."
I do so, and the "star" gives way to various mathematical symbols which I do not understand. I push harder, and the symbols give way to snakes. I push even harder, and the snakes give way to crystals.
"Do you know what that means?"

"No."
"Would you like to meet Estrella?"

Back in Bonn again. . . . Oh well, we'll make it through. I feel better
for having spent three weeks at home, more in touch with my life, less
isolated in the cocoon of cancer treatment. On the plane I wore a jacket
I hadn't used in awhile and found an unopened fortune cookie in the
right pocket; the fortune read "The result of your plans will be satisfac-
tory." That may sound like a rather faint fortune, not terribly enthusiastic, but on the eve of our departure for more chemotherapy it sounded
wonderful to me! When we arrived it turned out that Norbert had gone
on a four-week vacation without passing on this information—a rare
lapse for Norbert! Thus the hospital and the hotel were not expecting
us, and for awhile it looked like no room at the inn. . . . But all was
settled recently, sort of. Ken is in an attic room he can't stand up in,
waiting for another room to become available. Ah, the trials and
tribulations of support people!

It is now after midnight, and I am walking alone through the back
streets of Bonn. I still find it hard to meditate in Bonn, and so, as a
substitute, I walk for hours, very early in the morning, very late at night,
with nothing but brief and occasional glimpses of the Witness to keep me
company.

I pass a building with a large sign on the outside: "Nightclub," it says. I
had seen these nightclubs in several places, and wondered exactly what
they were. Not tonight, I decide, too tired. But eventually I pass another,
and then another. They are the only places in all of Bonn that seem to be
open at this hour. Bonn must have some incredibly hot nightlife, I decide.
I start laughing, almost out loud, at the thought of marauding bands of
swinging diplomats, as if that's not an oxymoron.

When I pass the fourth establishment labeled "Nightclub," I decide,
what the hell. I approach the building and am immediately struck by the
fact that the front door is locked, even though rather raucous music is
blaring inside. There is nobody on the streets. Next to the locked entry is a
doorbell, with a sign that says, I presume, ring for entrance. I do so.
Through a small window a pair of male eyes, with thick heavy brows,
stare at me. A buzzer rings, and the door opens.

I do not believe what I see. It looks something like a speakeasy from the
Roaring Twenties, but decorated perhaps by a crazed gipsy queen on acid.

Its walls are covered with gaudy purple velvet. There is something like a dance floor, with a round mirrored ball rotating slowly from the ceiling, scattering thin and sickly light rays across the faces of its inhabitants. It is otherwise incredibly dim. I manage to see, barely, that there are perhaps six men seated around the dance floor. All of them look slightly disheveled, none of them very attractive, and yet each of them accompanied by a rather striking-looking woman. Damn, I think, German women must be *really* grateful.

Everybody stops their muted talk and stares at me as I enter. I move slowly to the bar, which is an incredible forty feet long, with perhaps thirty barstools covered with the same crushed velvet that suffocates the walls, and not a single person is sitting there. I take a stool roughly in the middle of the bar. The rotating rays of sickly light now move across my face as well, and we all stand out as polka dots of light against the darkness of . . . of . . . of whatever the hell this place is.

"Hi, would you like to buy me a drink?"

"I've got it! This is a whorehouse, right? A brothel? That's what it is. I think. . . . Oh, I'm sorry. Do you speak English?" A rather beautiful woman has just joined me at the bar—I'm pretty sure it isn't because she can't find another stool—and I blurt out my obvious conclusion.

"Yes, I speak English, a little bit."

"Look, I don't mean any offense or anything, but this is a whorehouse, right? You know whorehouse?"

"Yes, I know whorehouse. This is not a whorehouse."

"It isn't?" I am now very confused. I keep looking for a door or some entrance through which the ladies and their, um, guests might go for a more private conversation, but I can't see any possible place where this might occur.

"This is not a whorehouse? Those women are not prostitutes? You know prostitutes?"

"Those women are definitely not prostitutes."

"Oh, man, I'm sorry. This is just a little weird."

"You want to buy me a drink?"

"Buy you a drink? Yeah, sure, a drink." I am completely flummoxed by the situation and by the utterly bizarre atmosphere in which it is all occurring. There is a dance floor and no one is dancing. It looks like a brothel but nobody is moving. Rotating rays of red and purple light stab holes in the dark, only to disclose a velvet-enclosed gallery of the weird. And what kind of place has a locked door and buzzer?

Two drinks arrive; they both look, and mine tastes, like watered-down champagne. "Look, I'm not a cop or anything, but you're sure. . . . Um, you know cop?"

"I know cop."

"I'm not a cop. Are you sure you're not a hooker? You know hooker?"

"You don't have to keep saying, 'You know question mark.' I am not a hooker, honest. Honest."

"Geez, I'm really sorry." And now I am really confused. "I know," I keep trying, "this is like a dance club, right? You know, men"—and I glance toward that motley collection of my gender—"men come here and pay and dance with pretty girls, right?" I feel utterly ridiculous.

"I'd like to dance with you if you want, but no, this is not a dance club. It's a nightclub. I come here every now and then when things get dull. My name is Tina."

"It's a nightclub. Oh geez. Hi, Tina. Ken." And we shake hands, and I drink my watered champagne, and my head begins to hurt.

"See, this is not a great time for me. My wife, Treya, is staying at the Janker Klinik. You know, um, are you familiar with the Klinik?"

"Yes, it's for Krebs, cancer. Your wife has cancer?"

"Yes." And for some reason I proceed to tell Tina everything about it— the cancer, the trip here, the difficult prognosis, about how much I care for my wife and how much I am worried. Tina is very concerned, and very kind, and listens intently throughout. I ramble on for maybe an hour. Tina tells me she is from Cologne, about thirty kilometers north; she comes down to the Bonn nightclubs when she gets bored. Such a beautiful woman has to come all the way down here for *this*? I keep watching the men, all covered in purple haze from the anemic light off the crushed velvet, all talking to lovely purple women, and none of them makes a move, not to dance, not to romance, not to nothing.

"Look, Tina, you're very nice, and it's been great to unload all this, really. But I have to go, it's two in the morning. See ya, okay?"

"You want to go upstairs?"

Aha! I knew it, I knew it, I knew it. "Upstairs?"

"Yes, we can go upstairs and be alone. I don't like it down here."

"Sure, Tina, let's go upstairs."

"To go upstairs we have to buy a bottle of champagne."

"A bottle of champagne. Sure, sure, let's have a bottle of champagne." The bottle comes, and I glance at the label, looking for the alcohol content—3.2%. Right. It's like the brothels in the States serving apple juice and charging for whiskey, so the ladies don't get drunk. I know I'm right. I leave the "champagne" on the counter.

Tina gets up and leads me across the dance floor, past the purple people, who all stare intently through the dimness. We turn a corner and there it is: a spiral staircase, hidden from the view of the bar, a spiral staircase that leads upstairs.

Tina goes first, and I follow. I feel awkward looking up, but I'm pretty sure she won't mind. At the top of the stairs I see perhaps six cubicles, all open, all with draw-curtains, all again in that wretched velvet. There is a bench in each cubicle, and a stack of towels. Soft music—Frank Sinatra, no less—is coming over the speakers, though Tina assures me that she will play any kind of music I want. "You got U2?" "Sure."

We sit down on the bench in the first cubicle, as Bono's voice fills the air. I notice there is an opening in the floor, through which you can see the dance floor below.

"Tina, there's a hole in the floor."

"Yes, Ken. It is so we can see the girls when they dance."

"When they dance? The girls dance?"

"Striptease. Mona goes on in a few minutes. We can watch."

"Tina, why didn't you tell me this was a whorehouse? You lied to me."

"Ken, this is not a whorehouse. There is no sexual intercourse here. It is illegal here and none of us, for no price, will do it."

"Then what exactly do you do? I know I'm naive, but I'm pretty sure it's not palm reading."

I hear a clunking on the spiral stairs, and up comes another rather striking-looking woman, who deposits our champagne on a small table in front of the bench.

"That will be sixty American dollars. You can pay downstairs. Have a pleasant time."

"What! Sixty dollars! Geez, Tina, I don't know."

"Oh look, Ken, Mona is going to dance." And sure enough, through the hole in the floor, we have a perfect view of Mona dancing, a long, wild, vibrant striptease, revealing a stunning body whose flesh, still purple-lit like everything else, does not now look insipid but alluring.

"Look, Tina . . ." And Tina stands up, and quickly but calmly takes off all of her clothes, and then sits back down beside me.

"So what would you like, Ken?"

I don't say anything. I just stare.

"Ken?"

I just keep staring. I don't know why, I just keep staring. And then it dawns on me. This is the first time in almost three years that I have seen two whole breasts on a woman. I look at Tina, and then I look down; I look at Tina, and then I look down. An enormous flood of conflicting emotions comes pouring over me.

"Look, Tina, you don't have to do anything. Let's just sit here a bit, okay?"

My mind is lost in a world of bodies, of flesh, and all that it can mean, and all that cancer can do to it. Sitting here, I'm now faced with both worlds. No doubt: Sex with cancer is a dicey proposition. Especially with a woman who has breast cancer, and then a mastectomy, there is first the whole problem of how the woman relates to her now "disfigured" body. It's no secret that in our society breasts are the most visible and "prized" symbols of a woman's sexuality, and losing one or both breasts can be devastating. I was always struck by how relatively well Treya had handled this difficulty. Of course she missed her breast, and of course she complained bitterly on occasion, to me and to her friends—it was a very difficult time. But by and large, as she often said, "I think I'll be okay." This is, in general, the most difficult and often agonizing problem for a woman with breast cancer. It can devastate her self-image and virtually nullify her sex drive, since she now often feels completely "undesirable."

This situation is compounded horribly if the woman is going through chemotherapy or radiation. She is often too tired, too exhausted, to be interested in sex at all, and then she feels terribly guilty about not being there sexually for her man. And so to undesirability is added guilt.

The situation is often greatly helped, or greatly hurt, by the response of the man in her life. Almost half of all husbands whose wives have mastectomies leave them within six months. He feels now he has damaged goods, and to that he can't sexually respond.

"Do you miss it?" she often asked after the operation.

"Yes."

"Does it matter a whole lot?"

"No." And the truth was, for the most part, it didn't. But it's not an all-or-nothing affair; it's more a matter of percentages. I'd say my sexual attraction for Treya was "dented" by about 10%; the simple tactile feel, the symmetry of two breasts, is definitely better than one. But the other 90% was so overwhelmingly positive for me that it just didn't matter that much. Treya knew this, she could tell it was honest, and I think it helped her more easily come to terms with her own self-image. That 90% was still the most beautiful and attractive woman I had ever known.

But during most of the Tahoe year, when Treya was undergoing chemotherapy and we were close to separation, we had sex not at all. Treya, understandably, felt it was largely because I found her "mutilated" body undesirable. But during that year it wasn't her body so much as *her* that I didn't like too much, and that naturally translated into sexual terms as well.

For the many men who do stay with their mates during cancer and its treatment, the feeling that comes up most often is fear. The men are frightened of having sex with their mates because they fear they might hurt them. In the men's support group at CSC, when the men were offered an outside expert, they chose a gynecologist. They just needed simple information—estrogen cream for vaginal dryness, for example—and that helped enormously with their fears.

Sometimes you go slow, and sometimes you go not at all. And it helps for men to hear that simple cuddling is sometimes the best "sex" you can have under any circumstances anyway, and cuddling is always allowed. Treya and I were champion cuddlers, and that went a long, long way.

Nevada has thirty-five legal brothels, all licensed and supervised by the state. The most famous, of course, is the Mustang Ranch, right outside of Reno, a mere forty-minute drive from Incline Village. During most of the time we lived in Incline, Treya was either on or recovering from chemo, and at one point she suggested I check out the Mustang.

"Really?"

"Why not? I don't want you to have to go without just because of stupid chemotherapy. I think, if you had an affair, I would be hurt by that. That would be very difficult, because it would be a personal thing. But I have no trouble with something like the Mustang. Twenty bucks for twenty minutes, isn't it?"

"Something like that." I personally think prostitution is a noble profession (if freely chosen), but it's just not my style. I had remained faithful to Treya throughout, and intended to stay so. But this is something each man has to decide for himself, I suppose. But I have often regretted, on theoretical grounds, not stopping in at the Mustang: just for the experience.

And there were definitely occasions when I missed that 10%, missed the fullness of two whole breasts, the lovely balance of it all.

And so here I am, staring at Tina, and that 10% is all that I see. I reach out and caress her breasts, and kiss them—both of them. I'm struck by how much I've missed that symmetry, the harmony of the figure, how good it feels, how erotic it really is, something to do with both hands. I'm very sad, sitting here with Tina, with her balanced body, her two full breasts, the sweetness on her face.

"Ken? Ken?"

"Look, Tina, I have to go, really. This has been great. But I gotta get."

"But we really haven't done anything yet."

"Tina, just what in the hell is it that you do do?"

"Hand-jobs, blow-jobs, that sort of thing."

"So no intercourse means you're not a prostitute, is that it?"

"Right."

"I gotta go. It's hard to explain, but, well, I've seen all I need to see, I guess. This has helped more than you might know, Tina. See ya."

I moved down the spiral staircase, back into the sickly purple haze with its dim inhabitants; and paid for the champagne; and wandered back into the cobbled streets of Bonn.

A few days later I told Treya of the experience, and she laughed and said, "You should have gone for it."

Rats.

"Hello, Fritjof."

"Ken? I don't believe it! What are you doing here?"

I was the last person Fritjof Capra expected to see sitting on the steps of the Janker. We hadn't seen each other since my wedding. He had brought his mother to the Klinik for treatment of a small tumor; the treatment was very successful, and she eventually returned to Innsbruck, where she lived. Fritjof and I have always had some theoretical differences, but personally I have always liked him very much.

"Treya's being treated at the Klinik. Recurrence to the lung and brain."

"Oh, I'm really sorry. I didn't know; I've been traveling and lecturing. Ken, this is my mother. She's being treated at the Klinik, too."

Fritjof and I made plans to meet later, and Mrs. Capra found her way to Treya's room. Mrs. Capra was a wonderful and quite impressive person. Famous as an author—poetry, biography, plays—she, like Edith, seemed to embody the grand wisdom of Europe, at home in the arts, sciences, humanities, the entire spectrum of human aspirations.

She and Treya met, and again, it was love at first sight.

Mrs. Capra is here being treated for early-stage breast cancer. What a delight she is! I really like her. Among many other things, she reads palms, and yesterday she read ours. Ken has a very long life line, all the way to the bottom of his hand! She pointed out this current "health crisis" in my palm quite clearly, but predicted it would soon clear up and I would live into my eighties. I like that, of course. Who knows if it's true, but I am aware of a stronger sense of wanting to do that. When I was most afraid of this recurrence, inundated with all the dire predictions from doctors, I thought I'd be grateful to get eight years instead of two. Today Ken read in a letter from a friend that his mother died of breast cancer at fifty-three; a month ago I would have thought, fifty-three minus forty-one (my age), that's twelve years, that sounds pretty good, I'd go for that. But today I thought God, that is young. I would like to live to eighty, to see the world change, to make my contribution, to watch my friends' children grow. Then I ask, is this wishful thinking? Or positive imaging of the future? Is it craving, grasping for more years? Or the manifestation of a will to live that will triumph over circumstances . . . or of a will to live that ignores real circumstances? I don't know; tune in next year and the year after that and the year after that. . . .

Perhaps it was that innocuous but touching palm reading, perhaps we had slipped into denial again, perhaps we just didn't care one way or the other, but by the time we saw Scheef for a review of Treya's present situation, we were both fairly optimistic. What he had to say was thus all the more disturbing.

Another down on the roller coaster. . . . Dr. Scheef had some completely unexpected news. The tumors in my lungs don't seem to have responded to the chemotherapy at all. One interpretation is that chemotherapy has reached all the cells that are active and the remaining tumor is now dormant or in a kind of steady state with my body. Some of what shows on the x-ray may also be swelling; he might do an MRI to find out what is swelling and what part, if any, is active tumor. "The danger here," he said, "is overtreatment. It takes a lot of experience to decide this; a doctor just out of medical school would not be able to tell." Overtreatment could make things worse. As he explained it, if 80–90% of the remaining cells are not growing, a third treatment would have a chance to kill only the 10–20% that are growing. But it would also temporarily suppress the immune system and thus make it possible for the now-dormant 80–90% to start growing; thus it might make the situation worse. He feels especially strongly about this. Ken and I were surprised and shocked.

We had known that the situation was quite serious, that some new spots had appeared on her lungs and liver. But Scheef had planned, for the third treatment, to switch from ifosfamide to cis-platinum, a very effective drug against this type of situation. And now he was telling us that even that wouldn't help and would probably hurt. He had valid reasons for this decision, and I admired his courage in refusing to do more chemotherapy, since our American doctors would most certainly have recommended more chemo, knowing full well it wouldn't help. But not Scheef; more treatment would just "damage her soul" and leave the cancer untouched.

Read it anyway you like, but Scheef was giving up on us, though he never put it like that. In fact, he was genuinely optimistic that the Kelley/Gonzales program, about which he was quite knowledgeable, might, just *might*, have an effect. But the fact is, he had used his big guns, and that wayward cell—the cell with a date on it—was unmoved.

We had our last conversation with this enormously likable man.

To stabilize my situation [hold the tumors in their present steady state], Dr. Scheef has started me on aminoglutethimide. It's a newly developed agent which has wider applicability than tamoxifen. He is also prescribing three unspecific biologicals—thymus extract (one suppository a day and two ampules a week), emulsified vitamin A (ten drops—150,000 IU—daily for three months out of the year; the liver stores enough for the remaining months), and Wobe Mugos enzymes. The thymus extract, not available in the States, is a nonspecific immune system stimulating agent. Its effectiveness has only been proven so far in animal experiments. Here they've found that where it might normally take 120,000 cancer cells to induce lung cancer in 50% of vaccinated animals, if they're given high doses of vitamin A, it takes one million cells to induce cancer. And if they're given thymus extract, it takes five to six million cells to do the same job! That's a pretty high level of protection. . . .

I reminded Dr. Scheef of my plan to start the Kelley program and he immediately said, with no hesitation, "Yes, of course, very good, very good." Ken said, "Would you send your daughter to him?" and Scheef smiled and said, "Absolutely." I'm especially glad to have the Kelley program as something to rely on now that treatment has stopped.

We asked what my prognosis was. "My feeling is not bad because your body is holding the tumors in steady state. This will give the other treatments you are considering time to work. The problem I see is if you get a cold or pneumonia, then your body can't fight cancer." He went on to say I should continue with my macrobiotic/Kelley program and suggested I look into Dr. Burzynski. The important thing is that all these programs might help and, since they are nontoxic, can't hurt. "You must always make the distinction between toxic and nontoxic," he said. Both Kelley and Burzynski are honest, he said, which is not true of some alternative cancer practitioners.

We gave Scheef one of Treya's glucoscan meters—a gift from one diabetic to another!—and said a sad goodbye. I went back to the Kurfürstenhof to begin preparations for our departure. Treya went off for a walk.

I left the hospital feeling quite down, concerned with what Scheef had said. The weather has been strange since our return, not a ray of sunshine, all clouds and drizzle and much colder than when we left in May, quite depressing. I started walking along Poppenheimerallee, a beautiful street with a wide, tree-lined, parklike esplanade down the middle. I looked at the buildings to my right—I'd seen them many times before—and felt a stir of interest in spite of my mood. I don't know when they were built—late 1800s?—but Bonn has some lovely houses, each painted a different color, each with balconies of various shapes and designs tucked into different angles, each with ornate plaster decorations and pediments and capitals and pilasters and moldings and embellishments of endless variety. Here was a light blue house, white moldings, pansies in window boxes along the second-floor balcony; next a weathered terra-cotta house, beige ornate moldings and carvings, with red carnations lining the second- and fourth-floor balconies; then a deep yellow house, a light green house, a creamy taupe house, each with handsome entrances, beautifully detailed windows and cornices and balustrades, some simple and classically elegant, others more ornate and baroque, all set off by the rich foliage of trees lining the sidewalk in front. An absolutely beautiful street. Across the wide parkway on the other side, I couldn't help but notice, were several modern apartment buildings; their blank surfaces, untrimmed square windows, bulky proportions, and gray paint showed no grace or beauty. But, reflections on modern life aside, they were overshadowed by their neighbors, by the rich green of the parkway, and I felt a tendril of joy begin to wind its way through my depression.

I was definitely feeling better. Was it my imagination, or were the clouds thinning a bit? Was that a bit of a shadow on the path in front of me? I walked on, toward a lovely old official building at the end of the parkway painted a rich yellow with deep beige trim. Suddenly I came across a strange group, eight- and nine-year-old girls dressed in tutus and white tights with odd little white hats perched on top of their heads, some older girls also dressed in ballet costume, some adults with video cameras. Alas, they were all just changing out of their ballet shoes; I had evidently missed the main performance but quite enjoyed the postperformance scene.

Yes, the sun was trying to come out and succeeding more and more. Suddenly I found myself walking next to a fence. On the other side was a lush, lovely botanical garden! I had never before stumbled across this in my wanderings and soon found myself inside the Bonn University Botanical Gardens that surround the official yellow building. What a discovery! Ancient trees with graceful drooping branches that gently touched the lush lawn. A waterway and ponds lined with old, graceful trees, populated by mallard ducks whose green heads glistened in the sunlight (yes, it was really out by now). Exotic species of all kinds in planting beds, carefully tended and carefully labeled. Here's a section for grasses, there a beautiful rose garden in the center. The pink roses seem to have bloomed first, now they're full and blowsy and overripe, dropping their petals on the lawn, framing the red roses which are just coming into their bright rich maturity. Behind them the tangerine roses are open just enough to identify their startling color. I wandered over every path in that garden, from the deep dark greenness of the statuesque trees to the bright open blazing colors of the flower beds in the center, and I felt wonderful by the time I returned to the Kur-fürstenhof.

I also reminded myself that I have other options. I had to remember my visualizations/meditations, since lately the tumors have been very quiet, no voices, images, or feelings coming from them. But, still, it wasn't until the walk in the Botanical Gardens that I felt at peace with the situation. This is the way things are. We'll do the best we can and take what comes. No way to predict, no need to hold on, no use in craving a particular outcome and feeling aversion to another, that only leads to suffering. It's a good life, Ken is my sweetheart, and just look at the color of those roses!

On our way out of Bonn, we stopped in Cologne and in Aachen to see their historic cathedrals, the last we would visit in Europe. But a hollow melancholy had set in.

There wasn't much to do in Aachen, especially since the stores in Germany close at two o'clock on Saturday (except the first Saturday of each month). We're tired of being here and anxious to get home now that no treatment is planned. Boredom very definitely set in, exacerbated by the food we were served. I was slightly entertained by two signs we saw—BAD ACCESSORIES and SCHMUCK U. ANTIQUITATEN—but only slightly. We're both tired of walking, walking and looking in windows. I certainly have my moments of wondering what life is all about, especially in the midst of such intense focus on treatment with all the time in between to be filled when we're in no position to do any work. Not an original question, to be sure. Still, my drive to be as well as possible seems so deep, like it comes from a cellular level, that my moments of being philosophically down don't much dent it, though they do make my shoulders sag and my delight in life grow dim. Before an altar to the Virgin Mary at the cathedral in Cologne, after we had lit some candles to join the already burning, dancing, flickering rows, I thought of how my love of life usually pops back unexpectedly, like when I feel sudden delight in a bed of roses or hear birds singing in boisterous competition. But today even those moments seemed flat, couldn't penetrate my mood or lift my drooping shoulders. Earlier that day I had commented to Ken that we might have to confront these moods more often than people who have children since children so constantly draw you into life, fill you with their sense of unbounded possibility and their hopes for the future, all at a time when your own sense of limitations looms larger, your body slows down, you become more "realistic" about life.

At this moment in church, kneeling before the masses of candles flickering in the soft gloom, the only thing I could think of that gives life meaning is helping other people. Service, in a word. Things like spiritual growth or enlightenment seemed like nothing more than concepts. Full development of one's potential also seemed trite and egocentric unless it leads (as it often does) to ideas or creations that help relieve suffering. What about beauty, my art work, creativity? Well, for today at least, it didn't seem very important, except perhaps for the art that adorns sacred places like this cathedral. Human relationship, human connections, indeed gentle loving relationship with all forms of life and all of creation, only that seemed important. Keeping my heart open, always my biggest challenge, letting down the defenses, being open to pain so joy can also enter. Does this mean I'll spend less time on my art and more on working with people who have cancer? I don't know. At the moment the book I'm working on with information that may be helpful to others meeting this challenge seems more worthwhile than fused glass plates. Though I imagine I'll find myself in a more balanced place at some point, where there's room for joy and beauty, when the clouds and my mood lift. . . .

We had a leisurely and luxurious departure, on the Lufthansa Airport Express train. They check your luggage through to your final destination when you board the train in Bonn, then serve quite a delicious meal with champagne for those who want it. This is our fifth time along this part of the Rhine and I finally have a guidebook that tells me a little bit about each castle—and there are many, twenty-seven mentioned in this guidebook—crowning the promontories along the way or guarding passage along the river. There's Drachenfels, Europe's most visited mountain (yes, Ken and I went there, Ken returned many times, and once took Vicky there), its core now held together with concrete bands after being dangerously weakened by quarrying; Der Pfalzgrafenstein, begun in 1327, a fortress built on an island in the middle of the river; the fortress of Ehrenbreitstein, first built in the tenth century to control the juncture of the Mosel and the Rhine; the narrow section of the Rhine where the Lorelei Rock, home of the enchantress, towers four hundred thirty feet above; Burg Gutenfels, erected around 1200, with steep, rock-terraced vineyards cascading down from its walls to the riverbanks. . . .

I must say it is quite a lovely trip down the Rhine. As much as anything else, I love to look at the family garden plots that pop up here and there on railroad land that would be otherwise unused. Sometimes there's only one or two, other times there's a large area with thirty or more plots, each with its own shed or tool room or tiny summer house, chairs positioned to catch the sun, some planted in vegetables I wish I could identify, others given over almost exclusively to bright-blossomed flowers. I wish it were Saturday instead of Tuesday so I could see people puttering around in the tiny plots scattered here and there along the tracks, looking just like colorful organic patchwork quilts covering special spots on the earth.

As we passed Drachenfels, I moved across the aisle to a window seat, and stared at the fortress until it faded on the horizon, which took a full ten minutes.

19

PASSIONATE
EQUANIMITY

❦

THE Kelley/Gonzales program is based on the simple premise that digestive enzymes dissolve all organic tissues, including tumors. And therefore, megadoses of enzymes, taken orally, will have a tumor-dissolving effect. That much is scientifically documented, and indeed, sports doctors have been using enzymes for years to dissolve diseased and injured tissues. The central part of the Kelley program is thus the ingestion of a large number of pancreatic enzyme pills six times a day (including once during the night). The enzymes need to be taken between meals, on an empty stomach, otherwise the enzymes would not enter the bloodstream to dissolve the tumors but would instead simply dissolve the food.

The Kelley program is now run by Dr. Nicholas Gonzales in New York City. Nick, as we knew him, is a highly intelligent, extremely knowledgeable physician who got his degree at Columbia and trained at Sloan-Kettering. While studying various cancer treatments, he came across the work of Dr. Kelley, a dentist who claimed to have cured himself, and some twenty-five hundred other patients, of cancer, using pancreatic enzymes in conjunction with diet, vitamins, coffee enemas, and other standards of the alternative health movement. But it was the pancreatic enzymes, in megadoses, that distinguished the Kelley approach.

Kelley eventually went rather bonkers—paranoid schizophrenic, from

336

what I can tell—and from what we could gather from Nick, Dr. Kelley is still out there somewhere, talking to little men from other planets. Far from upsetting either Treya or me, we found that part of the story strangely reassuring. We had tried all the treatments that sane men had come up with.

Nick looked through the thousands of case histories compiled by Kelley, and tossed out all the ones that weren't well documented, no matter how impressive they might have been. He settled on fifty representative cases that had ironclad medical documentation, and presented this as a thesis at Sloan-Kettering, with the chairman of his department serving as his advisor. Some of their results were astonishing. For example, the five-year survival rate for Treya's general type of metastatic breast cancer is exactly 0.0%. But in these fifty cases there were already three five-year-plus survivors (one seventeen years)! Nick was so impressed that he ran Kelley down and studied with him while he was still lucid. Only recently—about eight months before we first saw him—Gonzales had started his own practice based on Kelley's ideas. I would like to emphasize that this was not a Mexican fly-by-night clinic (although we would try those too if we thought they would help); Gonzales is a highly trained physician trying a very promising alternative approach to cancer management, fully complying with the laws of medicine in the United States.

The central diagnostic tool that Gonzales used was a blood analysis for various cancer markers in the body. This test claimed to be able to tell the location and extent of various tumor activities anywhere in the body. Before we met Gonzales, before we told him anything about Treya's case, this blood test indicated that she had extensive tumor activity in the brain and in the lungs, with probable involvement in the lymph and liver.

At the time of that test—we had just returned from Germany, and had just started the Kelley/Gonzales program—various orthodox tests performed at the Denver hospital indicated that Treya had: about forty lung tumors, three brain tumors, and at least two liver tumors, with possible lymph involvement.

The crucial score on the Gonzales test, however, was the overall or sum total of tumor activity, which ranged from 0 to 50. Gonzales considered 45 or above incurable, or terminal. Treya scored 38, which was very high but not outside the range of possible benefit, even possible remission.

The extremely disconcerting thing about the Kelley/Gonzales program was that, even when it was working, or especially when it was working, it created changes in the body that were medically indistinguishable from increased cancer growth. For example, when enzymes attack tumors and begin dissolving them, the tumors flare up—a standard histamine reaction—and this flare-up, on a CAT scan, looks exactly like the tumor is growing. There is simply no orthodox way to tell whether the tumor is increasing or flaring up as it dies (other than surgery and biopsy).

And thus we began what was by far the most nerve-racking, anxiety-inducing leg of this journey. As the enzymes began to have their effect, CAT scans showed what looked like massive tumor growth. And yet Gonzales's blood analyses showed Treya's overall cancer score unmistakably going down! Who are you going to believe? Treya was either getting better very fast, or dying very fast, and we couldn't tell which.

And so we settled into a very strict routine at home, and waited.

It was right at the beginning of this period that Treya underwent another major inner shift, a type of follow-up to the shift that had led her to change her name from Terry to Treya. This shift wasn't as dramatic or pronounced as the first, but Treya felt it was just as profound, perhaps even more so. As always, it involved the relationship between being and doing. Treya had always been in touch with the doing side of herself; the first shift was a rediscovery of the being side of herself—the feminine, the body, the Earth, the artist (that, anyway, was how she viewed it). And this recent shift was more the integration of both being and doing, the bringing them together into a harmonious whole. She hit upon a phrase—passionate equanimity—that seemed to perfectly summarize the entire process.

I was thinking about the Carmelites' emphasis on passion and the Buddhists' parallel emphasis on equanimity. This somehow seemed more important to me than the age-old argument about theism versus nontheism that these two groups usually engage in, and which seems beside the point to me. It suddenly occurred to me that our normal understanding of what passion means is loaded with the idea of clinging, of wanting something or someone, of fearing losing them, of possessiveness. What if you had passion without all that stuff, passion without attachment, passion clean and pure? What would that be like, what would that mean? I thought of those moments in meditation when I've felt my heart open, a painfully wonderful sensation, a passionate feeling but without clinging to any content or person or thing. And the two words suddenly coupled in my mind and made a whole. Passionate equanimity, passionate equanimity—to be fully passionate about all aspects of life, about one's relationship with spirit, to care to the depths of one's being but with no trace of clinging or holding, that's what the phrase has come to mean to me. It feels full, rounded, complete, and challenging.

This feels very right to me, very deep to me, very central to what I have been working on for many years, going back to the name change. It's like the first part of my life was learning passion. The life after cancer, equanimity. And now bringing them together. This feels so important! And it seems slowly but surely to be permeating all aspects of my life. I still have a ways to go! But it feels like I can finally see the road clearly, on that "journey without goal."

And as for the task before me, it means to work passionately for life, without attachment to results. Passionate equanimity, passionate equanimity. So appropriate!

By and large it was chop wood, carry water, which Treya approached with calm zeal. We let our awareness be filled with the various details of day-to-day life and the incredibly demanding aspects of the Kelley/Gonzales program. And we awaited the tests that would outline our future.

> Boulder
> July 1988

Dear friends,

We've been back from Germany for a few weeks now, and we're tremendously enjoying the ever-changing weather of the Rockies, the familiarity of America, the rough playfulness of our puppies, having friends and family nearby.

Obviously, healing myself as much as possible is now my primary focus. My program is a mixture of the Kelley Metabolic Ecology program (supplements, pancreatic enzymes, diet, various internal cleansing programs), meditation, visualization, spiritual reading, acupuncture with a practitioner from Taiwan (of the "if it doesn't hurt it can't be helping" school) through consultation with Michael Broffman [a San Francisco-based expert on Chinese and American medicine], judicious consultations and tests with the local oncologist, exercise, and being outside as much as possible. I've begun the process of finding a local psychologist to work with and have started doing a bit of yoga again.

A daily routine has emerged out of this combination of programs. Ken gets up around five and meditates for several hours before starting the daily chores of being a support person—cleaning, laundry, groceries, and lots of vegetable juicing! I sleep as late as I can, usually nine-thirty or ten (I can never seem to get to bed before twelve). Then I begin my morning routine, largely dictated by the rhythms of the Kelley program. By the time I actually get up I've already taken two of my seven daily doses of pancreatic enzymes (six capsules), one at 3:30 A.M. and one around 7:00 A.M. When I get up later I immediately take my diabetes medication and thyroid pills. I need to have breakfast right away or I can't fit the remaining enzyme doses and mealtime supplements (over thirty pills with each meal) into the remaining hours of the day. I start off with the fourteen-grain raw cereal (ground the night before and soaked in water overnight) and Ken usually makes me one or two eggs to go with the usual huge handful of supplements. Meanwhile I've made coffee for the morning coffee enema so it can cool while I eat; I'm also allowed one cup of coffee a day because it can be good for my metabolic type. (Slow to get started!) I must admit I look forward to it. . . .

While I eat and slowly savor my coffee and gaze out over the wooded valley below I read—lately it's been Becker's *Denial of Death*, Father Thomas Keating's *Open Mind, Open Heart: The Contemplative Dimension of the Gospel*, and Osborne's *Ramana Maharshi and the Path of Self-Knowledge* and *The Teachings of Ramana Maharshi*. It feels good to have constant reminders of different ways of looking at and approaching larger spiritual truths when I'm so constantly involved with my body and how it feels, so often frightened by the flashing in my eye or the numbness in my leg, somehow caught again and again in identifying with my body, tricked by my fundamental, basic will to live on the cellular level, again and again confusing Self with ego/body. It's tricky to put so much energy into healing, to fan the fires of life and my will to live without at the same time beginning to grasp after life, without at the same time becoming more attached to and identified with the life of this current agglomeration of living cells that this "I", whatever that is, so depends on!

After reading I do a little yoga and then meditate, simply as an offering of my time and attention to Spirit, an affirmation of my faith in something I find hard to articulate or explain. This approach helps keep me from falling into the ever-sticky trap of goal-oriented effort.

I also think of what Father Thomas Keating says: "The chief act of the will is not effort but consent. . . . To try to accomplish things by force of will is to reinforce the false self. . . . But as the will goes up the ladder of interior freedom, its activity becomes more and more one of consent to God's coming, to the inflow of grace." I usually have to insert the word "Spirit" where he says "God"; the latter is too loaded with male, patriarchal, and judgmental overtones, too much like a separate being or parent, while Spirit feels more like the all-encompassing One or Emptiness beyond form that I can somehow imagine myself absorbed into. But I like Keating's emphasis not on trying but on receiving, opening, consenting, an opening that is very active in its own way. He says, "Trying dilutes the basic disposition of receptivity that is necessary for the growth of contemplative prayer. Receptivity is not inactivity. It is real activity but not effort in the ordinary sense of the word. . . . It is simply an attitude of waiting for the Ultimate Mystery. You don't know what that is, but as your faith is purified, you don't want to know." This "active inactivity" is an example of what I think of as "passionate equanimity." Ken reminds me that the Taoists call it "wei wu wei," which literally means "action no action" and which is often translated as "effortless effort."

Keating recommends the use of a five- to nine-syllable "active prayer," rather like a mantra. The one I like (it's not on his list) is "Consent to the Presence of Spirit." I find that the word "consent" startles me, awakens me, surprises me each time because I so easily and so constantly fall into effort. It makes me pause in my activity, and a whisper of relaxation, of gentleness, of allowing moves through that pause. I still use the mantra "om mani padme hung" during the day [the mantra of Chenrezi, the Buddha of compassion], but it's nice to now have a mantra in English whose meaning always startles me into more awareness. I still wear the wooden rosary from the Snowmass Monastery on my left wrist and every time it catches on something, which is quite often, I try to pause, gently disengage it, notice the flash of irritation if that happens, and repeat to myself, "Consent to the Presence of Spirit." It creates a moment of stillness, of openness that I like.

After meditation it's time for the coffee enema, a generalized detoxification procedure that stimulates the liver and gallbladder to release stored toxins and wastes. It's a component of many alternative cancer treatments, including the Gerson program, and these enemas have been used safely for over one hundred years. I know that for me they feel good and intuitively right. I remember how years ago I let my oncologist at the time scare me away from them even though they provided a lot of relief from painful effects of chemotherapy on rectal tissue. He made a forceful, disapproving comment about these enemas causing electrolyte imbalances. Only later did I realize he probably didn't know much about them and that if such a thing had been proven it was probably in tests where enemas were given twenty times a day!

The enema takes about thirty minutes and I use the time for visualization, with a tape of Goenka chanting in Pali playing in the background. Depending on how things feel that day, I may visualize in a directive, goal-oriented way, seeing the tumors being digested, killed, and cleared away. At other times, when I feel the need to be open, to question and explore, I dialogue with the tumors, asking questions, seeing if they have anything to say to me.

In the first case, I actively imagine the enzymes attacking the tumors (I do this one at a time, starting with the brain tumor then moving on to the large lung tumor). I imagine the tumor being softened by the enzymes, which enter through the bloodstream but most strongly from the lower right. I imagine the cells being digested by the enzymes and at the same time imagine my immune system helping kill these weakened cells. I see the tumor being killed from within, the black area at the center growing larger, the surrounding swelling diminishing, and sometimes I see the tumor collapsing in on itself as more and more dead cells are cleared away from the center.

When I actively dialogue with each tumor, it's a different process with a different feeling tone. First I check to see if anything has changed since the last time. Then I may ask if the tumors have anything to say to me, such as confirmation of what I am doing or suggestions for something different. What I see and what I hear has been almost uniformly positive—I don't know if it means anything objectively, but at least it tells me I'm feeling hopeful on deeper, less conscious levels. The tumors have said things like "Don't worry, it's going to be OK," or "Don't worry if you get some strange symptoms, things will be changing in here, the shape of the tumor will change and press on different areas, but it doesn't mean anything, don't worry about it." Only a few weeks ago the brain tumor told me, somewhat apologetically, that it didn't want to hurt me, it certainly didn't want to kill me, and thus it was glad I was trying the enzymes because somehow it just couldn't give in to radiation or chemotherapy (it *has* proven fairly resistant to these) but it thought it would be able to give in to the enzymes, to please give this program a chance, at least three months!

Again, I hold all of this lightly. I don't know if the information and advice I get in this manner has any objective truth to it, but I find it helpful to connect with these different voices in myself, to better understand what is going on internally, below the level of everyday consciousness, and I do pay attention to the inner advice that comes in this way. Many times the tumors are silent or feel unapproachable. I always ask the help of Mother Mary and the Little Old Man of the Mountains (who looks suspiciously like a German doll I impulsively bought in the airport—he has a big gray beard, green loden-cloth jacket, and knapsack on his back). They have become my guides on this inner journey and are a most welcome source of comfort and companionship. If I wasn't inventive enough to have imaginary playmates as a child, I'm making up for it now!

After the coffee enema it's time for enzyme dose #3 (they have to be separated from meals by an hour or the enzymes will happily go to work on food and not make it into my bloodstream). I take the dogs for a short walk, clean up a little, and suddenly it's time for lunch, which Ken whips up. I was surprised by the diet Dr. Gonzales outlined. It's actually much broader than the semimacrobiotic diet I was on, which is a relief since I had anticipated an even narrower diet in some ways. I'm classified, on the basis of hair analysis and blood tests, as a Moderate Vegetarian Metabolizer, one of ten metabolic types (the program, especially the diet, is slightly different for each type). This means I do well with vegetarian protein (I've been a fish-eating vegetarian since 1972) but do better with some lean animal protein (eggs, cheeses, fish, poultry, occasional red meat). My only transgression on this program so far (I've been on it twelve days) is that I haven't gotten around to eating red meat yet! Quite a hurdle to overcome. I have to actually eat it! I wonder how it will taste . . . what it will be like to chew beef once again . . . and of course my father, a cattleman, is delighted by this strange twist!

The diet is 60% raw (I find this difficult to manage), at least four servings of vegetables a day, fresh vegetable juice almost every day (carrot juice for nondiabetics), whole grains, the fourteen-grain raw cereal five times a week, eggs and dairy products (my type can handle the cholesterol easily, but I'm to avoid yellow cheeses), nuts and seeds, lean poultry twice a week, lean red meat once a week. I'm also allowed three servings of fruit a day, but that's impossible for me unless I'm on insulin. I'm to avoid alcohol, especially for the first three months, though an occasional glass of wine is OK. Nutrasweet is considered unfit for human use, but a small amount of saccharine (this because I'm diabetic and can't use the fruits and honey that are allowed) is OK. I can't tell you how much difference that one package of sweetener makes to me on a daily basis. . . .

OK. With lunch another big handful of pills goes down again, though sometimes most reluctantly. I was once able to take a whole handful of pills in one gulp. No longer. Now they go down one by one or, if I'm feeling daring, two by two. Nothing like getting a pill caught part way down at 3:30 A.M., especially one whose contents are as delectable as pork pancreatic enzymes. With all of these procedures, including the enema, I use only water filtered by the reverse osmosis process or distilled water.

An hour or so after lunch I have dose #4 of the enzymes and two hours later dose #5 (no snacks or the enzymes get diverted). An hour after dose #5 I make a before-dinner glass of vegetable juice with the Champion juicer. Then we have dinner—Ken usually cooks something wonderful. He makes fabulous vegetarian pizza with a quinoa crust, scrumptious vegetarian chili and ratatouille, chicken primavera and Thai fish. He's still trying to figure out how to cook red meat! Then we watch videos and cuddle on the couch many evenings, dogs and all!

Ken does the shopping and the laundry and the house chores, which is extremely helpful because the enzymes make you so tired. He's always there for me, steady, available when I need him, cute, and loving. We cuddle together in the evenings and wonder what's happened to our lives. We're getting our wills in shape, just in case. It's just what is in our lives. We're furious and upset and angry that this is happening to us, that it happens to anyone at all, and we've also learned how to breathe deeply, how to accept what is (at moments, at least!), how to enjoy life as it is, how to appreciate the moments of connection and of joy, and how to use this terrifying, heart-wrenching experience to help us stay open to life and grow in compassion.

It's odd to buy a new car (a Jeep Wrangler) with a six-year warranty and wonder if I'll be around when the warranty runs out. It's odd to hear people making plans five years ahead and wonder if I'll be around then. It's odd to think I'd better not put something like terracing the garden off until next year because I may not be around to enjoy it. It's odd to hear friends talk about a trip to Nepal and realize that I can probably never go, that the risk of catching something that would divert my immune system from fighting the tumors is too great. Well, I've done a lot of traveling in my time, though never to Nepal. Ken's always saying I move around too much anyway, so this is my chance to see what changes staying closer to home will bring to my life.

To finish my pill-dominated day, three times a week I go for an acupuncture treatment, a process that takes around two hours. Then it's another blood sugar check and with dinner another handful of thirty more assorted pills. Enzyme dose #6 comes an hour later, then 45–60 minutes on the exercise bike, followed by enzymes #7 and a short meditation before going to sleep. I take a final set of pills at bedtime (this includes the anti-estrogen agent I take) and check to be sure the alarm is set for 3:30 A.M. This goes on for ten days, then I get five days to cleanse and rest when I take no vitamins or enzymes (though I continue enzymes and HCl with meals). This cycle of ten days on and five days off is the generally prescribed pattern, since during the time off the body can "catch up with the toxic load resulting from physiological repair and rebuilding." The first five days off I also do a "clean sweep protocol," taking high doses of psyllium seed husks and bentonite clay solution three times a day. The psyllium is supposed to work its way through the large and small intestines, forcing out wastes stuck in little nooks and crannies, while the bentonite absorbs toxins from the gut. I'm now on day #2 of this program. My next five days off I'm supposed to do a liver flush. Nondiabetics use apple juice but I will dissolve the ortho-phosphoric acid in plain water and drink four glasses a day. At the end I take Epsom salts, an enema, more salts, and then—whoopee!—a dinner of heavy whipping cream and fruit. Olive oil before bed, ugh. The acid is supposed to remove calcium and fats from arteries and soften and dissolve gallstones. Epsom salts relax the sphincter muscles of the gallbladder and bile ducts, allowing the stones to pass. The cream and oil make the gallbladder and liver contract, forcing wastes, bile, and stones into the small intestine. Quite a process . . . something to look forward to!

Ken and I both liked Dr. Gonzales. His office is a mere block and a half from my aunt's apartment in New York. He says 70–75% of his patients do well on the program, which I believe means they are eventually cured or manage to hold their own against the cancer for a long time. Since I have quite a lot of cancer in my body still, he says I probably have a 50% chance of responding well to the program, though he feels my chances are actually higher than that because of my determination and understanding of the program.

Through a special kind of blood test they test the strength of different organs and body systems and whether or not cancer is present. This shows the body's weak points and helps determine the vitamins and organ extracts prescribed. I won't go into the details, but the results of my test were completely consistent with where the cancer actually is and with the expected effects of chemotherapy; all of this before the doctor ever saw me or my records. They also give you an overall score for the amount of cancer in the body and this is the test they use to follow your progress on the program. Dr. Gonzales said most of his patients score between 18 and 24 and that he considers a score of 45 to 50 incurable. My score was 38, which is quite high but still with a good chance for a response. He said he's had patients who scored 15 who didn't make it and others who scored in the high 30s whose bodies were incredibly efficient at breaking down tumors once they started the program. We'll know more about my chances after a month on the program, he said. He'll probably do another blood test then, and how I feel will also tell us a lot about my response. Dr. Gonzales says that often people feel simply terrible on the program, almost like they're dying, before they start getting better. Every time I complain that I'm feeling tired, Ken says "gooood!"—no sympathy from that quarter. So far I have indeed felt quite tired, which means my exercise program has been curtailed and I've started taking insulin.

I do know that when I think ahead to the possible outcomes of this situation or when I think of the time of my death, whenever that moment comes, I know I will feel more at peace if I feel sure about the choices I made along the way, if I know that at the time I made each choice I was not unduly influenced by the beliefs of others around me, that the choice truly felt like *my* choice. I felt like the Scheef program and the Kelley program were my choice, definitely. But I felt I was too influenced by various doctors about having a segmental at first; I believe I would have chosen a mastectomy if I listened more to my own voice, and then gone to Livingston-Wheeler. My main advice is always to beware being knocked off center by what doctors say (they can be terribly convincing about what they do and terribly close-minded about nontraditional approaches), to take the quiet time to be clear about what you want and what you are intuitively drawn to, and to make a choice you feel is yours, a choice you can stand by no matter what the outcome. If I die, I have to know it is by my own choices.

I just completed the design of another fused glass plate, which feels satisfying. I now write "artist" when asked for my occupation!

I've taken as my practice lately (1) mindfulness and (2) surrender. Sort of combining a Buddhist practice and a Christian practice, in yet another way. I recently attended parts of Naropa's Christian and Buddhist Meditation conference and found it fascinating. For those who don't know, Naropa is a contemplative college here in Boulder originally founded by students of Chögyam Trungpa, Rinpoche. Ken is on the Board of Trustees, as is Lex Hixon, Jeremy Hayward, and Sam Bercholz. They have some very exciting and innovative programs, with a strong emphasis on psychology, the arts, writing and poetics, and Buddhist studies.

The main result of this conference for me was a growing sense that I'm beginning to cleanse Christian words and phrases and ways of describing mystical experience of the negative connotations that have always kept me from feeling comfortable with words like God or Christ or sin or surrender. In fact, I found the little phrase I use in meditation as my "Christian component" has changed from "Consent to the Presence of Spirit"—safe, ecumenical, no real buzzwords, though "consent" was even a challenge to me then—to "Surrender to God." Straightforward, direct, composed of what were once two major buzzwords for me. But now I love it! It is exactly what I need. The shock value, a holdover from what those words once meant to me, wakes me up. It brings me back to mindfulness. I find when I practice this, when I repeat this phrase, I suddenly let go of whatever was preoccupying me, my awareness opens and expands, and for a moment I suddenly see and feel the beauty and energy all around me, pouring into me, extending out to infinity, to all space, and the word "God" makes me think not of a patriarch but of vastness and emptiness and power and completeness and everlastingness and fullness.

Basically I'm doing quite well. My morning [spiritual] routine provides stability and comfort and constant reminders that, in spite of all the attention I pay to my body, I am not this body. I like being reminded of "the unconditioned, absolute Being that you really are," even if I'm far from directly experiencing that. I like being reminded that "all effort is simply to get rid of the mistaken impression that one is limited and bound by the woes of samsara (this life)." I like hearing Ramana Maharshi talk about trusting God, how "if you have surrendered it means that you must accept the will of God and not make a grievance of what may not happen to please you." I like being reminded that "You thank God for the good things that come to you but you don't thank Him for the things that seem

347

to you bad; that is where you go wrong." I do have the feeling that my having cancer has somehow "set my destiny in motion," a phrase a friend used about her own life that I responded to. I remember another friend who had cancer sharing his new artistic creation—I was blown away by its power and beauty—and afterwards saying "You know, I sort of hate to say this, but I wouldn't have found these depths within me but for this cancer."

I don't have any idea what lies ahead. It may get easier, it may get a lot tougher. I may be able to coast along for awhile, or a sudden change might find us in the middle of some other treatment. I realize that I haven't yet had to deal with pain or with impaired functioning of any kind, and I don't know how brave or how accepting or how calm or how thankful to God I'll be when/if that happens.

These letters were never intended to become a continuing series. I was simply too lazy to write to everyone individually but wanted to keep in touch. Now they've taken on a life of their own and even if no one else were to read them I'd probably still write them! And I have included all these details about tests and confusing results and conflicting opinions and difficult choices not because the numbers or the results or even the choices I've made are important but because the details of the dailiness of living with this disease brings alive generalities like "living with cancer is an emotional roller coaster," "treatment choices are harrowingly difficult," "we can't plan ahead past next week," and "this will go on and on until the end." Others' stories are different in numbers, details, pace, and outcomes but, all in all, not so very different in feel. It's a bumpy ride.

Certainly at those moments when I wonder if it's all worth it, is life really so great to be fighting so hard for more, maybe I'll just give up if it becomes too hard—and I do have those thoughts, quite regularly—one thing that sustains me, that makes me want to carry on, to explore deeper, is the process of committing what I experience and what I learn and the ways I am challenged to paper. In fact, Ken asked me just the other day if things got really bad, would I continue with these letters? I immediately said "Yes, of course. In fact, I've thought that this might be what would keep me going even if I were in pain, what would keep me from choosing an easier way out, keep me believing there was still value in living day by day even if I were in a lot of pain and the end was obviously near." I would still be trying to let you all know what it was like for me, still trying to use my experience to reach out to you in hopes that sharing might somehow, someday, be helpful to someone else.

Time to sign off and move on to the next letter! I apologize about not being better about answering letters or returning phone calls, but I'm sure each of you understands and I assure you that Ken and I feel the support of all of you out there every day in many ways!

> With much love,
> Treya

The bumpy ride—the really bumpy ride—began. Almost immediately conflicting medical reports started pouring in. Orthodox medical tests began showing rapid tumor growth in Treya's body. But these tests were also perfectly consistent with what we would expect to see if the tumors were being dissolved by the enzymes.

I had a scare yesterday, a bit of a restless night because of it. My Denver doctor called with the results of a test—the cancer embryonic assay, or CEA, which measures the amount of a protein in cancer cells circulating in the blood and thus indicates the amount of active cancer in your body. My test in January, when I was diagnosed, was 7.7 (0–5 is considered normal). After the first treatment in Germany it was 13 and just before I left in May it was 16.7. We're supposed to watch these tumor markers for indications that the tumors are growing, and if they are must consider the next step to take. Well, my latest test was 21. Did this mean things were active again? Did it mean that the brain tumor, which should stay stable for two to three years, was growing? That my immune system wasn't able to hold things steady? That I might have to reconsider ongoing, monthly chemotherapy? I've only been home two weeks, I said to Life. Come on, give me a little more of a break than this!

Fortunately Ken and I reached Dr. Gonzales in the morning. He said not to worry at all about the CEA. "I have patients with CEA's of 880 and 1300 who are doing fine. I don't even begin to be concerned with it until around 700." He warned me that on this enzyme program the levels might go much higher as cancer cells are broken down and release the protein the test measures. This is "no big deal," he said. "It

349

can go from 300 to 1300 in two weeks and orthodox doctors get freaky. Twenty-one indicates some activity but it is not high." You can imagine the wave of relief that flooded through me. I was also relieved when he assured me that the treatment works in the brain since the enzymes do pass through the blood brain barrier. (I've recently discovered that most of my "reserve" treatments—tumor necrosis factor, Burzynski's anti-neoplastins, and the monoclonal chemotherapy—do not, alas.) Dr. Gonzales sounded so confident, I immediately felt better. I hope he's right, I hope this treatment works. At least now I feel a little more secure about it, which will be important when we meet with my more orthodox oncologist next week to review all the tests and hear what he recommends next.

The orthodox recommendation was to immediately go on continuous chemotherapy; or, more drastically, to go on extremely high-dose chemotherapy—so high it would kill the bone marrow—and then do a bone marrow transplant (an overall procedure generally thought to be the single most grueling treatment around). We anxiously awaited the blood analysis from Gonzales, that special test that would determine, according to Gonzales, if the tumors were growing or in fact dissolving.

The enzymes seem to be working, hooray! The first good news we've had in a long time. I sent in another hair and blood sample after a month on the program and my cancer score dropped from 38 to 33— the biggest drop Dr. Gonzales has ever seen in only one month on the program. I also started taking anti-estrogens at the same time, so some of the reduction may be due to them (I spoke to one woman recently who said her lung spots disappeared completely when the only treatment was an oopharectomy [removal of the ovaries]). Ken and I were delighted at the news from Dr. Gonzales!

My enthusiasm was a little tempered by a new symptom in my right arm which may come from the tumor pressing in a new place, but I remember the visualization session where I was told not to worry if strange symptoms came up, they might be due to the tumor changing shape as it's eaten away. These inner communications continue to be positive and upbeat; the feeling that keeps coming up—even in the face of troubling symptoms—is "I'm going to be all right." This is not

> positive thinking, there's no feeling of force or even of intention behind
> these thoughts, the thoughts just come of their own accord. It's reassur-
> ing, even if it doesn't accord with orthodox test results!

This entire situation was driving me nuts. Who ya gonna believe? I took
the dogs for a walk that day, and this is what went through my mind:

I'm a trained biochemist, and what Gonzales says about the orthodox
tests makes sense. When tumors dissolve they do release the same types of
waste products as tumor growth; the orthodox tests can't easily differentiate them. Even a trained radiologist can't always differentiate tumor
growth, histamine flare-up, and scar tissue.

But what if he's just leading us on? Trying to make us feel good? But why
would he do that? Our orthodox oncologist thinks it's for money, but this is
ridiculous. Gonzales charges a flat fee up front. Whether Treya lives or
dies, he's already been paid!

Moreover, if he is feeding us "feel-good" news and it isn't true, he
knows we are going to find out soon enough and possibly become quite
legally nasty about it. Treya even asked him, as Treya would, "What if you
are wrong, and what if we decline orthodox treatment based on your
recommendation, and then I die? Can't my family sue the daylights out of
you?" And he said, "Yes, they can. But the reason this program is still
operating in the United States is that it has a very high success rate. If not,
then both me and the patients would be dead!"

Moreover, Gonzales has his own reputation to think of; when his
patients start failing on his program, he immediately recommends orthodox recourse. He wants Treya to live as much as anybody. And he is
confident Treya is not only not failing, but rapidly improving.

Either he's mistaken about the test, or he's lying. He's not lying—he's
got too much to lose. Is he mistaken about the test then? Why does he put
so much faith in it? I know he's worked with the test in hundreds of cases,
and he must have found, empirically, that the test has a very high rate of
accuracy. Not 100%, to be sure, but enough for him to hang his career
on, at least when combined with the other tests he uses. If the test didn't
work well, he would have definitely found out by now, or at least found out
its rate of error, which he would then most definitely take into account
when making recommendations that he will be held medically and legally
responsible for. Nobody puts as much on the line as he is, unless it's based
on something that you have worked with long enough and well enough to

be able to trust with good reason. We could without doubt hang him if he's wrong and he knows it!

And, from what we can tell from outside sources—his files are open to qualified researchers—about 70% of his patients either get better or stabilize. And in each case that we can determine, the blood test analysis matches accurately their status.

And that was when I began to realize that this crazy program just might work.

Treya, who made up her own mind on these issues anyway, also had the same realization. But neither of us would let ourselves believe it at this point. We continued to assume she had less than a year, simply because to assume otherwise would set us up for cruel disappointment. But moments of optimism started to creep through. And so we decided to spend a month in Treya's beloved Aspen, which was now only four hours away by car.

A month in Aspen!!! I see it as a month to rest, a month to enjoy life, a month to not have to call doctors or schedule tests or research options! A month's vacation from all this cancer stuff, a month to hike, a month to go to concerts, a month to see friends, a month to be outdoors, a month to be with my family . . . WHOOPEE! Just push all this stuff aside as much as possible, let the research papers on tumor necrotic factor and monoclonals molder on the shelf, and simply enjoy life!

At the last moment before our departure for Aspen Ken discovered a two-week Buddhist meditation retreat in northern Canada that he felt strongly called to do. I was delighted because he said it's the first thing he's excited about since the diagnosis of my recurrence in January. This whole year has been incredibly difficult for Ken—not just the pressure of being my main support person but also the constant stress of the possibility of my death, our discussions of the future, our review of our wills. So I was overjoyed that he discovered this retreat and I've spent this time with my parents and my sister and the puppies. It's been lovely, a nice break from Boulder where I felt I was beginning to lose my never-ending battle with details, details, details.

Will the enzymes work? Is Gonzales right, and they are? I don't know. I hope so, but I've had so many mixed feelings being here. It hasn't been a vacation, pure and simple. On my drive over I cried at the sheer majestic beauty of Independence Pass and the next day when I went to my meditation cabin I cried at the simple beauty of the sun shining through aspen leaves. Neither of those moments would have happened if I hadn't been aware I might not be around to see these things next year. All this beauty makes me so appreciate life that I just can't help but want more and more of it! It's hard not to cling, not to feel attached when I'm surrounded by things like the cleansing sound of a crystal clear stream shaded by tall cottonwoods, when I hear the distinctive soft flutter of a breeze through a stand of quaking aspen trees, when I'm mightily entertained by the bounding gracefulness of Kairos excitedly chasing critters through the green undergrowth, when I look up at night and gasp at the unexpected clarity and brightness of myriad stars in a sky that seems suddenly crowded. Yes, I sometimes feel *very* attached to life, especially in Aspen.

In being here I am constantly reminded not only of my attachments but also of my new limitations. That's hard. When I hear about exotic places my friends have been, or when Ken calls to tell me there's a retreat in Kathmandu he wants to take me to, I immediately think of the germs, the dirty water, the fact that I can't risk getting a simple cold: the troops are already fully engaged with cancer, no spare soldiers available for the common cold, much less something more exotic and challenging to the immune system! I'm afraid my travels will be limited from now on. . . .

When I go out, I need to do a lot of planning for each trip, each excursion, even for each day. I have to remember the insulin, time the enzymes, be sure I have all the pills and water with me, carry a sweet snack at all times in case my blood sugar goes too low, carry extra warm clothes everywhere, etc., etc. The need for all this planning tends to feed my obsessive side. I find the stray thoughts that distract me most in meditation go something like this: Did I take those early morning enzymes or not? . . . Let's see, if I took my morning pills at twelve then I have to eat by one or at least have a snack by then because of the insulin. . . . If I didn't take those early pills, how can I squeeze another dose in today? . . . Must remember to stock up on insulin and get a refill on both types of anti-estrogen pills before I go to Aspen. . . . I've got to go by the hospital for copies of those tests to send to M. D. Anderson. . . . Maybe I'll try changing the insulin dose tonight, my fasting sugars are too high . . . etc., etc., etc. It's all junk, my planning mind invading time set aside for other purposes, monkey mind, monkey mind. At times I'm irritated by it, at times amused, and sometimes it even shuts up for awhile!

The retreat I went on—the first time in almost three years that Treya and I had been apart for more than a few days—was a Dzogchen retreat. I returned to Aspen and joined Treya there. We still wouldn't let ourselves believe the enzymes would really work, and Treya wondered aloud if she would ever see another spring, but her joy and passionate equanimity seemed always to surface sooner or later, and I was even getting slightly giddy with happy thoughts.

Many wonderful things happened during my time in Aspen. One was John Denver's wedding to Cassandra—Ken and I both think she's wonderful and delight in her Australian accent. The wedding took place on a high meadow in Starwood almost completely surrounded with jagged mountain peaks dramatically lit by the late afternoon sunshine.

Another was Ken's return, revitalized and inspired after his retreat in Canada. Before Ken left, he said, I'm not really sure why I'm doing this. This was the first time I'd ever seen Ken just take off. He said he didn't understand it himself. But the retreat, given by Pema Norbu Rinpoche, turned out to be the highest transmission in all of Buddhism, a very rare and special event. It's been given in the West only twice, and there are only a few teachers in the world who can give it. The retreat itself sounded grueling. Ken received over a dozen empowerments, or spiritual transmissions, during those two weeks. He was very different when he returned, more at ease, more peaceful.

And other wonderful times. The time spent with my family just hanging out and allowing everything to be done for me. Yet another was the annual Windstar Foundation Symposium, Choices III, which this year was held in the Music Festival tent and was a wonderfully inspirational, joyful event.

On Saturday night Tom Crum, cofounder of Windstar, put together a special evening on the "State of Our Planet" which closed with a segment on changing perspective—statements by about six people on how changing their perspective helped them deal with personal challenges. About how inner psychological or spiritual shifts had helped with outer difficulties.

Tommy had asked me to be one of these people and I immediately knew I had to do it, much as I was unnerved by the whole situation! When I dialogued with my tumors during visualization/active imagination sessions, the lung tumor told me repeatedly that I need to speak out, especially about this cancer experience. The other voice that speaks through that tumor is quite terrified about doing this and says it needs to be convinced through experience, through my taking action, that speaking out is not as terrifying as it imagines. So, I accepted the challenge immediately if also somewhat fearfully.

Our talks were limited to three or four minutes. I gave mine and got a standing ovation! After my talk, John [Denver] sang "I Want to Live," a beautiful song, and when he was done he said, "That was for you." It was a wonderful, wonderful time!

Later we had dinner with John and Cassandra. Ken and John seem to really enjoy each other. When we got back to Boulder, Cassie came and had lunch with us on our balcony, and she broke the news: she's pregnant! I felt a little sad because that's out of the question for me, but I was so happy for Cassie and John! Ah, life goes on. . . .

Back in Boulder, we sent in another blood sample for Gonzales for yet another analysis. The results came back and, of all things, her score had dropped another five points! Gonzales himself couldn't believe it, and had the lab run it again. Same results. He attributed it to the "steady zeal" (passionate equanimity!) with which Treya pursued the program. Indeed, he began mentioning Treya to his other patients as an example of how to do it right. We began getting phone calls from people on the program, and we were glad to give advice where we could.

And how are the enzymes working, you may be wondering? Well, according to Dr. Gonzales's "funny little test" (that's what he calls it), very, very well. From a beginning point of 38 (he usually doesn't take patients with scores over 40), I'm down to 28 in a mere two and a half months!

I'm not going to get my hopes up, however. Work hard without attachment to results!, that's my motto. But it is wonderful to allow myself, every now and then, to think I might grow old, or at least a little older, with Ken, with my wonderful family and friends. I might even outlive the Jeep's warranty!

Treya's family came to visit us, and as they were leaving, I saw them to the door, and yelled after them: "You know, I just think she might make it! I really do!"

I poke my head into the room. "Treya?"

"Ken?!"

"Treya! Jesus Christ, where have you been? I've been looking everywhere for you! Where have you been?"

"Here." She looks at me tenderly. "Are you OK?"

"Yeah, sure." We kiss, hug, clasp hands.

"I see you brought him."

"Huh? Oh, more like he brought me."

"Now listen very carefully," the Figure says.

20

A SUPPORT
PERSON

❧❧❧

As the enzyme program continued to have its effect, the battle of the interpretations reached fevered pitch. On the Gonzales side: Somewhere beginning around the third month of the program, the patient will start to feel particularly exhausted; many feel like they are dying, we were told; at the least, "You'll feel like you were hit by a truck." This is because the enzymes are starting to break down tissues, including tumors, and the toxic waste products are accumulating in the system—hence the coffee enemas, the Epsom salt baths, and other measures designed to help rid the body of toxic buildup. Tumor markers will show what appears to be dramatic increase in tumor activity. And CAT scans will show all tumors to be proportionately larger.

That's what is *supposed* to happen if the program is working; virtually everybody on the Kelley routine who gets better goes through that first. And indeed, all of those things were happening to Treya. On the basis of those indicators, and the special blood analysis, Gonzales now gave Treya a 70% chance of turning it around—either stabilizing or actually going into remission.

The orthodox oncologists gave her two to four months to live.

It was an utterly impossible situation. As time wore on, and the test results became more and more dramatic, the two interpretations remained

357

diametrically opposed. I found that psychologically I simply split into two segments. One believed Gonzales, one believed the oncologists. I could find no completely convincing evidence that either side was definitely right or definitely wrong. Neither could Treya.

It was a Twilight Zone atmosphere: in a couple of months, you are either going to be well on your way to recovery, or you are going to be dead.

The enzymes made Treya feel exhausted, but apart from that she felt quite good. She looked quite good, quite beautiful, actually. She had no major symptoms—no cough, no headaches, no extra visual problems.

The situation was so preposterous that Treya often found it humorous.

What am I supposed to do? Pull my hair out? Don't have any. The fact is, my joy in life is there, and there are moments when I feel practically ecstatic just sitting on the deck and looking at the view out the back of our house and watching the puppies play. I feel so blessed in this moment. Each breath is so incredible, so joyful, so dear. What am I missing? What could be wrong?

And so Treya simply marched straight ahead. Like a tightrope walker, she took it one step at a time and refused to look down. I tried to follow, but I'm afraid I looked down a lot.

The first thing she did was give her talk at Windstar, which was voted the high point of the entire symposium. We videotaped it and watched it several times. What struck me most about this talk was that it seemed to summarize almost everything Treya had learned in her five-year battle with cancer, and managed to do so in under four minutes. It summarized her spiritual views, her meditation practice, tonglen, everything, but without once referring to "meditation" or "tonglen" or "God" or "Buddha." When Treya and I watched the video, we both noticed that at the point that she says, "My doctors have given me two to four years to live," her eyes go blank. She was lying. Her doctors had just given her two to four *months* to live. She didn't want to frighten her family or friends, so she decided to keep that information between us.

I myself was amazed that she could give the talk at all. She had forty lung tumors; four brain tumors; liver metastases; a CAT scan had just indicated that her main brain tumor had grown 30% (it was now the size of a large plum); and her primary doctor had just told her she would be lucky to live four months.

The other thing that struck me most about this talk was how absolutely vital and vibrant Treya was. She lit up the stage, and everybody there could feel it, see it. And through it all I kept thinking: This is what I have loved the most about her from the first day I saw her: this woman says LIFE, says it with her whole being, exudes it in all directions. That is exactly the energy that people find so attractive about her, that makes people light up in her presence, makes them want to be around her, look at her, talk to her, be with her.

When she stepped out on that symposium stage, the entire audience lit up, and I kept thinking, God, this is vintage Treya.

Hello. My name is Treya Killam Wilber. A lot of you here have known me as "Terry." I've been involved with Windstar from the early days.

Five years ago in this same month, in August of '83, I met and fell totally in love with Ken Wilber. I always called it, love at first touch. We were married four months later and then, ten days after our wedding, I was diagnosed with stage two breast cancer. We spent our honeymoon in the hospital.

In the five years since, I've had two local recurrences and many types of treatment, both conventional and alternative. But in January of this year we discovered the cancer had spread to my brain and my lungs. The doctors we consulted have given me two to four years to live.

So when Tommy asked me to speak at this event, my first thought was, but I'm still sick. The others who are speaking tonight have in some way overcome obstacles or forged something concrete from the challenges in their lives—as you'll hear from Mitchell, a dear friend I've enjoyed and admired for fifteen years.

OK, I thought, I'm still sick. Perhaps I can look at what I've done with my life since the diagnosis.

I've counseled hundreds of people with cancer, over the phone and in person. I cofounded the Cancer Support Community in San Francisco, which provides a wide range of free services and community for hundreds of people each week. I've written as honestly as I can about my experiences and inner explorations in a way that many say they have found helpful, and I plan to publish a book soon.

But when I finished this list of doing, I suddenly realized I'd fallen into an old familiar trap. I was equating success with achieving physical health against all odds, or with concrete accomplishments in the outer world. I feel instead that the shift in perspective that we're here to celebrate tonight, the choice of higher ground, is an inner change, an inner choice, an inner shift in one's being. It's easy to talk about and acknowledge doing in the world, but I'm more excited by my internal changes, my sense of increasing health on higher levels than the physical, by the spiritual work I do each day.

When I neglect this inner work I find that my life-threatening situation quickly becomes frightening or depressing or even at times, simply boring. With the inner work—and I'm quite eclectic, I draw on many traditions and disciplines—I feel continually challenged and excited, and deeply engaged in life. I find that the emotional roller coaster of advanced cancer becomes a wonderful opportunity to practice equanimity at the same time that my passion for life increases.

Learning to make friends with cancer, learning to make friends with the possibility of an early and perhaps painful death, has taught me a great deal about making friends with myself, as I am, and a great deal about making friends with life, as it is.

I know that there are a lot of things I can't change. I can't force life to make sense, or to be fair. This growing acceptance of life as it is, with all the sorrow, the pain, the suffering, and the tragedy, has brought me a kind of peace. I find that I feel ever more connected with all beings who suffer, in a really genuine way. I find a more open sense of compassion. And I find an ever steadier desire to help, in whatever way I can.

There's an old saying—it's popular among people with cancer—that goes: "*Life* is terminal." In a way I feel lucky. I always notice what age people are when they die. I always notice newspaper articles about young people killed in accidents; in fact, I used to cut these out as a reminder. I'm lucky because I've been given advance warning and the time to act on that warning. For this I'm thankful.

Because I can no longer ignore death, I pay more attention to life.

There were hundreds of people in the audience, and as they gave her a standing ovation, I looked around. People were openly sobbing and trying to cheer at the same time. The cameraman dropped the video. If only people could donate life force, I thought. We'd all give her enough for centuries.

A *Support Person*

It was during this period that I finally decided to write my own letter, a letter to complement the many that Treya was sending out, a letter on the trials and tribulations of being a support person. Here is a very condensed version:*

July 27, 1988
Boulder

Dear friends,

. . . As far as support people go, a particularly insidious problem begins to set in after about two or three months of caregiving. It is, after all, comparatively easy to deal with the outer and physical and obvious aspects of caregiving. You rearrange your work schedule; you get used to cooking or washing or housecleaning or whatever it is that you as support person have to do to physically take care of the loved one: you take them to the doctor's office, you help with medication, and so on. This can be fairly difficult, but the solutions are also fairly obvious—you either do the extra work or arrange for someone else to do it.

What is more difficult for the support person, however, and more insidious, is the inner turmoil that starts to build on the emotional and psychological levels. This turmoil has two sides, one private and one public. On the private side, you start to realize that, no matter how many problems you personally might have, they all pale in comparison to the loved one who has cancer or some other life-threatening disease. So for weeks and months you simply stop talking about your problems. You sit on them. You don't want to upset the loved one; you don't want to make it worse for them; and besides, in your own mind you keep saying, "Well, at least I don't have cancer; my own problems can't be so bad."

After a few months or so of this (I'm sure it varies from person to person), it slowly starts to dawn on the support person: the fact that your problems pale in comparison to, say, cancer, doesn't make your problems go away. In fact, they get worse, because now you have *two* problems: the original problem plus the fact that you can't voice the original problem and thus find a solution for it. The problems magnify; you clamp the lid down harder; they push back with renewed strength. You start getting slightly weird. If you're introverted, you start getting little twitches; you get shortness of breath; anxieties start creeping up; you laugh too loud; you have an extra beer. If you're extroverted, you start exploding at completely

---

* A complete copy of this letter is available from the Cancer Support Community. Please see page 421 for details.

inappropriate moments; you throw temper tantrums; you storm out of the room; you throw things; you have an extra beer. If you're introverted, there are times you want to die; if extroverted, times you want the loved one to die. If you're introverted, there are times you want to kill yourself; if extroverted, times you want to kill *them*. In any event, death hangs in the air; and anger, resentment, and bitterness inexorably creep up, along with terrible guilt about having any of those dark feelings.

Those feelings, of course, are completely natural and normal given the circumstances. In fact, I would worry considerably about a support person who didn't periodically have such feelings. And the best way to handle these feelings is to talk about them. I can't emphasize this too strongly— the only solution is to talk.

And here the support person runs into the second of the emotional-psychological difficulties that I mentioned: the public aspect. Once you decide you have to talk, the problem is: to whom? The loved one is probably not the best person to discuss some of your problems with, simply because they often *are* your problem—they are putting a heavy load on you, but nevertheless you don't want them to feel guilty about this, you don't want to dump on them, no matter how angry you might be with them "for getting sick."

By far the best place to talk about all this is in a support group of people who are going through similar circumstances, i.e., a support group for support persons. Also, an individual therapist might prove very valuable, as might couples therapy. But I'll talk about these "professional supports" in a moment. Because the average person, myself included, doesn't tend to take advantage of these agencies until rather late in the ballgame, by which time much damage has been done and much needless hurt suffered. For the average person does the normal and understandable thing: he or she talks to family, to friends, and/or to associates. And here the person runs smack into the public problem.

The public problem is this, as Vicky Wells puts it: "Nobody is interested in chronic." Here's what she means. I come to you with a problem; I want to talk, I want some advice, I want some consolation. We talk, you are very helpful and kind and understanding. I feel better; you feel useful. But the next day, my loved one still has cancer; the situation is not fundamentally better at all; in fact, it might be worse. I don't feel good at all. I run into you. You ask how I'm doing. If I tell the truth, I say I feel awful. So we talk. You are again very helpful and kind and understanding, and I feel better . . . until the next day, when she still has cancer and nothing is really better. Day in and day out, nothing really can be done about the situation itself (the doctors are doing everything possible, and she still might die). So day in and day out, you feel pretty rotten; the situation just doesn't change. And sooner or later you find out that almost everybody not actually faced with this problem on a day-to-day basis starts to find it boring or annoying if you keep talking about it. All but your most committed friends start subtly avoiding you, because cancer *always* hangs over the horizon as a dark cloud, ready to rain on any parade. You become a kind of chronic whine, and nobody wants to hear it, people get tired of hearing the same old problem. "Nobody is interested in chronic.". . .

So support people eventually begin to find that their private problems are multiplying, and the public solution just doesn't work very well. They begin to feel completely alone and isolated. At this point, one of several things tends to happen. They walk out; they break down; they get into substance abuse; or they seek professional help. . . .

As I said, by and far the best place to talk out your difficulties is in a support group for caregivers. When you listen to these groups, you find out that the main activity is basically bitching about the loved ones. You know—"Who does he think he is to order me around like that?" "What makes her think she's so special, just because she's sick; I got problems of mine own ya know." "I feel like I've totally lost control of my life." "I hope the bastard hurries up and dies." That kind of thing, things nice people don't say in public, and certainly don't tell the loved one.

The thing is, under all these dark feelings and anger and resentment is almost always a great deal of love, or else the support person would simply have walked out long ago. But this love can't really surface freely as long as anger and resentment and bitterness clog the route. As Gibran said, "Hate is love starved." There is a lot of hatred expressed in support groups, but only because there is so much love under it, starved love. If not, you wouldn't hate the person, you just wouldn't care at all. My experience with most support people (myself included) is not that they aren't *receiving* enough love, but they are finding it hard to remember how to *give* love, how to be loving under the difficult circumstances of being a caregiver. And since, in my experience, it is primarily giving love that is healing, support people really need to clear out the obstacles to love's presence— the anger, resentment, hatred, bitterness, even envy and jealously (I envy her having someone to take care of her all the time; namely me).

For this a support group is invaluable. . . . Failing that, or perhaps in addition to that, I would recommend individual psychotherapy, definitely for the support person, but also for the loved one as well. For you soon learn that there are some things that simply should not be discussed with the loved one; and conversely, there are some things the loved one ought not discuss with you. I think most of my generation believes that "honesty is the best policy" and that spouses should discuss every single thing that bothers them with the other spouse. Bad plan. Openness is important and helpful, but only so far. At some point, openness can become a weapon, a spiteful way to hurt someone—"But I was only telling the truth." I have had much anger and resentment at the situation that Treya's cancer has put us both in, but beyond a point, it does no good for me to constantly dump this on Treya. She hates the situation as much as I; in any event it's not her fault. But still I am angry and hateful and resentful. So you don't "share" that with your loved one, you don't dump that on them. You pay a therapist, and you dump the hell all over *them*.

This has the added advantage of giving the both of you room to be together without unexpressed resentment and anger on the caregiver's part and without guilt and shame on the loved one's part. You've already off-loaded much of that in the group or with the therapist. It also allows you to learn the gentle art of telling compassionate lies, instead of narcissistically blurting out what you "really feel" no matter how much it might hurt the other person. Not big lies, just little diplomatic ones, ones that don't gloss over any really important difficulties, but at the same time don't stir up a hornet's nest of unresolved issues just for the sake of so-called honesty. On some days you might be feeling particularly tired of being a caregiver, and your loved one asks "How are you doing today?" "I feel like hell and my life isn't mine anymore and why don't you jump off the bridge." Bad answer. Truthful, but real bad answer. Try instead: "I'm tired today, honey, but I'm hanging in there." Then hit the support group or therapist and let them have it. Absolutely nothing is gained by dumping on the loved one, no matter how "honest" it might be. . . .

You see, one of the strangest things I have learned about being a good-enough support person is that your primary job is being an emotional sponge. That is, most people think that your job is to give advice, to help the loved ones solve problems, to be useful, to give help, to make dinner and drive them around and so on. But all of those tasks take a backseat to the primary role of the caregiver, which is to be an emotional sponge. The loved one facing a possibly lethal disease is going to experience an overwhelming number of extremely powerful emotions; on occasion, they are going to be completely overwhelmed by those emotions, by fear and terror and anger and hysteria and pain. And your job is to hold the loved one, be with the loved one, and simply absorb as many of those emotions as you can. You don't have to talk, you don't have to say anything (there's really nothing to say that will help), you don't have to give any advice (won't help much anyway), and you don't have to do anything. You just have to be there, and breathe in their pain, or fear, or hurt. You act like a sponge.

When Treya was first ill, I thought I could make things all better by being in charge, by saying the right things, by helping choose medical treatments, and so on. Those were all helpful, but beside the point. She would get some particularly bad news—say a new metastasis—and she would begin crying, and I would immediately start in with things like, "Look, it's not certain yet; we need more tests; there's no evidence that this will change your treatments anyway," and so on. That was not what Treya needed. What she needed was simply for me to cry with her, and so I did; to feel her feelings; and thus to help dissipate them, or soak them up. I believe this occurs on a bodily level; talk is not needed, though you can talk if you want to.

Be that as it may, one's initial response, when a loved one is faced with terrible news, is to try to make that person feel better. And I am saying that is the wrong response, by and large. First, you empathize. The crucial point, as I began to see it, is simply to be present with the person, and not be afraid of their fear, or their pain, or their anger; to just let whatever comes up come up; and most of all, to not try to get rid of these painful feelings by trying to help the person, by trying to make the person "feel better" or "talk them out" of their worries. In my case, this "helping" attitude only happened when I didn't want to deal with Treya's feelings or with mine; I didn't want to relate to them in a simple and direct and uncomplicated way; I wanted them to go away. I did not want to be a sponge, I wanted to be AN ACHIEVER, and make the situation all better. I did not want to acknowledge my helplessness in the face of the unknown. I was as afraid as Treya.

Just being a sponge, you see, tends to make you feel helpless and useless, because you aren't *doing* something, you're just being there, doing nothing (or so it seems). And this is what so many people find so difficult to learn. I know I did. It took me almost a year to stop trying to fix things or make them better, and to just be with Treya when it hurts. I think this is why "nobody is interested in chronic," because you can't *do* anything about chronic, you can only *be* there. And so when people think they are supposed to do something to help you, and find out that doing is of no help, they're at a loss. What can I do? Nothing, just be there. . . .

When people ask me what I do, and I'm in no mood to chitchat, I usually say, "I'm a Japanese wife," which totally confuses them. The point is that, as a support person, you are supposed to be silent and simply do as your spouse wills—you're supposed to be a good "wifey."

Men find this particularly tough; I did, anyway. It took me, I don't know, maybe two years before I stopped resenting the fact that in any argument we had or decision we made, Treya had the trump card: "But I have cancer." Treya, in other words, would almost always get her way, and I was reduced to simply going along like the good little wife.

I don't mind this so much any more. For one thing, I don't just automatically "go along" with all Treya's decisions, particularly when I think they reflect bad judgment. Previously, I would tend to go along with her because she seemed almost desperately to need me to support her decisions, even if it meant lying about how I really felt. The way we work it now is that if Treya is making an important decision on, say, whether to try a new treatment, I give her my opinion as strongly as I can state it, even if I disagree with her, right up to the point that she finally decides what to do. From that point on, I agree with her, and get behind her, and support her in her choice as best I can. It's no longer my job to heckle her, or cast doubts on her choice. She has enough problems without having to constantly doubt her own course of action. . . .

For another, when it comes to day-to-day chores, I no longer particularly mind being the good little wife. I do the cooking, I clean up, I do dishes, I do laundry, I go to the supermarket. Treya writes really nifty letters, takes coffee enemas, and swallows handfuls of pills every two hours, so somebody's got to do all this junk, right? . . .

The existentialists are correct that within the realm of your own choices or your own doing, you have to affirm the choices you have made. That is, you have to stand behind the choices you have made that contributed to molding your own fate; as the existentialists say, "we are our choices." Failing to affirm our own choices is called "bad faith" and is said to lead to "inauthentic being."

For me this came in the form of a very simple realization: at any time in this difficult process, I could have walked out. Nobody was chaining me to the hospital wards, no one threatened my life if I left, nobody had tied me down. Some place deep inside I had made a fundamental choice to stay with this woman through thick and thin, no matter what, forever; to see her through this process come what may. But somewhere during the second year of the ordeal, I forgot about this choice, even though it was a choice I was still making, obviously, or I would have left. I was displaying bad faith; I was being inauthentic; I wasn't real. In my bad faith I had forgotten about my own choice, and therefore almost immediately fell into an attitude of blame, and consequently self-pity. Somehow, this all became very clear to me. . . .

It is not always easy for me to affirm this choice, or my choices in general. It doesn't automatically make the situation any better. I think of it like volunteering to go into combat and then getting shot. I might have freely chosen to go into combat, but I did not choose to get shot. I feel a little bit wounded, and I'm not happy about that; but I freely volunteered for the assignment—it was my choice—and I would freely volunteer again, knowing full well what it entails.

So each day I reaffirm my choice. Each day I choose once again. This stops blame from piling up, and slows the accumulation of pity or guilt. It's a simple point, but actually applying even the simplest points in real life is usually difficult. . . .

In addition to slowly getting back into writing, I have also returned to meditation, the whole point of which is really just to learn how to die (to die to the separate-self sense, or ego), and Treya's facing a potentially lethal disease is an extraordinary spur to meditative awareness. The sages say that if you maintain this choiceless awareness, this bare witnessing, moment to moment, then death is just a simple moment like any other, and you relate to it in a very simple and direct way. You don't recoil from death or grasp at life, since fundamentally they are both just simple experiences that pass.

The Buddhist notion of "emptiness" has also helped me a great deal. Emptiness (*shunyata*) doesn't mean blank or void; it means unobstructed or unimpeded or spontaneous; it also is roughly synonymous with impermanence or fleetingness (*anicca*). And the Buddhists say that reality is empty—there is nothing permanent or absolutely enduring that you can hold on to for security or support. As the Diamond Sutra says, "Life is like a bubble, a dream, a reflection, a mirage." The whole point is not to try to grasp the mirage, but rather to "let go," since there's really nothing to hang on to anyway. And again, Treya's cancer is a constant reminder that death is a great letting go, but you needn't wait for actual physical death to profoundly let go of your own grasping and clinging in this moment, and this moment, and this.

And finally, to bring this all back home, the mystics maintain that the type of action that one performs in this world, *if one lives by choiceless awareness*, is an action devoid of ego or devoid of self-centeredness. If you are going to die to (or transcend) the separate-self sense, then you have to die to self-centered and self-serving actions. In other words, you have to perform what the mystics call *selfless service*. You have to serve others, without thought of self or hope for praise; you simply love and serve—as Mother Teresa says, "Love until it hurts."

In other words, you become a good wife.

In other words, here I am, cooking dinner and washing dishes. Don't get me wrong, I'm still far from Mother Teresa status, but I increasingly see my support-person activity as being a major part of selfless service and therefore of my own spiritual growth, a type of meditation in action, a type of compassion. Nor does this mean that I have perfected this art; I still bitch and moan, I still get angry, I still blame circumstances; and Treya and I still half-kid (half-not) about holding hands, jumping off the bridge, and putting an end to this whole joke.

And all in all, I'd rather be writing.

Now, as a reward for reading through this long letter, and for all you other good wives out there, I'm giving out my world-famous recipe for vegetarian chili:

Ingredients

2–3 cans dark red kidney beans (drained)
2 stalks celery, chopped
2 onions, chopped
2 green peppers, chopped
2–3 T olive oil
1 28-oz. can whole tomatoes
3–4 cloves garlic
3–4 T chili powder
1–2 T cumin
2–3 T fresh parsley
2–3 T oregano
1 can beer
1 cup cashews
¹/₂ cup raisins (optional)

Heat oil in large pot; sauté onions until clear, then add celery, green pepper, and garlic; cook for 5 minutes or so. Add tomatoes (with juice; break the tomatoes into small chunks) and kidney beans; reduce to simmer. Add chili powder, cumin, parsley, oregano, beer, cashews, and raisins (opt.). Simmer as long as you want. Garnish with fresh parsley or grated cheddar cheese.

I can't remember if beer was part of my original recipe or I just dropped my beer in it once when I was cooking it; in any event, the beer is essential. Also, "T" does mean tablespoon, not teaspoon; the whole secret of this chili is in the large amounts of herbs.

À votre santé. Please eat it in good health.

Love,

Ken

As I said, this letter was picked up and published by the *Journal of Transpersonal Psychology*, where it got a response so large and so heartbreaking that we were all taken aback. But the response simply pointed out the desperate plight of support people everywhere, the people that are "silently wasted" because, since they aren't the "sick person," nobody thinks they have any real problems. Vicky Wells, who has been both a support person and a cancer patient, put it best, and in words I think every support person should hear:

> I've been in both worlds—I've had cancer and I've been a support person for Treya and others. And I would have to say that it is so much harder being a support person. Because, at least for me, when I was dealing with my own cancer, there were a lot of moments of sheer beauty and clarity and grace and reordering of priorities in life, and a reappreciation of the beauty of life. And I think that as a support person, that's really hard to find. The cancer person has no choice but to stay with it, but the support person has to choose to hang in there all the time. And it was real hard for me, as a support person, to get over the sadness, or get over the feeling of walking on eggshells around the person, or living with their treatment choices. What should I do and how should I support her? And should I be honest about what I really feel? It's like an emotional roller coaster for the support person. And what I usually come back to is, it's just love. Just love her, that's the most important thing.

After Treya's talk in Aspen, we went briefly to San Francisco, where we needed to consult with Peter Richards and Dick Cohen. While there, Treya gave a talk at CSC. On the day of the presentation, CSC was so crowded people were backed up into the street. Vicky summarized the whole thing: "I mean they were blown away by her. We're all a little bit in awe of her, you know. Her honesty, her courage."

"Yeah, I know, Vick. At this point, I think we're just the first in a long, long line of folks."

We returned to Boulder and our daily grind, waiting, waiting. By this time I was deeply involved in the practices of Dzogchen, given to me by His Holiness Pema Norbu Rinpoche, or Penor for short. The essence of Dzogchen (or maha-ati) is radically simple, and is in accord with the highest teachings of other of the world's great wisdom traditions, particularly Vedanta Hinduism and Ch'an (early Zen) Buddhism. In a nutshell:

If Spirit has any meaning, it must be omnipresent, or all-pervading and all-encompassing. There can't be a place Spirit is not, or it wouldn't be infinite. Therefore, Spirit has to be completely present, right here, right now, in your own awareness. That is, your own present awareness, precisely as it is, without changing it or altering it in any way, is perfectly and completely permeated by Spirit.

Furthermore, it is not that Spirit is present but you need to be enlightened in order to see it. It is not that you are one with Spirit but just don't know it yet. Because that would also imply that there is some place Spirit is not. No, according to Dzogchen, you are always already one with Spirit, and that awareness is always already fully present, right now. You are looking directly at Spirit, with Spirit, in every act of awareness. There is nowhere Spirit is not.

Further, if Spirit has any meaning at all, then it must be eternal, or without beginning or end. If Spirit had a beginning in time, then it would be strictly temporal, it would not be timeless and eternal. And this means, as regards your own awareness, that you cannot *become* enlightened. You cannot attain enlightenment. If you could attain enlightenment, then that state would have a beginning in time, and so it would not be true enlightenment.

Rather, Spirit, and enlightenment, has to be something that you are fully aware of right now. *Something you are already looking at right now.* As I was receiving these teachings, I thought of the old puzzles in the Sunday supplement section of the newspaper, where there is a landscape and the caption says, "The faces of twenty famous people are hidden in this landscape. Can you spot them?" The faces were maybe Walter Cronkite, John Kennedy, that kind of thing. The point is that you are looking right at the faces. You don't need to see *anything* more in order to be looking at the faces. They are completely entering your visual field already, you just don't recognize them. If you still can't find them, then somebody comes along and simply points them out.

It's the same way with Spirit or enlightenment, I thought. We are all already looking directly at Spirit, we just don't recognize it. We have all the necessary cognition, but not the recognition. This is why the Dzogchen teachings don't particularly recommend meditation, useful as that may be for other purposes. Because meditation is an attempt to change cognition, to change awareness, and that is unnecessary and beside the point. Spirit is already completely and fully present in the state of awareness that you have now; nothing needs to be changed or altered. And, indeed, the attempt to change awareness is like trying to paint in the faces in the puzzle instead of simply recognizing them.

And thus, in Dzogchen, the central teaching is not meditation, because meditation aims at a change of state, and enlightenment is not a change of state but the recognition of the nature of *any* present state. Indeed, much of the teaching of Dzogchen centers on why meditation doesn't work, on why enlightenment can never be gained because it is always already present. Trying to get enlightenment would be like trying to attain your feet. The first rule in Dzogchen: There is nothing you can try to do, or try not to do, to get basic awareness, because it already and fully is.

Instead of meditation, then, Dzogchen uses what are called "the pointing-out instructions." Here the Master simply talks to you, and points out that aspect of your awareness that is *already* one with Spirit and has always been one with Spirit, that part of your awareness that is timeless and eternal, that is beginningless, that has been with you even before your parents were born (as Zen would put it). In other words, it's just like pointing out the faces in the puzzle. You don't have to change the puzzle or rearrange it, you only have to recognize that which you are already looking at. Meditation rearranges the puzzle; Dzogchen doesn't touch a thing. Thus the pointing out instructions usually begin, "Without correcting or modifying your present awareness in any way, notice that . . ."

I cannot give the actual instructions, as those are the special province of the Dzogchen Master. But I can give you the Vedantan Hindu version, since they are already in print, particularly in the writings of the illustrious Sri Ramana Maharshi. As I would word it:

The one thing we are always already aware of is . . . awareness itself. We already have basic awareness, in the form of the capacity to Witness whatever arises. As an old Zen Master used to say, "You hear the birds? You see the sun? Who is not enlightened?" None of us can even imagine a state where basic awareness is not, because we would still be aware of the imagining. Even in dreams we are aware. Moreover, these traditions maintain, there are not two different types of awareness, enlightened versus ignorant. There is only awareness. And this awareness, exactly and precisely as it, without correction or modification at all, is itself Spirit, since there is nowhere Spirit is not.

The instructions, then, are to recognize awareness, recognize the Witness, recognize the Self, and abide as that. Any attempt to get awareness is totally beside the point. "But I still don't see Spirit!" "You are aware of your not seeing Spirit, and *that* awareness is itself Spirit!"

You can practice mindfulness, because there is forgetfulness; but you cannot practice awareness, because there is only awareness. In mindfulness, you pay attention to the present moment. You try to "be here now." But pure awareness is the present state of awareness *before* you try to do *anything* about it. Trying to "be here now" requires a future moment in which you will then be mindful; but pure awareness is *this* moment before you try anything. You are already aware; you are already enlightened. You might not be always already mindful, but you are always already enlightened.

The pointing out instructions go on like this, sometimes for a few minutes, sometimes for a few hours, sometimes for a few days, until you "get" it, until you recognize your own True Face, the "face you had before your parents were born" (that is, timeless and eternal, prior to birth and death). And it is a recognition, not a cognition. It's like peering into the window of a department store, and seeing a vague figure staring back at you. You let the figure come into focus, and with a shock realize that it's your own reflection in the window. The entire world, according to these traditions, is nothing but the reflection of your own Self, reflected in the mirror of your own awareness. See? You are already looking right at it. . . .

Thus, according to these traditions, basic awareness is not hard to reach, it's impossible to avoid, and the so-called "paths" to the Self are really obstacle courses. They prevent the recognition as long as they are engaged. There is *only* the Self, there is *only* God. As Ramana himself put it:

> There is neither creation nor destruction,
> Neither destiny nor free will;
> Neither path nor achievement;
> This is the final truth.

I should point out that although Dzogchen itself does not particularly recommend meditation, by the time you are introduced to the Dzogchen teachings, you are expected to have practiced to some degree most of the first eight stages of practice, which are all stages of meditation. And it is maintained that meditation is very important and very beneficial for increasing virtuous states of mind, powers of concentration, mindfulness, and insight, and meditation must be pursued vigorously as a training. It just has nothing to do with enlightenment per se. Any enlightenment that can be attained is not real enlightenment. Meditation is a training, and Dzogchen points out that training completely misses the point right in the first step, because it makes you try to move away from your present and prior awareness.

My own teacher would meet with students, and they would come in saying things like, "I just had the most amazing experience. My ego just disappeared and I was one with everything, and time evaporated and it was wonderful!"

And the Master would say, "That's nice. But tell me, did that experience have a beginning in time?"

"Yeah, it happened yesterday, I was just sitting there and all of a sudden . . ."

"That which has a beginning in time is not real. Come back when you recognize that which is already present, that which is not an experience, that which does not have a beginning in time. It has to be something you are already aware of. Come back when you recognize that *beginningless* state. You are giving me beginnings."

"Oh."

But once recognition has taken place in the student, *then* meditation is used to stabilize the recognition and to help bring it to all aspects of life. And this, indeed, is the hard part. There's a saying in Dzogchen: "Recognizing your True Face is easy; living it is hard." It was exactly these "living it" routines that I had begun practicing.

Treya's own practice was bringing her to a similar understanding, since she was working most with the teachings of Sri Ramana Maharshi, who is also my own favorite single teacher. And in particular she was realizing that the mystical experience she had when she was thirteen—and that she described as "the guiding symbol of my life"—was actually a glimpse or recognition of the everpresent Self, which is one with "all space." And that in dissolving into "all space"—which happened when she was thirteen, and which was happening in her meditation—she was really just rehearsing her own death.

I love the melting into spaciousness, into emptiness, of my meditation. Ken was saying this morning that just recognizing that spaciousness, or that identity with all space, is the only thing he is drawn to in terms of practice. This is my own strong pull as well. That immediately made me think of my experience as a thirteen-year-old, and I realized what a real help that is going to be for me at the point that I am dying. Because that was an experience and not a teaching, not something that I've learned or been told is true, but that just came to me spontaneously. I really think it will help me a great deal in terms of letting go, because I see myself expanding and eventually mixing completely evenly with all the atoms and molecules of the entire universe, being one with it all, dissolving back into it, realizing that as my real nature. This sometimes happens in meditation, but again, my original experience was unbidden, and therefore I really trust it. Somehow that's extremely comforting to me.

Gonzales warned us that as the lung tumors began to dissolve, Treya might find breathing difficult. In fact, some people on the enzyme program actually cough up dead and dissolved tumors, he told us, and indeed Bob Doty—our friend from the Janker Klinik who had recently had a relapse and was on the Kelley program—called us and told us he had coughed up a huge piece of what looked like liver, which amazed his doctors. And, we were told, if Treya found breathing difficult, she might have to go on portable oxygen.

Her orthodox doctors told her that she was dying of lung cancer and would soon have to go on portable oxygen.

In late October, Treya went on portable oxygen. We had a small oxygen tank that we refilled from a large barrel-sized container, and Treya carried this tank around with her everywhere she went. She wasn't fond of the arrangement, but did it slow her down? Each morning when I came up from my meditation I would pass her on her exercise walker machine, tank strapped to her back, walking at least three miles each day, passionate equanimity, joyful determination, written all over her face.

Her orthodox doctors quizzed her closely about her fear of death, because they were convinced that she was using the Kelley program as a massive denial of death and a refusal to follow their recommendations (which, of course, they admitted—when pressed—wouldn't work anyway). I remember one conversation vividly.

"Treya, are you afraid of dying?"

"No, I'm really not afraid of dying, but I am afraid of bad pain. I don't want to die in pain."

"Well, let me assure you we can handle that. Modern pain measures are very sophisticated. It's been a long time since I've had a patient die in pain, so I promise you that won't happen. But you're not afraid of dying?"

"No."

"Why not?"

"Because I feel that I'm in touch with a part of me, a part of everybody, that is just all that is. When I die, I'll just dissolve back into that. That's not frightening."

She was so obviously speaking her truth, I could see this doctor finally believed her. Then he got quite emotional; it was extremely touching.

"I believe you, Treya. You know, I've never had a patient like you. You have no self-pity. No self-pity. I've never seen anything like it. It's a real honor to work with you, may I tell you that?"

Treya reached out and embraced him, and with a big smile said simply, "Thank you."

"Have you seen the other rooms?" I say. "They are absolutely beautiful! One had these amazing crystals and mountains, and there was this jungle and, oh, did you see the stars? I think they're stars. Anyway—hey, where were you? Where were you when I was getting the tour?"

"Here. And am I ever glad you're here, too. You always promised you'd find me, you know, and I was beginning to wonder."

"Yeah, well, that's some cup of tea you went to make. I'd hate to see what happened if you made a whole pot."

"Who is he?"

"Don't know. Thought he was your friend."

"I can't see anything," she says. "Is there somebody there?"

"I'm not sure. I have a theory. I think this is a dream. We're in each other's dream. Is that possible? Anyway, I've just been going along with the guy, or the whatever it is. Just do what it says. It's kinda fun, actually."

"Listen very carefully to me," the Figure says. "I want you to hold hands and come this way."

"How?" I ask. "I mean, you've been giving instructions—push with your mind, that kind of thing. So how?"

"Just hold hands, and come this way."

Treya and I look at each other.

"Trust me," it says. "You must trust me."

"Why?"

"Because those stars were not stars, and because this dream is not a dream. Do you know what that means?"

"I told you, I don't know what any of this means. So why don't you . . ."

"I know what it means," Treya says. "Here, give me your hand."

21

GRACE AND GRIT

September/October 1988
Boulder

Dear friends,

The wind is blowing outside, quite mightily and unfortunately, because a large fire is raging in Left Hand Canyon, just over from our
house. Earlier reports said although the fire is out of control only a few
cabins were endangered, but the latest news flash said seventy-six homes
have been evacuated, primarily because of the smoke. They've been
unable to drop chemicals on the fire because of the high winds. We can
see flames quite clearly from our deck on top of the ridge and fear that
we, too, may have to evacuate. We'll probably load the car with a few
essentials before going to bed, half expecting to get an unwelcome
call in the middle of the night. And when will the fires in Yellowstone
end?

I find that situation highlights how I just don't get as upset by "bad" or
potentially bad events as I once did. I think being buffeted by so much
good then bad then uncertain news over the past five years since my initial
diagnosis has taught me something about moving with the tide, not
resisting, letting things be as they are, watching how things develop and
unfold with a certain calm but interested detachment, not trying to
envision or force a certain result but just watching and participating when
appropriate as the "isness" of life unfolds. If we have to evacuate, we have

377

to evacuate; I'll deal with that when and if it happens, and for now I'll watch the flames bright in the dark night, watch the red glow over the ridge beyond, and send good wishes to those who are evacuated.

Ken likes to say that the work we do on ourselves, whether it's psychological or spiritual, is not meant to get rid of the waves in the ocean of life but for us to learn how to surf. Under duress, to be sure, I've learned a lot about riding the waves. In Aspen last month I was reminded of how I used to be—how important everything seemed, what a "meaning and purpose" junkie I once was, how intensely I tried to figure everything out, how my new age perspective said clearly that everything was purposeful and planned and made sense. I remember a prayer that was popular at Findhorn and ended "Let the plan of love and light work out." Buddhism and having cancer have taught me so much about living with "don't know," about not trying to control the flow of life, about allowing things to be as they are, about finding peace among the upsets and disappointments of this life through letting be. I remember how attached I was to doing, how much my sense of self-worth depended on what I did, how busy I kept myself all the time, how I needed to fill each moment with activity.

During the Windstar Symposium I couldn't help but think of the Windstar student summer programs I ran (two-month residential for-credit programs). I thought with some regret of how full I kept those students' schedules, as if the program could only be good if they were busy and learning all the time (*my* neurosis imposed on them). I feel now like I didn't leave them much room to breathe, to integrate that rich, varied experience, to simply *be*, to enjoy each other, to bask in the beauty, colors, crisp air and starry nights of the Colorado mountains. I also saw, of course, how consistently I have done the same thing to myself over the years.

But, I'm learning. I've decided this next year, when the focus is totally on healing and the enzyme program, will be my "little old lady" year. I will sleep as late as I can and do as little as I can get away with and stop for a quiet cup of tea every afternoon. Travel as little as I can—only for treatment, retreats, and to see my family—since I hate the stress of packing and worrying about forgetting things and doing coffee enemas in a strange environment. I will build fires on cold winter evenings and curl up with Ken and the puppies to the crackle of the fire. I will drink my tea and look at the mountains rather than drink my tea and read. I will try to emulate the gentler rhythms of life at Findhorn (not the frantic, meeting-crammed dimension, which I think was introduced largely by the many Americans there, but the more civilized, slower British rhythm) where there's time to rest and meditate and reflect and visit with friends and walk in the garden and savor the late afternoon sunshine.

I think of a recent evening in Aspen spent sitting around a crackling fire in front of Bruce's cabin in Aspen, when Kairos crawled into Ken's lap and then mine to stay warm against the mountain chill. We were teaching a British visitor the technique for roasting marshmallows, and I will always remember her saying that her first impression of Americans was how frantic they seemed to her, with all their busyness and rushing around.

That's the kind of American I've always been, rather compulsive about "getting things done." I've always felt it was terribly important to contribute my energy and do the "right thing." For example, I was the kind of camper who, when we arrived at the campsite and most everyone else scattered to go play, I dutifully helped gather sticks and wood for the fire, helped unpack the horses, helped get the tents set up. I was almost always one of the "Honor Girls" commended at the end of the summer and awarded a silver and turquoise pin to add to the other rewards. Such a good little girl! But now, under the pressure of this illness and the tiredness that results from taking the enzymes, I feel my life becoming simpler, clearer, more spacious—airy rather than heavy. I find it easier and easier to get rid of "stuff," to give away all my photography equipment for example, instead of holding on to the possibility I might get into it again someday, to pass on clothes that once gave me pleasure and give away trinkets and fringed scarves and jewelry to the children of my best friends. There's room in my cupboards and my closets! Life feels less dense, less opaque, more airy and transparent and enjoyable—as the busyness to prove my self-worth subsides, as I give away more and more old "stuff," as errands get postponed and postponed and postponed again yet life doesn't unravel, as I spend quiet time with a cup of tea and a dog at my feet on the deck in the sunshine savoring the peaceful, expansive, wooded view that unrolls in front of me and constantly changes from dawn to dusk to moonlight.

September 26

I guess this next section could be titled "When Strangers Want to Help You—Don't Be Afraid to Say No; or, Learning to Trust Your Psychic Immune System!"

379

I don't know why I worry so much about people with cancer being made to feel bad or guilty or inadequate by people who think they've got it all figured out and are themselves invulnerable, but I do. Certainly it's because I've felt guilty and confused by all the advice and disguised judgment I have received from often well-intentioned people. The roots must go back to my strong feelings of inadequacy in childhood; I suppose I want to protect that little girl in myself and in everyone else, to help her see her own strengths, help her to sort out what's true about her failings and to recognize what's true about her strengths. And I suppose I want to do this for the vulnerable child within each of us, and particularly for the child within made even more vulnerable by virtue of now having cancer. "Don't listen to what everyone who thinks they understand has to say about you," I want to say. "Trust in yourself, filter their comments through your own understanding, and don't be afraid to reject those that you find are harmful or disempowering, those that weaken you and make you afraid or unsure of yourself. Keep your psychic immune system operating so you can accept helpful help and reject damaging 'help.'"

For example:

A friend of mine introduced me to two healers during the symposium. The first offered a free session, was quite gentle, and I trusted her. I somehow knew she wouldn't hurt or manipulate me for her own purposes. I had a second, very valuable session with her and the next day felt so energetic that I wanted to go dancing. (Ken and I did, at a disco that night!) And oh, how I ached to go skiing, snaking down the mountain, the wind blowing in my face!

The second woman, someone I had actually met briefly some years earlier, was a psychologist who ran est-type workshops. When I saw her first she was with my best friend Linda [Conger]—this was a brief break between speakers—and I was jabbering happily away with Linda about a dream I'd had the night before. This woman suddenly stopped me and said, forcefully, "Are you aware of a crying child inside at this moment?" I said "No, I feel happy right now." She said, "Oh, but there is. I sense her quite clearly, she's about two or three. And I sense a tremendous violence within you." "Anger?" I asked. "No, violence, a raging violence, something much stronger than anger." Well, there was nothing more to say because the next session was beginning. She later asked if what she had said was OK and my nice girl said, sure.

It took me until that evening to get in touch with how angry I was—at her! I took her aside the next day and explained as clearly as I could that whether her insight was true or not was not the point. The point was that I felt put down and disempowered and violated by her. I had not asked her to be my therapist, had never invited her in to my private world. There was no trust established between us, hardly an introduction. And, I tried to explain to her, she dumped this on me in a totally inappropriate situation. Moreover, she set it up for her to have the power and to be right—I think it would be a rare person who would have answered her question with a yes in that context. The whole scene made it very clear to me that she was not a therapist to be trusted; the exact opposite of my experience with the first woman. I'm glad my psychic immune system was working, but I wish it hadn't taken so long to kick in! Again, what she said may be true, I don't know, but the way she chose to communicate indicated clearly that she cared more about being powerful and right than about helping someone gain insight.

The first woman, the woman I trusted from the beginning, also runs weekend programs. I decided to go to one but immediately changed my mind when I spoke to one of her assistants. Again, I think my psychic immune system was working that day—the assistant I spoke to would call it resistance. The assistant suggested I get clear about what I wanted to work on and my goals for the weekend, and suggested I might feel resistance coming up (one's psychic immune system is often and, in my opinion, wrongly labeled resistance, a hard label to shed since efforts in that direction are often seen as only more resistance). Well, my resistance/ psychic immune system flared into action quickly when she said, "Well, if you have cancer you must have something eating away at you inside. Can you stand to face the truth?"

Ken was on the other line. He rarely gets really angry, but he blew up at this woman. I don't remember what he said exactly, something like, "What's eating her, ma'am, is assholes like you who don't have the faintest fuck of an idea what you're talking about." Anyway, he hung up the phone. I was thinking, "Oh God, please spare me from these simplistic interpretations. Is being around people like this going to help me, I asked, or hurt me?" I tried to explain to her just how much violence and aggression her seemingly innocent comment contained, but it was kind of hard after Ken's loving display! He says he's just had it with those people, and I agree, but I'm still trying to find ways to reach them and show them how much they are hurting people. Anyway, I hung up the phone, realizing this was definitely not for me.

I found that some of Jeremy Hayward's comments on Buddhist education (in a talk given at Naropa Institute) related to this whole issue. He said:

"From the Buddhist point of view there are certain essential marks of human existence which go altogether beyond, or before, culture. One of these is that all humans suffer. All of us, in the secrecy of our domestic security, are frightened . . . it is a fact that at any moment, as yet undetermined and certainly unknown, each and every one of us is going to die. And however slow, or however fast, the process of death may be in terms of illness or old age, the moment of death is sudden. . . . When, occasionally, we let this touch us it is very frightening. And this does not depend on culture. It is as true for the Inuit as for the Australian. . . . This is universal. . . . So, recognizing that fear and running from that fear—this balance continually goes on. Recognizing it is fearlessness. When you recognize it, when you stay with it, which means that you let yourself quake, feel the quaking, then there is fearlessness. And then running from it, in fear of fear, is cowardice. This is the constant play of mind. . . . At that moment, a realization might dawn of awareness encompassing both fear and fearlessness—joy . . . or confidence. So when you stay with that terror then you might discover confidence or joy, which comes from recognizing the indestructibility of awareness. . . .

"So the fundamental fact, then, is fear and fearlessness which joined bring confidence and joy. . . . The ground of humanness is goodness, in that sense of fundamental joy and fundamental confidence. Therefore we are free from guilt, free of sin."

He goes on to say that the basis of Buddhist education is absence of guilt, the basis is the inherent foundation of goodness. We need to "let go of guilt, let go of sin, let go of blame, let go of thinking that we made a mistake; stop looking for the problems that have to be corrected rather than the goodness and intelligence that can be nourished. . . . Recognizing the fear as well as the fearlessness in others, and helping others to recognize their fear and to discover fearlessness, this is compassion."

Now, as far as these workshops go, I fully recognize that they might be just the right thing for many people. But there are reports and criticisms beginning to filter to the surface of these workshops that they are harmful to some, sometimes coercive, and not based on compassion. I mention this series of events because I think people with cancer, in their search for a cure and in their attempt to investigate all possibilities, might be especially vulnerable to what these workshops promise. The woman on the phone had said that in the workshop I would find my "bottom line" and that would completely cure me. I'm glad Ken didn't hear that!

But in the maze of all these possibilities, so many of them unproven, I keep coming back to one thing, whether it's choice of physical treatment or choice of psychological work—the individuals must trust themselves in making a choice and never let themselves be coerced or unduly influenced by the preferences of others. I want to help people feel empowered to say "No, that's not for me" or "No, you're not the therapist for me" without always being afraid that some sort of unexamined resistance might underlie their choice. My message is simple, but hard-won: Trust yourself, trust your psychic immune system. Take time to find your center, the solid ground inside your being, do what works for you to stay in touch, whether it's meditation or visualization or active imagining or therapy or walks in the woods or journal writing or dream analysis or simply practicing mindfulness in your daily life. Listen to yourself, and take your own best advice!

God, I can't believe the state of mind I was in when I made decisions in my early days with cancer—the pressure, the fear, the frantic feeling, the confusion, the lack of knowledge—and I look back in wonder at how I motored ahead, being strong, but not taking the time to develop a relationship with my own inner wisdom and thus completely missing the sense of calm and peace that I feel now.

October 10

And how are the enzymes working? Fantastic! according to Dr. Gonzales's "funny little test." And apart from the tiredness, I feel quite good, quite joyful. Most of the time, that is!

Now, the view from the other side is not so good. All of my cancer markers are up in the last six weeks so my oncologist ordered another CAT scan just recently. He called early one morning to report that all the tumors had grown about 30%; would we please come in immediately to discuss the options? I didn't really panic (well, a little . . .) since I wanted to talk to Dr. Gonzales first and I remembered what a woman I spoke to had said about her bone scans. "They look worse than when I started the program," she said. "My doctors don't know what to think of it. . . . I had tremendous bone pain at the beginning and now I have no pain, so I believe what shows on the CAT scan is the healing reaction Dr. Gonzales talks about." Thank goodness we reached him that very morning. He was quite calm and confirmed that he thought this was also happening to me, that the enzymes were eating the cancer and the immune system was throwing all sorts of things into the battle, like macrophages, etc. A CAT scan picks up activity, he said, and it can't differentiate between growth, a healing reaction, or even scar tissue. "At least once a week," he said, "I have to talk one of my patients out of surgery or chemotherapy because their test results are worse." He asked me if my symptoms were any worse. I said no, not really, certainly nothing at all noticeable, which was reassuring since tumor growth of 30% should make me feel something. "OK," I said, "I sure hope you're right. But I'm not going to count on it or get my hopes up until you see the CAT scans yourself and say you still think it's a healing reaction."

Ken and I dashed off to look at the CAT scans; they looked terrible, but everything looked worse to roughly the same degree, which would seem to support Dr. Gonzales's interpretation, and there was no increased displacement in the brain (because of the large tumor and swelling in my right brain, it has pushed the left side a bit out of place). My symptoms are relatively minor—waviness in the left quarter of my left eye which makes me a little confused at times about what's there in my peripheral vision, occasional slight headaches, a strange feeling of fullness after meditation (so I spend more time doing yoga) or after sitting still for awhile while reading, an occasional sense of being slightly out of balance or disoriented. I sometimes have intense pain in the back of my eyes, which I attribute to the swelling. Since I've started sleeping on more pillows, however, this problem has almost completely gone away.

We called Dr. Gonzales after he had looked at the CAT scans and he confirmed his initial opinion about what they actually showed. He said he called in the radiologist, who has seen this many times, and the radiologist definitely thought, based on his prior experience with this situation, that what looked like growth was actually an inflammatory reaction due to tumor necrosis (or death).

So Dr. Gonzales advised me to carry on and I decided—especially since my other options are so completely uninviting (continuous chemotherapy, basically, though different drugs could be used)—that this was worth a shot. Dr. Gonzales talks confidently about the possibility of a cure, too, so it's worth the risk to me. In fact, I don't see it as risking much to turn down a treatment that only promises me some months and which I know will make me feel not so great. We'll do another CAT scan in mid-December, after I've been on the program close to six months. Dr. Gonzales says 60–70% of his patients show an improvement on CAT scans after six months. It would certainly be a nice Christmas present to get that kind of news!

I told Dr. Gonzales I admired him for sticking his neck out like this; it certainly demonstrates his faith in the program. Michael Lerner recently told me that there's something of a Gonzales boom going on around the country these days since both Patrick McGrady and Michael Schacter in New York are recommending him. Michael also said he'd heard nothing negative about him so far and, although Kelley himself seemed a combination of charlatan and healer, he met many people in small towns in Canada who got well on the Kelley program.

The enzymes still make me feel tired. I definitely look forward to cycling off of them twice a month (I do ten days on, then five days off taking no enzymes or vitamins to give my body a rest). I feel pretty good on day five!

Although there are two women at CSC who have done well on continuous chemotherapy—something like twenty months and twenty-four months—they both look like their constitutions are stronger than mine. I just have a sense it's not the right approach for me. I simply don't like the idea of getting weaker and weaker each month—even if I feel relatively well, clearly my body will be taking a beating and getting ground down a bit more each time. I remember how much worse my sixth chemotherapy treatment was compared to the first. I'm just glad there's another option out there that might work and that I have some confidence in. I *always* remind myself, however, that there are no clear statistics about this, that it may not work in spite of Gonzales's confidence (Dr. Scheef sounded very confident too), and that the danger is in beginning to cling to or count on some kind of positive outcome; what will be will be.

It looks like I'll be going on oxygen soon to help my lungs. More on that in a moment. . . .

Meanwhile, to turn to more trivial matters, my hair is growing in but very, very slowly. The combination of radiation and chemotherapy slows the whole process down. I wouldn't mind, really, except for this large area on the top of my head where the hair is growing in quite sparsely. This is the area where the radiation from each side overlaps so the skin gets, in effect, twice as much radiation as elsewhere on your head. They can correct for this near the end of the treatments, but by the time I remembered to ask it was too late, I only had one treatment to go. I don't understand why correcting for this isn't standard; I mean, people who have brain radiation have enough to go through without also having to deal with a large balding spot. I have enough hair elsewhere to go without a scarf or hat, but the thin area bothers me so I usually wear a baseball cap to cover it. If I survive and if this continues to be a problem, I'll seriously consider doing what a couple of my male friends have done [hair transplant]!

I continue to talk to people who have cancer on the phone, which is a bittersweet pleasure—I enjoy giving them a chance to talk, I enjoy sharing any insights of mine that seem relevant, but my heart breaks to hear their stories—single mothers, husbands who've left, ten years clear and suddenly a recurrence, happy lives constricted and contorted (and in many cases deepened) by this disease. Lately many of them call to ask my opinion of the Janker Klinik. This is a hard one to answer because I greatly respect Dr. Scheef but, although I can't say anything definite about the enzymes yet, Dr. Scheef's program is still chemotherapy, still quite toxic, and doesn't usually result in a cure. Also, although the results I got were less than we had hoped for, Scheef was not able to do his normal program with me because of my cold. Then of course you have to consider the expense and stress and time involved in going to Germany for so long, and you better have a support person as sharp as Ken or you're really in trouble. When all these elements are factored in, my endorsement comes out rather lukewarm. Dr. Gonzales says they do good work but he would only recommend such an extreme approach if someone only had three or four months left, i.e. to buy time for another treatment (presumably his!).

I had some wonderful massages while in Aspen, but what I especially liked is the prayer Janet began with each time (she is a former nun). It is from the Baha'i tradition, the short healing prayer, and it goes like this:

Thy name is my healing O my God,
Remembrance of thee is my remedy,

386

Nearness to Thee is my hope,
Love for thee is my companion.
Thy mercy to me is my healing and my succor
In both this world and the world to come.
Thou art verily the all bountiful,
The all knowing,
The all wise.

"Surrender to God" continues to be my mantra of remembrance.
Ramana Maharshi says "Surrender to Him and accept His will whether
He appears or vanishes. Await His pleasure. If you want Him to do as you
want, it is not surrender but command. You cannot ask Him to obey you
and yet think you have surrendered. . . . Leave everything entirely up to
Him. . . ." I find that the more I explore this quality of surrender in
myself—which I used to consider quite weak—the more I see that it
leads me to the same place as practicing equanimity, accepting things as
they are without trying to control or change them. Once again, Buddhism has helped strip away some of my reactivity to Christian terminology so I can recognize the common truths and teachings.

I really like the "always already" quality of Ramana Maharshi's
teaching. That we are always, already enlightened, always, already one
with Self, always already one with All Space. He says:

"People will not understand the bare and simple truth—the truth of
their everyday, ever present and eternal awareness. That is the truth
of the Self. Is there any one not aware of the Self? Yet, they do not
even like to hear of it, whereas they are eager to know what lies
beyond—heaven and hell and reincarnation. Because they love mystery and not the plain truth, religions pamper them—only to bring
them round to the Self in the end. Moreover, much as you may
wander you must return ultimately to the Self, so why not abide in
the Self here and now?

"But Grace is there all along. Grace is the Self. It is not something to
be acquired. All that is necessary is to recognize its existence. . . .

"If realization is not eternal it is not worth having. Therefore, what
we seek is not something that must begin to exist but only what is
eternal and present right now, present as your own awareness."

Effort: "One goes through all sorts of austerities to become what one
already is. All effort is simply to get rid of the mistaken impression that
one is limited and bound by the woes of *samsara* (this life).

"Now it is impossible for you to be without effort. When you go deeper, it is impossible for you to make effort."

October 20

I recently completed my second "Clean Sweep" and "Liver Flush." Very interesting to flush out bad things lurking in my colon and my gall bladder! This is part of the Kelley program, and since numerous friends have expressed interest in doing the two cleansing programs, I'm including the instructions and information on where you can order what you need. For me the Clean Sweep began as a process where for months I often passed what they call "mucus ropes" or strings in my stools. The first time I did the Liver Flush it was a failure, I think because I didn't drink apple juice. The second time I upped my insulin for the five days so I could eat a lot of apples, and ultimately passed thirty large gallstones (pea to large garbanzo bean size) and well over thirty smaller ones. And, yes, they're distinctively green just like I've always heard but never seen! A lot of people think everyone should do each of these once a year to maintain colon health. At the end of this process I joked to Ken "My life has been reduced to examining my stools!"

As for Ken, he does almost everything for me now, me in my little old lady mode. He's here for me in every way. He'll be embarrassed by this but I keep calling him "my champion." He cooks for me, he watches over me, he takes care of my diet, he gets me to the doctors, he helps me with my insulin, he even helps bathe me when I'm tired. He gets up at five each morning so he can meditate before he devotes the rest of the day to helping me. Something really wonderful is happening in his meditation. When he said to me that he had learned how to serve, his actions are proving it royally! When I tell him how sorry I am that cancer has "ruined" his career, he looks at me with his big browns and says, "I'm the luckiest guy in the world." What a sweetie!

How's the rest of my body doing?

Treya didn't have a chance to finish the letter, because she had gone blind in her left eye. Right about the time that she went on oxygen, I began noticing that she didn't respond well to things in her left visual field. Tests confirmed it: the tumors in her brain were affecting the optic center, and Treya had, probably permanently, lost all vision in her left eye.

Whether the damage was due to growing tumor or dying tumor, we couldn't tell. Of course, the orthodox said growing, Gonzales said dying. But for the moment, that wasn't the point; either way, the brain, not the lungs, had become our immediate concern; either way, the mass in the brain was expanding. Treya started taking Decadron, a powerful steroid that would control the brain swelling for perhaps a month or two. At the end of that time, it would cease being effective. At the end of that time, Treya's brain tissue would continue being smashed and destroyed. Rapid loss of function would ensue, and the pain would grow unbearable, making continuous morphine delivery a necessity.

It was now a simple race against time. If the enzymes were working, they would have to begin to turn the situation around within a month or two. And Treya's body would have to be able to dispose of the wastes in the brain, whether caused by growing or dying tumor cells, because if not, the pressure build-up in the brain would kill.

Treya listened to all this being explained—in the same dry terms I have repeated—and didn't blink once. "If this is a race," she finally said, "then let's get going."

Outside the doctor's office, I expected Treya to react, perhaps cry. But she just put her little oxygen tank on, got in the car, smiled at me and said, "Home, James."

Because Treya was now on oxygen almost continuously, including during sleep, we had her hooked up to a fifty-foot-long tether connected to the large oxygen barrel. There were now sixty spots on her lungs (new spots or old small ones flaring up due to enzymes?); her liver was swelling up, and now had pushed almost entirely across her abdomen, cramping her intestines (new liver cancer, or inflammatory reaction?); the pressure on her brain was slowly increasing; she still had to check her blood sugar five or six times a day, and give herself insulin shots; she had to take one hundred twenty pills a day, give herself six enemas, wake herself up in the middle of the night for more pills and enemas. And there she was, each day, getting on her walker machine and walking two or three miles, oxygen line over her shoulder, Mozart blaring in the background.

Her doctor was right: she had no self-pity, not an ounce. She had no intention of giving up, of feeling sorry for herself, of backing off in the least. She wasn't afraid of dying, by now I was convinced of that. But she wasn't about to roll over and play dead, either.

We talked about a very famous Zen koan that her attitude reminded me of. A student asked a Zen Master, "What is absolute truth?" And the Zen Master said only, "Walk on!"

It was during this period that Treya and I seemed to develop a genuinely psychic bond; and by "psychic" I mean paranormal (ESP). I personally don't put a lot of store in psychic events per se. (The "psychic level," as I use the term, simply indicates the beginning dimensions of the transpersonal domain, which may or may not involve actual psychic events; but they have nothing to do with its definition.) I'm sure they exist, they just don't interest me much, and in any event they have little to do with mysticism per se, and the charlatan "psychics" have given the whole field a bad name. So I'm a little reluctant to report all this.

But by this time every ounce of my energy, every second of my time, was for Treya. I began to anticipate her every need, so much so that I seemed to intuit her needs or desires before she spoke them, and sometimes, according to her, before she thought them. "Could you make me a three-minute egg?" "It's already in progress, sweetheart." "Today I think I need seventeen units of insulin." "It's right there by your leg." That type of thing. We both noticed it, talked about it. Perhaps it was just a series of lightning-fast, subconscious, logical deductions—the standard empiricist reply—but too many of the instances were illogical and unprecedented. No, something was going on. All I know is that it felt like there was just one mind, and one heart, in that house.

And why should that surprise me?

Treya was pretty much confined to the house by then, so we had her acupuncturist make house calls. His name was Warren Bellows, and he worked in conjunction with Michael Broffman. Warren was an old friend of Treya from Findhorn who was now living in Boulder. Warren was a godsend. Wise, gentle, caring, with a positively warped sense of humor—something for each of us. This was crucially important, because Treya's treatments took up to two hours daily. It was also important to me, because these two hours were the only time I had to take care of any personal business.

One evening as Warren was working with Treya, she began to feel extremely ill. She had horrible headaches, her whole body was shaking, she was having visual problems in her good eye. I called Gonzales at home. He had seen all the latest evidence, and he and his associates, all trained physicians, continued to be of the strongest opinion that all of Treya's symptoms were consonant with tumor decay and inflammation. She was having a toxic reaction he said. Take several enemas, work with the acupuncture, take an Epsom salt bath—anything to help cleanse the body out a little. Treya felt better just talking to him.

I did not feel better. I called the emergency room at Boulder Medical and asked them to set up an emergency brain scan, and called her local oncologist and asked him to be ready. Treya continued to deteriorate, and, fearing a brain seizure, I strapped the oxygen on her and rushed her to the ER. Fifteen minutes later she was on high doses of Decadron and morphine. The swelling in her brain was out of control, and, indeed she would have soon gone into convulsions.

A few days later, on November 10, with everyone's agreement (including Nick's), Treya went in for brain surgery to have the large mass removed.

Her doctors told her she would be in the hospital for at least five days, maybe more. Three days later, with her little oxygen tank strapped on her back and her Mütze on her head, she walked out of the hospital; and, at her insistence, we forthwith walked several blocks to the Wrangler restaurant for a barbecue chicken. The waitress asked if she was a model—"You are so beautiful!"—and where did she get that lovely cap? Treya whipped out her glucoscan meter, checked her blood sugar, gave herself an insulin shot, and polished off the chicken.

The brain surgery left Treya, not so much in pain, as in general and often agonizing body discomfort. But she stuck to her program with passionate equanimity: the pills, the enemas, the insulin, the diet, the clean sweeps, and the liver flushes. And each day, on her walker, cranking out the miles, oxygen line behind her.

The surgery also left her virtually blind. She could still see out of her right eye, but her entire visual field was fragmented. She tried to do some of her art work, but she couldn't coordinate the lines; the results looked like something I might come up with. "Not so good, huh?" is all she said.

What she didn't like, however, was that she could no longer read her spiritual books. So I got flash cards and in large bold letters wrote out dozens of her favorite "pith" phrases from her favorite teachings. Things like "Allow the self to uncoil in the vast expanse of all space," and, very simply, "Who am I?" These cards she carried with her everywhere, and I would see her, at various times of the day, sitting and smiling and slowly reading her cards, moving them around in her visual field, waiting for the lines to slowly form recognizable words.

We now had less than a month before the Decadron would wear off. Family and friends, assuming she was dying, all came by. The half of me that assumed she was dying wanted desperately to see Kalu Rinpoche, "our" teacher. Treya wanted me to see him, too, very much, and so she kept a stiff upper lip as she encouraged me to go, only to write in her journal the day I left: "I'm so miserable, I'm so unhappy, I hurt so much. If I tell him that he wouldn't leave. I love him so much—does he know how much I love him?"

I was gone for three days; Linda stayed with Treya. The half of me that thought Treya was dying wanted to reestablish our link with this extraordinary and enlightened and gentle man. All of the great wisdom traditions maintain that the actual moment of death is an extremely important and precious opportunity, and for this reason: At the moment of death, the person has dropped the gross physical body, and therefore the higher dimensions—the subtle and the causal—immediately flash in the deceased's awareness. If the person can recognize these higher and spiritual dimensions, then the person can acknowledge immediate enlightenment, and do so much more easily than when in the dense and obstructing physical body.

I'll be very specific here, because this is exactly the type of training that Treya had been practicing in preparation for her possible death. This explanation is based on the Tibetan system, which seems to be the most complete, but it is in essential agreement with the mystical traditions the world over.

The human being has three major levels or dimensions: gross (the body), subtle (the mind), and causal (spirit). During the dying process, the lower levels of the Great Chain dissolve first, starting with the body, starting with sensation and perception. When the body dissolves (ceases functioning), the subtler dimensions of mind and soul come to the fore, and then, at the actual moment of death, when all levels dissolve, pure causal Spirit flashes forth in the person's awareness. If the person can recognize this Spirit as his or her own true nature, then enlightenment is realized on the spot, and the person returns permanently to Godhead, as Godhead.

If recognition does not take place, then the person (the soul) enters the intermediate state, the "bardo," which is said to last up to a few months. The subtle level emerges, and then eventually the gross level emerges, and the person is then reborn in a physical body to begin a new life, taking with them, in their soul, whatever wisdom and virtue (but not specific memories) they may have accumulated in the previous life.

Whatever we might think about the notion of reincarnation or the bardo or afterlife states, this much seems certain: If you at all believe that some part of you partakes of the divine, if you at all believe that you have access to some sort of Spirit that transcends your mortal body in any sense, then the moment of death is crucial, because at that point the mortal body is *gone*, and if there is *anything* that remains, that is the time to find out, yes?

Of course, near-death experiences and near-death research seems to support this claim. But all I would like to emphasize is that there are specific meditation exercises that precisely rehearse this entire process of death and dissolution, and these meditative exercises were exactly what Treya was practicing when she described "dissolving into all space."

I wanted to reconnect with Kalu so my own mind might be more ready to dissolve or expand and help Treya with her own actual dissolution, as she and I had practiced. The traditions maintain that an enlightened teacher, since his or her mind is already "dissolved" or transcended, can be of enormous help in the dying process if a connection is established between your mind and the teacher's mind. Just being in the teacher's presence can establish this connection, and that is why I had gone to see Kalu.

When I returned, Treya began going through a period of trying to deal with her discomfort, which at times was severe, agonizing. The swelling in her brain was almost unendurable, causing not only pain but wreaking havoc on her emotions. Still, she didn't want any medication—no painkillers, no tranquilizers—it was just another dip on the roller coaster ride. She wanted to be clear so she could witness, so she could be aware, and aware she remained.

Vicky and Kati came to visit us. Late one night Treya called Vicky into her room, and for the next hour or two, in the most agonizing of terms, described to Vicky exactly what was going on with her—the precise sensations, the actual feel, of having a brain tumor slowly destroy all normal functions, detail by gruesome detail. It shook Vicky profoundly; when she came downstairs she was still shaking.

"She wants me to know what it's like, so I can better work with other cancer patients going through the same ordeal. She just gave me a precise map of the whole process so I can use it with others, so I can have more understanding and compassion for what they're going through, so I can help them better. I do not believe this." Treya was doing vipassana on her brain tumor, and describing the results to Vicky so she could use it at CSC.

The aftereffects of the brain surgery, combined with the continued swelling of the tumors in the lungs and brain and liver, were taking a terrible toll on Treya's body. And yet she maintained her program in all aspects and, yes, continued walking several miles a day on her walker. We continued to up her oxygen; we continued to up her Decadron.

We couldn't go home for Christmas, so family members, a few at a time, came to visit us over the holidays. When Rad and Sue left, they pressed this letter into my hand:

Dear Treya and Ken,

Yours is a true love story. Many can share blissful years together with a little adversity thrown in, but your life together started with a major problem that has almost constantly been with you. Your affection and devotion to each other is truly remarkable and each day regardless of the problems seem to grow stronger.

Ken, without you Treya would be completely lost. Your concern about her health, your constant attention to her needs, her aches and pains (and her dogs!) is a source of constant comfort to her and to us. We and she couldn't have picked a better son-in-law.

We hope the cancer has been turned and you, Treya, will be back to normal and in good health. If ever anyone deserves a full recovery it is you. Your attitude, your bravery, is an incredible inspiration to all who have been involved in your illness either by personal contact or through you and your letters. Now in a short time we feel that you will be working with CSC and all the many other organizations that you have been connected with that have as their objective making the world a better and more understanding community. For you, Ken, we hope that you will have time again to pursue your writing and scholarly thought (a lot of which we do not understand!) and give to the world your insight on the potential of the mind and soul.

We hope our visit has been of some help and as you know we and all the family support you both and will drop any and everything if you need us. We know this is going to be an unusual Christmas but it is going to be a good one—maybe not all of us together at the same time but the start of Treya's recovery.

Treya, we love you as a person and as a daughter. Ken, no one could have a better son-in-law or one more devoted to their daughter.

We shed a few tears when writing this because we love you both very much and you are always in our thoughts.

We pray this is the dark before the dawn. You've handled this dreadful illness heroically and we are so proud of you. No one could have a more wonderful daughter than you, Treya. And Ken will always be a member of our family. Christmas won't be the same without you, but you'll be in our hearts.

All our love,
Mom and Dad

On New Year's Day, when we were alone, cuddling on the couch, Treya turned to me and said, "Honey, I think it's time to stop. I don't want to go on. It's not so much that I feel like quitting, it's that, even if the enzymes are working, they aren't going to work fast enough."

Indeed, the Decadron was wearing off, and no matter how much we tried to adjust the dosage, we couldn't get it to work very well. Her discomfort, even agony, was increasing daily; and it certainly would get much, much worse before, and if, it ever got better.

"I'll support you all the way, sweetie. Just tell me what you want, tell me what you need."

"Do you think I have any chance at all?"

I knew Treya had already made up her mind, and as was always the case when that had happened, she wanted me to get behind her all the way, not haggle. "It doesn't look good, does it?" We were quiet for a long time. "I suppose I'd say, let's give it one more week. Just in case. You know, the brain tumor they removed was 90% dead tissue; the enzymes are having a definite effect; there might still be a chance. But you've got to decide. Just tell me what you want, and we'll do it."

She looked directly at me. "OK, one more week. I can do that. One more week."

Treya was very clear, very lucid. We talked in a matter-of-fact way, almost detached and aloof, not because we didn't care, but because we had been through all this so many times before, we had played this scene out in our minds a hundred times.

We got up and started to go upstairs, and, for the first time ever, Treya did not have the strength to walk up the stairs. She sat down on the first step, and dropped her oxygen line, and began softly crying. I picked her up in my arms, and began carrying her up the stairs.

"Oh, honey . . . I had hoped it would never come to this, I didn't want it to come to this, I wanted to be able to walk myself," she said, and buried her head in my shoulder.

"I think it's the most romantic thing in the world. You'd never let me do this under any other circumstances, so come on, let me carry my girl up the stairs."

"You trust him?" I ask Treya.
"I think so."

Treya kept her word, and for one week pushed through the extreme and rapidly growing, even alarming, agony—and stayed right with her program, every single exhausting detail of it. And refused morphine so she could be mindful and aware and present. She held her head high, and she smiled often—and she wasn't faking it. For her it was "Walk on!" And in doing so, I can say without the least exaggeration, she demonstrated a courage and an enlightened equanimity that I have never, *ever*, seen equaled, and doubt I ever will.

The evening that the week ended, she said softly, "I'm going."

At this particular point, all I said was "OK," and I picked her up to carry her upstairs.

"Wait, sweetheart, I want to write something in my journal."

I got her journal, and a pen, and in clear bold words she wrote: "It takes grace, *yes*—and grit!"

She looked at me. "Understand?"

"I think so." I paused for a long time. It wasn't necessary to say what I thought; she knew.

"Come on, gorgeous. Let me carry my girl upstairs."

The noble Goethe had a beautiful line: "All things ripe want to die." Treya was ripe, and she wanted to die. As I watched her write that entry, what I was thinking, what I didn't have to say, was: That summarizes her entire life. Grace and grit. Being and doing. Equanimity and passion. Surrender and will. Total acceptance and fierce determination. Those two sides of her soul, the two sides she had wrestled with all her life, the two sides that she had finally brought together into one harmonious whole— that was the last message she wanted to leave. I had seen her bring those two sides together; I had seen that balanced harmony pervade all aspects of her life; I had seen that passionate equanimity come to define her very soul. Her one, major, overriding life goal, she had accomplished; and that accomplishment had been brutally tested in circumstances that would simply shatter a lesser realization. She had done that; she was ripe with that wisdom; and she wanted to die.

I carried dearest Treya up the stairs for the last time.

22

FOR A RADIANT STAR

Dazed, uncertain, hesitating,
Wings still damp, bent, unfolded,
As if still molded
By darkness, change, confusion,
Bound still
In the emptied chrysalis.

The air stirs.
I tremble,
Feel still within that mold,
Shaped by a form I now
Vaguely sense
Is hollow, empty, spent,
Its work complete.

I only need to move—
One step, another, tentative,
And wait.

Feel the air dry this strange new form,
Watch tissue thin patterns of gold, black, orange,

Unfold into readiness,
Unfurl into openness,
As the air takes me,
Lifts me
Into surprise.

I know not what to do
Yet giddy with instinct
Throw myself out,
Caught by a current unseen,
Swoop low, glide high, dive
Into surrender.

A chrysalis stands now empty,
Drying in the sun,
Constraints forgotten by the life once served.

One day, perhaps, a child will come,
Will ask its mother,
"What strange creature one day lived
In such a tiny home?"

(Treya, 1974)

AND so began the most extraordinary forty-eight hours of our life together. Treya had decided to die. There was no medical reason for her to die at this point. With medication and modest supports, her doctors felt she could live another several months at least, albeit in a hospital, and yes, then she would die. But Treya had made up her mind. She was not going to die like that, in a hospital, with tubes coming out of her and continuous IV morphine drip and the inevitable pneumonia and slow suffocation— all the horrible images that had gone through my mind at Drachenfels. And I had the strangest feeling that, whatever else her reasons, Treya was going to spare all of us that ordeal. She would simply bypass all that, thank you very much, and die peacefully now. But whatever her reasons, I knew that once Treya had made up her mind, then it was done.

I put Treya in bed that evening, and sat down next to her. She had become almost ecstatic. "I'm going, I can't believe it, I'm going. I'm so happy, I'm so happy, I'm so happy." Like a mantra of final release, she kept repeating, "I'm so happy, I'm so happy. . . ."

Her entire countenance lit up. She glowed. And right in front of my eyes her body began to change. Within one hour, it looked to me as if she lost ten pounds. It was as if her body, acquiescing to her will, began to shrink and draw in on itself. She began to shut down her vital systems; she began to die. Within that hour, she was a different being, ready and willing to leave. She was very determined about this, and she was very happy. Her ecstatic response was infectious, and I found myself sharing in her joy, much to my confusion.

Then, rather abruptly, she said, "But I don't want to leave you. I love you so much. I can't leave you. I love you so much." She began crying, sobbing, and I began crying, sobbing, as well. I felt like I was crying all the tears of the past five years, deep tears I had held back in order to be strong for Treya. We talked at length of our love for each other, a love that had made both of us—it sounds corny—a love that had made both of us stronger, and better, and wiser. Decades of growth had gone into our care for each other, and now, faced with the conclusion of it all, we were both overwhelmed. It sounds so dry, but it was the tenderest moment I have ever known, with the only person with whom I could ever have known it.

"Honey, if it's time to go, then it's time to go. Don't worry, I'll find you. I found you before, I promise I'll find you again. So if you want to go, don't worry. Just go."

"You promise you'll find me?"

"I promise."

I should explain that, during the last two weeks, Treya had almost obsessively been going over what I had said to her on the way to our wedding ceremony, five years earlier. I had whispered in her ear: "Where have you been? I've been searching for you for lifetimes. I finally found you. I had to slay dragons to find you, you know. And if anything happens, I will find you again." She looked profoundly at peace. "You promise?" "I promise."

I have no conscious idea why I said that; I was simply stating, for reasons I did not understand, exactly how I felt about our relationship. And it was to this exchange that Treya returned time and again during the last weeks. It seemed to give her a tremendous sense of safety. The world was OK if I kept my promise.

And so she said, at that point, "You promise you'll find me?"

"I promise."

"Forever and forever?"

"Forever and forever."

"Then I can go. I can't believe it. I'm so happy. This has been much harder than I ever thought. It's been so hard. Honey, it's been so hard." "I know, sweetheart, I know." "But now I can go. I'm so happy. I love you so much. I'm so happy."

That night I slept on the acupuncture table in her room. It seems to me that I dreamt of a great luminous cloud of white light, hovering over the house, like the light of a thousand suns blazing on a snowcapped mountain. I say "it seems to me," because now I'm not sure whether it was a dream or not.

When I looked at her early the next morning (Sunday), she had just awoken. Her eyes were clear, she was very alert, and she was very determined: "I'm going. I'm so happy. You'll be there?"

"I'll be there, kid. Let's do it. Let's go."

I called the family. I don't remember exactly what I said, but it was something like, please come as soon as you can. I called Warren, the dear friend who had been helping Treya with acupuncture for the last few months. Again, I don't remember what I said. But I think that my tone said, It's dying time.

The family began arriving fairly early that day, and each member had a chance to have a last open talk with Treya. What I remember most was her saying how much she loved her family; how incredibly fortunate she felt to have each of them; how they were the best family anyone could want. It was as if Treya were determined to "come clean" with every single family member; she was going to burn as clean as ashes, with no unspoken lines left in her body, with no guilt and no blame. As far as I can tell, she succeeded.

We put her to bed that night—Sunday night—and again I slept on her acupuncture table so I could be there if anything happened. Something extraordinary seemed to be going on in that house, and we all knew it.

About 3:30 that morning, Treya awoke abruptly. The atmosphere was almost hallucinogenic. I awoke immediately, and asked how she was. "Is it morphine time?" she said with a smile. In her entire ordeal with cancer, except for surgery, Treya had taken a sum total of four morphine tablets. "Sure, sweetie, whatever you want." I gave her a morphine tablet and a mild sleeping pill, and we had our last conversation.

"Sweetie, I think it's time to go," she began.

"I'm here, honey."

"I'm so happy." Long pause. "This world is so weird. It's just so weird. But I'm going." Her mood was one of joy, and humor, and determination.

I began repeating several of the "pith phrases" from the religious traditions that she considered so important, phrases that she had wanted me to remind her of right up to the end, phrases she had carried with her on her flash cards.

"Relax with the presence of what is," I began. "Allow the self to uncoil in the vast expanse of all space. Your own primordial mind is unborn and undying; it was not born with this body and it will not die with this body. Recognize your own mind as eternally one with Spirit."

Her face relaxed, and she looked at me very clearly and directly.

"You'll find me?"

"I promise."

"Then it's time to go."

There was a very long pause, and the room seemed to me to become entirely luminous, which was strange, given how utterly dark it was. It was the most sacred moment, the most direct moment, the simplest moment I have ever known. The most obvious. The most perfectly obvious. I had never seen anything like this in my life. I did not know what to do. I was simply present for Treya.

She moved toward me, trying to gesture, trying to say something, something she wanted me to understand, the last thing she told me. "You're the greatest man I've ever known," she whispered. "You're the greatest man I've ever known. My champion . . ." She kept repeating it: "My champion." I leaned forward to tell her that she was the only really enlightened person I had ever known. That enlightenment made sense to me because of her. That a universe that had produced Treya was a sacred universe. That God existed because of her. All these things went through my mind. All these things I wanted to say. I knew she was aware how I felt, but my throat had closed in on itself; I couldn't speak; I wasn't crying, I just couldn't speak. I croaked out only, "I'll find you, honey, I will. . . ."

Treya closed her eyes, and for all purposes, she never opened them again.

My heart broke. Da Free John's phrase kept running through my mind: "Practice the wound of love . . . practice the wound of love." Real love hurts; real love makes you totally vulnerable and open; real love will take you far beyond yourself; and therefore real love will devastate you. I kept thinking, if love does not shatter you, you do not know love. We had both been practicing the wound of love, and I was shattered. Looking back on it, it seems to me that in that simple and direct moment, we both died.

It was at that moment that I began to notice that the atmosphere had become very turbulent. It took me several minutes to realize that it wasn't my distress or my grief that seemed to be so disturbing. It was the wind blowing wildly outside the house. And not just blowing. The wind began whipping up a ferocious storm; our ordinarily rock-solid house was shaking and rattling in the gale-force winds that hammered the house at exactly that moment. In fact, the newspapers reported the next day that at exactly four o'clock that morning, record-breaking winds—reaching up to an incredible 115 miles an hour—began to whip through Boulder (though inexplicably, no place else in Colorado). The winds overturned cars—and even an airplane!—all of which was duly reported in the headlines of the papers the next day.

The winds, I suppose, were coincidence. Nonetheless, the constant rattling and shaking of the house simply added to the feeling that something unearthly was happening. I remember trying to go back to sleep, but the house was rattling so hard I got up and put some blankets around the windows in the bedroom, fearing they would shatter. I finally drifted off, thinking, "Treya is dying, nothing is permanent, everything is empty, Treya is dying. . . ."

The next morning, Treya settled into the position in which she would die—propped up on pillows, arms at her sides, mala in her hand. The night before she had begun repeating silently to herself "Om Mani Padme Hung," the Buddhist mantra of compassion, and "Surrender to God," her favorite Christian prayer. I believe she continued to do so.

We had invited a member of the Hospice movement to come by and work with us, and in due course—around eleven that morning—Claire arrived. I personally had wanted a Hospice member to come by because I wanted to make sure that we were doing everything possible to insure that Treya could die painlessly and in peace, in her own bed, in her own way.

Claire was perfect. Looking very like a beautiful and peaceful angel (so beatific that Kati unconsciously kept referring to her as "Grace Dawn"), she entered the room and announced to Treya that, if it was OK with her, she was going to take her vital signs. "Treya," she said, "is it all right if I take your blood pressure?" I don't think Claire thought Treya would actually answer. The point, rather, was that Hospice members are taught that the dying person can hear quite clearly everything you say right up to the end, and perhaps beyond, so Claire extended this elemental courtesy to Treya. Treya herself had not really spoken anything for several hours. But when Claire asked that simple question, Treya abruptly turned her head (eyes still closed) and very clearly said, "Sure." From that point on, everybody knew that Treya, "unconscious" as she was, was in fact fully aware of everything that was happening.

(At one point, Kati, who like all of us had assumed Treya was "unconscious," looked at me and said, "Ken, she is so beautiful." Treya said very clearly, "Thank you." Those were her last words—"Thank you.")

The wind continued to howl, rattling the house severely. The family members maintained their vigil. Sue, Rad, Kati, Tracy, David, Mary Lamar, Michael, Warren—all touched Treya and many whispered final words to her.

Treya held her mala, a mala she had gotten at a meditation retreat with Kalu Rinpoche, a retreat in which she had taken a vow to practice compassion as her path to enlightenment. The spiritual name given to her at that time, by Kalu himself, was "Dakini Wind" (which means, "the wind of enlightenment").

By two o'clock that afternoon (Monday), Treya had ceased to respond overtly to any stimuli. Her eyes were closed; her breathing was following a pattern of apnea (shallow gasps with long pauses); her limbs had become cold. Claire took us aside and said that she thought Treya would die very soon, possibly within hours. She said she would return if at all necessary, and with the kindest of wishes, left us.

The afternoon stretched on; the winds continued rattling the house and contributing to the eeriest atmosphere. For hours I held Treya's hand and kept whispering in her ear: "Treya, you can go now. Everything here is complete and finished. Just let go, just let it happen. We're all here, honey, just let it happen."

(Then, uncontrollably, I began laughing to myself, thinking: "Treya has never done anything anybody ever told her to do. Maybe I should quit saying all this; she'll never let go if I don't shut up.")

I continued with her favorite pith phrases: "Move toward the Light, Treya. Look for the five-pointed cosmic star, luminous and radiant and free. Hold to the Light, sweetheart, just hold to the Light. Let go of us, hold to the Light."

I should mention that, in the year of Treya's fortieth birthday, a teacher of both of us, Da Free John, began saying that the ultimate enlightened vision was when one saw the five-pointed cosmic star, or cosmic mandala, pure and white and radiant, utterly beyond all finite limitations. Treya didn't know this was said at that time, but nonetheless that is exactly when she changed her name from Terry to Estrella, or Treya, which is Spanish for star. And it is held that, at the precise moment of death, the great five-pointed cosmic star, or the clear light void, or simply great Spirit or luminous Godhead, appears to every soul. It is my own belief that this vision had appeared to Treya some three years earlier—it had done so in a dream she told me of, right after an empowerment with the Very Venerable Kalu Rinpoche—the vision was unmistakable, and accompanied by all the classic signs, though she told no one of it. She did not change her name to "Treya" because Free John had talked about this ultimate vision; she had simply had this vision, of the luminous cosmic star, in a very real and direct way. Thus upon actual death, I thought to myself, Treya would simply be seeing her own Original Face, and not for the first time. She would simply be experiencing, once again, her own true nature as luminosity, as radiant star.

The only piece of jewelry she really valued was the five-pointed gold star pendant that Sue and Rad had made for her (based on a drawing Treya had made of exactly that vision). I thought to myself, about that star pendant, that it was, in the words of a Christian mystic, "The outward and visible sign of an inward and invisible grace." She died with it on.

I think everybody realized that their letting go of Treya was crucial to the process, and in their own individual ways, each person released her. I would like to report what transpired in those moments, as family members touched Treya, and softly talked to her, because everybody acted with such dignity and grace. I think that Treya would want me at least to say that Rad, who was beside himself with grief, touched her ever so gently on the forehead, and said, "You are the best daughter I could ever want." And Sue: "I love you so much."

I stepped out to get a drink of water, and suddenly Tracy was there, saying, "Ken, get up there immediately." I ran upstairs, jumped on the bed, grabbed Treya's hand. The entire family—every single member, and good friend Warren—made it into the room. Treya opened her eyes, looked very softly at everybody there, looked directly at me, closed her eyes, and quit breathing.

Everybody in the room was completely there and present for Treya.

Then the entire room began to cry. I was holding her hand, with my other hand over her heart. My body began to shake violently. It had finally happened. I could not stop shaking. I whispered in her ear the few key phrases from the Book of the Dead ("Recognize the clear light as your own primordial Mind, recognize you are now one with Enlightened Spirit"). But mostly we all cried.

The best, the strongest, the most enlightened, the most honest, the most beautiful, the most inspiring, the most virtuous, the most cherished person I had ever known, had just died. Somehow, I felt that the universe would never be the same.

Exactly five minutes after her death, Michael said, "Listen. Listen to that." The gale-force winds had completely ceased blowing, and the atmosphere was a perfect calm.

This, too, was dutifully noted in the next day's papers, right to the exact minute. The ancients have a saying: "When a great soul dies, the winds go wild." The greater the soul, the greater the wind necessary to carry it away. Perhaps it was all coincidence, but I couldn't help thinking: A great, great soul had died, and the wind responded.

In the last six months of her life, it was as if Treya and I went into spiritual overdrive for each other, serving each other in every way that we could. I finally quit the bitching and moaning that is so normal for a support person, a bitching and moaning that came from the fact that I had, for five years, set aside my career in order to serve her. I just dropped all that. I had absolutely no regrets; I had only gratitude for her presence, and for the extraordinary grace of serving her. And she quit the bitching and moaning about how her cancer had "wrecked" my life. For the simple fact was, we together had made a pact, on some profound level, to see her through this ordeal, come what may. It was a profound choice. We were both very, very, very clear about this, particularly during the last six months. We simply and directly served each other, exchanging self for other, and *therefore* glimpsing that eternal Spirit which transcends both self and other, both "me" and "mine."

"I've always loved you," she began on an occasion about three months before she died, "but recently you have changed in very profound ways. Have you noticed?"

"Yes."

"What is it?"

There was a long pause. This was the period right after I had come back from the Dzogchen retreat, but that wasn't the main cause for the change she had noted. "I don't know, kid. I love you, so I'm serving you. It seems very straightforward, don't you think?"

"There's an awareness about you that has kept me going for months. What is it?" She kept repeating, as if it were very important, "What is it?" And I had the strangest feeling that it wasn't a question, really, but more of a test, which I did not understand.

"I think it's just that I'm here for you, sweetheart. I'm here."

"You're why I'm alive," she finally said, and it wasn't a comment about me. The point was that we kept each other going, and we became each other's teacher during those last extraordinary months. My continued service to Treya generated in her almost overwhelming feelings of gratitude and kindness, and the love she had for me in return began to saturate my being. I became completely full because of Treya. It was as if we were mutually generating in each other the enlightened compassion that we had both studied for so long. I felt like years, maybe lifetimes, of karma was being burned out of me in my continued response to her needs. And in her love and compassion for me, Treya also became completely full. There were no empty places in her soul, no corners left untouched by love, not a shadow in her heart.

I'm no longer sure exactly what "enlightenment" means. I prefer to think in terms of "enlightened understanding" or "enlightened presence" or "enlightened awareness." I know what that means, and I think I can recognize that. And it was unmistakable in Treya. I'm not saying this simply because she is gone. That is *exactly* how I came to see it, over those last few months, when she met suffering and death with a pure and simple presence, a presence that outshone her pain, a presence that clearly announced what she was. I saw that enlightened presence, unmistakably.

And those who were with her in those last few months, they saw it, too.

I had arranged for Treya's body to remain undisturbed for twenty-four hours. About an hour after her death, we all left the room, mostly to compose ourselves. Because Treya had propped herself up for the last twenty-four hours, her mouth had hung open for almost a day. Consequently, due to insipient rigor, her jaw was locked in an open position. We tried to close her jaw before we left, but it wouldn't shut; it was locked tight. I continued whispering "pith sayings" to her, then we all left the room.

About forty-five minutes later, we went back into the room, only to be met with a stunning vision: Treya had closed her mouth, and there appeared instead on her face an extraordinary smile, a smile of utter contentment, peace, fulfillment, release. Nor was it a standard "rigor smile"—the lines were entirely and totally different. She looked exactly like a beautiful Buddha statue, smiling the smile of complete release. The lines that had been deeply etched on her face—lines of suffering and exhaustion and pain—had all completely disappeared. Her face was pure, smooth, without wrinkles or lines of any sort, radiant, glowing. It was so profound that we were all taken aback. But there she was, smiling, glowing, radiant, content. I couldn't help it, I kept saying out loud, as I gently leaned over her body, "Treya, look at you! Treya, honey, look at you!"

That smile of contentment and release remained on her face for the entire twenty-four-hour period that she was left in her bed. Her body was finally moved, but I think that smile is etched on her soul for eternity.

Everybody went up and said goodbye to her that evening. I stayed up that night and read to her until three that morning. I read her favorite religious passages (Suzuki Roshi, Ramana Maharshi, Kalu, St. Teresa, St. John, Norbu, Trungpa, the *Course*); I repeated her favorite Christian prayer ("Surrender to God"); I performed her favorite sadhana or spiritual practice (Chenrezi, the Buddha of compassion); and most of all I read to her the essential pointing-out instructions from the Book of the Dead. (These I read to her forty-nine times. The essence of these instructions is that, to put it in Christian terms, the time of death is the time that you shed your physical body and individual ego, and become one with absolute Spirit or God. Recognizing the radiance and luminosity that naturally dawns at the time of death is thus to recognize your own awareness as eternally enlightened, or one with Godhead. You simply repeat these instructions to the person, over and over again, with the very likely assumption that their soul can still hear you. And so this I did.)

I may be imagining all this, but I swear that, on the third reading of the essential instructions for recognizing that your soul is one with God, something audibly clicked in the room. I actually ducked. I had the distinct and palpable feeling, at that utterly dark 2:00 A.M., that she directly recognized her own true nature and burned clean. In other words, that she acknowledged, upon hearing, the great liberation or enlightenment that had always been hers. That she had dissolved cleanly into All Space, mixing with the entire universe, just like in her experience as a thirteen-year-old, just like in her meditations, just like she hoped she would upon final death.

I don't know, maybe I'm imagining this. But knowing Treya, maybe I'm not.

Some months later I was reading a highly revered text of Dzogchen which describes the stages of dying. And it listed two physical signs that indicated that the person had recognized their own True Nature and had become one with luminous Spirit—that they had dissolved cleanly into All Space. The two signs?

> If you remain in the Ground Luminosity,
> As a sign of that, your complexion will be nice . . .
> And it is taught also that your mouth will be smiling.

I stayed in Treya's room that night. When I finally fell asleep, I had a dream. But it wasn't a dream, it was more of a simple image: a raindrop fell into the ocean, thus becoming one with the all. At first I thought that this meant Treya had become enlightened, that Treya was the drop that had become one with the ocean of enlightenment. And that made sense.

But then I realized it was more profound than that: I was the drop, and Treya the ocean. She had not been released—she was *already* so. Rather, it was I who had been released, by the simple virtue of serving her.

And there, there it was: that was exactly why she had so insistently asked me to promise that I would find her. It wasn't that she needed me to find her; it was that, through my promise to her, she would therefore find me, and help me, yet again, and again, and again. I had it all backwards: I thought my promise was how I would help her, whereas it was actually how she would reach and help me, again, and again, and forever again, as long as it took for me to awaken, as long as it took for me to acknowledge, as long as it took for me to realize the Spirit that she had come so clearly to announce. And by no means just me: Treya came for all her friends, for her family, and especially for those stricken with terrible illness. For all of this, Treya was present.

Twenty-four hours later, I kissed her forehead, and we all said goodbye. Treya, still smiling, was taken for cremation. But "goodbye" is the wrong word. Perhaps *au revoir*—"till we meet again"—or *aloha*—"goodbye/hello"—would be better.

Rick Fields, a good friend of both Treya and myself, wrote a very simple poem upon hearing of her death. Somehow, it seemed to say it all:

For a Radiant Star

First we're not here
Then we are
Then we're not

You looked into
Our coming and going
Face to Face

Longer than most of us
With more courage and grace
Than I have ever seen

And you smiled
All the way—

This is no hyperbole, it is a simple statement of fact: I have never known anyone who knew Treya who did not think that she had more integrity and honesty than any person they had ever known. Treya's integrity was absolute, unimpeachable by even the meanest of circumstances, and overwhelming to virtually all who knew her.

I don't think any of us will ever actually meet Treya again. I don't think it works that way. That's much too concrete and literal. Rather, it is my own deepest feeling that every time you and I—and any who knew her— that every time we act from a position of integrity, and honesty, and strength, and compassion: every time we do that, now and forever, we unmistakenly meet again the mind and soul of Treya.

So my promise to Treya—the only promise that she made me repeat over and over—my promise that I would find her again really meant that I had promised to find my own enlightened Heart.

And I know, in those last six months, that I did so. I know that I found the cave of enlightenment, where I was married, by grace, and where I died, by grace. This was the change that had come over me that Treya had noticed, and about which she kept saying, "What is it?" The fact is, she knew exactly what it was. She simply wanted to know if I did. ("And as for the Heart, it is Brahman, it is All. And the couple, now one, having died to themselves, live life eternal.")

And I know, in those last few moments of death itself, and during the night that followed, when Treya's luminosity overwhelmed my soul, and outshone the finite world forever, that it all became perfectly clear to me.

There are no lies left in my soul, because of Treya. And Treya, honey, dear sweet Treya, I promise to find you forever and forever and forever in my Heart, as the simple awareness of what is.

Treya's ashes came back to us, and we had a simple passing-over ceremony.

Ken McLeod read passages on the development of compassion, which Treya had studied under Kalu's guidance. Roger Walsh read selections on forgiveness from *A Course in Miracles*, which Treya had practiced daily. These two themes—compassion and forgiveness—had become the path that Treya most valued as the way to express her own enlightenment.

Then Sam performed the final ceremony, during the course of which a picture of Treya was burned, representing a final letting-go. Sam (or as Treya called him, "dearest Sammy") was the only person that Treya had wanted to perform this ceremony.

Some there spoke final words of remembrance about Treya, and some remained in silence. Twelve-year-old Chloe, Steve and Linda's daughter, wrote this for the ceremony:

Treya, my guardian angel, you were a star on earth and gave us all warmth and light, but every star must die to be born again, this time in the heavens above, dwelling with the eternal lightness of the soul. I know you are dancing upon the clouds right now, and I'm lucky enough to feel your joy, feel your smile. I look at the sky and I know you're shining, with your brilliant, radiant soul.

I love you Treya and I know I'll miss you here, but I'm so happy for you! You have shed your body and your pains, and are able to dance the dance of true life, and that is the life of the soul. I can dance with you in my dreams, and in my heart. So, you are not dead, your soul still lives, lives on a higher plane, and in your loved ones' hearts.

You've taught me the most important lesson, what life and love is.

Love is complete and sincere respect for another being . . .

It is the ecstasy of the true self . . .

Love extends beyond all planes and is limitless . . .

After a million lives, and a million deaths it still lives . . .

And it only dwells in the heart and soul . . .

Life is of the soul, and of nothing else . . .

Love and laughter ride with it, but so do pain and anguish . . .

For a Radiant Star

WHEREVER I GO
AND WHATEVER I SEE
IN MY HEART AND SOUL
YOU'LL ALWAYS BE WITH ME

I looked at Sam, and I found myself saying to those assembled:

"Not many people remember that it was here in Boulder that I proposed to Treya. We were living in San Francisco at the time, but I brought Treya here to meet Sam, to see what he thought. After meeting with Treya for just a few minutes, Sam laughed and said something like, Not only do I approve, I'm worried about her getting shortchanged. I proposed to Treya that night, and she said only, 'If you didn't ask me, I was going to ask you.' And so, in a very special sense, our life together began here, in Boulder, with Sammy, and it ended here, in Boulder, with Sammy."

We would eventually have a memorial for Treya in San Francisco—with remembrances spoken by Vicky Wells, Roger Walsh, Frances Vaughan, Ange Stephens, Joan Steffy, Judith Skutch, and Huston Smith—and in Aspen—with eulogies by Steve and Linda and Chloe Conger, Tom and Cathy Crum, Amory Lovins, Father Michael Abdo, and the monks from Snowmass Monastery. But somehow Sam summarized it all in just two sentences that day:

"Treya was the strongest person I have ever known. She taught us how to live, and she taught us how to die."

In the following days, letters began to arrive. What struck me most was how many of them reported essentially the same events that I have recorded here. It seemed to me, perhaps in my grief, that maybe hundreds of people had participated in the remarkable events of those last two days.

Here is a letter from my family—a poem, actually, that an aunt had sent to me. ("This is a favored poem and symbolic of Treya we think, and one day we will all be reunited. Of this we are absolutely sure.")

I found, in all the letters, a repeating of the words "wind," and "radiance," and "sunlight," and "star." I kept thinking: How did they know?

The "favored poem . . . symbolic of Treya," my aunt had sent to me, was very simple:

Do not stand at my grave and weep;
I am not there. I do not sleep.

I am a thousand winds that blow;
I am the diamond glints on snow.
I am the sunlight on ripened grain;
I am the gentle autumn's rain.
When you awake in morning's hush,
I am the swift uplifting rush
Of quiet birds in circled flight.
I am the soft star that shines at night.
Do not stand at my grave and cry,
I am not there. . . .

Here is a letter, from a woman who had met Treya only once, a woman who was nonetheless overwhelmed by her presence (I kept thinking: This is so typical, because all you had to do was meet Treya *once*)—

"The dream came on Monday night the 9th, before I knew Treya was in the last hours of her life.

"As with most everyone, I felt so much the presence of her great soul and have carried it, like the light that was all around her, with me since then. The only other time I've seen and felt that kind of light around people was in the presence of Kalu Rinpoche."

(When Kalu learned of her death, he performed a special prayer for Treya. For Dakini Wind.)

"Maybe that's why the path was open to dream of her 'out of nowhere' that night. She touched so many of us so deeply.

"In the dream, Treya was lying—floating—on air. . . . As I looked on, a great sound came, and soon I realized that it was the wind coming. It blew all around her body, and as it did, her body began to stretch out, becoming finer, until it became translucent and took on a soft glow. The wind kept blowing around her and through her with a sound that was also somehow music. Her body became more and more transparent and then began slowly blending into the snows on the side of the mountain . . . then up and up with the wind into that fine, crystalline powder that 'smokes' off the mountaintop to become a trillion stars, and eventually the sky itself.

"I woke up crying that morning, filled with awe and beauty. . . ."

So the letters went.

After the passing-over ceremony, we all watched the video of Treya speaking at Windstar. And an image went through my mind, the most difficult image I will ever have, an image that will never leave me: When we first received this video from Windstar, I played it for Treya. She was sitting there, in her chair, too tired to move, hooked to oxygen, in much discomfort. I played the video, the video of her speaking so straightforwardly and so strongly, just a few months ago, the video in which she had said, so clearly, "Because I can no longer ignore death, I pay more attention to life." The speech that had made grown men weep and people clap with joy.

I looked at Treya. I looked at that video. I saw both images together in my mind. The strong Treya, and then the Treya crippled by this cruel disease. And then Treya said to me, through her great discomfort: "Did I do all right?"

I have seen, in this lifetime, in this body, the great five-pointed cosmic star, the radiant star of final release, the star whose name will always be, for me . . . "Treya."

Aloha, and Godspeed, my dearest Treya. I will always, already, find you.

"You promise?" she whispered yet again to me.

"I promise, my dearest Treya."

I promise.

SELECTED READINGS

⋘⟐⋙

Achterberg, Jeanne. *Imagery in Healing*. Boston and London: Shambhala Publications, 1985.

Anthony, Dick; Bruce Ecker; and Ken Wilber. *Spiritual Choices: The Problems of Recognizing Authentic Paths to Inner Transformation*. New York: Paragon House, 1987.

Arieti, Silvano. *The Intrapsychic Self*. New York: Basic Books, 1967.

Assagioli, Roberto. *Psychosynthesis*. New York: Hobbs, Dorman, 1971.

Aurobindo. *The Life Divine*. Pondicherry: Centenary Library, 1982.

Becker, Ernst. *The Denial of Death*. New York: Free Press, 1973.

Bellah, Robert, et al. *Habits of the Heart*. Berkeley: University of California Press, 1985.

Blanck, Gertrude, and Rubin Blanck. *Ego Psychology II: Psychoanalytic Developmental Psychology*. New York: Columbia University Press, 1979.

Broughton, John. "The Development of Natural Epistemology in Adolescence and Early Adulthood." Doctoral dissertation, Harvard University, 1975.

Campbell, Joseph. *The Masks of God*, vols. 1–5. New York: Viking Press, 1959, 1962, 1964, 1968.

Capra, Fritjof. *The Tao of Physics*. New York: Bantam Books, 1977. Boston: Shambhala Publications, 1985 (2nd ed.), 1991 (3rd ed.).

Clifford, Terry. *Tibetan Buddhist Medicine and Psychiatry*. York Beach, Me.: Samuel Weiser, 1984.

Coomaraswamy, Ananda. *Time and Eternity*. Ascona, Switzerland: Artibus Asiae, 1947.

A *Course in Miracles*. Tiburon, Calif.: Foundation for Inner Peace, 1975.

Cousins, Norman. *The Healing Heart*. New York: Avon, 1984.

Da Free John. *The Dawn Horse Testament*. Clearlake, Calif.: Dawn Horse Press, 1986.

Eckhart, Meister. *Meister Eckhart*. Trans. by Edmund Colledge and Bernard McGinn. New York: Paulist Press, 1981.

Erikson, Erik. *Identity and the Life Cycle*. New York: International University Press, 1959.

Faye, Martha. *A Mortal Condition*. New York: Coward-McCann, 1983.

Fowler, James. *Stages of Faith*. San Francisco: Harper & Row, 1981.

Frankl, Viktor. *Man's Search for Meaning*. Boston: Beacon Press, 1963.

Freud, Sigmund. *Civilization and Its Discontents*. New York: W. W. Norton, 1930, 1961.

————. *The Ego and the Id* (1923). Standard Edition, vol. 19. London: Hogarth Press, 1961.

————. *A General Introduction to Psychoanalysis*. New York: Pocket Books, 1971.

Gilligan, Carol. *In a Different Voice*. Cambridge: Harvard University Press, 1982.

Goddard, Dwight. *A Buddhist Bible*. Boston: Beacon Press, 1966.

Grof, Stanislav. *Realms of the Human Unconscious*. New York: Viking Press, 1975.

Habermas, Jurgen. *Communication and the Evolution of Society*. Boston: Beacon Press, 1979.

————. *The Philosophical Discourse of Modernity*. Cambridge: MIT Press, 1990.

Hart, William. *The Art of Living: Vipassana Meditation as Taught by S. N. Goenka*. San Francisco: Harper & Row, 1987.

Hayward, Jeremy. *Shifting Worlds, Changing Minds: Where the Sciences and Buddhism Meet*. Boston and London: Shambhala Publications, 1987.

Hegel, Georg. *The Phenomenology of Mind*. J. Baille (trans.). New York: Harper & Row, 1949.

Hixon, Lex. *Coming Home: The Experience of Enlightenment in Sacred Traditions*. Los Angeles: Jeremy Tarcher, 1989.

Hoffman, Edward. *The Way of Splendor: Jewish Mysticism and Modern Psychology*. Boston and London: Shambhala Publications, 1981.

Hume, Robert (trans.). *The Thirteen Principal Upanishads*. London: Oxford University Press, 1974.

Huxley, Aldous. *The Perennial Philosophy*. New York: Harper & Row, 1944.

Jampolsky, Gerald. *Love Is Letting Go of Fear*. Millbrae, Calif.: Celestial Arts, 1979.

John of the Cross. *The Dark Night of the Soul*. Garden City, N.Y.: Doubleday/Anchor, 1959.

Jung, C. G. *Analytical Psychology: Its Theory and Practice*. New York: Vintage Press, 1961.

————. *Man and His Symbols*. New York: Dell, 1964.

————. *The Portable Jung*. Joseph Campbell (ed.). New York: Viking Press, 1971.

Lax, Eric. *Life and Death on Ten West*. New York: Times, 1984.

Levenson, Frederick. *The Causes and Prevention of Cancer*. Chelsea, Mich.: Scarbrough House, 1986.

Kalu Rinpoche. *The Gem Ornament of Manifold Oral Instructions*. San Francisco: KDK, 1986.

Kapleau, Philip. *The Three Pillars of Zen*. Boston: Beacon Press, 1965.

Keating, Thomas. *Open Mind, Open Heart: The Contemplative Dimension of the Gospels*. New York: Amity, 1986.

Kernberg, Otto. *Borderline Conditions and Pathological Narcissism*. New York: Jason Aronson, 1975.

Kohlberg, Lawrence. *Essays on Moral Development*. San Francisco: Harper & Row, 1981.

Kohut, Heinz. *The Restoration of the Self*. New York: International University Press, 1977.

Kongtrul, Jamgon. *The Great Path of Awakening*. Trans. by Ken McLeod. Boston and London: Shambhala Publications, 1987.

Krishnamurti, J. *The First and Last Freedom*. Wheaton, Ill.: Quest, 1954.

Lama Shabkar. *The Flight of the Garuda*. Kathmandu, Nepal: Rangjung Yeshe Publications, 1988.

Lasch, Christopher. *The Culture of Narcissism*. New York: W. W. Norton, 1979.

Levine, Stephen. *Healing into Life and Death*. New York: Doubleday/Anchor, 1987.

Locke, Steven, and Douglas Colligan. *The Healer Within*. New York: E. P. Dutton, 1986.

Loevinger, Jane. *Ego Development*. San Francisco: Jossey-Bass, 1976.

Mahler, Margaret; Fred Pine; and Anni Bergman. *The Psychological Birth of the Human Infant*. New York: Basic Books, 1975.

Maslow, Abraham. *The Further Reaches of Human Nature*. New York: Viking Press, 1971.

Murphy, Michael, and Steven Donovan. *The Physical and Psychological Effects of Meditation*. San Rafael, Calif.: Esalen Institute, 1989.

Norbu, Namkhai. *The Cycle of Day and Night*. Barrytown, N.Y.: Station Hill Press, 1987.

Piaget, Jean. *The Essential Piaget*. Ed. by Howard E. Gruber and J. Jacques Voneche. New York: Basic Books, 1977.

Ramana Maharshi. *The Collected Works of Ramana Maharshi*. Ed. by Arthur Osborne. York Beach, Me.: Weiser, 1970.

————. *The Spiritual Teaching of Ramana Maharshi*. Boston and London: Shambhala, 1972, 1988.

————. *Talks with Sri Ramana Maharshi*. 3 vols. Tiruvannamalai: Sri Ramanasramam, 1972.

Reynolds, John Myrdhin (trans.). *Self-Liberation through Seeing with Naked Awareness*. Barrytown, N.Y.: Station Hill Press, 1989.

Ring, Kenneth. *Life at Death*. New York: Coward, McCann & Geoghegan, 1980.

Schuon, Fritjof. *Logic and Transcendence*. New York: Harper & Row, 1975.

Smith, Huston. *Forgotten Truth*. New York: Harper & Row, 1976.

Sontag, Susan. *Illness as Metaphor*. New York: Vintage Books, 1979.

Suzuki, D. T. (trans.). *Lankavatara Sutra*. Boulder: Prajna Press, 1978.

Suzuki Shunryu. *Zen Mind, Beginner's Mind*. New York: Weatherhill, 1970.

Teilhard de Chardin, Pierre. *The Phenomenon of Man*. New York: Harper & Row, 1964.

Trungpa, Chögyam. *The Myth of Freedom*. Berkeley: Shambhala Publications, 1976.

Tsele Natsok Rangdrol. *The Circle of the Sun*. Hong Kong: Rangjung Yeshe Publications, 1990.

Tulku Thondup Rinpoche. *Buddha Mind: An Anthology of Longchen Rabjam's Writings on Dzogpa Chenpo*. Ithaca, N.Y.: Snow Lion, 1989.

Vaughan, Frances. *Awakening Intuition*. Garden City, N.Y.: Doubleday/Anchor, 1979.

————. *The Inward Arc: Healing and Wholeness in Psychotherapy and Spirituality*. Boston and London: Shambhala Publications, 1986.

Walsh, Roger. *Staying Alive: The Psychology of Human Survival*. Boston and London: Shambhala Publications, 1984.

————. *The Spirit of Shamanism*. Los Angeles: Jeremy Tarcher, 1990.

Walsh, Roger, and Deane Shapiro (eds.). *Beyond Health and Normality: Explorations of Exceptional Psychological Well-Being*. New York: Van Nostrand Reinhold, 1983.

Walsh, Roger, and Frances Vaughan. *Beyond Ego: Transpersonal Dimensions in Psychology*. Los Angeles: Jeremy Tarcher, 1980.

Watts, Alan. *The Supreme Identity*. New York: Vintage Books, 1972.

Wei Wu Wei. *Open Secret*. Hong Kong University Press, 1965.

Wilber, Ken. *The Spectrum of Consciousness*. Wheaton, Ill.: Quest, 1977.

————. *No Boundary: Eastern and Western Approaches to Personal Growth.* Boston and London: Shambhala Publications, 1979.

————. *The Atman Project: A Transpersonal View of Human Development.* Wheaton, Ill.: Quest, 1980.

————. *Up from Eden: A Transpersonal View of Human Evolution.* Boston and London: Shambhala Publications, 1982.

————. *A Sociable God: A Brief Introduction to a Transcendental Sociology.* Boston and London: Shambhala Publications, 1983.

————. *Quantum Questions: Mystical Writings of the World's Great Physicists.* Boston and London: Shambhala Publications, 1984.

————. *The Holographic Paradigm: Exploring the Leading Edge of Science.* Boston and London: Shambhala Publications, 1985.

————. *Eye to Eye: The Quest for the New Paradigm.* Boston and London: Shambhala Publications, 1990.

Wilber, Ken; Jack Engler; and Daniel P. Brown. *Transformations of Consciousness: Conventional and Contemplative Perspectives on Development.* Boston and London: Shambhala Publications, 1986.

Zukav, Gary. *The Dancing Wu Li Masters.* New York: Morrow, 1979.

ABOUT THE CANCER
SUPPORT COMMUNITY

I F you are moved by Treya's story and would like to help with her vision, I urge you to support the Cancer Support Community. Based in San Francisco, CSC (a nonprofit organization) offers a wide range of services, information, and support to many hundreds of cancer patients a week, and their families and friends, all *entirely* free of charge. Treya and Vicky decided early on that they would not burden a cancer patient with yet another financial worry. The only way this can be done is through gifts and donations.

Any amount will help.

Treya and I gave CSC permission to reprint the following:

1. "What Kind of Help Really Helps?" by Treya Killam Wilber
2. "On Being a Support Person" by Ken Wilber
3. "On Visualization" by Treya Killam Wilber
4. "Health, Wholeness, and Healing" by Ken Wilber

For a donation of $15 each, CSC will be glad to send you reprints of any (or all) of them. Please indicate which you would like.

Although CSC is located in San Francisco, it is fast becoming a premier center on which other support communities, in other cities, can model themselves. And thus the benefits of supporting CSC are by no means confined to the Bay Area.

Treya always considered CSC her "child." I ask you to join me in supporting this extraordinary endeavor, one of the very finest examples of selfless service that I have ever seen.

Donations are tax-deductible, and can be sent to:

The Cancer Support Community
401 Laurel Street
San Francisco, CA 94118

Phone: (415) 929–7400